Curriculum Handbook For School Executives

edited by
WILLIAM J. ELLENA

Published by
AMERICAN ASSOCIATION OF SCHOOL ADMINISTRATORS
1801 North Moore Street • Arlington, Virginia 22209

Library of Congress
Catalog Card Number: 73-75242

Single copy, $6.
Quantity orders:
2-9 copies, 10 percent discount;
10 or more copies, 20 percent discount.

AASA Stock Number: 021-00372

FOREWORD

Sound decisions about the kind of education that is good for a given people at a given time in history rest upon information that is pertinent and accurate, upon thinking that is rational and objective, and upon values that are clear and compelling. Today a special urgency dictates educational reappraisal.

Most institutions, including the schools, do not adapt easily to change. The planning and substance of change tend to block instantaneous adjustment and create a lag between society's needs and desires and the operations of social institutions. However, this slowness of adaptation also provides society with a degree of desirable stability, especially necessary in emergencies.

Many of the fundamental knowledges, abilities, attitudes, and ideals require relatively little adjustment from year to year. Much of the past has stood the test of time. The successes of the past must not be discarded until we have assurance of something better. Although the future rests with our imaginations, and science is constantly changing the world drama, we must guard against illusions.

New understandings about people and about the learning process are constantly emerging, and they must be applied in the classrooms if the schools are to serve the children of this nation effectively. Major curriculum studies abound. School administrators are besieged with information, claims, and counterclaims about new curricular concepts in every conceivable subject. The educational vocabulary is being swollen with a bewildering array of initials, acronyms, and abbreviations denoting various curriculum studies or developments.

The dilemma of the school administrator is this: He cannot afford to accept recommendations uncritically, but neither can he afford to reject them without thoughtful consideration. This is a monumental problem in view of the numbers of materials and recommendations being generated. Nevertheless his decision must rest upon information that is pertinent and accurate and upon thinking that is rational and objective.

The Executive Committee of the American Association of School Administrators believes that school administrators are in urgent need of a clear, concise source of information about the many new curriculum developments that must be considered and studied before sound decisions can be reached. Consequently, it enlisted the help of specialists and organizations in numerous areas in the preparation of this handbook.

The Committee asked the authors to identify, for their particular fields, the emerging concepts in curriculum concept, the emerging concepts in the organization and application of knowledge, and the emerging methods of instruction. Subject areas chosen were adult education, art education, business education, career education, early childhood education, English language arts education, foreign language education, health education, home economics education, industrial arts education, mathematics education, music education, physical education, safety education, science education, and social studies education.

We believe that this handbook will serve a significant need for AASA members by presenting an overview of the surfacing curriculum developments about which school executives must be knowledgeable if they are to ensure vital instructional programs to meet the rising demands on the schools.

Paul B. Salmon
Executive Secretary
American Association of
School Administrators

ACKNOWLEDGMENTS

Curriculum Handbook for School Executives is the result of a major exercise in cooperation, involving the unfailing efforts of scores of people and 14 national organizations. While the American Association of School Administrators assumes full responsibility for any errors of fact, omission, or commission, we gratefully thank the many people who gave so generously of their time and energy in the preparation of this document.

Particular appreciation is extended to the 14 national associations, each of which cosponsored the preparation of a chapter, and to the individuals selected by or representing the associations for their scholarly and painstaking work in preparing manuscripts:

Chapter 1 NATIONAL ASSOCIATION FOR PUBLIC CONTINUING AND ADULT EDUCATION, James R. Dorland, Executive Secretary
Authors: James R. Dorland and Carrol A. Word, Program Coordinator, NAPCAE

Chapter 2 NATIONAL ART EDUCATION ASSOCIATION, John Mahlmann, Executive Secretary
Authors: John Mahlmann, Executive Secretary, NAEA, Washington, D.C., and Stanley Madeja, Director, Aesthetic Education Program, Central Midwestern Regional Educational Laboratory, St. Ann, Missouri

Chapter 3 NATIONAL BUSINESS EDUCATION ASSOCIATION, O. J. Byrnside, Jr., Executive Secretary
Author: O. J. Byrnside, Jr.

Chapter 4 Reprinted from *Career Education,* U.S. DEPARTMENT OF HEALTH, EDUCATION, AND WELFARE Publication No. (OE) 72-39

Chapter 5 AMERICAN ASSOCIATION OF ELEMENTARY-KINDERGARTEN-NURSERY EDUCATION, D. Dwain Heam, Executive Secretary
Author: Margaret Z. Lay, Associate Professor, Syracuse University, Syracuse, New York

Chapter 6 NATIONAL COUNCIL OF TEACHERS OF ENGLISH, James R. Squire, Executive Secretary
Author: James R. Squire. This manuscript originally appeared in the 1967 AASA publication *Curriculum Handbook for School Administrators.*

Chapter 16 NATIONAL COUNCIL FOR THE SOCIAL STUDIES, Merrill F. Hartshorn, Executive Secretary

Author: James Becker, Director, Social Studies Diffusion Project, Social Studies Development Center, Indiana University, Bloomington

Chapter 17 PLANNING AND ORGANIZING FOR IMPROVED INSTRUCTION

Author: Margaret Gill Hein, Head, Department of Teacher Education, Mills College, Oakland, California

The positions cited above are those held at the time each manuscript was submitted.

The Association is deeply indebted, too, to Ann Kidwell Kurzius for assuming responsibility for handling the numerous details involved in preparing the manuscript for the printer and to Mrs. Carol Epstein for critically reviewing the entire document. Their advice was frequently sought and always generously given.

To all of the people listed above, to the associations without whose help this document could not have been prepared, to the dozens of others who contributed to this publication, and especially to former AASA executive secretary Forrest E. Conner, who saw the need for a publication of this kind and authorized its preparation, the AASA says thanks much.

CONTENTS

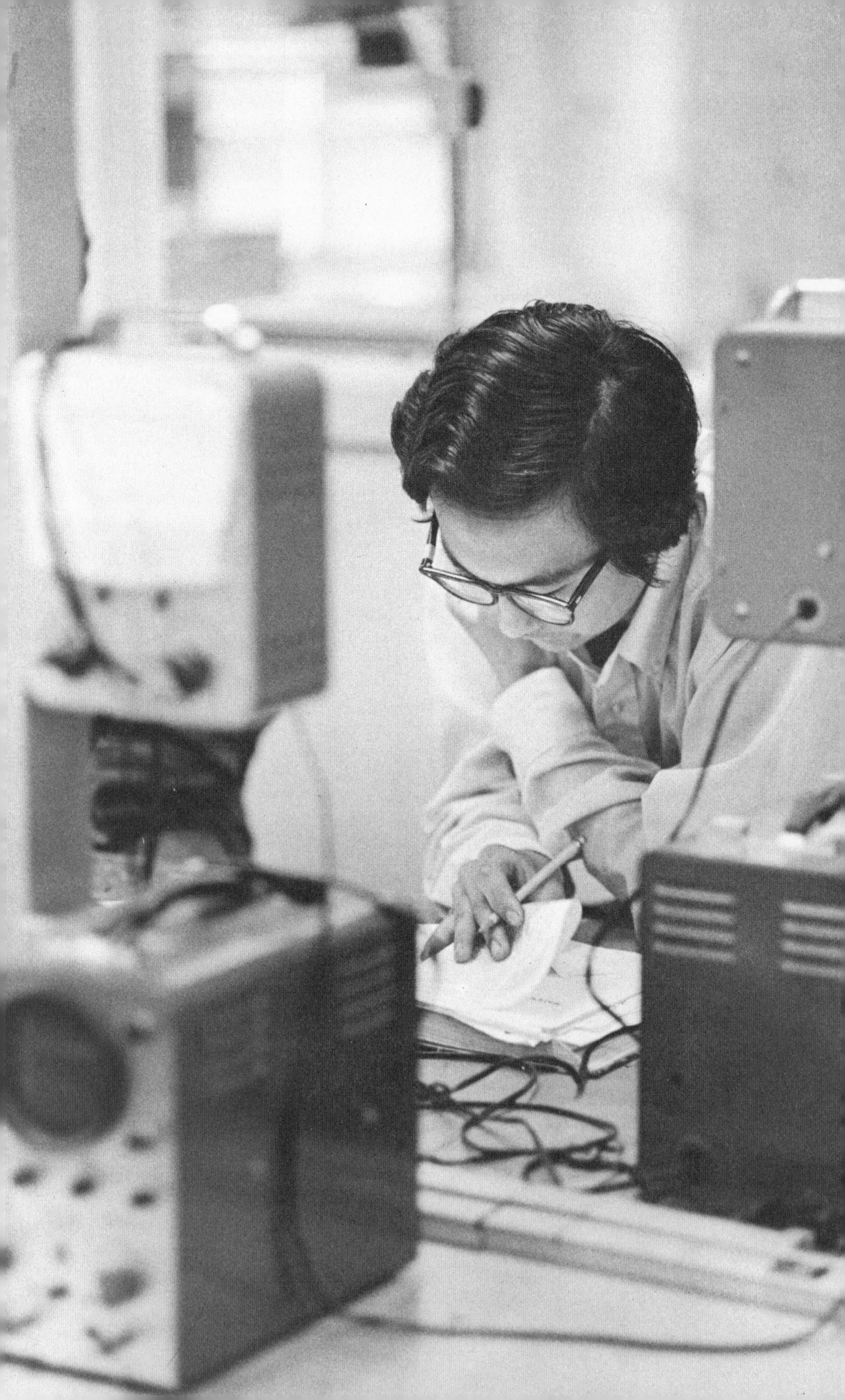

1

Adult Education

Adult education is one of the fastest growing fields of American education. Retraining needs, increased community use of schools, the availability of more and more leisure time—these and other factors have given impetus to adult education activities. Unfortunately, many educators have had little or no training or experience in adult education.

Emerging Concepts in Organizing Adult Education Programs

Certain trends in the development of public school adult education programs can be identified:

1. *Broadening the scope of the program.* An analysis of current program announcements shows a new breadth, depth, and diversity of activities and educational services. A limited, stereotyped program cannot adequately meet the varied and changing interests and needs of today's adults. (An exception to this trend is the intensification of effort in a few limited areas, such as vocational education and manpower development.)
2. *Offering educational opportunities for specific groups.* People want adult education programs that are intimately connected with their needs. Young adults, senior citizens, persons with deficient educational backgrounds, parents and homemakers, factory workers, professional workers, and others need learning activities tailored to fit their particular problems.
3. *Creating partnerships with community groups.* Cosponsorship with the PTA, labor and business organizations, and other professional and civic groups not only provides sources of leadership but also ensures support for the undertaking.
4. *Extending programs into the community.* Although sponsored and financed by the public schools, more and more adult education activities are being held in libraries, churches, homes, factories, offices, government buildings—wherever the instruction can best be given.

5. *Providing adult education around the clock and around the year.* Full-time community adult schools and occupational centers open from 8 a.m. to 10 p.m. all year long are increasing the flexibility and variety of adult education services.
6. *Offering more creative educational services.* Discussion groups, team teaching, field trips, educational tours, clinics, demonstrations, consultations, reading and informational services, home study courses, workshops, forums, lectures, and instruction by TV are bringing a more imaginative, innovative, and creative approach to adult education.
7. *Expanding counseling and guidance programs.* More and more programs are responding to the need for experienced counseling services to guide adults more efficiently into the world of work and to help them make wise use of expanding leisure time.
8. *Selecting more highly trained instructional personnel.* In response to the expansion of continuing education services and activities, the instructional staff is becoming increasingly diverse in terms of talents, training, experience, and personality.

The Setting of Adult Education

For many years, public elementary and secondary schools were the primary locations for adult education classes. However, this arrangement eliminated the possibility of a daytime program for adults. With the constant increase of students and the broadening of program objectives, adult education classes began to spring up in a variety of "off-campus" locations.

Today adult education is not confined to schools, colleges, and other educational institutions, nor is it confined to courses and classes. It takes place in a variety of settings, and it assumes such varied forms as courses taken for credit, instruction on the job, home study, and demonstrations in the home, shop, or office. The "classroom" may be an empty apartment in a housing development, a recreation room in a senior citizen complex, a Sunday school room in a church, a student's home, or even the great outdoors.

The trend toward placing adult classes in nonschool settings throughout the community is a response to more than merely a lack of space in public school facilities. It reflects an awareness of the special needs and concerns of adult students—whether psychological, financial, or environmental. It is in keeping with the objectives of adult education and lends support to the community school concept. The advantages of locating classes throughout the community are obvious. First is accessibility to the public. Conducting classes in students' "backyards" tends to build community interest and support. Offerings can be diversified and tailored to meet the needs of the community—a major objective of adult education. Finally, familiar surroundings can be an important factor in drawing people into an adult program. Affiliation with the church in which adult education classes are held may be sufficient reason for some to enroll.

The number of year-round adult schools is increasing throughout the country. Such schools can now be found in most large cities. The impetus for them has come from manpower development and training programs. The new, full-time adult centers are housed in good buildings where good lighting, equipment, and food (prepared by food-service training classes) create an atmosphere conducive to adult learning.

Essential Considerations in Designing Adult Education Programs

Building Community Ties

Many factors distinguish a great adult education program from a merely good one: creative planning, meaningful formats, outstanding faculty, and strong community ties. Most well-known adult education programs have come about at the request of the people who wanted them, who petitioned (or sometimes even stormed) the offices of those in control, pointing up the need and requesting that the educational institution expanded its operations into the adult field.

It is most often the people themselves who come to the defense of adult programs threatened by budgetary considerations or lack of understanding on the part of the education power structure. Sometimes it seems that no one wants adult education except the people themselves. Their desire is a big plus for the adult education administrator. He or she must strive to maintain, strengthen, and build on it, constantly developing new channels for better two-way communication with the community.

Identifying Needs and Resources

The adult education administrator's first task is to identify the educational needs and resources in the community. He cannot determine staff, facility, or budget requirements until he knows the elements or dimensions of the program he should provide to meet the community's real educational needs.

Organizing an Adult Education Advisory Committee or Task Force

The adult education administrator must develop lines of communication that will provide him with current information on the needs and problems of various segments of the community. Citizen advisory committees can be the eyes and ears of the administrator and his program. They represent one of the best forms of help in determining educational needs and planning successful adult education programs. Advisory committees are usually small, averaging six to ten members who represent particular social, economic, business, and industrial groups within the community. Members are carefully chosen on the basis of their occupational competence and on the extent to which they are accepted and respected by their colleagues and fellow workers in the community.

Tasks normally assigned advisory committee members include the following:

1. Contacting employers to find out what kinds of jobs they have available, what deficiencies they find in applicants that could be remedied by adult education, what kinds of inservice opportunities would help present employees upgrade themselves
2. Talking with newspaper editors to get ideas on how the adult education story could be better told on their pages
3. Holding coffee hours for present participants in the program and asking for their ideas about how it could be improved
4. Contacting local professional groups such as the county medical society to explore the possibility of some kind of cooperative adult education program in a health education area
5. Serving as liaison representatives on community action councils, councils of social agencies, or other coordinating groups
6. Visiting adult classes and using the break to talk with participants about what other courses might interest them
7. Evaluating the adult education budget and attending open hearings on the public school budget to defend the allotment for adult education
8. Discussing new course ideas and whittling them into a shape that would appeal to their acquaintances and friends

9. Finding space in the community for daytime classes
10. Contacting state or federal legislators from the community to express support for special adult education legislation.

Community people who have served actively on adult education advisory committees report great satisfaction from their work. They enjoy knowing and working with the other members. They can see the results of their deliberations when new programs are started around ideas that have been mulled over by their committee. They feel closer to the education system because they have worked on a part of the school program. And they identify strongly with adult education because it is not bound up in as much legality, red tape, and educational jargon as most other parts of education.

Establishing Community Partnerships

The administrator of the public school adult education program should strive for full cooperation with other adult education programs in the community. Good communication among the various programs will help them avoid duplications and omissions.

Scores of community agencies and programs—including county welfare departments, Neighborhood Youth Corps, Model Cities, and Opportunities Industrialization Centers—are now receiving federal funds for education and work training of out-of-school youth and adults recruited from among their clienteles. More and more public schools are conducting adult classes on a contractual basis with such agencies, supplying the buildings, equipment, staff, or technical know-how they need to make the most of the funds available to them.

The public school is the one agency best suited by tradition and circumstances for establishing an atmosphere of cooperation in the total adult education effort in the community. It represents the public. Because it is nonpartisan, professional, and noncompetitive, it is the natural candidate for the leadership role. Where the school accepts this role and implements a policy of cooperative stewardship of the community's adult education fortunes, the entire public benefits.

Selling the Program to the Community

Reared in the climate of the public schools, the adult education administrator often has difficulty understanding the need to merchandise education as a commodity. All the public education he has ever known was dispensed, free of charge, to a captive audience that lacked the right of refusal. But in adult education, where the customer has the choice of accepting or refusing the curriculum, educational salesmanship becomes necessary.

The potential customer may not be aware that he is in need of educational assistance. He must be motivated to give up a portion of his time to attend school. Whether we like it or not, the adult in our society has the legal right to live out his life in blissful ignorance. Convincing him to give up that right often takes plain, unadulterated salesmanship.

The adult education administrator has many avenues of promotion open to him, including press releases, brochures, radio and television, open houses, and speeches before community organizations. His relations with the *press* should involve more than a perfunctory delivery of class schedules and other routine announcements to the newspaper office. He should strive to create a warm, friendly rapport with the editor. Human interest stories and news items emanating from the program keep the image of adult education before the public. The *brochure* outlining the roster of adult education offerings plays a major role in the public appraisal of the program. Good brochures are to adult education what attractive menus are to a restaurant: they help to sell the product. *Open houses* at the end of the semester or year afford the people of the community an opportunity to see some of the products of the adult classes. Finally, the ingenious administrator will avail himself of every opportunity to appear on the programs of other *community groups* and organizations to interpret his program. It is amazing how little is known about the field of adult education, even by those who work side by side with it in the same community. Salesmanship, promotion, interpretation—call it what you will—requires relentless attention to the task of acquainting the public with the nature and purpose of adult education.

Providing Inservice Training

In recent years there has been an unprecedented increase in student enrollment in adult education programs. The survival and expansion of these programs depend upon the recruitment and retention of new and effective teachers who bring to adult education professional and vocational skills and who have (or, more often, acquire) the special skills necessary to teach adults. For the foreseeable future it is likely that the part-time teacher who comes into adult education will depend upon local inservice education programs for his orientation and training for work with adults. If we believe in the adult education process—if we believe that people can and do change through education—then we will stop looking for "born" teachers and will plan adequate, sequential programs of inservice education to help good teachers of children become good teachers of adults.

The Planning Committee. The inservice education program must meet all the training demands of the total adult education program, complex and diverse though they may be. To accomplish this, most administrators will want to form a planning committee, made up of members of the adult education faculty, to help plan and conduct a balanced program of inservice education. Such a committee ensures a democratic atmosphere and so generates support for the final plan.

The committee should include nonprofessional teachers and one or more members of the day school administrative and instructional staff, as well as the director of adult education. The best inservice education program results when the administration, planning committee, and faculty are all involved in its planning and execution. The planning committee, working closely with the administration, can develop a program consistent with teacher needs and, at the same time, build faculty support for inservice education. Such a committee may also strengthen the program by making recommendations to the school board for compensatory time or for faculty participation in the inservice program. All things considered, an interested planning committee is an invaluable asset for gaining administrative and community support.

Where possible, the committee should be allowed several weeks' lead time before the beginning of the school year to plan a year's program. While the program administrator should be vitally interested in the work of the committee, he must give committee members freedom within their areas of responsibility. A committee will not function effectively if its plans are not implemented or if the members see themselves as mere rubber stamps.

Identifying Institutional Goals. In planning the inservice program, the committee should have a statement of the philosophy, goals, and objectives of the adult education program. This statement should serve to broaden the scope of the inservice program and should foster the idea of a continuing effort using all community resources. If there is no such statement, the committee may wish to develop one as a first order of business.

The goals of the adult program can then be translated by the committee into a range of activities and programs that will add up to vital, effective inservice education. The committee should have the responsibility for determining not only the scope and extent of the year's program, but also its content. All too often inservice sessions consist of speakers whose contributions may not fit the critical needs of the local program.

Planning the Inservice Education Program. What follows is a representative, though by no means exhaustive, list of core topics appropriate for any inservice education program for adults. These topics can lend continuity to the program and can be geared to any level of sophistication.

- The instructional program of the adult division
- Adult learning competencies
- Methods and techniques for teaching adults
- Adult interests
- Personal qualities of a successful adult teacher
- Population study of enrolled students
- Differences between teaching children and adults
- Physiological and psychological aspects of aging
- The philosophy of adult education in a technological society
- Leadership training
- Group dynamics
- School-community relations
- The adult counseling process.

Specialized adult education programs will require additional inservice topics. In inservice courses on teaching in adult basic education (ABE) programs, for example, the reading program and the culture of the disadvantaged should be added to the list of topics, to help faculty members adjust rapidly to a new clientele.

Although the activities of the planning committee should not end with the beginning of the inservice education program, primary responsibility for implementing the committee's plans should rest with the adult education administration. Those administrators fortunate enough to have a full-time faculty do not have as much difficulty in scheduling inservice programs as their colleagues whose faculty is part-time. However, the latter should arrange a schedule that is best for the individual program and that provides continuity. Some administrators schedule workshops on Friday afternoon and Saturday morning several times a year. Others plan monthly meetings in the late afternoon before evening classes begin. Still others schedule programs two evenings a week at times when each faculty member can attend at least one of them.

Each activity in the inservice program should meet the criteria set by the planning committee and should relate to the overall purposes and objectives of the adult education program. Since it is a sacrifice for the faculty members to work a meeting into their already full schedules, it would be better to cancel a meeting than to meet without a clear objective.

Effective Use of Resource People. Resource people for inservice education programs can be found in many places. Consultants in almost every phase of adult education will be found in the state university, the state department of education, and such national agencies as the U.S. Office of Education and the National Association for Public Continuing and Adult Education (NAPCAE). These consultants will often assist without charge. In addition, state and local health and welfare departments often have on their staffs adult educators who can make a valuable contribution. Psychologists, sociologists, and extension personnel from universities or private agencies can also be called upon for specialized topics.

Supervisors and teachers from the local day program are a frequently overlooked source of help in the inservice program. They can often make a particularly valuable contribution because they are acquainted with the community, with local problems, and with school operations and programs.

When resource persons are used in the inservice program, their instructions and assignments should be specific. Materials describing the adult education program, the purpose of the inservice program, other consultants used, or topics to be discussed should be sent to consultants in time for them to make appropriate preparations. When the program is scheduled to run for more than a day, it is helpful to have the consultant arrive a day early so that he can observe the activity in progress and discuss his presentation with the program chairman.

Another important resource is the local board of education, which has the basic responsibility for developing a forward-looking policy of inservice education. The local board can be most effective in implementing inservice education for adult programs if it—

- Develops policies with the participation of teachers, administrators, supervisors, and other school officials connected with the adult program.
- Makes adequate budgetary provisions to pay the cost of inservice activities and consultants.
- Develops salary policies that reflect the desirability of continuous professional growth.
- Provides adequate compensatory time.

Activities for Inservice Programs. The inservice program need not and should not be limited to meetings. The *workshop* is frequently a useful activity and is ideally suited to inservice education. By actively working on some facet of the curriculum, participants learn more than they would as passive listeners.

Because of the wide range of subject matter covered in inservice education, the use of *committees or study groups* is frequently helpful. These groups can work independently, reporting to the entire faculty from time to time. Working on a study group or committee can provide a depth of experience that is difficult to achieve in meetings of the faculty as a whole. In addition, study groups provide flexibility in working with new teachers, subject matter groups, and special projects.

Individual instruction should not be overlooked in planning the inservice program. Access to a good adult education library is important here. The administrator may wish to assign new faculty members to experienced colleagues for special help. However, it remains the administrator's responsibility to see that the new teacher is given every opportunity to prepare to work effectively with adults. Close communication and support during the first critical weeks of classes will give the new teacher confidence in his ability to teach adults.

University extension courses give the teacher the threefold opportunity to work toward an advanced degree, meet state certificate requirements, and participate in an inservice program. When the university course is to take the place of the local inservice program, the adult education director and the university professor should collaborate in planning the course content.

If teachers of special groups—such as seasonal farm workers or residents of slum areas—have little concept of the living conditions of their students, a *field trip* is the first step toward making them more perceptive. Another method of bringing about a better understanding of special problems, needs, and attitudes is to schedule *joint inservice education sessions* with welfare case workers and other social workers. Such sessions also have the beneficial side effect of achieving better agency cooperation in working with the disadvantaged.

Attendance at meetings of local, state, and national organizations (e.g., NAPCAE) can be an important means of inservice education for the teacher of adults, offering a unique opportunity to become acquainted with new materials and resources.

Facilities, Equipment, and Materials. As the trend toward day as well as evening programs accelerates and full-time facilities are constructed or remodeled for adults, thought should be given to the need for a professional library and for a meeting place for the inservice program. An informal setting with comfortable furniture is desirable. If school facilities are used, adequate classroom and conference space suitable for adults should be made available. If school facilities are not available, consider a meeting room in a local bank, labor organization, church, or other public or private organization, which may actually be more centrally located and more comfortable.

There should be a library of professional books, periodicals, and teaching guides in addition to a library of audiovisual materials. The inservice program should also have access to typing and mimeographing facilities. Textbooks, manuals, workbooks, teaching guides, course outlines, instructional materials, standardized and teacher-made tests, and other evaluation materials should be available.

Attention should also be given to demonstrating new instructional materials and equipment developed for use in the adult program. Many adult educators remember the days when there were few instructional materials specifically for adults. Fortunately things have changed. One byproduct of federal programs in adult education has been the development of new and better materials. Programmed materials and adult education texts are now available from a number of publishers.

However, determining the suitability of available materials is a matter of concern and an important topic for the inservice program, because publishers' claims are not always dependable. Readability charts and annotated bibliographies, which have been developed for adult educators by several universities, are better criteria for evaluating publications and should be available in the professional library. (One such readability scale is contained in *Teaching Reading to Adults,* an NAPCAE publication.)

Careful attention should be given to the criteria for selecting materials for the inservice program as well as for the adult program itself. Whenever possible, a faculty committee should be given time during the summer to examine materials and make recommendations about those that might be useful in the adult program. They can then be studied and further evaluated in the inservice program.

In addition, demonstrations to acquaint teachers with videotape recorders, teaching machines, and other new teaching materials are appropriate for inservice sessions, even though it may be some time before the items will be perfected or available for use in the local program.

Providing Preservice Training

No teacher should be employed in an adult program without preservice training. Several adult basic education programs in Florida require a program of preservice education for prospective teachers before they are employed. Intensive preparation is given in all facets of the instructional program, the culture of the disadvantaged adult, methods and techniques for teaching adults, and characteristics of the adult learner. The preservice program also serves as a valuable screening device: those teachers who demonstrate a lack of qualifications or potential for teaching adults are not employed.

Ideally, a preservice program for adult teachers should be scheduled for two weeks or more, but it does not seem likely that this ideal situation will come about in the near future. In those systems where there is a two-week preservice program for all teachers before school opens in the fall, the superintendent will often allow parts of several days for the adult teachers to meet. One alternative is to use the first week of school for an inservice education program. For the adult students to miss a week of classes is preferable to beginning classes with teachers who are unskilled in working with adults.

As a last resort, the administrator may conduct informal preservice programs individually by giving the new adult teacher such reading materials as *When You Are Teaching Adults, In-Service Training for Teaching Adults, Swap Shop,* and *Teaching Techniques* (all published by NAPCAE) and discussing the materials with the teacher before classes begin. Other devices for individualized preservice education will doubtless be designed by the imaginative, innovative director.

Providing for Continuous Program Evaluation

The purpose of program evaluation is program improvement. Planning and implementing an effective adult education program is a complex task. If the administrator is to provide leadership in program improvement, there must be provision for systematic feedback of information on program effectiveness to policy makers, teachers, and learners, so that they can make sound judgments regarding future programs. Continuous program evaluation is the process by which evidence regarding program effectiveness is systematically collected, analyzed, and used to improve programs of continuing adult education. The extensive literature on educational evaluation contains many ideas and principles that can be helpful to adult educators.

Emerging Concepts in Curriculum Content in Adult Education

The impact of change, the new morality, modern technology, and the social revolution have all given rise to urgent concerns for the curriculum of public school continuing and adult education. The development of modern and dynamic curriculum offers a great challenge to the administrator of an adult education program. This challenge was well expressed in the following statement made by former president Lyndon Johnson at the AASA Convention in 1966:

> Tomorrow's school will be a school without walls—a school built of doors which open to the entire community. Tomorrow's school will reach out to the places that enrich the human spirit—to the museums, the theaters, the art galleries, to the parks and rivers and mountains. It will ally itself with the city, its busy streets and factories, its assembly lines and laboratories—so that the world of work does not seem an alien place for the student. Tomorrow's school will be the center of community life, for grown-ups as well as children—"a shopping center of human services." It might have a community health clinic or a public library, a theater and recreation facilities. It will provide formal education for all citizens—and it will not close its doors anymore at three o'clock. It will employ its buildings round the clock and its teachers round the year. We just cannot afford to have an $85 billion plant in this country open less than 30 percent of the time.

The knowledge and skill that the administrator of the public school continuing and adult education program can bring to bear on this challenge will determine the direction of public adult education in the years ahead.

Certain fundamental principles underlie the process of curriculum construction in adult education. The experience of many administrators over many years indicates that a good curriculum meets the following criteria:

1. *It is continuously evolving.* To be viable and effective, the adult education program must have continuous evaluation and reappraisal. A program must adapt its educational activities and services to meet the needs of a modern and dynamic community. A curriculum that is at all sensitive and responsive to the needs of a changing society can never be settled once and for all. The effort to evaluate aims of education in terms of current realities should be only a part of the continuing effort of adult educators to reflect the needs of the individual and the society in their curriculum offerings.
2. *It is based on the needs of people.* It is imperative in developing a program to begin with those most concerned—the adult students. They bring to the classroom many years of experiences that can be woven into the fabric of the classroom presentation. Opportunity should be provided for student participation in developing the curriculum and also in assessing its effectiveness. In adult education, we do not plan a curriculum *for* people, we plan it *with* them.
3. *It is democratically conceived.* The minds and energies of many people who are in intimate contact with the interests, needs, and resources of the community will create a more effective product than the individual director could possibly provide by working alone.
4. *It is the result of long-term effort.* Enthusiasm for a proposed curriculum activity often impels proponents to push for immediate action. But a class or service that is begun hurriedly and folds quickly may hurt the long-term continuance of the program.
5. *It is a complex of details.* Good program planning provides the proper instructional equipment and meeting places that are most conducive to adult learning. A friendly social setting, good student-teacher relationships, effective guidance opportunities, and a favorable attitude on the part of individuals, groups, and organizations within the community are necessary ingredients for a successful program.
6. *It provides for the logical sequence of subject matter.* Classes and activities in adult education should be planned so as to achieve an orderly development of subject matter and step-by-step progress of the learner. A familiar principle in adult

education philosophy holds that we begin with the student "where he is," whether he is illiterate or the holder of a graduate degree. Curricular flexibility is required to accommodate the various levels of educational attainment usually found in the adult student body. Curricular content should be devised in such a way as to provide the student with a progressive pattern that offers opportunity for further study in those areas of learning important to him.

7. *It complements and cooperates with other programs of adult education in the community.* The public school should not try to monopolize the adult education scene at the community level. Its major concern should be to see that the job gets done, regardless of who does it. The administrator of the adult program ought to familiarize himself with course offerings in the community and offer his assistance in the improvement of ongoing programs, rather than start a similar one of his own. He should determine gaps and omissions in the total community effort and initiate those courses that are lacking. Cooperative effort toward this end will accomplish more than competitive zeal.
8. *It has educational quality.* The curriculum must be made up of offerings that pass the test of good, sound education. The reason is obvious: the public supports the program financially, and the taxpayer has a right to expect his money to be well spent.
9. *It has administrative flexibility.* The curriculum in adult education, whenever possible, should be freed from the formal rigidities of time and place. There should be no season when the program is automatically closed down, no reasonable time of day when an activity cannot be scheduled, no convenient location in the community where a class cannot be held. The program of activities should be determined by the needs, available time, and convenience of the students—not by fixed administrative policy.

There has been a steady progression of adult education in tune with the times and needs of the people. Current and predicted curriculum and program concerns include adult basic education, parent and family life education, high school completion, public affairs education, occupational training, and "education about education."

Adult Basic Education

Federal efforts to eliminate poverty and the ensuing legislation aimed at raising the economic and social levels of disadvantaged adults have stimulated the education world and, more specifically, the adult educator to recognize the high correlation between proficiency in the basic skills (reading, writing, and arithmetic) and job opportunities and job success. Many studies have shown that children from families of low educational achievement usually repeat the pattern. Adult basic education can help alleviate these problems.

The vast differences in the populations to be served should be considered in the development of adult basic education curriculums. No one curriculum can serve all segments of our disadvantaged population. For example, a program for the disadvantaged in urban ghettos cannot be implemented on an Indian reservation in the Southwest, nor can an English-as-second-language program designed for recent immigrants from Puerto Rico be used for the native-born, French-speaking adults in some of our Northeastern states. Therefore, curriculums must be designed to meet specific objectives and to respect the cultural differences of the population to be served. However, there are enough commonalities so that guidelines for the development of a meaningful curriculum can be stated.

Seven years of intensive efforts at developing literacy skills have taught that there is no such thing as "instant literacy." The time span for the development of the communication skills can and must be compressed, but aspiring to bring functional literacy levels to total illiterates in a matter of hours with our present-day knowledge of materials and techniques is not realistic. Program designs must reflect an understanding of the time and intensity of instruction required to produce results.

Adults from disadvantaged groups are often reluctant to seek literacy education, primarily because there has traditionally been little relationship between their economic and social problems and the curriculum of adult basic education programs. To attract these adults, the curriculum must not only offer opportunities to develop their literacy skills but also provide supportive services that help them put these skills to use.

A viable adult basic education curriculum cannot be developed and implemented in a school situation isolated from the rest of society. It must be developed in cooperation with social, welfare, labor, employment, and other governmental agencies. Continued communication with the industrial community, through personnel specialists in industry, is also highly essential.

As an integral part of the basic skills program, the curriculum should provide opportunities for the adult to gain knowledge and understanding of the social living skills such as health and nutrition, the world of work, family life, and practical government. It is unrealistic to expect adults with low levels of literacy to develop sophisticated concepts in these areas primarily through reading. Discussion groups, group counseling, and the use of audiovisual materials can be highly productive.

Parent and Family Life Education

Adult basic education is only one of the developing frontiers open to adult educators as they plan their programs for the future. Family life education, a rapidly expanding field in which numerous agencies are becoming involved, is a natural program area for public schools and colleges. It may take various forms, such as programs of guided observation for parents of preschool children or of children with learning and behavior problems, psychological studies of teenagers and the hazards they face in affluent suburbs as well as culturally deprived areas, or studies of the nature of violence. Family life education might include courses to help parents know what their children are studying and how to work with them at home. There might be discussions of the school curriculum, or how to prepare one's child for college, or the importance of education for advancement in work and life.

For a society in the process of great change, strong families and effective parents are imperative, and education for the parental role is an urgent necessity. Although the need is broadly recognized and a wide variety of agencies and organizations offer programs, education for family living is neither generally understood nor universally available. Many of the offerings in this area are considered supplementary and involve fragmented and disparate approaches. Frequently, program goals are not as broad as they might be. Available education for parenthood tends to be restricted by the particular emphasis of primary agency goals.

A society that blames the family for many of its social ills without providing adequate education for child rearing and family living is not meeting its obligations. A program of adult education that does not make parent and family education obtainable is incomplete.

High School Completion

The millions of adults without a high school education find many doors closed to them. The labor market for the worker who cannot produce a high school diploma or its equivalent is shrinking. In many employment offices it is no longer sufficient for an applicant to *say* that he has a secondary school education; evidence is often required in the form of the actual diploma or some other piece of paper attesting to the truth of his statement.

One answer lies in adult courses leading to a high school diploma. Such courses have been increasing rapidly in recent years as job qualifications have been raised. (Usually these courses also admit persons who want specific instruction rather than credit.) Evening high schools established in larger cities a hundred years ago offer a complete, formal high school program to adults. In smaller districts, the adult education program offers high school credit in selected courses for which there is a demand. Most of the students are fairly recent high school dropouts who need a diploma to improve their employment status, or who are simply seeking a second chance after failing or forfeiting their first one.

Another answer lies in the high school equivalency certificate program, an alternative for the more mature adult. No courses are required, although districts frequently offer a high school refresher course for candidates. The underlying thought is that a person can learn on his own from the job he holds and from all his other experiences. If he learns enough and can pass a general achievement examination, he is granted an equivalency certificate.

One problem sometimes facing the administrator of a secondary education program for adults is the question of who gives credit. Many times the adult division cannot grant secondary credit even though it administers the program. Before embarking on a secondary program, administrators should get clarification of legal requirements and should obtain the complete cooperation of secondary school officials in the district. In most cases only a certified secondary school teacher may teach a course that carries secondary school credit. Local regulations should be checked and board policies determined.

In many cases, courses are of approximately the same length for adults as for children. But there is variation in this practice, and there is ample evidence that accelerated courses are desirable and practicable for adults.

Public Affairs Education

Public affairs includes such things as citizen participation in the civic and public matters that affect their lives; local, state, and national issues; trends in world affairs; comparative political systems; world religions; current crises; the United Nations; and the numerous problems and issues arising from poverty. One of the major goals of adult education is the development of an informed citizenry willing to make judgments about local, state, and national problems and issues. Courses and activities with subject matter ranging from small local problems through urban renewal plans to our most complicated national and international problems—including questions about public education itself—have increasingly appeared in adult education programs throughout the country. Schools are no longer avoiding controversial issues but are accepting them as an educational challenge.

Administrators find this one of the most difficult areas of the adult curriculum. People do not stand in line demanding to be kept informed. They must be attracted to school offerings in some manner, or else the programs must be taken to them. As in the case of parent education, all forms of adult education must be used and the cooperation of other groups obtained. Here, too, the use of press, radio, and television and the exploration of new ways of working with voluntary associations may hold some of the answers for the future.

Civic and public affairs education should not rely exclusively on classes and courses. It has been amply demonstrated that, while adults will come to school two nights a week to learn arc welding, complete a high school education, study French, or find out why Johnny cannot read, they will not generally come to school on a regular basis to learn more about their community, problems in urban redevelopment, the structure of political parties, air pollution, the duties of a good citizen in helping to solve transportation problems, or many other kinds of civic questions. They go instead to their clubs and organizations for this kind of education. They participate in civic clubs, in luncheon clubs, in political parties, in parent-teacher associations, and in numerous other groups. The responsibility of the public schools in this area is not to provide the educational experience itself (unless a specific request is made), but rather to help civic leaders—through program clinics and personal consultation—perform their educational functions as efficiently as possible.

One example is the service performed by a director of adult education when he consults with the mayor and his director of housing on the educational implications of a community conference on housing. Neither the mayor nor his housing expert are presumed to be experts in adult learning, but the director of adult education certainly should be. Services of this kind rendered to public agencies provide an important community service and at the same time enhance the school system's prestige.

"Education About Education"

Today education is one of the key civic and social issues. It is front page news much of the time in most communities, yet most voting citizens of a school district probably do not know the tax rate that applies to education and are unclear as to whether a school teacher is legally an employee of the municipal government or of the state. Many new practices that have been well documented by research are not put to use in the schools in part because of public undereducation about education.

In one midwestern city, the board of education held neighborhood conferences on education in all but a few of the elementary schools of the district. The purpose was to enable citizens to communicate points of view to—and discuss them with—school officials. Then representatives from each of the elementary schools went to the junior high schools, where community forums were held. Eventually the members of the board of education, the superintendent of schools, and civic leaders appeared on a television program in which they commented to the total community on the exchange of points of view that had developed through these channels.

Occupational Education and Training

Any concept of the adult education curriculum must include adult vocational and technical education, even though the administrator of adult education is not always directly responsible for this area. In certain states and districts a special administrator of vocational education, an associate or assistant superintendent, or a director of vocational education is in charge of both child and adult vocational work. But the administrator of adult education is still required to be informed about the vocational work of the district.

Vocational and technical courses make up a large part of the total adult curriculum. In large cities they are usually conducted in evening trade vocational schools, which compare to the evening high school. Elsewhere, they are taught in the vocational facilities of special buildings or of the regular high school.

Basic curriculum areas in vocational or occupational education, derived from the formulations of the American Vocational Association, may be described as follows:

- *Trade and industrial courses* provide instruction for the purpose of developing basic manipulative skills, safety judgment, technical knowledge, and related occupational information. These may be preemployment courses or courses designed to upgrade or retain workers employed in industry. Examples include courses in machine shop, auto mechanics, blueprint reading, and power saving. Many of these courses are now taught in an expanded curriculum under provisions of the Manpower Development and Training Act.
- *Apprentice training* is a special program to provide the manipulative skills and technical or theoretical knowledge needed for competent performance in skilled occupations. Because apprentices learn craft skills through on-the-job work experiences as well as in the classroom, the program usually involves cooperation among school, labor, and management. The minimum terms and conditions of apprenticeship are regulated by state and local statutes and agreements. Some of the apprenticeable trades are carpentry, plumbing, electrical work, and sheet metal work.
- *Business education courses* equip the adult with marketable skills, knowledge, and attitudes needed for employment and advancement in business occupations. The business curriculum includes stenographic subjects (typing and shorthand), bookkeeping, clerical practice, and office machines.
- *Distributive education courses* offer training in the selling, marketing, and merchandising of goods and services for the purpose of improving distribution and upgrading distributive workers, including employees, managers, and owners engaged in distributive occupations. Typical courses include real estate, small business management, salesmanship, insurance brokerage, and merchandising.
- *Supervisory training* assists foremen and supervisors in industry and business in various phases of their work, such as the training of workers, personnel relations, and legislation. Commonly offered courses include foremanship training, management training, industrial relations, and quality control.
- *Agricultural courses,* designed to improve farm methods and rural living, cover such areas as soil conservation, increased production, and marketing. A few examples are farm mechanics, dairy management, crop improvement, farm management, and pest control.

- *Technical courses* provide technical information and understanding of the laws of science and technology to prepare adults as technicians or to give them knowledge necessary to an occupation or profession. Common course titles include technical mathematics and physics, electronics, refrigeration, and metallurgy.

Traditional Curriculum Areas

The cultural enrichment area of the adult program includes oil painting, composition, understanding and appreciating music, ceramics, antiques, portraiture, photography, dance, acting, poetry, scenic design, piano instruction, creative writing, American literature, English, English as a second language, and numerous foreign languages.

In the practical crafts and homemaking area, classes are offered in sewing, tailoring, dress design, wood- and metalworking, knitting, gardening, interior decoration, family finance, and numerous other areas.

Business courses include typing and shorthand, accounting, advertising, computers, business management, analysis of business problems, marketing, merchandising, effective listening, business psychology, world trade, economics, and the stock market.

There are also numerous special interest courses in such areas as swimming, judo, and driver education, as well as special daytime classes for senior citizens.

Expanding Opportunities—Community, Junior, and Technical Colleges

A new educational institution has appeared in recent years to reinforce the efforts of public school adult education. Actually, community, junior, and technical colleges have always been with us in one form or another, whether they were called academies or institutes or just schools or colleges. But in the last decade their numbers have increased significantly. Public support for these institutions grew in a period in which four-year colleges were jammed and college costs were soaring. Their primary purpose is to provide low-cost, two-year college programs for commuter students.

Many of the community colleges were operated by local school boards, while others had their own community college boards but were supported by public funds. So it was only natural for them to search for new ways of being useful to the local adult community and to come up with adult education and community service programs.

For the most part, the courses and programs are quite different from the usual courses available through the public schools. For one thing, they are on a more advanced level, particularly in the technical areas. The result is that coordination between adult educators on the public school and community-technical college level can provide the adult student with a continuous study series so that he can strive toward ever higher levels of competence in a planned sequence.

Prospects for further growth in the numbers of community-technical colleges—and therefore for increased educational service to adults—are certain. All administrators of adult or continuing education, regardless of their institutional loyalties, should be aware of and concerned about the program offerings and the clientele of neighboring institutions and should make a genuine effort toward cooperative program planning.

Special Interest Groups

In attempting to meet individual needs in the various curriculum areas, administrators discovered the great diversity of adults in training, experience, and motivation. Homogeneous grouping seemed to provide a partial answer. Special groups were formed in the schools, not around subject matter but around common interests and needs. As early as 1926, Eduard Lindeman foresaw this development:

> The approach to adult education will be via the route of situations, not subjects. . . . Every adult person finds himself in specific situations with respect to his work, his recreation, his family life, his community life, etc.—situations which call for adjustments. Adult education begins at this point. Subject matter is brought into the situation, is put to work, when needed.

Senior Citizens

Senior citizens make up a constantly increasing proportion of our population. Government has tried to solve some of their basic problems through social security and welfare programs. Community agencies and the public schools are making their contribution by organizing activities for the aging. Through adult education the schools have either organized and supported senior citizen groups or served them with educational programs that have been organized by some other agency.

What is the curriculum for the aging? There are classes and activities in at least five areas:

1. *Vocational training to help the retired person earn a supplementary income.* Training provided in various handcrafts is on a level higher than for a nonvocational course, because the product must be salable. Production methods, pricing, and marketing are also taught. Frequently, a cooperative marketing procedure is developed. Other courses of a vocational nature are taught, such as typing and bookeeping—skills that can be used for part-time employment.
2. *Cultural activities to enrich living.* These activities include training and practice in the arts and crafts. Less common is the study of philosophy, psychology, and science.
3. *Health education* to help the older person recognize what is normal in aging and what is not normal. Subjects range from accident prevention and nutrition to common degenerative diseases and emotional disturbances.
4. *Family life education* to help the aged person make a better adjustment to changed family and social relationships.
5. *Community service* to help the retired person feel useful, have status, and consider himself part of the community.

The administrator of adult education must permit in his work with the aged a degree of informality and autonomy not present in other parts of the program. He who can afford to employ and can find a competent coordinator for this work is fortunate, for the problems are many. But the response of the aged to such special programs has been most gratifying.

Handicapped Adults

Courses developed for physically and mentally handicapped adults include speech correction, lip reading, therapeutic swimming, remedial reading, and general skills for the retarded adult. Cooperation with such agencies as the Vocational Rehabilitation and Employment Service can suggest to the administrator the types of courses needed.

Second Careers for Mature Women

A look about the business, distributive, professional, and industrial worlds quickly reveals that women comprise a substantial portion of the nation's work force. Programs to orient mature women for reentry into the world of work, followed by skill training programs, have received enthusiastic response in many parts of the country when offered as part of the total curriculum of continuing education for adults. The enterprising adult educator seeking new avenues of individual and community service with a high rate of guaranteed response and effectiveness will be well advised not to overlook career planning for women who are approaching the end of their child rearing years.

Emerging Methods of Instruction in Adult Education

Historically, administration of units in adult education has duplicated traditional class patterns of the American elementary and secondary school. There is now an urgent need for innovative scheduling approaches to encourage the use of methods and techniques leading to individualized instruction. Methods must be based on the objectives of the program planners, instructors, and enrolled adults to ensure use of the best method for the specific content areas and course objectives.

Individualized Instruction

Individualized instruction has gained rapid acceptance in continuing education, where time for study is frequently at a premium, student motivation is high, and what is learned has immediate application for job opportunities.

Encouraging students to accept greater responsibility for learning has been talked about for years. What is new are the methods and techniques that stimulate self-directed learning. Learning is an individual process. Students learn at different rates. Individualizing instruction allows the student to discover his own errors, correct his own mistakes, and reset himself before his efforts are checked by the teachers.

Individualized instruction is a direct move away from the imitation and fact memorization that characterize much classroom learning today. Many educational authorities have long believed that learning can be enhanced by relating facts to problem situations relevant to students. Unfortunately, it was difficult to apply this long-talked-about principle when the lecturer or textbook simply dispensed facts and students were tested on assimilation of facts rather than on problem solving. Under individualized guided study it is easier for the student to succeed than to fail. It is not surprising that many less able students, including those in their teens, appreciate this "special privilege." And the more able students appreciate the privilege of moving ahead at their own pace.

Perhaps the most innovative approach to individualized instruction in programs of adult basic education is the learning laboratory. Originally designed to serve adults functioning at a level lower than eighth grade, the laboratories are also used to help adults gain educational improvement in areas of their own choosing. The programed instructional materials used are not only for credit toward elementary or high school completion but also for personal improvement.

The learning laboratory can best be defined as a systems approach to providing the academic knowledge and skills needed or desired by an individual. It is an accumulation of commercially available instructional materials designed for maximum effectiveness with adults and so organized that any adult can attend at a time convenient to him, stay as long as he can, work at his own most efficient pace, use the materials most effective with him, and study only the subjects that serve his own particular purposes. He is never compelled to work beyond his comprehension level and must master each concept before progressing.

Discussion Groups

Group discussion has become an important method in adult education in recent years. It represents a shift from the almost exclusive use of the lecture method and indicates a basic change in philosophy and direction in adult learning. The student will enjoy the course more and get more from it if he participates actively in the classroom discussion. Group discussions should be carefully planned so that they relate directly to the problems and concerns of the students.

Buzz Groups

Most people find it easier to talk to a few people than to a large group, easier to speak informally than to make an address or even a report. The buzz group is a way of setting up face-to-face communication within a large audience, by creating subgroups of from four to ten persons. It enables all the people in a large group to participate in planning, in setting a course of action, and in talking something over more thoroughly than is possible in a large group. Buzz groups usually report their thinking or recommendations to the total group by asking one person to summarize their discussion and to indicate minority as well as majority opinion. What is said in the reports may be noted on a chalkboard or newsprint and used for further discussion.

Team Teaching

The team approach to adult education is receiving increased attention, especially in the areas of basic and vocational education. The team may be composed of a master teacher and a beginning teacher, a master teacher and a teacher aide, a basic education teacher and a vocational teacher, or some other combination. Guidance counselors, employers, and welfare personnel often contribute to the team effort. Input from representatives of the various program components allows for the development of a more comprehensive program suited to the needs of the individual student.

Educational Television

Adult education programs have been using educational television (ETV) on a comparatively limited basis. In the near future, however, more communities will have the opportunity to benefit from television as an instructional medium. Administrators will want to be prepared to make the best use of ETV—telecourses, public affairs programming, creative arts, information programs, etc.—because those who have had experience with the medium consider it a most effective tool for certain types of adult learning.

Forum

A forum—also called a lecture-forum or lecture-discussion—is any meeting given over to general public discussion of some particular issue or closely connected group of issues. Its purpose is to air issues, explore ideas, and interpret information. This kind of program presents a greater challenge to the leader than other types do, because more people are taking an active part in the discussion and the outcome is less predictable.

In some forums, a film is used to present the essential background information. Someone may explain the purpose of the film, suggest how it can be used, and call attention to particular things to note in it. After the film has been shown, audience members may comment or raise questions. It is essential to preview any film or filmstrip before presenting it to an audience. Preparations must also be made to prevent mechanical failure of the projector and equipment.

Debate

The debate is suitable only for "either-or" issues. A debate is usually followed by questions from the audience.

Panel

The panel is made up of three to six people who exchange views on some problem or issue. The program is unrehearsed and informal, and the discussion has the give-and-take of conversation. Panel members may put questions to one another, and they may differ with one another. Planning in advance exactly what each person will say defeats the purpose of a panel discussion, which is not to give speeches but to explore a subject together. The panel members should have more than a casual knowledge of the subject they discuss.

The chairman or leader of the panel, sometimes called the moderator, opens the discussion with a statement about the problem or topic to be explored. It is his responsibility to introduce the panel members or ask each one to introduce himself. At the close of the discussion, he throws the meeting open to the audience for brief comments or questions directed to the panel in general or to individual panel members.

Symposium

Like a panel, a symposium is made up of several speakers. The difference is that they give short prepared talks—perhaps 15 minutes in length—on various sides of the same subject. To make the best use of their time, the speakers should know in advance what ground each will cover. The talks may follow one another without any break, limiting audience participation to a discussion after the last talk, or there may be both a short question period after each speaker and a general question period at the end.

Brainstorming

Brainstorming was designed by Alex Osborn, an advertising executive, to develop radically new ideas. To be successful, it depends on an uninhibited atmosphere and spontaneity. It may be used with small or large groups, but groups of 12 seem most popular. The problem to be attacked must be an important one that concerns action rather than policy.

The first step is to state the problem clearly. Once it has been satisfactorily defined, members of the group voice every solution that comes to mind, regardless of how simple or complex, radical or unrealistic. A recorder writes the suggestions on a blackboard or piece of newsprint. Only after the group has exhausted all possible ideas does it begin to evaluate them in open discussion. Some ideas will be quickly discarded, but many will be retained that under ordinary conditions might never have been advanced.

Circular Response

The members of the group—10 to 20 are preferred—are seated in a circle. The chairman or leader proposes the question. The person at his right has the first opportunity to express his views, followed by the person at *his* right, and so on until the discussion has gone around the circle. No member of the group can speak a second time until his turn comes again. For example, the person sitting fourth from the leader's right may express his views on the subject or on the opinions advanced by the leader and the three before him. If, however, the person who follows him says something that arouses his ire, he has no chance for rebuttal until the next time around.

The circular response does wonders to correct the bad manners and monopolistic practices that often mar a group discussion. Extreme views presented in a belligerent manner are modified by the restraints imposed. The timid person speaks more freely when he knows that it is his natural right as a member of the group.

Demonstration

The technique of demonstration, in most cases, is quite simple. But demonstrations need a certain amount of advance preparation in order to be worthwhile. A checklist for planning a demonstration follows:

1. Prepare in advance by analyzing everything that is to be done.
2. Be ready to begin without delay by having all tools, materials, and supplies in readiness on your desk or table.

3. Have the class gathered around you so that the students can see clearly everything that takes place.
4. Prepare the students by explaining in advance what is going to happen, calling attention to the key points to be noticed.
5. Be sure the demonstration is given slowly and deliberately so that each step can be clearly seen and understood.
6. Explain each step after its completion.
7. Provide an opportunity for questions after each step, even if they interrupt the demonstration.
8. Conclude with a final summary; then immediately answer questions and evaluate.
9. If at all possible, let each student operate the demonstration himself.

Field Trips

The field trip should be an opportunity to gather information that cannot be gotten as completely in any other way. If it is not, it is a waste of the students' time. The trip can have a variety of benefits: it can be an upgrading experience, helping the adults to set new goals and to see these goals as realistic; it can show them new jobs for which they can later compete; it can broaden their horizons with new ideas about working, living, learning, and enjoying. To be effective, the field trip must be directly related to the concepts to be learned and must be carefully planned and organized.

The effective adult education program will incorporate a variety of instructional methods. Discussion groups, team teaching, demonstrations, field trips, filmstrips, learning laboratories—all can introduce variety. These methods, of course, should be selected on the basis of intended educational outcomes for a given target population with certain attributes or needs.

ADDITIONAL SOURCES OF INFORMATION

Adult Education Association of the U.S.A.
1225 Nineteenth Street, N.W., Washington, D.C. 20036

Adult Services Division, American Library Association
50 East Huron Street, Chicago, Ill. 60611

American Society for Training and Development
P.O. Box 5307, 517 N. Segoe Rd., Madison, Wis. 53705

Association of University Evening Colleges
University of Oklahoma, Adult Admission and Records
1700 Asp Avenue, Norman, Okla. 73069

National Association for Public Continuing and Adult Education
1201 Sixteenth Street, N.W., Washington, D.C. 20036

National University Extension Association
One Dupont Circle, N.W., Washington, D.C. 20036

Bureau of Adult Education
New Jersey State Department of Education
333 West State Street, Trenton, N.J. 08618

BIBLIOGRAPHY

1. Crabtree, Arthur P. *The Curriculum in Adult Education.* Trenton, N.J.: State Department of Education, Bureau of Adult Education, 1968.
2. Johnstone, John W. C., and Rivera, Ramon J. *Volunteers for Learning: A Study of the Educational Pursuits of American Adults.* Chicago: Aldine, 1965.
3. Knowles, Malcolm S. *The Modern Practice of Adult Education: Androgogy vs. Pedagogy.* New York: Association Press, 1970.
4. National Association for Public Continuing and Adult Education. *Administration of Continuing Education: A Guide for Administrators.* Washington, D.C.: the Association, a national affiliate of the National Education Association, 1969.
5. Smith, Robert M.; Aker, George F.; and Kidd, J. R., editors. *Handbook of Adult Education.* New York: Adult Education Association of the USA, 1970.

2

Art Education

The invitation to write a chapter in this curriculum handbook for school administrators stressed the need for a "clear and concise" statement. For art educators this is indeed a challenge and, in some cases, might precipitate an apology, for art education often seems far from "clear and concise." However, the apparent lack of consistency is in fact a reflection of the discipline's greatest asset and should not be judged without more in-depth evaluation. Art education is by its very nature a distinctive and inherently individual process; but while it often demands a greater flexibility and freedom than other disciplines, it does contain consistencies as a discipline. In other words, guidelines and directions are available. There are serious and valuable concerns in art, beyond simply learning facts or developing mechanical skills or techniques. Those concerns fall within the affective domain and deal with the encouragement of feeling, thinking, appreciation, and sensitivity in human beings. They cannot be measured or discussed with the calculation that might afford a neat treatment.

In a book that has made a recent impact on educational thinking, *Crisis in the Classroom,* Charles Silberman outlines a need for the development of the entire individual, including the emotions, feelings, and intuition often overlooked in the rush to meet the technological demands of a mechanistic society. Silberman cites the understanding of the ancient Hebrews (7, p. 8):

> . . . the biblical verb *yadah,* "to know," signifies a unification of intellect, feeling, and action. . . . Contemporary psychologists have the same understanding; in Jerome Bruner's phrase, "the scientist and the poet do not live at antipodes." On the contrary, the artificial separation of these aspects or modes of knowing—the false dichotomy between the "cognitive" and the "affective" domain—can only cripple the development of thought and feeling. If this be so, then poetry, music, painting, dance, and the other arts are not frills to be indulged in if time is left over from the real business of education; they *are* the business of education.

Art educators share a commitment to this "total" concept of parallel rather than dichotomous domains.

One of the most encouraging signs to art teachers has been the vocabulary of education in recent years, exemplified by such phrases as "quality of life." The implication, it seems, goes far beyond a simple concern for the physical needs and comforts of humanity and begins to suggest attention to the kind of values that are nurtured by art education. Perception, sensitivity, critical awareness, and creative problem-solving abilities—all items high on the priority list of any art educator—are beginning to receive increasing emphasis as we strive for true quality and appreciation of life in an increasingly complex environment. Obviously, one must also pay heed to other recurring words in today's educational vocabulary—such words as *accountability, assessment, relevancy,* and *priority.* These words challenge art education and all other disciplines to come to grips with some of the pressing needs of today's society and to assess their own effectiveness in meeting educational needs.

Curriculum Content

Certain guidelines have been established that outline the need for an art program in the schools and suggest a general curricular rationale. The National Art Education Association (3) has adopted as its official policy that—

1. Art experiences are an essential part of schools' programs of education.
2. All children and youth must be afforded a carefully planned program in art from kindergarten through high school.
3. Such a program should be developmental in character.
4. To provide such a program it is necessary to have well prepared personnel, adequate curriculum content, and sufficient time.
5. Physical facilities, equipment, and material should be available in sufficient quality and quantity so that the art personnel can provide art experiences that will result in the full development of the potentialities of each individual.

Background and Rationale for Art in General Education

Art, of course, has been a part of public education for well over a hundred years, starting with the activities of William Morris in the late nineteenth century, and has progressed through the child study movement, the psychological dimension of the artistic experience as outlined by Dewey and later Lowenfeld, the functional aspects of the art form as characterized by the Owatonna study in the 1930's, and other movements. All of these movements had generalizable characteristics for education, but art was still considered a subject outside the context of general education and not concerned with the basic learning skills supposedly needed by the typical elementary or secondary child.

Art to many administrators and teachers was, and unfortunately often still is, considered a subject apart from the mainstream of education. In fact, it is usually considered something for the highly skilled or talented and has the connotation of an elite subject. The talented few for whom art may have some career potential should not be overlooked, but they are only one concern of the art educator. Such a narrow focus excludes the majority of students, for whom the art experience is a significant educational asset.

The false connotation of art in the public school is not difficult to understand, for often the decision makers in public education—the administrators—have not had any formal education in the arts. Often the values that elevate art education to a priority position among subjects are neither enumerated adequately by the discipline nor fully comprehended by the administrator. Realizing this problem, art educators are increasingly concerning themselves with the problem of placing art in the mainstream of general education. The support generated within a particular school system for the art program usually determines whether it continues to exist.

Art educators prefer to think of art as an essential part of the education of every student. General education in art would encompass the first nine years of the student's program and include the kinds of arts learnings useful not only to students preparing for professional careers in art but also to students who will take positions in business, education, or technology. In stressing general rather than specialized education in art, the aims are (a) to develop the student's skills in the areas of making esthetic judgments about man-made as well as natural phenomena, (b) to give him a general knowledge of the characteristics and function of art forms and an understanding of how the arts perpetuate and maintain a culture, and (c) to provide a range of esthetic experiences through the production and analysis of art objects.

John D. Rockfeller III (6) has aptly summarized the case for a general education in the arts for all students:

> Arts education is considered a separate matter, not woven into the fabric of general education. Our present system is to involve some of the children—usually those who demonstrate special interest or talent—with one or two of the arts. Theatre, dance, film, architecture are virtually nonexistent. As a result, the teaching of history remains distinct from art history. Our children graduate without understanding that the creative scientist and the creative artist have a great deal in common. Segregated and restricted in scope, the arts are a kind of garnish, easily set aside, like parsley.
>
> A clear-cut conclusion emerges: we need to expose all of the children in our schools to all of the arts, and to do so in a way that enriches the general curriculum rather than reinforcing the segregation of the arts.

Mr. Rockefeller's concern is that the value system in our society should be changing, that the arts should play a significant role in the changing of this system, and that education could and should be the vehicle for this change.

Art education can be seen either as a separate discipline within the total school program—the art class as opposed to math, social studies, science, and so forth—or as esthetic education—the development of that aspect of the individual that embodies the feelings, emotions, and thinking in a totally sensitive and creative process. The second focus is not really separate from the first.

Art Education as a Discipline

While there has been concern for relating art to other arts disciplines in order to provide an area of study for all students, there has also been a significant movement toward defining the content areas in art that are appropriate for the art program itself. The emphasis in the elementary and secondary art programs of the 1950's was solely on those activities that resulted in an end product, the art object. The production of art and the creative process are exciting for the student and intrinsic to a good art program, but the emphasis on "just making art" (without understanding what the process is for or what the object means when it is created) did not generate the comprehensive art learning that most art educators thought was essential in an art program. Therefore, in recent years there has been an intensive effort to help the student to make critical judgments about art objects and to look at the historical and cultural implications of art in our society as well.

The addition of these two emphases places more stress on the whole work as an esthetic phenomenon to be studied, analyzed, and discussed. Many of today's art educators believe that the student should not only have the experience and develop the skills to produce art, but also be able to talk intelligently about the purposes, processes, and end products in the very broadly based discipline of art. Art educators have attempted to develop curriculums at all levels, from kindergarten to college, which reflect this broadened emphasis. They see art as not only an activity-centered discipline but also one with an academic dimension provided by the areas of art history and art criticism, formerly emphasized only at the college level. This academic dimension has now moved down into the high school and the elementary school.

Guidelines for Teacher Preparation, compiled by the National Art Education Association in 1970 (5), outlines the content areas in art education with which the teacher should be concerned:

> Throughout the two major components of content to be taught, the productive (studio) and the appreciative (history and criticism), conscious efforts should be made to alert students to two overarching premises: (a) The uniqueness of works of art, from inspiration to completion, is determined by the individual, his purposes, his culture, the media and tools he selects and his methods and procedures. (b) It is critical to develop sensitivity to—and skills in—description, analysis, and evaluation of art forms.
>
> 1. The Studio Component
>
>   Basic concepts and skills related to processes, organizational structure, technical aspects, expressive content, communicative qualities, technological knowledge are to be developed through studio experiences. The creation of expressive forms should include: drawing, painting, printmaking, photography, film making, graphic communication, sculpture, and crafts (fabrics, wood, metal, clay, etc.). Instruction should include traditional as well as newer technological developments.
>
> 2. The Art Appreciation Component: Aesthetics, Art, History, and Criticism
>
>   The program should include study of contending philosophies of art, the developments of past and contemporary art forms, and examination of theories of criticism.
>
> 3. The Advanced (In-Depth) Work Component
>
>   The program should require extended work in at least one or more studio and/or art appreciation areas (competencies built upon and beyond the above areas listed in 1 and 2).

While additional areas of concern and supplementary knowledge are quite extensive, it is adequate here to stay with these three major components.

Studio Component. Active participation in the making of art is an exceptionally valuable part of the art experience in education. The chance for a student to solve creatively some artistic problem from beginning to end, from selection of materials to completion of work, is an exceptionally valid and increasingly rare experience in education. Too often our compartmentalized society and school curriculum force students to think and develop in fragmented fashion. The art experience allows a student to initiate a project; explore the possibilities; choose solutions; and examine, evaluate, and verify his conclusions in a personal and unique way. New materials that are introduced, whether they be fabric or metal or wood, bring to the student their inherent characteristics which he must evaluate and, through sensitivity, use to their best advantage in his own expressive act. Creative expression growing out of new and challenging barriers works toward the development of an increasingly sensitive human being, aware of textures, forms, shapes, and colors as well as arrangements, structures, and orders in the world around him. Such a human being is better equipped to cope with the great majority of today's problems—problems that demand creative solutions.

Art Appreciation Component. The study of art history enables the student to appreciate and learn from the art of the past, to explore the art of the present, and to develop a deeper cultural understanding of his own heritage. It can help him develop a healthy self-image—something that is increasingly important in an often impersonal technological age. The gap that often seems to exist between students and art is being bridged in many communities by such innovations as traveling exhibitions of art work and visiting lecture and performance series by local professional artists. Coupled with effective teaching, these innovations help students see art as no longer some strange, mystical force or special museum possession but rather as a strong, dynamic, and viable force in the lives of human beings.

Advanced Work Component. "Advanced work" usually refers to the development of teacher expertise, but it can likewise be offered to students in elementary and secondary schools. For as a student progresses from elementary to secondary levels, he works on an increasingly independent basis for his own satisfaction and development. The obvious implication is a need for greater flexibility in scheduling, organization, and facilities for this individualistic component in art education.

Esthetic Education and Interdisciplinary Studies

If art is considered part of the general education of every student, how then can this type of program be implemented in a school setting? A number of projects and programs have been devoted to the idea of art as general education and to the broadening of the context of art into fields of study such as esthetic education, interdisciplinary education, and allied arts. In a 1969 National Art Education Association publication on exemplary programs in art (4), the largest section was devoted to interdisciplinary programs. Such programs expand the range of the discipline with which art is combined; they usually bring together such arts disciplines as visual arts, music, literature, dance, or film.

The trend throughout elementary and secondary education in recent years has been away from discipline orientation and toward broader areas of study which relate or juxtapose the disciplines. An example of such an area of study is esthetic education. No one is suggesting that the study of philosophical esthetics, a subject area usually found at the college level, should be moved down into the elementary and secondary schools. On the contrary, esthetic education implies the generalizability of esthetic phenomena to all students and at all levels of instruction. Esthetic education, with its larger frame of reference, encompasses all the arts disciplines: literature, music, theater arts, dance, film, and the visual arts. The student in an esthetic education program would be involved in a broadly based program in the primary grades. As he moved through the program to the intermediate grades, the junior high, and the senior high, the separate disciplines would emerge at appropriate times depending on their requirements for early student involvement and the needs of the student at a particular level of instruction. Such a program would logically parallel the patterns of instruction now existing in the social sciences or mathematics and would provide a manageable solution to the dilemma that there is not enough time in the school day for all the arts as separate disciplines. It should be noted that this is an emerging idea; it has not been tested in a total school setting. However, many art educators are now initiating and testing programs based on this concept.

On the national level, the John D. Rockefeller III Foundation initiated three pilot projects through its Arts and Education Program. These pilot projects have formed the basis of a program that has as its main objective the bringing of all the arts to all the students in the context of general education. Other programs geared to similar objectives include the IMPACT Project and the CEMREL Aesthetic Education Program, a curriculum development effort to develop instructional materials for esthetic education. (CEMREL is the Central Midwestern Regional Laboratory, Inc., in St. Louis, Mo.—one of 11 educational laboratories supported by the U.S. Office of Education.) These programs and projects have started to bring the arts into closer proximity with one another in the context of the curriculum at both the elementary and the secondary levels.

Environmental Studies and the Changing Classroom Environment

The esthetic condition of our environment is a significant facet of esthetic education and should be one of the concerns of an art program. There is general agreement that we have neglected the esthetic dimension of our environment, as evidenced by the strip developments in most cities and their chaotic visual images, by the boxlike suburban homes that offer little visual variety and provide a universal sameness from city to city, or by the freeways—concrete albatrosses that sever the city sociologically and visually. These problems and their implications for the visual dimensions of both the man-made and the natural environment are becoming content areas for art education programs. In one sense, the total environment becomes the learning environment for the visual arts, for it is from perceptions of our surroundings that creative expression receives its impetus. The types of activities that students engage in are varied. However, the program usually begins with developing the total environment as a reference for visual problem solving. The student at some point also deals with the urban environment as if he were an urban designer and relates to the problems of designing a new city or town or recreating an existing urban area. The American Institute of Architects has stimulated the development of such projects as *Our Man-Made Environment,* by GEE! (Group for Environmental Education) in Philadelphia, *Our Cities,* by June McFee, to cite but two examples of materials used to teach environmental concepts in art education.

Another very important facet of our environment is the school itself, which can become subject matter for an art program. Providing an exciting visual environment for learning is a genuine concern for art education at all levels. It is disheartening to realize that most public school buildings in the United States are very bleak, austere, uninteresting places in which children are supposed to do exciting things. There have been many innovations in school construction in recent years, as exemplified by the work of the Educational Facilities Laboratories, but these innovations have not filtered down into schools as rapidly as one might expect or hope. Many art education programs have taken on the task of redesigning the school environment as a part of their study of the environment. Letting students paint the halls with supergraphics and fill lunchroom and classroom spaces with images gives the school some personality and makes it reflect the students it serves. This is a difficult concept for some administrators to understand, because it is almost sacrilege to mark or change any part of the school building. However, enlightened administrators are coming to realize that the environment has a significant effect on how a child learns, and that having a part in altering the learning environment can enhance the learning process.

Newer Media

Another emerging trend in art education is the treatment of film as an art form. Students today are exposed to the moving visual image on the television screen for hours on end. This exposure has implications for education, although there remain many unknowns. However, it seems clear that the media should become a part of the art education program, if only because of such exposure. The student should be able not only to deal with the production of the art object through the traditional modes of drawing, painting, sculpture, or the crafts, but also to orchestrate and judge visual images produced through the media.

Recording happenings or events is one way of using the film medium; another method, which introduces a creative dimension, is using film to produce a work of art. The student of today is media-oriented and enjoys learning to manipulate visual images using film and sound. Even kindergarteners have successfully made films and used still cameras. Programs in many parts of the country are demonstrating that filmmaking can become an integral part of the elementary and secondary curriculum. Making films or visual presentations, whether to produce an art form or to better understand how the media convey information, is a skill pertinent to our time.

Instructional Methodology and Organizational Patterns

Many an adult can still recall the "artistic" experiences of his early school years: such activities as tracing his hand to make a turkey for Thanksgiving, cutting out duplicate daisies for window decoration, or coloring in a teacher-drawn and duplicated picture—being careful not to go outside the lines, of course. We can only hope that such activities, which have "turned off" countless people to the excitement of art, are finally disappearing from the classroom. The kinds of school structures that encouraged such "training" have given way to innovative structures better suited to implementing truly creative art programs.

Art teachers, like educators in all disciplines, are concerned and involved with nongraded schools and programs, team teaching, flexible and nonpermanent groupings, differentiated staffing, and other emerging patterns and organizations of educational activity. To attempt to focus on a specific direction as the best for art in the schools would defeat the very purpose of these innovations in curricular organization and instructional methodology, which are aimed at maintaining flexibility and adaptability in the program. Neil Atkins (1) puts this issue in perspective when he explains (p. 98),

> The question isn't "How shall a school be organized?" but "What kind of learning environment does it produce?" The question isn't "How are the schools staffed?" but "What are the people who staff it doing?" The answer to the second half of both questions depends upon the refocused objectives of the school. If indeed the focus is on individual performance rather than group categorization, then the way children and adults are deployed in school must make it possible for the individual to take precedence over the group; the organization has to encourage, not inhibit, people who are a part of that organization to behave in ways that will personalize rather than generalize the learning process. But first they must know what they want to do before they can organize to do it.

The art teacher's involvement with organizational patterns and methodologies, then, is not so different from that of teachers in other areas. The search for implementation structures depends largely on the objectives of the discipline itself and explores the best means of providing a learning-centered environment to meet those objectives. In the case of art education, there is increasing focus on assessing objectives and evaluating programs so that the organization and staffing of the programs can be best implemented to answer the need.

One specific national effort toward assessment of the effectiveness of art education systems in terms of desirable goals and objectives is the National Assessment in Art (9), now scheduled for 1974 and 1975. The ongoing process of assessment, of course, is not waiting until 1974 but is being carried out by teachers on a day-to-day basis as they continually evaluate their goals and methodologies in their individual situations.

Attempts to structure curriculum exist in programs such as the Kettering Project, the major goal of which was "the development of an effective art curriculum supported by useful instructional materials for children of elementary school age" (2, p. 1), or projects similar to those of CEMREL, Inc., that developed curriculum packages that likewise provide structure and activities to meet goals. Such projects contain evaluative components that assess strengths and weaknesses and point to new structures and methodologies in art education. Perhaps the very fact that one ideal pattern of school organization cannot be formulated to answer all situations is the strength of current educational thought. The firmly structured educational patterns of the past have given way to new arrangements, just as the "coloring book" idea of art has given way to meaningful creative expression and esthetic understanding and appreciation.

In talking with a group of art teachers, Herbert Thelen (8) made the following point (p. 17):

> We must assume that there is an aesthetic aspect of all the activities of man. Art is the endeavor in which this aspect is most explicit, demonstrable, and manipulative. Basically art activity is a refinement of, and a response to, the whole host of structure-seeking behaviors of men, and art education should facilitate these natural, valuable, and inevitable processes.

It is to be hoped that school administrators, realizing the need to encourage, develop, and foster the basic esthetic aspect of human endeavors, will lend support to the development of art education as a fundamental and vital part of the school curriculum. Art educators (3) stress that administrators can help ensure the continued growth and quality of the art program in the school by—

1. Providing an adequate number of art teachers.
2. Scheduling art as a regular part of the total school program.
3. Controlling student-teacher ratios in art classes.
4. Providing time and space for inservice education of teachers of art.
5. Maintaining facilities for an effective art program.
6. Securing opportunities for using community resources.
7. Encouraging art teachers to take an active part in local, state, and national professional art education associations.

With the quality of life a priority item on the education agenda, we can hardly overlook the affective domain embodied so well in the art program, for it encourages appreciation of the quality of life. It would indeed be unfortunate if art, an integral part of human endeavor and human behavior, were thought a "frill." To eliminate art for short-term expediency would prevent us in the long run from reaching the real goal—education.

BIBLIOGRAPHY

1. Atkins, Neil P. "Changing Concepts of Schoolhouse Activity: Organizational Life and Supervisor Behavior." *Supervision: A Mandate for Change.* Report on the Seminar for Improving the Effectiveness of Supervisors in Art Education. Washington, D.C.: National Art Education Association, 1970. pp. 87-99.
2. Eisner, Elliot W., and others. *Teaching Art to the Young: A Curriculum Development Project in Art Education.* Dayton, Ohio: Charles F. Kettering Foundation, November 1969.
3. National Art Education Association. *The Essentials of a Quality School Art Program.* Washington, D.C.: the Association, 1967.
4. ———. *Exemplary Programs in Art Education.* (Edited by Stanley Madeja.) Washington, D.C.: the Association, 1969.
5. ———. *Guidelines for Teacher Preparation.* Washington, D.C.: the Association, 1970.
6. Rockefeller, John D., III. *The Arts in Education: All the Arts for All the Children.* Address before the General Assembly of the Arts and Education Council of Greater St. Louis, April 17, 1969. New York: John D. Rockefeller III Foundation, 1969.
7. Silberman, Charles E. *Crisis in the Classroom.* New York: Random House, 1970.
8. Thelen, Herbert A. "From Individual Behavior to Classroom Activity: An Inquiry into Art Education." *Supervision: A Mandate for Change.* Report of the Seminar for Improving Effectiveness of Supervisors in Art Education. Washington, D.C.: National Art Education Association, 1970.
9. Wilson, Brent. "The Status of National Assessment in Art." *Art Education* 23:2; December 1970.

3

Business Education

As its purposes have expanded and its technology has increased and been refined, business education has constantly undergone changes in both organizational structure and content. Because its programs on all levels have made use of independent and diverse operational procedures, the possibilities for innovation and the opportunities for leadership development have been great. Recognizing that rigid centralization of thought and practice only appears to lead to achievement and that too much regimentation ultimately results in the stifling of individual initiative, business education has steered a course away from conformity. The aim has been to maintain flexibility in business programs from their initial planning through their implementation and evaluation.

The goals of business education are (a) to provide effective programs of occupational instruction for students desiring careers in business, (b) to make an important contribution to the economic literacy of all students, and (c) to provide programs for students requiring postsecondary education in the field of business.

An individual's education is incomplete unless career goals and an understanding of occupational possibilities give purpose to his learning. There are common and unique elements in each phase of education, and it must be always kept in mind that it is important for students to learn not only how to live but also how to earn a living. Business education is one element in the total education program that serves both the general and career objectives of young people and adults.

The immense value of business education may be lost if we fail to provide adequate counseling for all students. Occupational information and assistance in interpreting it should be provided through the guidance department as well as through personal conferences with business teachers. Every student should be helped to develop an awareness of his own interests and capabilities so that he may plan his career and prepare for it in the most efficient and effective manner.

The time devoted to preparation for business careers should depend upon the student's abilities, interests, and personal qualities. The sequences of learning experiences should be planned so that the student will achieve his highest occupational competency upon completion of his program.

In general, the business curriculum is pursued by students in junior high schools, secondary schools, area vocational-technical centers, and adult or continuing education centers. These schools may be located in urban, suburban, or rural surroundings. Their programs must meet the needs not only of the "average" student but also of the gifted and the disadvantaged. Programming, scheduling, and instructional methods must be flexible in order to meet the needs of students in varying circumstances and with varying abilities. No business program should lead to a "dead-end" career or prevent the student from continuing his education in a post-secondary institution.

Unrealistic academic requirements established by institutions of higher learning can be and often are detrimental to the business education program at the secondary level. These arbitrary requirements tend to screen out many good students and make it difficult for them to gain the necessary competencies for business employment. The school administrator can have tremendous impact on those who are responsible for establishing standards for admission and graduation in our schools and colleges. Business teachers should work closely with school administrators to provide the information on which action can be taken to remedy this situation. The major problem that faces educators today, including many business educators, is the false assumption that everyone will graduate from high school and enter college or be employed.

This problem can only be solved through an effective education and implementation program for all teachers and administrators involved in the articulation of business programs from the junior high school through graduate school. Business programs must be designed on the premise that business education is a part of the total educational program, which must provide for the needs of all students, in all communities, at all educational levels.

Administrative Organization

For any business program to function properly, curriculum leaders must keep the school administrator abreast of the changing curriculum patterns and needs of the business department. Busy school administrators, charged with responsibility for the total educational program, often have neither the time nor the opportunity to gain insight into the activities and goals of the business department. Therefore, it becomes the responsibility of business teachers and supervisors to provide the information needed in a concise form. A plan of action for the business department for the current year and the foreseeable future should be summarized effectively in an instrument that translates the educational program into dollars and cents.

The Business Department Head

Every business department in every school must have a department head to provide general direction and leadership for the department and to coordinate it with the total school program. Even in a school with only two business teachers, one should be designated the department head or chairman. In order to carry out the duties required, the department head should be given a reduced teaching load, additional compensation, or a combination of these.

This specialist in the field of business education serves as a liaison between the administration and the department, interpreting the school's goals to the department and representing the department's point of view to the school administrator. He should provide not only for effective implementation of educational programs but also for the orderly conduct of scheduling and budgeting. The office of the department chairman and the classrooms, laboratories, and storage rooms should be models of efficient business management. An effective system of internal control for equipment, maintenance, textbooks, and supplies must be initiated and maintained. One of the most important challenges of the department head's job is to stimulate the professional growth of his staff members by opening new horizons for them in program offerings and in service to the business community.

Another responsibility of the business department head is to serve as the coordinator of business education on the adult or continuing education level and/or in the evening high school. The same classrooms, equipment, and teachers are typically used for adult education and evening high schools. Coordination of the overall program, including maintenance and effective use of equipment and instructional materials, is necessary to avoid possible conflicts between the regular day program and the adult or evening program.

The business department head should be an active member of the school cabinet, participating in the formulation of school policies and objectives and in the continuous evaluation of the total school curriculum. He should formulate long-range plans for departmental development, examine current programs and courses for possible revisions, develop plans for new programs deemed essential, determine adequacy of departmental facilities and equipment for existing and proposed programs, secure a realistic indication of possible funding, and submit a prepared budget to the appropriate school administrator. Of course, in carrying out these duties, the effective department chairman must constantly involve his business teachers and keep them informed of progress toward desired goals.

Local Supervision and Administration

Most city and large county school systems employ a supervisor of business education, who is responsible for the overall improvement of the business program, including curriculum guides, instructional aids, and methods of teaching. It is his job to provide assistance to school administrators and teachers through professional meetings, classroom visits, conferences, and demonstration lessons. In addition he assists school administrators with a number of administrative details concerning the total school program: physical facilities, enrollment statistics, funding, purchase and maintenance of equipment, etc.

The most important of the local supervisor's functions is coordination. In order to design and conduct a business program to fit the needs of students and the business community, a close liaison must be maintained between business education and the business and civic organizations within the school district. Careful plans for a continuous program of public relations must be made for the entire school year.

Advisory Committees

Business community involvement is vital. It is the responsibility of the supervisor of business education to coordinate the activities of each school in forming an advisory committee and obtaining members for it. There should be one member representing each of the curriculums the school offers. An overall district-level advisory committee could be made up of one member from each of the local advisory committees. School administrators should be a part of these advisory committees to represent school management.

State Supervision and Administration

The state supervisor assigned to the division of vocational-technical education of the state department of education is responsible for the statewide program of business education. Like the local supervisor, he must provide the leadership needed for curriculum improvement, but he must also deal with a number of administrative concerns unique to the state department of education.

Of particular concern to school administrators is the development of the business education section of the state plan for vocational-technical education. Once this state plan has been approved by the U.S. Office of Education, it serves as the operating policy under which the business education service will function. It concerns itself primarily with authorization for federal funds and the allocation of these funds to local school districts offering programs of vocational-technical education.

Federal reimbursement for programs offered at the local level is authorized through the Vocational Education Amendments of 1968 and the Elementary and Secondary Education Act. These federal legislative acts provide the guidelines under which the state plan for vocational education is developed and implemented. Problems are frequently created for school administrators when state departments of education spend all their time working with reimbursable programs and neglect schools in the nonreimbursable category, which may need their professional assistance even more. Even if the state supervisor of business education has a portion of his salary reimbursed by the federal government through one of the legislative acts mentioned above, he must remember that he is on the state payroll. Federal funding should not and must not determine which school administrators, teachers, and students are served. It is the responsibility of the business education service to work for all the people in all the communities throughout the state.

Teacher Preparation and Qualifications

Institutions preparing business teachers offer basic content instruction as well as needed professional education courses. Most business teachers are graduates of four-year colleges or universities.

In some cases a five-year program (one year beyond the bachelor's degree) is required for certification to teach business subjects. Usually there are special certification requirements for business teachers, which include a broad background in the field of business administration, courses in professional business education, and a required number of courses in each business subject or group of subjects the student proposes to teach. Prior to their graduation and certification, all prospective business teachers serve a part-time internship as student teachers in an approved high school under the direction of an experienced teacher. In some cases, business teachers are certified to teach on the basis of a successful score on the National Teacher Examinations. Temporary certificates are issued to persons who have received a highly specialized type of training that did not require a bachelor's degree—e.g., computer programming—and who wish to enter the teaching field. Once they have taken some professional education courses, including methods of teaching and educational psychology, these individuals with highly specialized skills can make a very important contribution to the business department.

Full-time or part-time occupational experience in his teaching area is very desirable for a teacher, because it provides an overall view of the knowledge, skills, and competencies required in the job for which he is training future employees. Work experience enables the teacher to go beyond the typical textbook experiences and to bring a more businesslike atmosphere into the classroom.

Inservice education is offered during school vacations by colleges and universities working with local school boards. These inservice programs, which are coordinated by the local supervisor of business, sometimes offer credit toward a master's degree.

Journals and yearbooks published by professional associations also help to keep the teacher up to date on trends and developments in the business field. Teacher growth and development is essential if business education teaching methods are to keep pace with technological changes in the business and industrial community.

Arrangement of the Business Program

The business program may be divided into several specialized areas to provide students with training for a cluster of business occupations: (a) secretarial-stenographic, (b) bookkeeping and accounting, (c) business data processing, (d) clerical skills, (e) marketing and distribution, and (f) administrative management and supervision, as well as more specific clusters within any one of these categories. Flexibility must be maintained to allow students to transfer from one cluster to another on a semester or quarter basis. Students should be guided by business teachers into specific programs best suited to their interests, needs, and abilities. Sequencing courses within a particular program is the key to providing the most efficient program to prepare young people for careers in business.

In sequencing courses for a specific occupational program, it is important to remember that students need to have a thorough knowledge of our free enterprise system and how it operates. The basic or general business course and other prevocational courses such as consumer education and economics instill economic concepts that help ensure future success in a business career program. Offering such courses in cooperation with the social studies and home economics departments is most desirable.

Cocurricular Youth Activities

Business-oriented youth organizations can add immeasurably to a regular business program. Although formal classroom learning still constitutes the backbone of business education, it is important to recognize that what takes place outside the classroom often makes a more lasting impression on one's habits, attitudes, and future life. Future Business Leaders of America-Phi Beta Lambda was founded (and continues to function) for one specific purpose—to provide business students with the experiences and leadership training necessary for future success in their business careers. Within the framework of this organization, teachers can stimulate interest in many relevant activities and projects that are not feasible in a classroom situation. There is no better way for business students to gain an understanding of the American free enterprise system. In a very personal and practical way, they themselves conduct and become actively involved in projects that extend beyond normal classroom instruction. The business teacher serves in an advisory capacity only and provides guidance to each individual member of the group in relationship to the overall project. Phi Beta Lambda provides an opportunity for many students to gain firsthand knowledge from experts in the field of business, to "belong," to be of service to other people, and to gain recognition from teachers, other adults, and their peers.

Instructional Designs and Scheduling

Major attention has been given in recent years to individualized instruction, modular scheduling, simulation, and other instructional innovations. The school administrator, in conjunction with the business department head, must decide whether the goals of the business program can be best met through traditional, modular, or block-time scheduling; whether simulation of a model office or a cooperative program will best serve the needs of students in preparing for business careers; whether programed instruction, team teaching, or the project method will fit the availabilities and preferences of his teaching staff. Each design and schedule has a unique contribution to make, and no one design or schedule is the answer for all students. The final choice must be based on the needs of the students to be served. Perhaps a combination of two or more of these methods would best suit the needs of a particular school or school system.

Traditional Scheduling

A traditional schedule (standard-length class periods offered on a daily and weekly cycle regardless of subject matter) is still effective in providing business programs to business students. Usually, teachers in the business program are assigned to subjects they are best qualified to teach. One of the major considerations in implementing the traditional schedule is to give top priority to business students. If additional class space is available after these students have been accommodated, other students who wish to take the subjects on an elective basis are admitted. Traditional scheduling is better suited to the needs of the nonbusiness student than the other types of scheduling are, because it does not involve large time segments.

One of the hazards of a traditional schedule is the possibility of having a "cafeteria-style" program emerge. Courses must be sequenced properly, and successful completion of the introductory or beginning-level courses should be established as a prerequisite for admission to advanced classes. Allowing students to take various business subjects without having a planned sequential program does them a disservice. It can also lead to dissatisfaction when employers discover that job-seeking graduates are inadequately prepared.

Block-Time Scheduling

Under block-time scheduling, two or more subjects that would ordinarily be taught separately are replaced or combined by two or more regular class periods. The courses to be combined into integrated blocks may vary. A three-hour block secretarial program could combine the subject matter and skills typically taught in the traditional advanced typewriting, advanced shorthand, and office procedures classes. A two-hour secretarial block might combine the areas covered in advanced shorthand and office procedures. A clerical block could be set up to include advanced typewriting and office procedures, with a larger block of time provided for low-ability students.

The major advantages of block-time scheduling are the integration of subject matter and the flexibility in activities and instruction. Block-time scheduling of business subjects offers the opportunity to train students for an occupation rather than teach only the skills required in one subject area. The block-time scheduling of beginning shorthand and advanced typewriting, for instance, provides a situation for carrying on office-type transcription activities. A block program combining the study of office machines with clerical office procedures provides the necessary time to make full use of a simulated office setup. In general, block-time scheduling reduces emphasis on fixed time allotments and period changes, makes possible more continuity in learning experiences, and reduces instructional duplication.

Modular Scheduling

Modular scheduling, because it divides the day (and the week) into a large number of component units, is probably the most flexible form of scheduling. Class periods are composed of any number of modules, depending on the length and frequency of class time required for proper teaching of the content and skills involved. Because it provides the possibility of varying the duration of classes, modular scheduling can be used effectively in block scheduling or in arranging other types of multiple periods for specialized programed learning, films, projects, or cocurricular activities that best fit the needs of business students. In addition, "unscheduled" modules allow students free time for such activities as using a shorthand dictation laboratory, getting extra practice in typewriting and on other office machines, or receiving the individual attention needed to develop skills and knowledge. The modular schedule approach can also foster the establishment of enrichment programs—such as an accounting seminar or a course in computer programming—for high-ability students.

Simulation

Whatever scheduling system is decided upon, the business department should consider various methods of instruction. Simulation is one method used to bridge the gap between the classroom and the business community. A simulated office makes use of a business office's basic functions, equipment, and interactions. It is a "real" organization of students, formed under the direction of the teacher, that carries on integrated office functions at a level and in a facility that correspond very closely to the typical business office. The simulated office can do the same work as a business office, thus enabling students to apply their knowledge and skills to the kind of work situation they will find when they are actually employed. The fundamental difference between a simulated office and an actual office is that the various company departments, products, and clients are fictitious. Students, however, compose "real" business communications, prepare invoices, keep track of inventory, and perform the many other tasks involved in operating an actual business.

Simulation emphasizes group learning. The primary relationships in simulation are among the several people in the group. They learn together how to work successfully in office groups. Training in a succession of office tasks enables all members of a group to grasp the concept of an office as an operating system with many interrelated parts and functions.

The Cooperative Method

The cooperative method of instruction, which combines classroom instruction with on-the-job training, offers business students an excellent way to meet their occupational objectives. The increasing complexity of modern business equipment and the scarcity of competent office workers point up the value of cooperative work-training programs. These programs, which expose students to realistic interpersonal relationships and the latest office procedures, techniques, and equipment, offer a higher quality learning experience than can be provided in a simulated office situation.

The term "cooperative" describes the relationship between the school and the employing business: they work together to prepare a student for his vocation. The classroom serves as the instructional center of the program, while the employing agency provides the needed laboratory experiences. The student benefits from the simultaneous presentation of theory and actual working practice. School administrators and teacher-coordinators in a cooperative program must exercise judgment in both the selection of students to participate in the program and the placement of these students in a working environment conducive to learning. Career development is affected by the experiences the student has on the job. If the teacher-coordinator, the student, and the job training supervisor jointly plan the training program, the student is likely to receive diversified and meaningful occupational training. The teacher-coordinator and the job training supervisor must work together to follow the plan, revise it, and prepare the student for meeting the planned objectives.

The Project Plan Laboratory

The project plan laboratory is especially suited to the needs of business students. Learning objectives are prescribed for each learner rather than for homogeneous groups. Each student is involved in his own business project and participates in integrated and interrelated work experiences and other learning activities necessary to develop occupational competence for his chosen career. The individualization of this approach results in variations in classroom organization, teaching techniques, instructional materials, facilities needed, use of the teacher's time, and evaluation procedures.

Types of learning experiences that can be provided through the project plan include in-school laboratory experiences, related instruction, related field experiences, and cocurricular youth activities. It is up to the teacher to correlate these activities with a planned, purposeful program in order to meet each student's individual needs, interests, and career objectives. The teacher must plan laboratory resources to include facilities and equipment designed to meet the objectives. He must also allow time in the schedule for whole-class, small-group, and individual activities. Since the teacher does not have the same control over a project plan laboratory as he would over a class using a more traditional instructional method, there must be constant evaluation and reinforcement of the goals.

Team Teaching

Team teaching can be readily applied to many business classroom situations. It has been found to improve the quality of teaching by allowing a more practical use of each instructor's specialized talents, interests, training, time, and energy. It also provides an arrangement for student grouping that more effectively gears instruction to individual student abilities. Team teaching can be used in conjunction with a variety of curriculum organizations, such as the project plan or simulated office laboratory, as well as in a traditional classroom. It provides an ideal teaching arrangement in a block-time class or in a modular schedule where adequate time is available for large-group instruction followed by small-group discussions and problem solving.

The most effective team teaching is accomplished when the team members plan the total effort together before the course begins. Team members must establish behavioral objectives as well as minimum levels of student performance for each objective. These objectives must be designed in light of current business, industrial, and manpower needs, and they must lead to the development of competent future businessmen and businesswomen. They must, however, be flexible, and the related learning steps must be changed regularly to meet the current and future needs of the student.

Programmed Instruction

Programmed instruction is effective in the regular business classroom and is especially valuable in a team-teaching or laboratory situation. The student has an opportunity to receive remedial help, gain extra practice, or widen the scope of his learning experience. Programmed materials may be commercially packaged kits, or they may be teacher-made tapes or other multimedia materials. Cassette recorder and playback units are especially useful for dictation practice in the shorthand classroom, allowing every student to work individually at his or her own pace.

In a modular schedule, programmed business materials can be used by students who have available time and wish to learn a business skill or related subject at their own convenience and speed. "Short courses" in various areas of the business curriculum can be taught through programmed materials.

The teacher who uses programmed materials will have more time to work individually with students who need assistance in problem areas. Programmed instruction minimizes the chance of boring the talented students or discouraging students with lesser abilities. Programmed business mathematics is currently a required course in general mathematics in many school districts.

Equipment for the Business Classroom and Laboratory

Instructional efficiency in business programs is dependent to a great extent upon adequate equipment and physical facilities. It is not possible to prepare one model layout or a particular list of equipment to fit the needs of every school. However, a detailed plan should be drawn up, showing number of rooms, size of each room, proposed layout for the work stations, and placement of desks, furniture, and equipment at each station. Occupational training is most effective when it uses the same operations, tools, and machines as the occupation itself. The proposed facilities and equipment plan should explain the educational program and describe present activities and anticipated programs. Furniture, equipment, special instructional materials, and any special utility services that will be required in the future should be described in these specifications.

The business teacher, the business supervisor at the local level, and the state supervisor of business education should be called upon to assist the school administrator in developing the educational specifications for facilities and equipment needed by the business department. In order to maintain modern business equipment, detailed budgets for the purchase, maintenance, and replacement of machines should be prepared by the business department. Complete records should be kept to serve as a basis for replacing equipment that requires extensive repairs, has outlived its usefulness, or has been replaced in the business world by new and updated machines.

Business teachers and supervisors at the local and state levels should make recommendations for the selection of business equipment, furniture, textbooks, audiovisual materials, and supplies, basing such decisions on a survey of the types of equipment used by businesses in the employment community. Business machines should definitely be the same as those used by business and industry and *not* machines that have been stripped down and labeled "educational equipment." It is false economy to purchase business equipment simply on a low-bid basis. Some business equipment is not suited to instructional purposes. Details and specifications should be drafted and adhered to in soliciting bids of any type, and these specifications should correspond to the equipment being used in business and industry.

An example of an unwise purchase based on a low bid is a manually operated 10-key adding machine. If the adding machine is not electric, the entire principle of the touch system used in 10-key adding machines and printing calculators is nullified. *All office machines purchased for the business machines laboratory should be electric.* It is recommended that electric typewriters be available for second-year typing students. Enough typewriters should be available for transcription in both the first- and second-year shorthand courses, regardless of whether the shorthand system being taught is manual or machine-touch.

In the business machines laboratory, the following equipment is typical for a class of 21 students:

- 10-key adding-listing machine (1)
- Printing calculators (2)
- Full-keyboard adding-listing machines (3)
- Rotary calculators (3)
- Dictating-transcribing machine (1)
- Transcribing machines (2)
- Stencil-duplicator (1)
- Fluid duplication (1)
- Offset printer (1)
- Proportional spacing typewriters (3)
- Manual typewriters—13″ carriage (5)
- Manual typewriter—16″-18″ carriage (1)
- Bookkeeping machine (1)
- Keypunch machines or simulators (2)

This equipment should be used on a rotation plan developed by the business department. Each student enrolled in business machines must be allowed to gain the necessary knowledge and skills to operate this equipment at the job-entry level.

Placement and Follow-Up of Business Students

The secondary school's business department, in cooperation with the guidance department, should maintain a close liaison with business, industry, and government agencies in order to find available opportunities for employment or further education for its graduates. A placement service not only helps students but also serves to keep the business department abreast of the changes in the business and industrial world and provides the information on which to base necessary changes in the business curriculum. It also serves as an excellent public relations program for both the business department and the school. Constant contact with community businessmen and businesswomen enables the business department to draw from their knowledge and experience, seek their advice in the development of new programs, and help them develop standards for employment. Advisory committees, comprising businessmen and -women and school administrators, serve a useful function for the business department and the business placement service.

Follow-up studies of students graduating from the business program will be useful in determining whether the program adequately prepared them for entry-level jobs and opportunities for advancement. An evaluation of the program by graduates who have had some practical experience in business and industry can serve as a basis for maintaining, improving, and developing new approaches and new programs.

Recent Research Affecting Business Programs

One of the major research projects in business education is the "New Office and Business Education Learning System" (NOBELS). This project is an attempt to determine what constitutes appropriate preparation for current and emerging business and office careers. It will also provide mechanisms for continual updating of curriculums in response to changes in occupational opportunities and requirements. NOBELS comprises several research subprojects:

1. *Developing a taxonomy of office activities for business and office education.* Besides the taxonomy, this report includes (a) systematic guidance for the observation and analysis of office activities, (b) a common language for describing office activities, (c) a basis for consolidating data from many locations and occupations, and (d) a basis for writing performance goals.
2. *Developing performance goals for a new office and business education learning system.* The major purpose of the NOBELS study is to develop performance goals based upon basic job tasks performed by office workers 16 to 24 years old (from current beginning to intermediate-level office jobs) who have earned less than a bachelor's degree. From the basic task data, performance goals are developed.

When the process of steps making up a basic task involves more than a straight line or sequential flow, flow-charts are included with the performance goals. A preliminary report of the data is available through the ERIC system.

3. *Writing performance goals: strategy and prototypes.* This report gives an overall procedure or system for preparing performance goals, including simple sets of performance goals for various areas of business education as well as other areas of vocational education.

4. *Improving business education for the emergent office.* The two major purposes of this study were (a) to identify high-priority, commonly acceptable abilities that are presently emerging and increasing in importance in offices across the United States, and (b) to develop general and specific instructional plans to help business and office instructors prepare students for the emergent office. Analysis of the data collected in this project revealed nine emerging activities applicable to all levels of office personnel. The second group of six emerging activities relate to clerical and supervisory and professional-technical personnel. A third group of 15 emerging activities relates in particular to managers, professional-technical personnel, and supervisors.

5. *Analyzing hardware used by office workers and social interaction critical incidents.* The data showed that 91 items of hardware were used by beginning office workers. These 91 items were divided into 11 categories. Typewriter keyboard machines, communications machines, and adding-calculating machines accounted for 60 percent of hardware usage. Typewriter keyboard machines and mailing equipment were the only types of hardware used by workers of all job titles. The only hardware classification that occurred in all 10 activity areas was typewriter keyboard machines. Computers and data processing represented 52 percent of the changing tasks reported. Of these changing tasks, 94 percent were found in metropolitan areas of over 100,000 population.

An analysis was also made of 829 social interaction critical incidents uncovered in a survey of office supervisors. These critical incidents related to both effective and ineffective behaviors of office workers. A classification scheme was developed, based on the worker's perception of social role expectations within the formal or informal company system. A majority of the incidents reported involved the worker's use of social sensitivity in dealing with customers, peers, and superiors. In situations involving reaction to stress and judgment in decision making, the incidence of ineffective behaviors was almost twice that of effective behaviors.

The field of research and development in business education has only recently begun to receive the recognition it deserves. If efforts in this field are to have an impact on business education practices in our schools, the business teacher must play a crucial role. The research cycle cannot be complete unless teachers are informed of research findings and actively apply them in their classroom practice. The lag between the formulation of new ideas and their acceptance and application must be reduced if the business program is to provide a dynamic, forward-looking instructional program for tomorrow's students.

The Future

Dynamic leadership will be required to help business education benefit fully from new instructional techniques and the new depth, scope, and variety in the curriculum. Through its leadership, the business program will be able to meet the challenge of providing a solid foundation for total career development instead of preparing students for entry-level jobs only.

The content and structure of the business curriculum will continue to be determined to a large extent by the nature of existing jobs, but it is important to be aware of the new jobs that are constantly emerging. Appropriate performance goals and behavioral objectives will be further developed and refined, based on task analyses of specific jobs in the business and industrial community. New developments in computers and business data processing will necessitate an expansion of programs in this area. The major research referred to in this chapter should serve as a basis for many of the curriculum changes that will be needed.

The business curriculum of the future will increasingly rely on individualized instruction. Certain technical skills, such as typewriting, shorthand, and machine calculation, can be best developed when each student is allowed to progress at his own rate through job-training sequences suited to his needs, interests, and abilities. Other skills and concepts—for example, communication, human relations, and personal development—are more effectively taught to students in groups.

The accuracy of our projections is extremely important. We must not only understand and accept the changes that are evident today but also anticipate those that are on the horizon. If we fail to do this, we will find ourselves unprepared to cope with the demands of our leadership roles as teachers and administrators. The most important aspect of the overall business program will be its continued flexibility and adaptability, which will permit each school district to meet the needs of its students and the business community it serves. The effectiveness and vitality of the business curriculum will quickly vanish if an attempt is made to establish one standard curriculum or one basic design. The continuing experimentation by individual teachers in the classroom, more sophisticated research techniques and applications, and the introduction of new kinds of instructional materials and equipment will generate a wave of innovations and educational methods that will make business education a relevant and vital part of the total school program.

BIBLIOGRAPHY

1. *Business Education Forum,* October 1970—May 1971.

2. The Eastern Business Teachers Association. *The Office Practice Program in Business Education.* Forty-Third Yearbook. Somerville, N.J.: the Association, 1969. 318 pp.

3. National Business Education Association. *Contributions of Research to Business Education.* Ninth Yearbook. Washington, D.C.: the Association, 1971. 374 pp.

4. ———. *Criteria for Evaluating Business and Office Education.* Seventh Yearbook. Washington, D.C.: the Association, 1969. 324 pp.

5. ———. *The Emerging Content and Structure of Business Education.* Eighth Yearbook. Washington, D.C.: the Association, 1970. 322 pp.

6. ——— and Joint Council of Economic Education. *Two Decades of Partnership in Economic Education.* Washington, D.C.: National Business Education Association, 1969. 79 pp.

4
Career Education

The Need for Educational Reform

A fundamental purpose of education is to prepare the young to live a productive and rewarding life. For far too many young Americans our schools are failing in this essential mission.

In typical schools throughout the country young people complain that curriculums are dull and irrelevant, that their education is not opening pathways to a fulfilling adulthood. Substantial numbers of students score below their grade level in basic skills; high dropout rates, absenteeism, academic failure, drug abuse, vandalism, and assaults on administrators, teachers, and pupils signal their discontent.

It is a rare high school that equips all its students to make the choice upon graduation of entering the job market with a salable skill or of continuing their education. Too often the graduate has neither option, let alone the opportunity to select one or the other.

Nearly 2.5 million students leave the formal education system of the United States each year without adequate preparation for a career (chart I). In 1970, not counting enrollment in homemaking, only about one high school student in six was enrolled in occupational preparation. More persons are graduating from a 4-year college with a bachelor's degree than there are jobs for degree holders. By the end of this decade eight out of 10 jobs in America will not require a baccalaureate degree.

More appropriate curriculums must be developed, validated, and installed, and they must be used more realistically if we are to meet the needs and desires of students and serve the purposes of society.

A Solution: Career Education

The fundamental concept of career education is that all educational experiences, curriculum, instruction, and counseling should be geared to preparation for economic independence and an *appreciation for the dignity of work.*

The main thrust of career education is to prepare all students for a successful life of work by increasing their options for occupational choice, by eliminating barriers—real and imagined—to attaining job skills, and by enhancing learning achievement in all subject areas and at all levels of education.

Career education recognizes critical decision points at which students must be prepared and equipped to decide whether to pursue a job, seek further education, or choose some combination of both.

Dr. Marland has pointed out that conventional economic success is not necessarily compatible with every student's goal:

> Some young people—and perhaps there will be more as the seventies progress—are not necessarily impressed with the economic advantages implicit in work. Those young people who march to a drumbeat different from the economic rhythm of their fathers often possess a deep commitment to the service of their fellowman. They too are the concern of career education, for the essential message of this program is a *useful and fulfilling life.* They will be better able to serve their fellowman if qualified as skilled artisans, health technicians, accountants, social work aides, teachers, environmental technicians, engineers—to mention a few fields of usefulness and fulfillment.

In scope, career education encompasses educational experiences beginning with early childhood and continuing through the individual's productive life.

In early childhood it provides an awareness of the world of work as well as direct experiences to motivate and captivate the learner's interest. As the child moves through school he increases his familiarity with the world of work and acquires knowledge necessary to obtain meaningful employment upon leaving school. Career education prepares the individual for employment and, later in his career, upgrades his skills, updates his knowledge, retrains him for a new job.

The Goals of Career Education

Career education, in the words of Commissioner Marland, will eliminate the artificial separation "between things academic and things vocational."

The Commissioner has observed that:

> Educators must be bent on preparing students either to become properly and usefully employed immediately upon graduation from high school or to go on to further formal education. The student should be equipped occupationally, academically, and emotionally to spin off from the system at whatever point he chooses—whether at age 16 as a craftsman apprentice, or age 30 as a surgeon, or age 60 as a newly trained practical nurse.

Career education increases the relevance of school by focusing on the learner's career choice. It gives students informed guidance, counseling, and instruction throughout their school years.

It demands no permanent bondage to a career goal. Rather, it reveals to students their great range of occupational options and helps them to develop positive attitudes toward work.

Career education will enable nearly all persons who complete secondary school to obtain immediate employment or go on to technical school or college. Placement services in the school system will assist every student, especially the student leaving before he completes the 12th grade, to plan the next step in his development. Job entrance will be just as important as college entrance to counselors and teachers. Skill credentials, universally recognized, will be just as valid as the commonly accepted credentials for college entrance.

There will be no "dropouts," only individuals who choose to go to work or to pursue a different kind of education. Entrance and exit requirements will be flexible enough to enable all persons to acquire—at any time they choose—the educational and occupational experiences that meet their needs.

The Career Education Concept

The current categorization of school curriculums into "vocational," "general," and "college preparatory" education makes it difficult for a school to meet the real needs of students and society.

A school system offering career education, however, could make it possible for students to pursue an individualized year-

CHART I

The Problem

Nearly 2.5 million students leave the formal education system of the U.S. each year without adequate preparation for careers. In 1970-71, there were:

850,000   Elementary and secondary school dropouts; many found school irrelevant

750,000   General curriculum high school graduates who did not attend college

850,000   High school students who entered college in 1967, but did not complete the baccalaureate or an organized occupational program

TOTAL 2,450,000 (est.)

CHART II

A Solution . . .

An Example of a **CAREER EDUCATION** Model

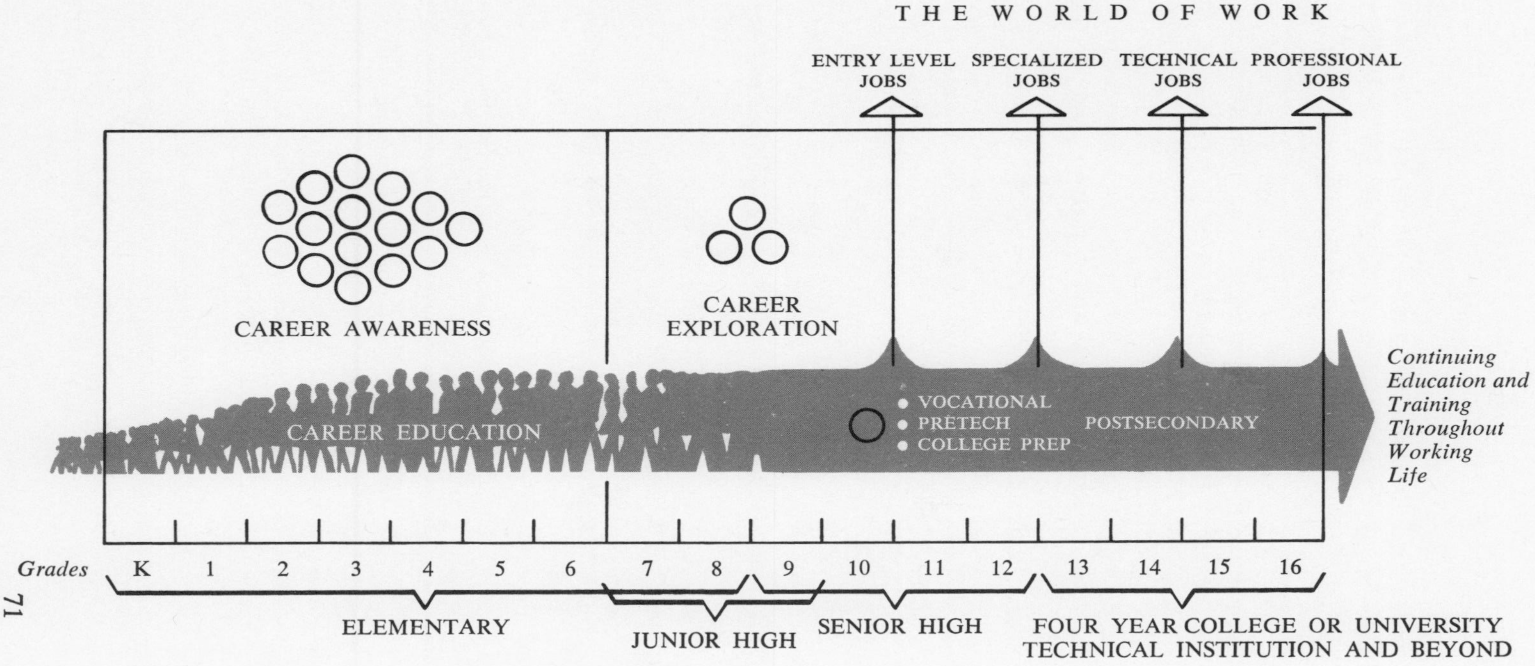

round program. Students could leave or reenter school at almost any time to further their education or sharpen their job training.

A few schools and school systems have installed career education elements. But none has adopted a curriculum that cuts across all of a student's educational experience and runs throughout the entire elementary and secondary spectrum. This total approach is the essence of career education. It should at this time extend at least through 2 postsecondary years of school.

Under the career education concept, every child gets the same educational bill of fare up to a certain grade, usually the 6th. Besides learning how to read, write, and compute, the career education student studies history, languages, and the physical and social sciences. (See chart II for an example of a Career Education model.) Simultaneously, he explores the world of work through a wide spectrum of occupational "clusters." For example, in the "transportation occupations" cluster, he becomes aware of such diverse occupational areas as aerospace, pipeline, road, and water transportation. He is made aware of the hundreds of job categories in each and their relationship to each other as well as to himself and his fellow members of society. The same exposure is provided in the "health occupations" cluster and its service possibilities in accident prevention, pharmacology, and medical and dental science.

In the middle grades, 7 through 9, the student examines more closely those clusters in which he is most interested. By the end of the 10th grade he develops elementary job entry skills—as a typist, for example, or construction helper, social work aide, service station attendant, or environmental technician aide—skills he can pursue if he does not complete the 12th grade. If he does complete the 12th grade, the student is prepared to enter the world of work or to continue his education at a postsecondary institution—college, technical institute, or other—suitable to his needs, interests, and abilities.

All students have the opportunity to enjoy actual work during their high school years. This is accomplished through cooperative arrangements with business, industry, and public institutions. Extensive guidance and counseling activities assist the student to discover and develop his particular interests and abilities and match them against potential careers.

A student preparing for postsecondary education while in high school would have less time for in-depth occupational preparation. Nevertheless, as a participant in a career education program, he would acquire entry-level job skills through some courses in school and through on-the-job or work center experience.

It is important that each student master the skills he will require to live by. Whether these skills are labeled "academic" or "vocational" is beside the point. The essential need is that every student be equipped to live his life as a fulfilled human being. If he is to live his life with machines, he must know how to use them. If he is to live with a slide rule or a computer, he must understand its magic. If he is to combat diseases that afflict mankind, he must know a great deal about the human body and mind and all the ills they are heir to.

Costs and Meaning to the Educational Establishment

Obviously, to put a career education program into action requires a profound rethinking of missions and restructuring of operations by all who are concerned with American education.

School board members and the general public will have to make some fundamental decisions. Career education's initial installation costs, including inservice training and new curriculum materials, could increase school budgets fairly substantially the first few years. However, after a school system has retooled and converted to a career education program, the continuing costs of its maintenance and operation should decline nearly to previous levels.

In most school systems it will be necessary to employ more counselors, paraprofessionals, and others. Administrators, teachers, counselors, and paraprofessionals will require inservice training to become familiar with career education concepts. They will need to learn the effective use of new laboratories, instructional materials, and media.

Teachers and guidance counselors will have to make substantial changes in their knowledge banks and accept the career-oriented learner as equal in value to the traditionally more fashionable college-oriented student. They should broaden their own actual work experiences so that they can help students more effectively to prepare to live and work in a great variety of situations.

There will be large rewards for educators and students in a career education program. School administrators and teachers will gain a renewed sense of accomplishment in giving students realistic, effective preparation for life in the society into which they will be graduated. Schools will become animated, joyful places rather than the fortresses of despair that so many of them are today.

Examples and Progress

The career education concept is being developed through State-level curriculum laboratories and State vocational research coordinating units. This process of development and diffusion at the State level is increasing.

The U.S. Office of Education is conducting a series of "capstone" projects in which schools with partial career education programs will be able to increase and hasten their efforts to install comprehensive programs. The "capstone" programs will serve as models and working demonstrations of career education in action.

For the past 2 years the Office's Bureau of Adult, Vocational, and Technical Education has funded exemplary *vocational* education programs in many States. Some of these programs have developed breakthroughs that are being incorporated into emerging model *career* education curriculums.

The bureau has identified and codified 15 occupational clusters in all. Aside from the transportation and health occupation clusters already mentioned, they are: agri-business and natural resources, business and office communication and media, consumer and homemaking education, construction, environment, fine arts and humanities, hospitality and recreation, manufacturing, marine science, marketing and distribution, personal services, and public service. These clusters are being modified and adapted to fit some local situations, and in some cases are being adopted virtually completely. For example, the Arizona State Board of Education made $1.9 million available to install career education in 15 school systems starting in September 1971. The Office of Education's 15 occupational clusters are playing a key role in this conversion program.

Other States with outstanding examples of local efforts to install career education programs include Delaware, Georgia, Mississippi, New Jersey, North Dakota, and Wyoming. Large-city school systems turning to career education as their basic design include those of Dallas and San Diego.

These are promising first steps—but only first steps—on the long road to nationwide educational reform. Speaking before the Council of Chief State School Officers in June 1971, Commissioner Marland described the concepts of *career* education as they were being formulated in the Office of Education. He added, significantly:

> Career education cannot be defined solely in Washington. Revolution doesn't happen because government suggests it. We can ask many of the questions, we can help with funds, but if career education is to be the revolutionary instrument that the times demand it will be defined in hard and urgent debate across the land by teachers, laymen, students, and administrators in months to come. Let that debate start now.

The Chief State School Officers, without a single exception, agreed to commit themselves to the educational revolution that is now taking form.

The future of that revolution will depend on the support it receives from the people of America—especially from its educators.

BIBLIOGRAPHY

1. *Abstracts of Instructional Materials in Vocational and Technical Education.* Summer 1970. (ED-042-930).

2. American Vocational Association. "Career Development: K-14." *American Vocational Journal,* December 1969. (Entire issue)

3. Bottoms, Gene. *Orientation to New Concepts and Programs of Career Orientation and Occupational Education for Students in Rural Areas.* Raleigh, N.C.: Center for Occupational Education, North Carolina State University, December 1970.

4. ———, and Matheny, Kenneth B. *A Guide for the Development, Implementation, and Administration of Exemplary Programs and Projects.* September 1969. (ED-040-301).

5. ———, and O'Kelley, George L. "Vocational Education as a Developmental Process." *American Vocational Journal* 46: 21-24; March 1971.

6. *Career Guidance, Counseling, and Placement.* Proceedings of the National Conference on Guidance, Counseling, and Placement in Career Development and Educational Occupational Decision Making. October 1969. (ED-041-143).

7. *Career Opportunities for Technicians and Specialists.* Chicago: J. G. Ferguson Publishing Co., 1970. (5 vols.)

8. Dreves, Fred. "An Episode . . . Is 'Fun' Learning." *Industrial Arts and Vocational Education Magazine* 60: 24-26; February 1971.

9. Dunn, C. J., and Payne, Bill F. *World of Work; Occupational-Vocational Guidance in the Elementary Grades; A Handbook for Teachers and Counselors.* Dallas, Tex.: Leslie Press, 1971.

10. Elliot, Ian. "Occupational Orientation Means Work for You." *Grade Teacher* 88: 60-65; April 1971.

11. ERIC Clearinghouse on Counseling and Personnel Services. "Intensive High School Occupational Guidance Approaches for Initial Work and Technical School Placement." November 1969. (ED-033-254).

12. ———. "Orientation Approaches to Increase Student Awareness of Occupational Options." November 1969. (ED-033-255).

13. ERIC Clearinghouse on Vocational and Technical Education. "Intensive Training for Job-Entry Skills: A Selected Bibliography for Use in Program Development." November 1969. (ED-034-061).

14. ———. "Work Experience for Broadening Occupational Offerings: A Selected Bibliography for Use in Program Development." November 1969. (ED-034-062).

15. *Facilitating Career Development: An Annotated Bibliography.* Springfield, Ill.: Division of Vocational and Technical Education, Illinois State Board of Vocational Education and Rehabilitation, July 1970.

16. *A Guide for Cooperative Vocational Education.* September 1969. (ED-037-564).

17. *A Guide for the Development of Curriculum.* June 1969. (ED-037-535).

18. Laws, Lee. *Elementary Guide for Career Development; Grades 1-6.* Austin, Tex.: Region XIII Educational Service Center. 1970.

19. Marland, Sidney P., Jr. *Career Education: More Than a Name.* Speech delivered before the annual meeting of the State Directors of Vocational Education, Washington, D.C., May 4, 1971. (ED-050-295). (Mimeo.)

20. ———. *Career Education Now.* Speech delivered before the convention of the National Association of Secondary School Principals, Houston, Texas, January 23, 1971. (ED-048-480). (Mimeo.)

21. Mississippi State University, Curriculum Coordinating Unit. *Occupational Orientation: An Introduction to the World of Work; Teacher's Handbook; Preliminary Draft.* August 1969. (ED-050-279).

22. Morgan, Robert L. *An Approach to Evaluation: A Model for Evaluating the North Carolina Exemplary Program.* July 1970. (ED-042-910).

23. ———. *The Plan for Implementation of an Exemplary Occupational Education Program in a Rural Community.* 1970. (ED-050-296).

24. Rhodes, James A. *Vocational Education and Guidance: A System for the Seventies.* Columbus, Ohio: Charles E. Merrill Publishing Co., 1970.

25. Smith, Howard. "Now It Pays To Talk About Tomorrow's Jobs." *Industrial Arts and Vocational Education* 60: 20-22; February 1971.

26. Tennyson, W. W. "Career Development: Who's Responsible?" *American Vocational Journal* 46: 54-58; March 1971.

5

Early Childhood and Elementary Education

Emerging Patterns of Early Childhood Education

Enthusiasm, flux, and diversity characterize the recent curriculum activity in the early childhood field. A strong influence toward change was exerted by Bloom (3), Hunt (10), and other researchers in the early 1960's who described intelligence (previously considered an invariant, innate "given") as substantially the function of early experiences. This changing concept of abilities, coupled with societal concern over the continuing "cycles of poverty," brought funding and fervent activity to early childhood education.

Beginning in 1965, the massive Head Start efforts and other related programs significantly altered the public conception of the scope of public education. In 1966 only 30 percent of America's approximately 12.5 million children were actually enrolled in either nursery school or kindergarten programs; since that time the trend has been to extend public school opportunities to all children at an earlier and earlier age.

In 1968, for example, James E. Allen (1), then commissioner of education, envisioned an education system in which—

> there would be available in the school district a Central Diagnostic Center to which, at age 2½, a child would be brought by his parents or guardian. The purpose of the Center would be to find out everything possible about the child and his background that would be useful in planning an individualized learning program for him. . . . Part of his prescription during this period (from 2½ to 5) would include spending some time in what might be called a Good Start Center, where he would learn to work and play with children of various backgrounds. In addition, some children would receive specialized help.

Although we are still far from the situation described by Allen, many regular school programs for three-, four-, and five-year-olds are now operating under a variety of funding arrangements. Several states that had previously begun public education at first grade have moved to inaugurate kindergartens—a major stride toward public acceptance of the responsibility for education of the young child. What is more, certain states—New York, for example—are moving toward the provision of universal opportunity for school experiences for all four-year-olds.

State departments and local school districts all across the nation have been deeply involved in providing prekindergarten experiences for children with special characteristics—the culturally disadvantaged, the migrant, and so on. With all of this activity in a variety of settings and with advice from various groups of professionals—educators, child development and family specialists, psychologists, sociologists, medical and health personnel—we should not be surprised to find considerable diversity in the kinds of programs now actually provided for children. The differences extend across several dimensions, some of which will be discussed in this chapter. Most developers of curriculums for young children agree that it is vitally important to plan carefully the experiences of the young, since the early years pass so quickly and affect later achievement so significantly.

Functions of Early Childhood Programs

Traditionally, there were two relatively distinct functions for early childhood centers. There were, first, *supplementary programs,* typified by the middle class (in fact, largely upper-middle class) "nursery schools," which supplemented a relatively rich home experience by providing opportunities for work and play with peers in a group setting. Second, there were *custodial programs,* which had no particular concern for educational stimulation or guided social development but provided safe and healthful care outside the home. These were especially prevalent during World War II.

In the 60's Americans became very much aware of a third function of early childhood programs, *compensatory education.* Typified by Head Start, compensatory programs focused primarily on providing learning and experiences judged necessary to successful societal participation—of which school entrance was considered the first step. School readiness was thought to develop in informal ways in most middle class homes but not at all in some "disadvantaged" homes.

By the beginning of the 70's the distinctions between *supplementary, custodial,* and *compensatory* programs were blurring. Although most of the activity and change in early childhood curriculums in the last decade have been initiated within compensatory programs, the materials, methods, and innovative structures have been quickly assimilated into many of the programs with supplementary or custodial functions. Any visit to a middle class nursery school or a suburban kindergarten will disclose an abundance of the materials designed for use in programs for the "disadvantaged." The current emphasis in day care is almost always either a combination of custodial *and* supplementary for middle class children or custodial *and* compensatory for low-income children. The increasing emphasis on strengthening the family milieu and involving and guiding the parents in the education of their own young children brings even programs for "disadvantaged" groups out of the category of compensatory and into closer alignment with those labeled supplementary.

Goals of Early Childhood Programs

For the sake of clarity, three groups of curriculum planners will be identified, although in actuality there are many subdivisions and cross-groupings.

One group of program designers feels that the goal for prekindergarten or kindergarten programs should be to provide as rich an experience as possible for each child through activities appropriate to his age and stage. James Hymes (11) is perhaps the most eloquent spokesman for this approach, which holds firmly that by selecting materials and experiences according to what children of a given age are known or thought likely to enjoy and participate in with a minimum of adult manipulation, the groundwork will be laid indirectly for the next age/stage without ever focusing directly on it. The evaluation of program effectiveness is made on the basis of how involved the children become within the program in either material manipulation or social interaction. If the children seem uninvolved, restless, or bored, the curriculum planner for this type of program searches for new materials, new equipment arrangements, and new experiences. If, however, the children are busily playing with sand, dress-ups, blocks, art media, or whatever, the proponents of this approach are satisfied that their intentions for programming are well met.

A contrasting group of program planners takes into account very directly the demands that children will encounter in ensuing years. The designers of the Academically-Oriented Preschool, Carl Bereiter and Siegfried Engelmann (2), typify this point of view. They discount the value of child-selected play-oriented activities, however involving they may be to the child, and concentrate instead on using the most direct means possible to build competency in academic areas of reading, arithmetic, and language in preparation for the demands of elementary school. The evaluation of the program is based on how successfully children evidence a command of the competencies necessary for elementary grade achievement. Although this program—packaged in commercial form by Engelmann as Science Research Associates' DISTAR program—was designed for the "disadvantaged," it has had some direct influence on curriculum for children in advantaged circumstances as well.

Planners in the third category are also very concerned with the demands of the next stage but focus on developing prerequisite skills, vocabulary, and attitudes rather than on actually teaching academic skills at the preschool level. These designers often include "free play" periods in the daily program, but during these periods teachers focus their attention on engaging individuals and small groups in skill-oriented games and activities. The choices for activity are arranged to ensure that children will have experiences in visual and auditory discrimination, manipulation of number and word forms, classification, development of vocabulary, and similar pursuits. Proponents of this approach are dubious that the children's own choice of activities would provide sufficient conditions for optimal learning without effort on the part of the teacher to construct and/or select appealing games and activities to accomplish specific objectives. In this situation, the curriculum will often also include some whole-group sessions in which puppets, pictures, films, games, stories, and learning exercises are used to further concept attainment, perceptual-motor development, listening skills, vocabulary development, and the like. The curriculum is designed to add gradually to what the child knows and can do within a relatively child-centered and noncoercive setting. The objectives for each child are formulated in terms of building attitudes (e.g., task persistence, attention, achievement motivation) and specific skills or knowledge thought to be prerequisite to successful school participation.

These three general types of curriculums might be considered anchor points on a continuum upon which most early childhood curriculums could be placed according to their degree of direct concern with preparation for later school experiences.

Specificity of Objectives in Early Childhood Programs

As one would anticipate, there are concomitant differences among the three groups of planners along another dimension—the degree of specificity of curriculum objectives. Whereas most of the second group and some of the third would feel it essential to specify in operational terms the expected educational outcomes of their programs, the first group would be more likely to emphasize the overall arrangement of facilitating circumstances while avoiding any predetermination of what and/or when particular learnings will occur. This difference among groups of program planners is well illustrated by the statements of Parker and Whitney (16), in which they contrast their own Discovery program with other early childhood programs. The Discovery program is said to have 1,800 specified behavioral objectives keyed to materials and learning experiences. Parker expresses amazement and distress that in reviewing hundreds of other early childhood programs he learned that most did not have an operational statement of their curriculum—did not, in fact, have a written curriculum.

There are several possible reasons. Some programmers are perhaps by personality and personal philosophy more comfortable in considering their goals in less precise terms. Although lack of precision renders goals less easy to attain, they feel that to formulate narrow objectives would lead them away from their preferred holistic style of perceiving children's development.

Others who are unlikely to focus curriculum on specific objectives are influenced by the belief that if children are given choices of a variety of play situations they will become involved in the manipulation of various objects and media in ways that may be quite unpredictable but highly beneficial in laying the groundwork for later formalization with full comprehension. When adult-imposed objectives are stressed at this age level, they feel, the result is only parroting or mimicking by the children. These persons often base their beliefs on the concepts of Piaget. Although they might agree that it will not harm the child to be involved in a curriculum focused on accomplishing specific objectives and that it may indeed be necessary to arrange direct instruction toward specific goals in areas of diagnosed deficiencies, they doubt the lasting efficacy of these procedures. They would instead concur with Kohlberg (13), who elaborated on Piaget's ideas and concluded that limited specific training cannot replace the massive general types of experience accruing with age. They prefer a relatively nonfocused program to bring "preoperational" children into contact with materials providing rich multisensory experiences.

Methods and Strategies in Early Childhood Programs

There are striking differences in the extent to which program planners are willing to predict the appropriate methods for all children or even for subgroups of children. Some published curricular models come equipped with what could be considered nearly "teacher-proof" directions, carefully prescribing sequences of utterances and actions; others supply only a basic philosophy, general guidelines, and a series of resource publications or inservice programs from which teachers must design curriculums to fit their children as they go.

Admittedly, we know far too little about providing teachers (let alone the children in their classes) with the optimal balance of structure and flexibility to allow their potential to emerge. One does not have to look far to see evidence of the kind of teaching that leads administrators to seek "teacher-proof" materials. The problem with these materials, however, is that they may also be proof against the development of teachers who can take advantage of the learning potential of a particular situation for a particular child. Weikart's (18) curriculum model comparisons led him to conclude that a program involving daily planning and evaluation on the part of the teacher is more effective than a program lacking this participation by the teacher.

The last few years have provided an interesting array of teaching strategies for early childhood. These are quite well represented in the Office of Child Development's planned variation program (12), which is designed to provide information about the impact of various preschool curriculums on Head Start children. The study includes systematic evaluation of the following models:

- The Bank Street College model, a developmental approach providing both group and individual activities and much opportunity for children to investigate objects and explore materials freely. Explorations are interrelated with functional and expressive use of language.

- The behavior-analysis model, using systematic reinforcement procedures and programed materials in reading and math.
- The Academically-Oriented Preschool model, providing structured sessions and programed materials to produce achievement in concepts and operations in reading, arithmetic, and language.
- The cognitive model, based on Piaget's theories and providing (a) activities to help children develop abilities to think about physical and logical relationships, (b) active teacher involvement in developing the program, and (c) home cooperation.
- The pragmatic action-oriented model inspired by the British infant schools, attempting to provide a flexible curriculum and schedule and to fashion classroom environments responsive to the individual needs of children and the equally individual talents and styles of teachers.
- The Institute for Developmental Studies model, emphasizing concept formation, perception, language, self-image, and social-emotional growth through individualization, continuous teacher assessment, and work with small groups.
- The Florida Parent Education Model, using a mother from the local community as a parent educator who visits parents at home and presents them with weekly tasks and also assists in the classroom.
- The Primary Education Project Model, which provides an individual progress plan for each child, allowing him to work through finely graded curriculum sequences emphasizing basic skills and concepts.
- The Responsive Model, which encourages children to explore and find answers from people and from responsive materials and equipment.
- The Responsive Environment Corporation model, which uses specially designed learning materials and educational technology (e.g., a teaching machine that reads to children) within a flexible classroom structure.

When centers adopt program materials, games, particular curriculum sequences, perceptual-motor training series, packaged units of instruction, learning devices, and so on, the teacher is consequently cast into particular roles. With the diversity of approaches represented in the field of early childhood today, the buyer or adopter should give thought to the compatibility of curricular materials with desired teaching methods prior to acquisition or commitment.

Decision Making About Early Childhood Programs

Choice of the program to be adopted or developed should ideally be based on the capabilities and preferences of the teachers to be involved and on the assessed needs of the prospective learners. For example, if the children are known to lack language competency, a language program focused on their specific needs would be justifiable, but there would be little justification for using the same program in a situation where young children come to school with rich and varied verbal competencies; a highly structured, presequenced program would certainly be a more reasonable choice for an inexperienced or untrained teacher than for a creative, capable, and experienced one.

In addition to attempting to match program objectives and local capabilities and needs—which is far more difficult than one might suspect, despite the wealth of available curriculum materials—decision makers should ask themselves the following questions when examining an early childhood curriculum:

- To what extent does the curriculum prescribe the appropriate times for certain kinds of behavior?
- How much variety does a child encounter in terms of equipment, settings, peers, and teachers?
- To what extent is accommodation made for individual diversity in behavior and progress?
- To what extent does the curriculum permit encouragement of and responsiveness to child initiations and explorations?
- To what extent are child encounters simplified and sequenced (as contrasted with encounters of unaltered complexity)?
- What motivational strategies are used?
- To what extent does the curriculum accommodate or encourage the teacher's drawing comparisons for children between novel stimuli and their own previous personal experiences?

Stating these questions is in no way meant to imply that there is a proper answer to each one. Programs must still be based on some educated guesses as to what conditions will fulfill broad goals for children from various experiential backgrounds. For example:

- Provision of a healthy and safe setting
- Easily accessible facilities and/or provisions for physical needs—elimination, thirst, hunger, rest, activity

- Regularity in the daily pattern of snack, rest, outdoor play, story, and similar program offerings, but with a minimum of coercion to participate in these activities
- Considerable space and/or time where there is a minimum of adult restriction on exploratory and motor behavior
- Diversity of materials and equipment that (a) provide opportunity for manipulation and experimentation, (b) provide for multisensory experiences, (c) are "responsive" in that the child receives some information as to the effectiveness of his actions, and (d) can be used autonomously with a minimum of adult assistance
- Frequent positive recognition of individual accomplishments or characteristics via verbal comment and/or nonverbal expression
- Frequent adult verbal interaction with individual children about their activities, which should include relevant comparisons between current encounters and prior experiences
- Change in equipment and materials, adults, and peers encountered as program progresses
- For children with diagnosed developmental deficiencies, specialized programs (direct instruction, special facilities, simplified and/or sequenced encounters) designed for a low ratio of children to adults
- Visits to other settings in very small groups with adults who can demonstrate and verbalize about salient characteristics of the new environment.

Anyone involved in the selection or evaluation of early childhood curriculums should formulate a similar set of guesses, discuss them with others knowledgeable in the area, and observe and examine curriculums to see how and why they agree with or deviate from these guesses. There is still no consensus among educators as to which is the "best" of the many approaches to programming for young children.

The experience of the last few years in compensatory education has indicated that it is far from easy to make meaningful and lasting changes in a child's level of performance. Although many programs show gains in IQ of 10 to 14 points on the Stanford-Binet or comparable tests after a year of early intervention, these gains are dissipated after a year or more of nonintervention.

It is of interest to note that some of the programs including heavy components of parental involvement in a total intervention effort were relatively successful in maintaining effects. Both the Early Training Project of Peabody's DARCEE program (8,9) and the Weikart program (18) in Ypsilanti, Michigan, engaged the parents in working toward educational objectives and found test scores of the youngsters involved still higher than those of control groups at the end of third or fourth grade. There would seem to be substantial empirical precedent as well as popular appeal and logical consistency in the conclusion of the 1970 White House Conference on Children that a top national priority should be "comprehensive family-oriented child development programs."

A variety of parent involvement designs are currently in operation. Community-controlled programs probably ensure the highest degree of commitment and concern—although perhaps not necessarily the greatest potential for changing parent behavior, should this be an objective. In some situations, home visitors (professional educators, social workers, or paraprofessionals who have received special training) coordinate home and school efforts.

Elsewhere parental participation is arranged through paid or voluntary classroom participation, through arrangement for parallel training and/or social activities within the school setting, or through distribution of a series of "take-homes" intended to enlist parental support and aid in accomplishing educational objectives. A program for young children that does not have some provision for either receiving guidance from parents about their concerns or for enlisting parental support for the concerns of the school is likely to be missing out on a component of the total curriculum of the young child. The finding by the evaluators of *Sesame Street* that children whose parents watched the program with them gained more than those who watched it by themselves is simply another confirmation of the value of parental participation.

The assumption of public responsibility for some aspects of the young child's experience should not be thought of as parental abdication of responsibility, but rather as the *sharing* of responsibility among the child's parents, siblings, other relatives, community, and school. The special equipment and experiences facilitating learning are finding their way into homes through television (*Sesame Street* style), educational toy lending libraries, mobile preschool units, program "take-homes," and home educator visits. The distinctions between home learning and school learning are gradually fading at the early childhood levels.

Summary

There has been enthusiastic activity in arranging varieties of programs for the nation's young children over the past few years.

Old classifications and expectations have in many respects given way, but there is little consensus to date on such matters as the nature of the goals of early education for all children, the desirability of specifying objectives in operational terms, the most effective methodologies, or the characteristics of the "ideal" early childhood program for any given educational purpose. Perhaps one of the few areas of consensus will for some time continue to be the belief in the value of continued searching and questioning regarding optimal experiences for the young.

Emerging Patterns of Elementary Education

Deliberate efforts have been made in most of our schools to keep them close to the people. We continue to struggle with ways to solicit greater public understanding of and involvement in the work of the school. Administrators concerned with elementary education are constantly bombarded with questions: "What are children learning?" "What do elementary school children need in order to achieve in secondary school?" "What knowledge is of most worth?" "How can education affect the lives of people in more penetrating ways?" These questions are illustrative of our concern for keeping education alive and for having it make its maximum contribution. Unfortunately, we know much more about quality elementary education than we currently practice. There is a kind of crisis confronting elementary education today, suggesting the great need for overhauling many practices, curtailing some trends, and recharting the course.

The complex social problems of our time have increasingly found their way to the schoolhouse door, piling mammoth burdens upon the education system. These burdens have ranged from the administration of meat stamps and gas coupons during World War II to the current efforts to deal with drugs, school-related suicide, and delinquency. Today we also find the schools concerned with major problems of racial integration. In a way, the fact that major problems have been turned over to the schools is indicative of the continuing vitality of the school system. The schools have not shirked their responsibility as service agencies as well as learning centers. Yet the result has been one of the continuing problems of education—lack of clarity about the central purpose of the school.

Over the years we have seen many new programs, new emphases, new materials. As they have appeared, disappeared, and reappeared, they have left a stockpile of practices that can be thought of as appropriate and sound. Persisting concerns that have stood the test of time are needs, values, and creativity; today these may be seen as the major strengths of many elementary education programs—programs based on the *needs* of the people, guiding children to develop *value* systems, and emphasizing the *creative* process and its dynamics.

Out of the numerous attempts to state the basic purposes of the school, there has tended to emerge as a primary purpose that of *helping each individual to develop and maintain his potential.* This powerful statement of philosophy can give direction to our programs. It is more than an abstraction; it is an aspiration!

Emerging Patterns of Curriculum

Rather than review the extensive literature concerning specific projects, programs, and developments, we prefer to highlight the major emerging emphases that seem to be giving focus and direction to elementary school curriculum work.

Clarification of Curriculum Theory. One of the profound developments of recent years has been the increased emphasis on the importance of a rationale or design for the development of curriculum. The work of Herrick and many of his graduate students, like the work of Beauchamp, has stressed the importance of curriculum theory and its concern with new insights. Such developments have provided a new focus for the curriculum field, giving curriculum decisions greater prominence and greater internal consistency. The teacher is still recognized as curriculum decision maker, but the process is no longer a casual one. It is hoped that the teacher is making such decisions in terms of some logical construct, based on the question, What do we believe are the essential elements of a theory that gives meaning, consistency, and specific direction to the curriculum?

Development of a Variety of Curriculum Projects. Since Sputnik, a number of curriculum projects, sponsored by universities, foundations, and agencies, have been developed for various subject areas. These projects form a new foundation for the curriculum field. Eisner (5, p.1) states, "These projects are important not only in their own right, but also because they provide the necessary conditions for building the empirical foundations of the field of curriculum."

Certainly the various projects have demonstrated the necessity for updating content, for seeking the advice of specialists, and for developing greater insight into the structure of each of the disciplines. Yet their impact upon effective and efficient curriculum practices is questionable. In many cases they lead to greater specificity of content and more concentration upon textbooks, workbooks, and ready-made materials. In some cases the emphasis is on process, but the child's application of the process to local problems, local conditions, and local understandings is limited or nonexistent. The emerging pattern generating the most optimism is the tendency for local groups to study existing projects and programs and to remake their own tentative guide or plan. Encouragement should be given to local groups to study, evaluate, and experiment with proposed new projects. Opportunities should exist for local people to develop extensive background and expertise in these innovations.

Clarification of Objectives. Increased concern is being shown for the cognitive development of children. There are those who believe that the elementary school exists primarily for this dimension of an individual's growth. The current emphasis on behavioral objectives resulting from cognitive learning reinforces such a point of view for many people. Too many leaders seem to be emphasizing cognitive objectives to the exclusion of affective or psychomotor objectives. Emphasis on cognitive behavior is not new. Leaders in elementary education have long been concerned with modifying the behavior of children, but this concern has assumed even greater importance today. The emphasis on behaviorally oriented objectives resulting from cognitive learning leads to more precision in identifying content.

We face an important dilemma. As teachers specify objectives within a single content area and work primarily for such objectives, they run the risk of forming major gaps in a child's growth. Objectives must be considered in terms of particular children, rather than in terms of particular subjects. A more penetrating course of action would be for each school faculty to recognize the needs of the particular school and then attempt to formulate purposes to be achieved for a particular group and/or individual. Methods of achieving purposes would then include opportunities for each discipline to contribute to development in other disciplines. *Learning to Feel—Feeling to Learn* (14) and *Freedom To Learn* (17) are current titles that see objectives as universal and that suggest the interrelationships of various curriculum areas. Teachers are providing rich experiences for their particular groups of students by drawing from a variety of disciplines.

On the one hand, there is the curriculum pattern that is highly structured, highly organized, and highly subject-centered. On the other hand, there is the tendency toward a curriculum that begins with concerns of the learner and involves a multisensory approach. This is a far more human approach. We look, feel, exhibit, try out, explore, communicate, and learn in many ways.

Renewed Focus on Learning. Teachers are increasingly recognizing that children learn in many ways, that many resources are useful in facilitating learning, and that many of these resources are available locally. Out of the materials dealing with learning has come the idea that learning is an active process and that total involvement of the learner is imperative. Teachers now recognize that children learn at different rates and that they do not all start from the same place. Individualization of instruction has become a prominent concept in curriculum circles, and teachers recognize the importance of this concept as they conceive of the curriculum. More and more teachers are realizing that learning is a multisensory activity and that youngsters need to feel, hear, move, construct, listen, and dramatize as they engage in learning activities.

This realization has contributed to renewed prestige for such areas as art, music, dance, physical education, home economics, and industrial arts. A variety of pilot studies have underscored the importance of these areas as sources of rich learnings for many children. There has been a nationwide surge of interest in elementary physical education in recent years, and exciting things are happening in schools around the country. For many years the physical education curriculum was limited primarily to games, sports, conditioning activities, and some folk dance. Now there is momentum for structuring the physical education curriculum around basic movement, whereby a child can be helped to manage his body in many different situations. The trend is away from isolated activities and toward a comprehensive developmental program with basic movement as a core, facilitating achievement, a sense of belonging, and involvement. Teaching methods emphasize the interrelationships of movement experiences with other fields of knowledge and skills. Out of physical education may come vocabulary building and reading, as well as illustrations of science or social science concepts.

The same type of development is occurring in both art and music. Increasingly we are recognizing in the elementary school that these areas are not isolated within themselves but are useful as a means of helping people to communicate ideas in a variety of ways. For example, out of work on pollution can come a chant, a song, a dance, or a dramatization, followed by careful analysis of the multiple scientific and social concepts related to pollution. Learning becomes exciting, and children develop new interests and perceive new dimensions of knowledge from their learning activities.

Curriculum Design. In *Curriculum for the 70's: An Agenda for Invention,* Arthur W. Foshay (7) calls our attention to three curriculums operating in our schools: Curriculum I is the formal academic offering; Curriculum II has to do with social development; Curriculum III concerns self-development. If we would break down the barriers between these three curriculums and think increasingly of the school as a humanizing agency, this analysis could provide for an important extension of our curriculum activities.

Curriculum I, the formal academic offering, consists mainly of school subjects organized around the disciplines they represent. As Foshay indicates, this curriculum connotes a cool, detached, objective version of what it means to be a human being.

The latent curriculum, Curriculum II, has to do with the nature and function of authority in life, with the problems of preparation for making one's own decisions, and with social development in general. Most curriculums do not fulfill their obligation to enhance the social development of the individual. The lack of reality in the social studies curriculum is quite apparent on the present scene. Our schools need very much to offer more opportunities to help children grow in human understanding.

Self-awareness and self-development, Curriculum III, has been neglected. Persistently we find art and music being taught as isolated areas of the curriculum. Dance is often separated from the work in physical education. Self-awareness could provide an entirely new ingredient for helping the schools modify the basic behavior of children.

Now is the time for administrators to look at the curriculum of the elementary school in a more analytical manner. No longer is it appropriate to raise the question, "Should the school teach the children to read, to quantify, or to understand the heritage of our culture?" Thoughtful administrators have long recognized the importance of these components, but perhaps we have been too busy with isolated fragments of the school—namely, reading, arithmetic, geography, and history—to concern ourselves with the massive interrelationships among these areas of content. There are probably few children who do not wish to learn to read. There are probably few children who do not want to become responsible. But all children need help and guidance. Teachers need sensitivity and direction. These needs give direction to overall curriculum design.

Educational literature has been spotty. There have been curriculum movements—the "activity" movement, the "unit" movement, the "project" movement. Each of these is good in its own way; each has something to offer. But at this point what we need is a penetrating look at every child in terms of how best to develop competencies that help him to become more human, to assume some responsibility for his role in today's world, to see meaning in today's life. We must help our youth develop respect for their world and develop their individual maturity and security.

Emphasis on Esthetics. Chandler Montgomery, in *Art for Teachers of Children* (15), places great emphasis on esthetics. He says that producing art is not the aim of his approach. Rather, the aim is to develop an appetite for what is lively, vivid, and personally felt. The teacher who has lasting effects on children must have deep roots in experience if he is to bring the distilled quality of his living into productive relationships with children.

Many teachers today are concerned with trying to generate the esthetic outlook in their students. This outlook appreciates the beautiful as distinguished from the moral and the useful. The concern is with the individual's esthetic experiences, with his own active doing process rather than with comparisons of his products with those of other children or with a "standard" for a given age group. Administrators need to make it increasingly acceptable for schools to provide opportunities for children to engage in meaningful and vivid activities that foster esthetic qualities, thinking, and valuing.

Relevant Content. Van Til's article, "The Key Word Is Relevance" (19), made quite a case for relevant content selected on the basis of the social realities of the student's environment. There is no substitute for knowing the learner as an individual. Many of the current activities in the curriculum field seem to crowd out this process.

Evaluation in Curriculum Practice. More and more current developments in curriculum planning have their roots in evaluation activities.

> Evaluation may be thought of as providing a basis for curriculum planning. It is more than testing; it is more than meas-

> urement. There are those who tend to place evaluation in a terminal position rather than to conceive of it as a vital part of the entire educational activity. It is proposed that evaluation might well become the central ingredient around which the work of curriculum planning emerges.
>
> The process of evaluation is the same whether it serves an entire school faculty or the individual teacher. The faculty may use this process in planning ways of improving the program; the individual teacher may use it as she studies a group of children and plans ways of helping them. It is also the same process for an individual teacher who works with an individual child to determine his weaknesses and charts ways of helping him to overcome them. Evaluation makes it possible for one to describe or summarize status at a given time. This seems vital as a basis for making judgments as to future changes which are needed. This is essential in curriculum planning. (6, p. 495)

Efforts to diagnose an individual's status, to determine needs, and to involve him in meaningful learning experiences have an evaluation base. Evaluation is no longer a terminal enterprise. Evaluation is ongoing and continuing; in its most effective role it is an initial facet of curriculum planning. Extensive efforts at formulating "prescriptions" for learning are based on evaluative efforts. Evaluation needs the attention of administrators.

As teachers become increasingly alert to individual children—their anxieties, fears, worries, concerns, interests, and participation—they attempt to secure more and more evidence concerning each one's status. Self-evaluation activities hold much promise for letting teachers view a child in a more comprehensive manner. Perhaps our greatest hope is for evaluation that is extended over a period of time and that makes more valid judgments concerning one's programs.

Emerging Patterns of Organization

Leaders in elementary education over the years have been impressed by the importance of the learning environment. School organization has been a matter of concern to many during recent years. Numerous organizational models have arisen out of the concern for providing organizational features that offer greater flexibility and enhance learning. The Dual Progress plan implemented in several schools demonstrated that organization could be modified significantly without detriment to the quality of students' learning or growth.

In the early 1960's, there was a great debate concerning the relevance and value of the self-contained classroom. The debate often resulted in modifying the structure as an attempt not only to make education more relevant but also to make better use of school personnel. The nongraded school has long been advocated as an important organizational plan. There are probably as many versions of nongradedness as there are schools with such a label. The concept of team teaching likewise has emerged as a means of better using teachers' competencies and of developing greater flexibility in the work of the school. The focus should be placed on "team planning" as much as on team teaching. Multi-age groupings, too, have certain desirable features, when they are based on careful screening, assessment, and status identification. More recently, many have advocated the "open" school, in which there are many centers of interest and in which children can work in their own manner using whatever resources the school has to offer.

It would be difficult to endorse any of these plans as "best." Yet we know that the organizational structure of the school affects the potency of its program. *Organization should be a function of purpose.* Schools should seek those organizational qualities that make possible the realization of the purposes they seek. Movable walls, adjustable furniture, flexibilty of schedule, lack of rigidity of time, and more openness in space are laudable qualities. *Perhaps elementary schools should not be saddled with one organizational scheme but should draw from the entire available list those organizational factors that enhance their purposes.* Selection of organizational pattern on this basis returns us to the importance of continued planning on the part of the faculty as a means of fulfilling the requirements of the educational program, as opposed to using an organizational scheme that is fixed, specific, and maintained at the cost of other purposes to be achieved.

Conditions in many schools create organizational blocks. Older buildings with fixed structures pose numerous problems for administrators seeking to promote flexibility. On the other hand, in newer buildings with open space there can be many barricades which teachers have constructed to "fence themselves in." Many of the more traditional schools still have a library period or a physical education period or a music period scheduled on a highly organized basis in complete isolation from the balance of the program. Such rigidity in organization poses major hazards to the instructional program. The newer arrangement is to have a multimedia center, providing books, phonograph records, films, filmstrips, television, radio, and reference materials of all kinds in one central location. The center, which becomes a kind of core for the school, is characterized by diversity of materials, flexibility and openness of space, and availability to the children.

It is too bad that a fluid organizational scheme allowing for continuing modification in terms of purpose has not emerged. The requirements for effective organization are daily faculty assessment of program needs, daily planning, and maximum utilization of both faculty and space. We need a school plan with much time for planning and conferring among teachers, special services personnel, and administrators. The administrators who advocate a four-day teaching week with a day for planning may well be on the right track.

Emerging Patterns of Instruction

The individual child is more clearly in focus in instructional activities today than ever before. It may be that the typical school has at last found the child. Today's teacher appears to know more about each child than ever before. School records, although still grossly inadequate, contain important information about the individual, his home and family, his interests, and his status. It could well be that much of this knowledge is not used adequately, but it is a start in planning for an individual.

Teachers are making increasing efforts to individualize instructional procedures. The diversity of materials now available in our schools makes such efforts possible. Abundant materials have been developed in recent years that enable children to engage in exploration and discovery, sharpen their ideas, and communicate them in their own way.

The concept of *exploration* is an exciting one. Providing dynamic opportunities for exploration "turns on" the student and promotes automatic involvement. Exploration occurs with "things" —an idea, a book, a situation. In the child's response the teacher has a great opportunity to observe his status, perceptions, and work habits, as well as to find clues to fruitful further learning steps. To be sure, no discoveries are made without exploration. The elementary classroom is becoming more and more a work center, a learning center, a problem-solving center, offering children opportunities to work in multiple ways with many materials.

Conceptual systems are now identifying relationships among complex and interacting disciplines and/or areas of content. Teachers are increasingly using instructional procedures based on large concepts in contrast to the kind of instruction that only dispenses factual material isolated from a meaningful setting.

Although evaluation was emphasized as an element in curriculum practice, it also comes into focus in relation to instruction. Evaluation has become a central element in instructional practices. Evaluation of teaching has been employed at all levels of the instructional enterprise. *Testing is but one element of the evaluative operation.* Observations, listening, and analysis of student work are becoming prominent in evaluation materials. More important, a child's progress is used as a basis for assessing his studies and, therefore, as a basis for planning his program.

Among the instructional practices conspicuous in our schools are the following:

1. Greater concern for firsthand experiences—trips, walks around the block, discussions with resource people.
2. Greater diversity of instructional materials, art supplies, books, and references; a variety of science equipment, television, tapes, phonograph records.
3. Greater emphasis on esthetic experiences—painting, music, dance, dramatics.
4. Greater attention to enrichment experiences drawing from the arts, science, dramatics, and field experiences.
5. Greater acceptance of technology and of using products of technology—television, audiovisual materials, computers.
6. Greater concern for comprehensive evaluation employing many sources of data, formal and informal.

Instruction now takes place in many ways and at varying rates, using a diversity of materials. More teachers than ever before seem concerned with finding ways to facilitate learning.

The emerging instructional pattern of the recent decade has centered around the concept of humaneness. As Combs (4, p. 174) says, "What makes people human are matters of feeling, beliefs, values, attitudes, understanding. Without these things a man is a nothing."

Learning has two phases: the acquisition of new knowledge or experience and the discovery of its meaning. Attempts at curriculum refinement often overemphasize the information side of the learning equation. Instruction must help us to bring about greater balance. Teachers who see themselves in essentially positive ways, who perceive themselves and their world accurately and realistically, and who develop deep feelings of identification with other people, should be able to draw on such qualities for instructional procedures.

Directions for the Future

Our elementary schools are not as they should be or as they could become. Our programs are often ineffective, and our instruction often misses the point. Administrators could well ask, "How do we help people to live better? How do we plan educational programs that respect the dignity of people and provide opportunities for them to know themselves better, to interact with their peers more effectively, to develop dreams and hopes and aspirations, to enhance their thirst for knowledge, and finally, to develop the qualities that make for democratic living in a well-ordered society?" There are no formulas or prescriptions. But there are aspirations and wishes. A promising development could be the open-access curriculum. Another could come with freeing the capacity to learn and recognizing human variability in learning. In all these lovely phrases we see the essential ingredients of faith in oneself, faith in people, faith in tomorrow, and faith in human dignity. After numerous philosophical statements about the structure of knowledge, organizational patterns that foster learning, and relevant methodology, the essential questions remain: What turns people on? What challenges and stimulates individuals? What motivates them to want to become all that they can become? As one wrestles with such questions, the following "shoulds" for the elementary school of the future seem of high priority:

1. A school should be inviting, attractive, and stimulating—a place where children like to be, a place where each can find himself.
2. A school should be staffed with adults who care. The school needs people who are open, responsive, imaginative, and sensitive to the young and to their parents.
3. A school should have a storehouse of raw materials, to be used for creating and communicating ideas.
4. A school should recognize that it exists in today's world and should analyze, study, refine, and understand today's people, resources, and problems.
5. A school should be cognizant of its community, which should be a library and a storehouse of problems, cultural heritage, and vast interrelationships and interdependencies.

6. A school's faculty should recognize that knowledge is unfolding daily, to be understood, to be interpreted, to be used. The newspaper, the news broadcast, the events of the day, the movies should all find their place in the modern school.
7. A school should provide its students with opportunities to share their talents and to provide social service to others: the aged, the young, the sick, etc. These experiences should begin at an early age.
8. A school should make it possible for students to be responsible for their activities. Assuming responsibility contributes to personality development, to citizenship practices, and to value education.
9. A school should make it possible for students to discover latent competencies, to find out "what I can do." To paint a picture, to participate in a dance, or to create a new set of relationships provides security and maturity. Each day should contribute to the student's stockpile of competencies and to his own feelings of adequacy.
10. A school should provide opportunities for each child to realize his own power; to identify progress; to verbalize his limitations without fear; to accept his status as a benchmark of adequacy, a basis for continued learning, and an element of positive mental health.
11. A school should be led by an administrator who is sensitive to people, sensitive to learning, skilled in leadership, and comfortable with change.

This is what school is all about. Those who are preoccupied with this or that body of content, type of school organization, or piece of instructional gadgetry miss the point. Let us not become so engrossed in the trivia of our profession that we lose sight of the dynamics of our opportunity. To help people live better, to help people communicate with greater clarity, to help people strive for something, to help people help themselves—these are objectives of the highest order. They require neither massive legislation nor new sources of money. They reflect a deep commitment to basic human values and the recognition that the school is the one agency in our culture best prepared to nurture humaneness, to foster growth, to develop competencies, and to enrich life.

BIBLIOGRAPHY

1. Allen, James. "To Move the Mountain." Address before the Thirtieth Annual Convention, National School Boards Association, San Francisco, Calif., April 1970.

2. Bereiter, Carl, and Engelmann, Siegfried. *Teaching Disadvantaged Children in the Preschool.* Englewood Cliffs, N.J.: Prentice-Hall, 1966.

3. Bloom, Benjamin. *Stability and Change in Human Characteristics.* New York: John Wiley & Sons, 1964.

4. Combs, Arthur W. "An Educational Imperative: The Human Dimension." *To Nurture Humaneness.* (Edited by Mary-Margaret Scobey and Grace Graham.) 1970 Yearbook. Washington, D.C.: Association for Supervision and Curriculum Development, 1970. pp. 173-88.

5. Eisner, Elliot W. *Confronting Curriculum Reform.* Boston: Little, Brown and Co., 1971.

6. Fleming, Robert S. *Curriculum for Today's Boys and Girls.* Columbus, Ohio: Charles E. Merrill, 1963.

7. Foshay, Arthur W. *Curriculum for the 70's: An Agenda for Invention.* Schools for the 70's, Preliminary Series. Washington, D.C.: National Education Association, Center for the Study of Instruction, 1970.

8. Gray, Susan W., and others. *Before First Grade: The Early Training Project for Culturally Disadvantaged Children.* New York: Teachers College, Columbia University, 1966.

9. ———. *Research, Change, and Social Responsibility: An Illustrative Model from Early Childhood Education.* ERIC Document ED 032 922. Nashville, Tenn.: George Peabody College for Teachers, 1967.

10. Hunt, Joseph McVicker. *Intelligence and Experience.* New York: Ronald Press, 1961.

11. Hymes, James. *Teaching the Child Under Six.* Columbus, Ohio: Charles E. Merrill, 1968.

12. Klein, Jenny. "Planned Variation in Head Start Programs." *Children* 18: 8-12; January 1971.

13. Kohlberg, L. "Early Education: A Cognitive-Developmental View." *Child Development* 39: 1013-62; December 1968.

14. Lyon, Harold C., Jr. *Learning to Feel—Feeling to Learn.* Columbus, Ohio: Charles E. Merrill, 1971.

15. Montgomery, Chandler. *Art for Teachers of Children.* Columbus, Ohio: Charles E. Merrill, 1968.

16. Parker, Ronald K., and Whitney, D. C. "A Systems Approach to Early Education: The Discovery Program." *Educational Technology* 11: 22-28; February 1971.

17. Rogers, Carl R. *Freedom to Learn.* Columbus, Ohio: Charles E. Merrill, 1969.

18. Weikart, David, and others. *The Cognitively Oriented Curriculum: A Framework for Preschool Teachers.* Final Report. ERIC Document ED 044 535. Ypsilanti, Mich.: Ypsilanti Public Schools, 1970.

19. Van Til, William. "The Key Word Is Relevance." *Today's Education* 58: 14-17; January 1969.

6

English Language Arts Education

The past decade has seen a continued search for clarification of English as a subject for study in schools—clarification that establishes proper priorities, that specifies concretely what the English teacher is to do, and that increases opportunities for developing good sequential programs from elementary grades through high school to college undergraduate levels. In major experimental curriculum centers throughout the country, a number of models for the curriculum in English are under study. In at least one center, the model is a language-based curriculum, and composition and literature are treated as the two highest and most artistic manifestations of language; in a second, separate but related strands of language, literature, and composition are being organized into a K-12 sequence. Another popular model is the literature-centered curriculum, with the sequence based on the reading of particular works and with study of writing, speaking, and language growing from reading and discussion. Also receiving attention, especially at the elementary level, is a curriculum emphasizing cognitive processes, the mental operations involved in reading and in the uses of oral and written language. These and other models are being tested continually. In the next few years experimentation with many patterns of organizing instruction in English rather than the adoption of any uniform national pattern will probably be evident.

Despite the diversity in approach and sometimes in definition, curriculum builders now widely accept certain principles. Primary is their recognition that English instruction involves both content and skills. Regardless of emphasis or approach, curriculum leaders today agree that the teaching of English is concerned with the content of literature, language, and composition (i.e., the principles of rhetoric), and with the supporting skills of speaking, listening, reading, and writing. In most programs, skills are developed as the content is explored.

To overstress the skills of English to the exclusion of its content places an almost insurmountable barrier between elementary and secondary programs and provides no intellectually valid context for teaching skills. For example, when the teaching of reading is overstressed during elementary years, it can too easily slide into a separate program alienated from other English instruction and organized without commitment to any content. On the other hand, overemphasis on the content of language and literature, especially at the secondary level, can lead to the neglect or even the abandonment of either reading skills or the uses of oral language.

Though imbalances are possible in either content or skill, a curriculum limited to the teaching of skills may create greater dangers. Since the teaching of reading, writing, speaking, and listening is quite properly the goal of general education, everything contributing to this goal can be regarded as "English"; and every teacher can be regarded as "a teacher of English." Such a view explains attempts to stress the basic processes of communication in teaching in all subject areas, but it also may partly account for the insufficient emphasis on specialized preparation in English. Elementary teachers, for instance, who spend 40 to 60 percent of their time teaching skills embraced under the general term *English,* spend only 8 percent of their preprofessional course time on preparation for this task (17, p. 96). Faulty preparation to teach content, as well as skills, also contributed to the findings reported in Robert C. Pooley's three-year Wisconsin study of K-12 English programs that few planned literary experiences were introduced between the end of grade 3 and the beginning of high school. In the absence of any concern with literature, elementary teachers stress reading almost exclusively as a set of skills. Once children become independent readers after the primary grades, reading becomes only practice to maintain or improve efficiency and a means to gather information in other content fields. It is important that all reading and study skills needed by children be carefully taught; it is no less important that the content of English receive necessary attention.

To rejuvenate awareness that English is a content subject as well as a skills subject is one of the major aims of the profession's current efforts in curriculum. An awakening to the integral relationship of the two parts of English is directly related to new understanding of concept development and the psychology of thinking. In proper balance, skills and content should help lead each student to use language effectively and to find in literature a storehouse of human understanding, as well as extend each individual's knowledge about language, literature, and composition.

Emerging Concepts and Applications in Teaching Language

No aspect of English is changing more dramatically than the teaching of oral and written language. Insights into the nature of language and language development of children have modified our basic perceptions about the content that we teach and how we should organize instruction.

In the past, many teachers taught English as a series of separate subjects: reading from 9:00 to 9:20 A.M. and spelling from 11:00 to 11:20 A.M., or literature on Monday, grammar on Tuesday, and composition on Thursday. They failed to see that the processes of reading, spelling, speech, and applying usage and grammar are bound together through an awareness of basic linguistic processes. Teachers strengthen the entire K-12 sequence when they relate its various parts to a central view of language study.

The field of reading can serve to illustrate how language is a major consideration in everything we teach. New programs in reading are based not only on physiological, psychological, social, and experiential factors, but on linguistic factors as well. In teaching children to read, we are newly aware that we are teaching the mastery of a written language system. Most linguists and many reading specialists agree that programs of beginning reading should be based on the consistent structures of sound in the English language as we know them to exist. To achieve proficiency in reading and spelling, the child must learn how the sounds of English are translated into written symbols, something quite different from the reverse process of translating specific but arbitrary letters into specific sounds.

To help children most effectively, teachers need a basic understanding of the relationship between pronunciation and reading and the systems of phonemics and phonetics. Linguist C. C. Fries calls reading "the process of transfer from *auditory* signs for language symbols, which the child has already learned, to the *visual* signs for the same symbols." The ways in which the child learns to associate sounds with written symbols in reading then relate to the ways he masters spelling. Clearly a sharpening of relationships between reading and spelling is emerging from present work on finding the true consistencies of sounds and letters in the language codes.

When a child enters school, oral language is *the* language. It is the only method of communication he knows. Instruction in written language and reading must accordingly be built upon the oral language that the child brings to school, not on more formal written language that is unrelated to what the child uses every day. Hence, increased attention is given to aspects of language as these are involved in teaching the child to read; e.g., dialect study of the culture groups whence children come, study of children's language habits, readiness instruction that includes more attention to speaking and listening, and a relaxation of rigid vocabulary control so that sentences more closely resemble those the child hears.

The importance of oral language is best illustrated in programs for teaching the disadvantaged. Head Start instruction throughout the nation, the Wilmington Project on Changing Neighborhoods, the Bernstein studies at the University of London—all demonstrate the importance of two-way oral language in improving the thinking and language skills of children. Through the work of sociolinguists, schools are recognizing that teaching English to the disadvantaged involves not piecemeal remedial processes but the teaching of a second, overlying language system in addition to the one such children habitually use. Some specialists recommend that the schools, particularly in the primary grades, conduct much classroom learning in the oral language familiar to children, even while attempting to develop children's facility in using language patterns of a more socially approved type.

Abundant evidence shows, too, that our early and most successful readers generally profit most from a rich background of oral language. For poor readers today, as well as for disadvantaged children, the path to improvement may lie not so much with remedial work in reading, but with frequent and effective oral experiences to make up for the deprivation. How far existing programs need to go in strengthening experiences in speaking and listening is suggested by a recent study finding that conventional language arts textbooks for children devote less than 25 percent of their content to speech activities (3).

Oral language is not the only aspect of language instruction receiving attention today. Of equal importance in improving elementary instruction are applications of studies of sentences used by children, studies revealing that most children beginning school, even those from disadvantaged areas, have mastered orally most of the sentence patterns they will use even as mature adults. No longer is the teacher seen as one who presents a new, correct language; rather, his role is one of expanding and activating the linguistic repertoire which the child already possesses. New reading materials introduce children to a rich variety of sentences; wide reading of many books helps supplement and extend a restricted basal program; and experiences with oral literature provide children with rich and imaginative uses of language. These are some hallmarks of our new language programs.

Ability to manipulate the possible variations within the English sentence distinguishes the articulate child from the inarticulate, the effective from the ineffective. The implications are clear. The need in schools, especially in elementary schools, is for more emphasis on sentence building through purposeful discussion, conversation, reporting, and dramatizing and less emphasis on sentence analysis; more stress on achieving variety in writing and speech and less on restricted correcting of printed sentences that seldom resemble the child's own.

Nor is meaning forgotten in newer approaches to language study. Since studies show that children entering school have spent, on the average, more than 1,500 hours before a television set, hearing thousands of new words with only limited understanding, attention to the meaning in communication becomes increasingly critical. The newer English programs display extensive concern with multilevel meanings of words in various contexts, with persuasive language, with metaphorical or imaginative language, with informational and evaluative language, and with the purposes to which language is put.

Literature, too, is important in the language development of young people. As Ruth Strickland has observed, "It is through exposure to literature that children learn the possibilities of their language. In everyday communication, they hear the language used for utilitarian purposes. In literature they encounter it in more artistic and creative forms. . . . And listening to the teacher's reading of good literature is especially important to the child who comes from a substandard language background." (26)

If understanding of the nature of language provides a new perspective on the development of children's language, it also makes us ask what should be taught about language itself and how. Most English specialists have clearly rejected the notion that the only purpose of language study is the improvement of writing, speaking, listening, and reading. Language, as the study of one of man's most characteristic modes of behavior, has a content which is profitably taught in itself, much as is the content of biology or history. The questions before the profession today are, How much study, when, and of what kind?

The study of the history of the language as related to dialect growth and change and evolution of its structure is one facet currently receiving new attention. From such study young people learn how our language has changed and what forces have promoted change and continue to influence the development of the language. Some specialists argue for attention to linguistic history early in the curriculum. In considering the expansion of the American West, for example, fifth-grade children may trace the westward movement of the English language and the changes which occur: the pioneer terms, the Spanish influences, the regional place names, the regional pronunciations like "creek" and "crick." For the secondary school, special units on the history of language are being developed to accompany the study of literary history. One new development is the publication of selected historical texts showing pupils the forms in which English has appeared over the centuries, i.e., selected printed passages and authoritative oral (or recorded) readings of Old English and Middle English passages.

Young people who will live in the rich diversity of the American culture need to develop deep respect for the variety of English tongues. A special concern is the teaching about English and American dialects, the variations of English deriving from social and geographical influences. Awareness of linguistic differences, of what such differences signify and do not signify, is important to a mobile population in a land characterized by social change. Listening to recordings of dialect samples in intermediate classrooms; studying dialects of "live" speakers in the elementary, junior high, and senior high schools; and studying lexicography, that is, dictionaries, dictionary makers, and what dictionaries are for—all are important.

One product of the "great dictionary controversy" of the early sixties has been an increase in the attention schools give to the nature of English usage. Modern teachers are trying to explain what appropriate language is: language that effectively communicates meaning to a specific, stipulated audience. To understand this, children must learn that the effectiveness of language varies with the context in which it is used, and our programs must help them learn to adjust their own language to each immediate occasion while they are, for other purposes, learning the common usage of educated adults in their own region.

The grammar of English is now studied as subject matter in its own right, not as a means of improving speech and writing. Forty years of research in education has shown that the study of grammar, when narrowly conceived, does not contribute observably to the improvement of the way students write. Although experimental efforts to demonstrate the relationship between grammar and writing continue, specialists today argue for grammar instruction which contributes to the child's understanding of the structure and operation of his language rather than an allegedly "functional" instruction which confuses grammar and usage. Some newer approaches attempt to improve the possibilities of transfer of grammatical study to actual use. The creation of sentences (the writing of examples of structure) has values that mere analysis of someone else's sentences does not have. The rewriting of papers enables students to use grammatical knowledge at the moment when it may have the greatest potential for transfer.

At least three grammars are being introduced in new school programs—scholarly, traditional grammar; structural grammar; and transformational grammar. Until recently none of these had been widely taught as a discipline in schools. The "school grammar" of recent decades, too often a confused blend of usage and grammatical rules, has been referred to as "traditional" grammar because it was traditionally taught in the schools, but seldom in a coherent, systematic way. Such "school grammar" has been universally denounced by scholars. Specialists are not yet agreed on what kind of grammar should be presented in the classroom, but they generally agree that teachers themselves should understand at least two methods of grammatical description, if only to free themselves from dependence on a single approach.

Structural or descriptive grammar provides a valid description of the relationship among words and the patterns of word groups (syntax); the forms of words (morphology); and the sounds of the language, including such features as intonation, stress, and pause (phonology). Transformational grammar, on the other hand, is a rigorous description of the regular, internalized structural and semantic systems through which individuals produce English sentences. Scholars differ in their views of these two newer grammars. Some regard transformational grammar as a logical extension of structural approaches, while others view the two as incompatible in many ways. Most modern programs of language instruction derive from one or both of these grammars; transformational analysis has perhaps attracted the most recent attention.

Still widespread are differences of opinion about the place of grammatical instruction during the first six years of school. Many specialists argue that school should vigorously provide for expanding and enhancing the child's own repertoire of linguistic behavior rather than for studying theoretical principles of grammar. These specialists argue that to pause for grammar study is to deny the time needed for stimulating language growth. Programs of instruction should provide for creative expression as well as for the more practical uses of language. The teacher must understand that children need a wide range of experience in conversation, discussion, reporting, and dramatizing which will build toward later attempts to generalize about language. The formal study of English grammar should be delayed until secondary school when, according to these observers, children would be so conscious of the possibilities of language that the study of grammar would not encourage empty verbalization.

Some recently published textbooks, however, introduce sequential study of grammar early in the intermediate grades. For some children, such carefully organized programs may provide useful and interesting knowledge about the nature and operation of language without necessarily interfering with language growth. Supporters of this approach argue that there are limits to what schools can do to stimulate language growth, which, it is believed, is but one part of total growth.

In any event, however it is introduced, a carefully defined sequence of grammar instruction is characteristic of many new programs being developed in school districts and in textbooks, whether the sequence begins in the late elementary school or in high school. The curriculum study center at the University of Oregon, for example, introduces principles of transformational grammar in grades 7 and 8, then expands its concerns over the subsequent years to include such aspects of language as its history and regional and social variations.

Concerned about the needless repetition of instruction in language from grade to grade and aware of the confused relationship between knowledge about and use of language which fragmented many programs of the past, curriculum specialists are moving to create curriculums in language which inform young people about language while teaching them to use it more effectively. Because of the help offered by numerous institutes and inservice programs, elementary and secondary teachers should know more about the full dimensions of language, and schools of the future should be far better prepared (a) to evaluate the purposes, possibilities, and limitations of the new programs and textbooks prepared for children's use and (b) to create and teach language programs in keeping with what is known and is appropriate to their pupils.

Emerging Concepts and Applications in Teaching Composition

Programs today tend to stress planned, cumulative experiences in writing. A remarkable development recently has been the stress on composition at almost every grade level, including even the primary school. An important byproduct of initial teaching alphabet programs in reading, although the occurrence is not confined to these programs, has been the stimulation of much writing by children. Introduced to new words and new ideas by their early independence in reading, children begin writing very early. Experiences with new media and new books also generate an early interest in writing. The "writing approach to beginning reading" is based on the dictation and reading of children's own stories almost from the first moments of school. Such early creative experiences serve in turn as a foundation of literary sensitivity—children write their own literature, read and listen to the literature read by others, and shape their experiences through artistic expression.

At the intermediate level, writing continues and is related both to reading and to oral expression of ideas. Although still uncertain about how much direct writing instruction to give in the upper elementary school, specialists agree that both imaginative and objective writing should play some part at this level.

New programs in the secondary school, while devoting more attention to writing than did the old, place more emphasis on the composing process itself, often by using short selections for analysis that develop conceptual understanding of how the material is put together. Often considerable help is given in planning and organizing a paper and in revising and polishing. Instruction in spelling, drills on conventions of writing, vocabulary work, grammar, the study of English usage—these are not substitutes for writing, for they too often direct attention away from writing itself. Particularly in junior high school programs, where teachers traditionally have substituted so-called exercises for actual writing, new programs are resulting in significant changes.

Formal statements stipulating what amount of practice in writing should be required have not had widespread support. The "theme a week" proposal of a few years back was more an appeal for increased attention to composition than a carefully reasoned position. No doubt students should do some writing almost every week. But heavy teaching loads still handicap teachers who could otherwise offer their students thoughtful, creative instruction. Because of these heavy loads, few teachers can develop major weekly assignments with care and find time to evaluate the resulting mountain of themes. When they casually introduce unmotivated weekly writing assignments, their pupils seem to experience little permanent growth in ability to write. In such circumstances, it is preferable that students write less frequently if their writing is therefore more thoughtfully and carefully conceived and their teachers have time to read papers carefully and offer constructive help. According to one recent study of successful programs, only 15.7 percent of high school time is spent on composition, an emphasis considerably less than most authorities would recommend, but perhaps not inadequate if the time is carefully spent (23, p. 192).

Writing of a composition by a student and reading of it by a teacher should be a process which begins at the level of ideas, not at the level of conventions of sentence analysis. Since any writer must have something meaningful to say before writing an acceptable essay, even a child's writing should indicate that he has done some thoughtful reading or that his personal experiences have led him to form some thoughtful conclusions. Writing is a skill which demands constant practice, but this practice must be in expressing ideas and feelings. Thus the emphases in a program of composition are on wide reading, discussion, and the relationship between writing and the reading of literature. It is hardly possible, then, to separate writing from reading and literature. Children who have read and experienced little, and who have thought or fancied even less, may find the writing of a meaningful story, poem, report, or essay well beyond their powers.

Little evidence exists that reliance on workbook exercises or drills or meticulous sleuthing through student papers for missing commas or misspelled words encourages growth in writing ability. Indeed, an education overemphasizing mechanics and conventions in writing can lead to other problems. A student sacrificing ideas in order to write what he considers to be a "perfect" or "safe" paper—one which the teacher can't attack because it is written in simple declarative sentences, all properly punctuated and capitalized—has missed the point; he has not understood that the purpose of the communication should determine the structures and conventions of writing and not vice versa. And the teacher is derelict in grading papers if he fails to indicate that thinking and organizing are matters of primary importance and that errors in mechanics are not evils of and by themselves but are simply obstructions to the flow of thought within the essay which should be overcome through revision.

Sequence, now seen as important to good composition programs, must be based on psychological rather than logical patterns of organization. Long before Jerome Bruner evolved his carefully considered construction of a spiral curriculum, philosopher Alfred North Whitehead discussed the "rhythms of education" at various education levels and insisted that the sequence through which effective education is best achieved is not necessarily that leading from the simple to the complex. It is still common for teachers to argue that children should master the paragraph before proceeding to the essay, should master the sentence before proceeding to the paragraph, should master the parts of speech before proceeding to the English sentence. But linguists have now reiterated that the structural and semantic properties of words have meaning only in larger language units—phrases, clauses, sentences, and paragraphs. Parts of the communicative process can be studied only in relation to the whole communication. Modern elementary teachers find that children's ability to compose is enhanced by experiences in building and manipulating sentences, in clarifying sentences, and in changing them to achieve a pleasing variety or repetitive sound, often before much word study has been introduced. Similarly, today's secondary teachers learn that concepts of the paragraph and even longer units of writing develop slowly and require recurrent study.

The usual method of writing instruction followed in many schools proceeds from student writing of compositions to teacher "correction" and subsequent return of the essays—in many cases to be revised and resubmitted. No doubt this time-honored system will continue to be practiced by many teachers. It emphasizes instruction through correction after writing and is supported by the belief that success depends upon adequate annotation of student papers. Unfortunately, recent studies of teachers' annotations on students' writings have revealed startling deficiencies. Examination of one sampling of thousands of papers returned to students revealed that one third had not been annotated in any way; in another third, only "gross errors" of spelling and usage were corrected (23, p. 193). The basic problems of expressing and organizing ideas, problems which should receive major stress, are too often ignored.

Without a doubt, heavy pupil loads often prevent teachers from carefully annotating themes. If as much as 8.6 minutes is the median time required to mark a 250-word paper intended to teach "writing and thinking" (8, p. 4), then a teacher with 125 to 150 students, the national average in secondary schools, will devote about 19 hours per week to correction of papers if he requires students to write a "theme a week." Few teachers can sustain such an outlay of time. When teaching loads cannot be reduced substantially, most specialists recommend giving writing assignments less frequently. But they emphasize that the annotation of this writing should be focused more upon quality of ideas and organization and effectiveness of presentation than upon conventions of writing (22).

Nevertheless, instruction in composition after the act of writing may be less effective than what the teacher does with children before they write. The composition assignment is thus developed with care, and students are urged to explore the composing problems involved before putting pen to paper, not to write in a rush and repent at leisure. Extended writing laboratory periods give classes sufficient time to develop ideas before beginning to write and also afford the teacher opportunity to assist individuals with problems in composing at the time when problems occur.

New programs are placing great emphasis, also, on both principles of rhetoric—that is, the principles of effectiveness in expression and communication—and methods of rhetorical analysis derived from the restudy of classical rhetoricians and from modern scholarship in communication. In a few programs, too, teachers are relating such principles and methods to both oral and written discourse, seeing in the composition program a way of developing understandings pertinent to speech as well as writing. Although they have only limited value, models of good writing by both students and adults are frequently introduced. The use of models may help children recognize the unity of parts in a whole composition before they emulate in their own writing the models provided.

Attention to the rhetorical problems of composing means greater attention to the "inventing" of subtle topics and to methods of organizing and expressing ideas. Before ideas are organized and expressed, however, problems in determining a speaker's attitude toward his subject, his purpose, and his awareness of audience and selection of detail must be stressed in modern programs. Most important of all in rhetorical approaches is the stress placed on composing as the writer's way of shaping and communicating ideas through language.

Establishing arbitrary differences between personal (imaginative, subjective) and practical (factual, expository, business) writing seem less important than providing balanced experiences in writing during a total curricular sequence. On certain occasions, students wish to describe their feelings; on others, to narrate vicarious or personal experiences or convey information; on still others, to grapple with abstract ideas and to analyze the ideas and perceptions of others. In the hands of children, the impersonal can become personal, the expository become imaginative. Exaggerated stress on allegedly different modes of adult discourse, the tendency to avoid imaginative writing, and the practice of overemphasizing one particular kind of analytical writing represent considerations that are external rather than internal (e.g., the need to communicate). Children progressing through the schools should have a variety of opportunities to write; inevitably their writing will become increasingly impersonal as experience and maturity lead them toward control of more abstract discourse. Yet reasonable balance between the development of personal and of practical writing should be provided.

Writing is the attempt of an individual first to clarify for himself and then to express his personal attitudes, ideas, and feelings. Here, perhaps more than at most points in the curriculum, emphasis should be placed on the individual. Those programs in writing that subordinate the individual either to abstract and sometimes fallacious notions about composition or to the group—in what is assigned, in what is expressed, in what is taught, in how sequence is achieved—will ultimately be less successful in encouraging effective composing than are programs designed to free individual expression.

Emerging Concepts and Applications in Teaching Literature

For many years now the quality of literary experiences provided children and young people has concerned the profession. The inadequacy of organized programs in literature for elementary children, the paucity of adequate literary materials in conventional basal reading programs, and the substandard selections from literature in conventional high school curricula have recently been attacked. Conditions are already improving, however; elementary schools are introducing programs in literature for children; new elementary school readers include far more literary content than the old; high school anthologies have been substantially improved by weeding out the peripheral and dull selections; and the paperback revolution in the publishing industry has provided schools with extensive and relatively inexpensive resources for literature of quality which allow great latitude and imaginative planning.

Traditionally, elementary schools have introduced literature as only one aspect of the program in reading or have relegated it to being merely enrichment for other subjects, such as social studies. These approaches can be justified in part and almost certainly will continue. But most curriculum leaders today feel a compelling need to organize developmental programs in literature for children, programs designed to introduce literature for its own sake, for its inherent cultural values, and for the delight which it conveys.

Effective curriculum planning in the elementary schools begins with attempts to increase children's enjoyment and understanding of literature of many kinds. Instruction to help boys and girls learn to critically analyze well chosen works also is important, but such instruction must be so planned as to enhance appreciation rather than to kill it. Providing extensive opportunity for personal reading from the abundance of worthwhile literature for children is crucial throughout primary and intermediate levels and even more so in junior high school, when most people will read more books than at any other time in their lives. Thus the development of organized programs in literature for the first eight grades emerges as an important curriculum need and a trend which is evident today.

Model programs to encourage further change are being tested in the schools. For example, a sequence for grades 1-12 has been developed by the curriculum study center at the University of Nebraska. The sequence introduces children to representative literary genres: parables, fables, picaresque tales, myths and epics, comedies, poetry, and romances are presented throughout the curriculum; increasingly complex selections appropriate to the age and interests of the children are introduced every two or three years to achieve a cumulative effect.

Another approach stresses the education of the imagination. The child not only reads stories, dramas, and poems, but also tells them or acts them out. Personal experience and creativity, involvement, and engagement are vital ingredients. Less attention to reasoning and the analytic skills at an early age and to the acquisition of knowledge about literature are characteristic of this second approach.

Still a third model for the elementary curriculum supports wide personal reading by direct study of the elements of literature: character, theme, plot, style, diction, tone, and figurative language.

Differing in emphasis, the paradigms are similar in stressing a common core of literary experiences as central to educating the imagination of children. However these common experiences are achieved, their quality and richness are as important in elementary as they are in secondary education. Insistence on quality does not mandate rigid teaching of a fixed list of books. The extensive resources of literature in English and literature in translation are available to both teachers and students. Valuable annotated book lists and collections of appropriate reading should be available in every school library, textbook room, and English classroom. From such resources teachers can select those literary works which promise to offer most to the young people in their classes. Pseudo-literature, potboilers, and pap, writings which communicate no genuine experience and no sense of artistic form, have no place in any program. Under an avalanche of adverse criticism, classroom use of adapted or rewritten versions and snippets or bits of longer literary works—whether of children's literature or standard classics—is disappearing. A good, well-written contemporary work appropriate to the interests and abilities of a child can provide far more genuine experience in literature than does a rewritten classic, no matter how venerable.

Although specialists in English agree on no canon of literary works which all children must read (and there is no likelihood that they will), they do agree that programs should incorporate literature of many kinds. Some literary forms have clearly been neglected; recent study of high school literature anthologies, for example, indicated that an average of only 2.7 percent of the content of these books is devoted to the essay (5). Also, recent recognition of the importance of the myths and folktales, which form the background of allusion for other adult works of literature, has created an impetus to introduce such genres in elementary programs. This reading, however, should supplement, not replace, the reading of such superb modern works for children as *Charlotte's Web* and *Make Way for Ducklings.*

To achieve a well balanced program, teachers must assign priorities. Because of the scope of literature, most students will have gaps in their reading, but better readers at least should have some contact with classic myths; Arthurian tales; stories from the Old and New Testaments; Shakespeare; major New England writers like Ralph Waldo Emerson and Nathaniel Hawthorne; and representative modern writers like Robert Frost, William Faulkner, Ernest Hemingway, and George Orwell. Just because no national curriculum compels the teaching of specific titles, teachers should not assume that "anything goes."

How, then, should literary works be selected? The prevailing sentiment is that the literature program in every school should be arrived at through a consensus of the English teachers, at least a consensus of those teachers informed about both literature and the available literary resources, sensitive to the individual readers, and knowledgeable about contemporary criticism and the newer practices of teaching literature to young people. Only if teachers know why they teach each selection are they likely to be responsible and effective. As the Commission on English writes,

> To accept the fact of unavoidable variety is merely to recognize that curriculums in literature must respond to the needs and interests of teachers and students in varying communities and in changing times. In the individual curriculum of a particular school—or of a school system—the achievable consensus on literature finds its center. (4, p. 46)

Significant imaginative experiences in the classroom are apparent, too, in programs for the non-college-bound student. The excessive emphasis on the technical, "practical," and scientific which has characterized many English programs for "the lower tracks" is yielding as educators realize that oral reading and interpretation by the teacher of selections which pupils cannot read on their own will excite the imaginations of such young people. Further, the literature of the film can evoke significant and surprising aesthetic response. The curriculum study center at Hunter College has developed a three-year sequence of literary units for disadvantaged boys and girls in grades 7 to 9. For young people whose access to aesthetic and cultural achievement is sometimes limited by restrictive social environments, the education of the imagination can provide significant release.

For some decades teachers have concerned themselves with whether arrangement of selections by historical period, by theme or topic, by genre, by author, or by individual work might offer the greatest teaching possibility. Each approach has its dangers; each its own possibilities. All are being used effectively with some students today, though direct emphasis on literary history or thematic organization seems less in favor now.

More important than any particular system of organization is the attention given to individual selections. The unique quality and instructional demands of the work itself and the relationship of the work to the student should govern what is done in the classroom. Careful reading of a particular text with close attention to the interrelationship of idea and form and language is fundamental. Historical and biographical matters, background information often overstressed in programs of the past, can then be introduced as necessary to illuminate the reading of the text. Newer programs do not present a steady diet of such information.

The literary work itself is the center of study. Recognition of the cruciality of the text has led to a de-emphasis on coverage and to stress on close reading of a smaller number of selections with extensive personal reading following class study. Such literary pieces are taught in their entirety so that readers may sense their total impact. Historical surveys of English and American literature, even geographic surveys of world literature, are less important than concentration on literature itself.

But the close reading of literary texts will never promote lifetime habits of reading until schools find better ways to encourage wide personal reading. Indeed, attention to close reading alone may restrict the interests of individuals as well as their freedom in book selection. Thus, supplementary textbooks, small sets of books for group reading, classroom book collections, and improved school libraries are needed for modern programs. Library corners in elementary classrooms, special reading rooms and reading hours in the secondary school, and efforts to bring the "outside" reading inside—these are significant new developments. Research and experience have convinced many teachers that young people will develop permanent appreciation only with the opportunity to expand their interests. As T. S. Eliot once wrote, "Wide reading is valuable because in the process of being affected by one powerful personality after another, we cease to be dominated by any one, or by any small number."

Another trend in teaching literature is to a renewed interest in oral literature. To all students, not only to the disadvantaged, teacher readings of myths, fables, and fairy tales provide an important source of aesthetic pleasure. Moreover, oral interpretation is virtually a necessity in dealing with genres meant to be read aloud, such as poems and plays. Creative dramatics, role playing, and dramatic improvisation also stimulate active response to literary expression and contribute to the development of sensitivity.

Administrators and curriculum specialists have long worried about the need to integrate the learning of many parts of the curriculum. The interdisciplinary relationship of all art forms is reflected in new humanities courses, many of which provide contrastive and comparative experiences in literature, art, and music. The study of films as literature, an art form developed in this century, seems likely to open new opportunities for the study of modern drama. Recent attention to the emerging English-language literatures of Africa and Australia communicates to young people a sense of the urgency and universality of the literary experience. Our new programs in literature introduce young readers to some of the best literature of our time and to some of the best of all time, striving always to cultivate heightened taste and interest in reading.

Emerging Methods of Instruction in English

New content for English programs has demanded new methods of instruction. English, more than most fields of study, has felt the impact of new theories of teaching and learning. As a consequence, at least five basic trends are apparent.

The learning of English is now seen largely as a process of inquiry and discovery. In placing greater emphasis upon the intellectual development of children, teachers have become increasingly aware of fundamental mental processes. Learning in English becomes learning to compose rather than learning about composition, learning to engage in literary experience rather than learning facts about literature, learning to manipulate the elements of the English sentence rather than learning isolated principles and rules of grammar. The Commission on English of the College Entrance Examination Board in its final report says that the fundamental goal of English in the high school is "criticism," and by this the Commission intends substantially more than criticism of literature or language. Rather it intends the development of a critical and evaluative attitude toward literature and toward life itself. Learning in English becomes the learning of the processes of criticism.

This change in perception requires the establishment of criteria for judging learning different from mere reliance on the number of correct answers on a weekly spelling test or a quiz on the author's life and times. Instead, the processes of learning English are emphasized: students learn how to spell rather than memorize spellings, how to read books and discover what is in books of varying kinds, how to respond critically to a Shakespearean drama rather than recall a collection of facts about the work and its background.

The quality and the depth of each learning experience are important, the extent to which it reaches the intellectual base of the learner and cuts through to his emotional, psychological, and philosophical consciousness. Our classrooms for this new English should be remembered not as places where 50 sentences were diagrammed each day or 50 facts about the French Revolution memorized as a result of reading *A Tale of Two Cities,* but rather as places where young writers first discovered how unity brings effectiveness to communication and where they were brought to the edges of their seats with excitement about the inferential qualities of words.

New approaches to learning English concentrate on concepts related to the "structure of the subject" and avoid attempting to cover the entire field. In English as in other subject fields, knowledge is being generated rapidly. Consequently, more and more, programs are designed to help the student discover basic unifying ideas which offer insight into the nature of the discipline (or the several disciplines of literature, language, and rhetoric). Through study of significant examples, rather than through broad coverage, the learner may gain sufficient understanding to make it possible for him to cope with future knowledge.

In language, too, selectivity of content is important. New programs for grammatical instruction restrict attention to fundamental insights, introduced in a careful sequence. One attractive feature of transformational grammar, for example, is its reduction of most English sentences to a few basic patterns. Furthermore, the study of linguistic history and geography focuses on basis concepts which assist young people in understanding historical changes in language and varieties of language they will later encounter on their own.

New methods of teaching English require a variety of learning and teaching materials. Learning today provides seriously for anticipated differences in individuals, involves the full repertoire of linguistic processes, and depends upon intelligent use of a great variety of materials. If young people are to read extensively on their own, strong school libraries are essential—at an invitational national conference, high school English chairmen called for book collections of 500 titles for every English class (14, pp. 13-14). Important, too, is a more diversified supply of textbook materials, especially a wide range of supplementary textbooks suitable for group and individual use.

But more than books and printed materials are needed in a modern English classroom. The overhead projector, record player, and tape recorder (perhaps equipped with earphones for use by groups within the classroom) enable teachers to use promising visual and auditory means for providing linguistics and literary experiences. In the presentation of sample passages for the study of composition, transparencies shown on the overhead projector have long demonstrated their unique value. Also widely used to extend the experiences of children are motion pictures, filmstrips, slide projectors, and television receivers.

Possible uses of educational technology are promised by new experimental programs such as programed individual drills on English usage presented orally through specially designed machines, the use of programed instruction for the expansion of language patterns, individual listening carrels for recorded experiences in literature, computerized instruction in basic reading skills or in the mechanics of English, and short, single-concept cartridge films for reinforcement of classroom learning.

The time devoted to English studies varies with individual need. The learning of language, so central in man's behavior, is affected by a constellation of factors: the learner's social and cultural background, his motivation and capacity, psychological and emotional factors, and the context provided for learning. Individual differences in the learning of any subject are considerable; in language, they are probably greatest of all. Of all the subjects taught in the schools, English least lends itself to the traditional age-grade sequence of progression.

To achieve necessary flexibility to accommodate individual differences, time adjustments are being made in the school day. For example, programs in which slower students devote twice as many hours to English as do their more advanced peers are not uncommon. Flexibility is further achieved through independent study for able students. For disadvantaged children or those learning English as a second language, special pattern practice in English language laboratories can be assigned. Seminars and tutorial sessions also enable teachers to tailor instruction to individuals. English laboratory periods can be scheduled in specially equipped classrooms supplied with books and equipment for individual study and work such as typewriters, self-instructional aids, reference works, writing tables, and reading areas, which provide centers for instruction. Reduced teaching loads and flexible schedules release teachers for conferences with individual students. For more than a decade, national studies of the teaching load of secondary teachers of English have recommended not more than four classes or 100 students per teacher; concern over the pupil load of elementary teachers also seems to be growing. In short, new patterns of administrative scheduling and staff utilization, planned in relation to the needs of learners and nature of the subject, offer possibilities for redesigning the teaching of English.

The interrelated content and skills of English must be taught in a continuous, unified program. Recent reappraisals of the curriculum in English, from preschool to college levels, suggest the need for an integrated sequence from beginning reading instruction based on children's own oral language through writing instruction that gains strength from the reading of literature and discussion experiences in oral language sparked by the reading program to studies of rhetorical principles which apply to both oral and written discourse. In the future, focus will be on particular skills and content at different levels and for different children, but this attention will not be so exclusive as to constitute neglect of other outcomes.

A continuous developmental program in general English is a first priority. Such a program would be provided all students and might embrace the first 10 years of education; it should provide for the spiral reteaching of basic skills not only in English classes but in all subjects, reinforced by all teachers. A second-phase program, appropriate for schools which have begun this minimal program even when it is not fully in force, is the establishment of small classes to meet special needs—corrective reading classes, advanced reading instruction for the able, honors work, and special instruction in writing and speech. In increasing numbers of schools, the final years of English provide diversified courses approximate to individual pupil goals: intensive study of literature and expository writing for some, opportunities for creative expression for others; assured work in language and literature for vocational students; interest courses in humanities; technical, journalistic, and scientific writing; and speech and theatre work.

But before these final years, English should be regarded as a unified subject, taught as a unified subject, presented with appropriate attention to the general language development of each child. This means that teachers of English at any level can no longer neglect the teaching of reading and teaching of speech; it means also that specialized instruction in reading or writing or detailed attention to spelling, vocabulary, and English usage will be a strength only if related to a carefully designed overall developmental program.

The Case for an Intelligent Pluralism

This, then, is English teaching today: a profession aware of modern psychological theory, concerned with contemporary scholarship in literature and language, seeking more economical ways to teach important concepts and skills in the classroom, and exploring new avenues to learning. The explosion in curriculum development, promoted by almost thirty regional curriculum study centers; the changes in teacher education stimulated by NDEA English institutes for advanced study; the upheaval in publishing created by American technology—all promise ideas, personnel, and materials capable of transforming the teaching of English, the nation's largest educational enterprise, into dynamic new programs for tomorrow's youth. During the next few years, our elementary and secondary schools will encounter more attractive alternatives for new curricula, more information from scholarship and research, and a greater array of competing choices than could possibly have been imagined a few years ago. Faced with conditions which will demand intelligent pluralistic planning, school administrators may find the outline of trends and possibilities in this report useful as a guide in curriculum planning.

BIBLIOGRAPHY

1. Bennett, Robert A., editor. *Summary Progress Report of English Curriculum Study and Demonstration Centers.* Champaign, Ill.: National Council of Teachers of English, 1966.
2. Braddock, Richard; Lloyd-Jones, Richard; and Schoer, Lowell. *Research in Written Composition.* Champaign, Ill.: National Council of Teachers of English, 1963.
3. Brown, Kenneth L. "Notes on an Analysis of the Speech and Listening Content of Selected Pupil Textbooks in the Language Arts for the Elementary School: Grades Three Through Six." Papers presented at the meeting of the Speech Association of America, December 1965. (Mimeo.)
4. College Entrance Examination Board, Commission on English. *Freedom and Discipline in English.* New York: the Board, 1965.
5. Commission on the English Curriculum. *Language Arts for Today's Children.* New York: Appleton-Century-Crofts, 1954.
6. Corbin, Richard. *The Teaching of Writing in Our Schools.* New York: Macmillan Co., 1966.
7. ———, and Crosby, Muriel, editors. *Language Programs for the Disadvantaged.* Champaign, Ill.: National Council of Teachers of English, 1965.

8. Dusel, William J. "Determining an Efficient Teaching Load in English." *Illinois English Bulletin,* March 1956.

9. Frazier, Alexander, editor. *Ends and Issues: 1965-1966 Points of Decision in the Development of the English Curriculum.* Champaign, Ill.: National Council of Teachers of English, 1966.

10. ———, editor. *New Directions in Elementary English.* Champaign, Ill.: National Council of Teachers of English, 1967.

11. Goldstein, Miriam B. *The Teaching of Language in Our Schools.* New York: Macmillan Co., 1966.

12. Hogan, Robert F., editor. *The English Language in the School Program.* Champaign, Ill.: National Council of Teachers of English, 1966.

13. Holbrook, David. *English for the Rejected.* Cambridge, England: Cambridge University Press, 1965.

14. Lacampagne, Robert, editor. *High School Departments of English: Their Organization, Administration, and Supervision.* Champaign, Ill.: National Council of Teachers of English, 1964.

15. Lynch, James J., and Evans, Bertrand. *High School English Textbooks: A Critical Examination.* Boston: Little, Brown and Co., 1963.

16. Mackintosh, Helen K., editor. *Children and Oral Language.* Champaign, Ill.: ACEI, ASCD, IRA, NCTE, 1964.

17. National Council of Teachers of English, Committee on National Interest. *The National Interest and the Continuing Education of Teachers of English.* Champaign, Ill.: the Council, 1964.

18. Reeves, Ruth. *The Teaching of Reading in Our Schools.* New York: Macmillan Co., 1966.

19. Shugrue, Michael F. *How the "New English" Will Help Your Child.* New York: Association Press, 1966.

20. Shuy, Roger W. *Discovering American Dialects.* Champaign, Ill.: National Council of Teachers of English.

21. ———, editor. *Social Dialects and Language Learning.* Champaign, Ill.: National Council of Teachers of English, 1965.

22. Sister M. Judine, editor. *A Guide for Correcting High School Composition.* Champaign, Ill.: National Council of Teachers of English, 1964.

23. Squire, James R., and Applebee, Roger K. *A Study of English Programs in Selected High Schools Which Consistently Educate Outstanding Students in English.* U.S. Department of Health, Education, and Welfare, Office of Education, Cooperative Research Report No. 1994. Urbana: University of Illinois, 1966.

24. Squire, James R., and Gwynn, Frederick, editors. *Source Book on English Institutes for Elementary Teachers.* Champaign, Ill.: National Council of Teachers of English, and New York: Modern Language Association of America, 1965.

25. Steinberg, Erwin R., and others. "The Inductive Teaching of English." *English Journal* 55: 139-57; February 1966.

26. Strickland, Ruth G. "The Contributions of Structural Linguistics to the Teaching of Reading, Writing, and Grammar in the Elementary School." *Bulletin of the School of Education, Indiana University* 40: 19-20; January 1964.

7

Foreign Language Education

School administrators at all levels are seeking answers to questions, exploring new trends, and searching for new directions so that they may make wise decisions concerning foreign language programs under their jurisdiction. The following seem to be some of the major questions:

- How do foreign language programs fit into the total curriculum?
- How can school administrators effectively evaluate their foreign language programs?
- Does the study of foreign languages help in developing better interpersonal relationships in the community?
- When is the best time to begin the study of a foreign language?
- What is the value of FLES (Foreign Languages in Elementary Schools)?
- What are the new developments in foreign language curriculum?
- How important is the role of local supervision in upgrading instruction in foreign languages?
- How relevant are foreign language course offerings for students?

Probably the most basic question deals with the rationale for foreign language instruction in today's increasingly crowded curriculum. A world drawn closer by technology has made exposure to at least one foreign language generally accepted as an important part of every student's education. However, goals, courses, length of sequence, and methods and materials of instruction are all part of the fluid state of education in general and of foreign languages in particular.

In any transitional period, certain basic tenets begin to emerge, and the following appear to represent the current status of foreign language instructional patterns:

1. The goal of foreign language instruction is communication.
2. Foreign language instruction embraces both linguistic and cultural activities.

3. Attitudes of intercultural understanding may be fostered by the study of foreign languages at all school levels.
4. In order to take advantage of the special language proclivities of young children, foreign language instruction should begin as early as possible.
5. An interdisciplinary approach to the teaching of foreign languages can add greater relevance to the instructional program and deeper significance to such subject areas as social studies and literature.
6. A foreign language should be offered to all students at some point in their educational careers.
7. The changing nature of foreign language offerings has brought about variations in programs: long sequences, courses for specific purposes (comparative literature, travel, reading, etc.), mini-courses, individualized programs, and courses for independent study.
8. Bilingual programs and the teaching of English as a second language have become part of the broadened scope of foreign language education.
9. A modified audiolingual approach—providing instruction in the four skills of listening, speaking, reading, and writing but stressing the first two—is widely used.
10. The changing nature of course offerings has brought about varied goals and objectives. No longer is "mastery" the expected outcome of all sequences; behavior is specified in terms of "an understanding of . . .," "an appreciation of . . .," "the ability to ask directions . . .," "fluency in ordering a meal in a restaurant . . .," "the ability to understand a native speaker on the telephone . . .," and so on.

Emerging Curriculum Concepts

There has been a revolution in the teaching of foreign languages in recent years. Since 1959, instruction has undergone major changes in both objectives and methods. Prior to that time, stress had been placed upon the teaching of reading skills, the analysis of grammatical rules, and translation, with little emphasis upon listening and speaking skills. Furthermore, foreign language study was reserved for college-bound students—the intellectual elite. In the 60's, the focus shifted from the grammar-translation method first to the audiolingual approach and finally to the fundamental skills approach, an eclectic philosophy that values highly the listening-speaking aspects of instruction yet maintains a harmonious balance of the four skills of listening, speaking, reading, and writing. This, then, is the current framework for instruction in the foreign language curriculum.

The structure of the foreign language curriculum is based on the major premises of linguistics, psychology, anthropology, and physiology. Linguists have told us that language is primarily oral, that language consists of a sound system and of a system of structural patterns, and that the prime function of language is communication. Furthermore, they have noted that the natural order for learning the skills of a language is listening and understanding first, then speaking, and finally reading and writing.

Psychologists have theorized that language is a complex set of habits and that first (native) language habits interfere with the acquisition of second language habits as the child matures. Psychologists also stress that learning should involve a multiple-sense appeal so that each of the senses can provide reinforcement for the others.

The cultural dimension of foreign language instruction follows the findings of anthropologists who note that students are interested in the activities of their peers in foreign cultures, particularly from the point of view of similarities and differences in modes of behavior. If by *culture* we mean the total number of activities and experiences of a people, then it follows that learning their language is one route to participation in their "culture"—a first step toward understanding a little about their way of life and their way of looking at reality.

The field of physiology indicates to us that young children have a plasticity of brain and vocal functions and that the optimum time to begin the study of a foreign language may be before age 10. In educational, psychological, and linguistic terms, the early introduction of a foreign language to elementary school children is highly desirable and important if we are to help them live in a culturally pluralistic world. Interested in all new experiences, the child in the first decade of life is uniquely receptive to the linguistic patterns and cultural role playing that language instruction provides. The study of a foreign language can be integrated easily and appropriately into the social studies curriculum, the language arts sequences, and the humanistic areas of art, music, and literature.

School districts faced with economic difficulties can still provide basic foreign language study in the early grades if they exploit such possibilities as the team-teaching approach.

Methods of Teaching Foreign Languages

Methods of teaching foreign languages vary greatly, since a number of factors determine what happens in the classroom: objectives of the course, materials of instruction, teacher fluency, teacher personality, student interest and motivation, type of evaluation of the program, and the textbook. Too frequently the text or the final examination determines the methodology to be used. When this happens, unfortunately, not enough attention is given to the objectives of the program and the specific needs of the students. *The focus should be on the goals of the program and how they can best be achieved.*

The current thinking of the profession leans toward the four-skills developmental program for the standard course, with heavy emphasis on the aural-oral skills (listening and speaking). Mindful of the recommendations of linguists, many foreign language teachers first present new work orally and then proceed to practice in speaking, reading, and writing. Formerly it was deemed important to maintain a time lag of a week, several weeks, or several months (or even years for the FLES level) between the initial oral presentation to the students and the subsequent viewing of the written word. The time lag has now been considerably shortened, depending upon the age and maturity of the students and their mastery of the sound system. Some secondary school teachers, for example, present a new dialogue at the beginning of a class period and, after sufficient repetition and drill, show the written form of the dialogue to the students at the end of the period. Some FLES teachers present new material orally in one class period and present the written form of this material in the next class period. Others wait until the material is thoroughly familiar and memorized or nearly memorized before introducing the written form.

Listening and Understanding Skills

Pupils do not acquire listening and understanding skills merely by hearing the foreign language in the classroom or language laboratory. They need a variety of ear-training activities if they are to learn to discriminate among the various sounds of the language, especially those that differ from similar sounds in English, and to become familiar with the rhythm, pitch, stress, and intonation of the language. Such activities often include repeated directions, chain drills, recordings and tapes, songs, dialogue sequences and adaptations, question-and-answer procedures, contrastive pairs of words and sentences, and purposeful listening practice in the language laboratory, classroom listening corner, or electronic classroom.

Speaking Skills

Pupils acquire speaking skills in the foreign language by first imitating the basic sounds and intonation patterns in a dialogue, song, or poem. Generally speaking, the younger the pupil, the more accurately and more freely he will pronounce the foreign sounds and patterns. Speaking skill, however, implies more than imitation and the ability to recite memorized material. It includes the ability to select from a reservoir of learned material the appropriate response to comments or questions. Thus, speaking skill consists of pronunciation and intonation skills and the correct manipulation of language in functional speech, within the limits of learned material.

Reading Skills

Reading skills are developed through a sequence that starts with reading labels and short sentences, proceeds on to reading familiar material (memorized dialogues, songs, or poems), and continues through analysis of sound–symbol correspondences to the reading of recombined and unfamiliar material. Through contrastive exercises and phonic drills, attention is given to maintaining a high standard of pronunciation after reading has been introduced. As language skills are developed, intensive reading lessons stress comprehension of the written word, determined by questions, summaries, pictures, matching activities, and true-false and fill-in items. Reading material of high interest and wide variety, such as newspapers, cartoons, magazines, and pen-pal letters, should be available.

Writing Skills

The ability to write in a foreign language depends upon previous experience in understanding, speaking, and reading the language. Early activities involve copying correctly, labeling, writing from dictation, and directed composition. Since material that pupils write should be corrected so that poor habits are not reinforced, it is wise to keep such activity to a minimum or at least limited to an amount the teacher can easily correct until students have been trained in proofreading skills.

More sophisticated writing activities include writing in the foreign language for creative and functional purposes: writing stories and poems for the school paper, writing pen pal letters, working on puzzles, writing book reports, writing for information, and so forth.

Cultural Awareness

One of the prime outcomes of foreign language study is an understanding of the people who speak the language and an attitude of openness toward them. Numerous class opportunities, therefore, are planned for the inculcation of cultural awareness. Dialogues, for example, reflect aspects of the life of the people; reading material deals less with factual items such as mountains, rivers, and cities than with current information about sports, television, heroes, student protests, ecology—in short, topics of interest to students.

Where there are large numbers of people in the community who speak a foreign language, there may be opportunities for representatives of these groups to come into the schools as paraprofessionals or visitors. They can work with small groups for remediation or for enrichment lessons, bringing personal glimpses of their life in the foreign country to the students. Very often, such involvement helps to promote unity within the community as the self-image of these ethnic groups is raised.

Presentation of New Material

Following a warm-up review (which may include a review dialogue, a poem, a song, a rapid chain drill, a series of questions and answers, or a directed dialogue), the teacher presents new material orally. There may be a very brief explanation in English at first, and then the new material is presented in the foreign language, with gestures, pictures, puppets, overhead transparencies, visuals on the chalkboard, maps, and various objects used as aids to convey meaning directly. The teacher is the model as the class repeats the materials (as soon as checks for comprehension have been made). Choral repetition may be in the form of whole class, half class, boys, girls, or row repetitions. Questions and answers that personalize the new material complete this stage of the introduction of new patterns. A visitor to the class would hear student talk, teacher talk, small-group talk, and large-group talk, for language learning is spirited and noisy.

Grammar (Structural Patterns)

Language consists of vocabulary, idiomatic expressions, and structures. In order to learn how to use language, students have to learn how to manipulate these elements and understand how and why they change. Structural patterns are taught through pattern drills, and a generalization of the particular point being drilled is elicited from the students and explained. Some pattern drills that may be used in foreign language classrooms follow:

1. Repetition drills
   The teacher presents a pattern and the students repeat it.
   Teacher: *I am going to the park.*
   Students: *I am going to the park.*
2. Substitution drills
   The teacher presents a pattern and then gives a cue for students to substitute in the pattern.
   Teacher: *I am going to the park . . .* (cue) *movies.*
   Students: *I am going to the movies.*
   Teacher: *bullfight.*
   Students: *I am going to the bullfight.*
3. Transformation drills
   The teacher presents a pattern and indicates how the students are to change the pattern (to a different tense, to the negative, to the interrogative, etc.).
   Teacher: *I am going to the park . . .* (cue) *tomorrow.*
   Students: *Tomorrow I will go to the park.*

When the grammatical structures are handled with ease, further practice may include more creative activities in the form of directed dialogues, games, and conversational adaptations on topics of interest to the students.

The Textbook Series

Many of the current textbooks have been revised to reflect the new directions in foreign language teaching. They abound in dialogues, pattern drills, exercises, and culturally authentic and interesting material; they have numerous supplementary components such as tapes, take-home records, charts, pictures, transparencies, filmstrips, films, and the like. Teachers and local supervisors should be invited to inspect new textbooks and materials, but for purposes of articulation (which will be discussed later), it is best to select one series for use throughout the foreign language sequence.

Since foreign language lessons are most effective when they are dynamic, teachers should be encouraged to depart from the textbook for time to time in order to adapt some of its lessons to a different format or to take advantage of the vast array of newspapers and current materials.

Multimedia Resources

Language training benefits from all types of media, including resource centers, language laboratories, programmed learning, and computer-assisted instruction (CAI). Research indicates that people learn differently, some perceiving content more readily by one sense than by another. Consequently, the best approach would be multisensory—training students to express themselves orally, derive meaning aurally, comprehend written materials, and communicate in writing. Concentration on a single point through several sensory techniques has a greater impact and aids memory and implementation.

When the pure audiolingual approach was at the height of its popularity—from the late 50's to the middle 60's—the language laboratory was considered an indispensable adjunct to the classroom presentation. But experience over the years showed that the sheer repetition of uncomprehended patterns or dialogues created very little ability to use language freely, and the formal language laboratory in the high school underwent a change in function. The high schools, borrowing from the universities, now assign the laboratory facilities largely on an individual basis rather than for lockstep class drill. Dial-access laboratories have the potential for providing immense quantities of information and drills to several schools from a single central location.

The facilities of the standard laboratory are designed to channel several programs simultaneously. Some students may be reviewing materials missed when absent, while others listen to tapes of plays they have studied, and still others study independently a language not offered as a course. Where there are not sufficient tape programs, either the teachers may work in the summer to prepare them or the school may tie in with a central dial-access facility.

Mechanical devices such as films and tapes bring a new dimension to the language program by introducing the language as spoken by natives in a culturally correct setting. Computer-assisted instruction individualizes the course work and frees the teacher from time-consuming drill to work with students in creative conversational or evaluative groups. Programmed courses (12) have not yet proved fully effective, but experimentation with some shows great promise; we can expect to see greater use made of such courses in cases where the enrollment is small or the student is motivated to progress at his own speed.

The resource center is perhaps the fastest growing innovation in foreign language facilities in the schools today. Ideally, it is provided with comfortable chairs, study carrels, tape recorders, a supply of current periodicals in many languages, encyclopedias, reference materials, the texts used in the courses, books about the countries being studied, drills on tape (with the answers), old tests for review, and film loop machines with tapes to accompany the films. Most important, native aides, paraprofessionals, or teachers are assigned to the center to direct the students in their search for information, recreation, or experience in using their language skills.

The tape recorder, phonograph, radio, television, videotape recorder, electronic classroom, listening corner, and language laboratory have tremendous value in the foreign language program. Live and recorded sequences can furnish listening practice, an intimate confrontation with the foreign culture, and the opportunity to bring excitement into day-to-day lessons. The electronic equipment may serve one group of students who need specific drills while the teacher works with another group. Individuals who need remedial work or enrichment can profit from "software" planned, prepared, or selected by the teacher with the assistance of paraprofessionals who are native speakers of the language. With the trend toward small-group instruction, individualized instruction, and independent study, optimum use of electronic equipment is a necessity in helping to provide disparate learning situations, for foreign language instruction no longer takes place in a conventional classroom at all times.

An active and interested teacher should be given enough preparation time to develop suitable and exciting materials for use with the multimedia equipment.

Use of English

The use of English should be minimal in the foreign language classroom. There will be times, however, when clarification is needed, when comprehension checks need to be made, or when explanation is required before the presentation of new work. The teacher may use English, but student use of English should be discouraged.

Translation is generally not part of the first few years of foreign language instruction, although occasionally a translation drill may be used for practicing idiomatic expressions. Translation is considered a highly technical skill and is usually reserved for the more advanced levels of study.

Bilingual and TESOL Classes

In many areas, two major programs that involve children whose native language is not English have been added to the school curriculum: Bilingualism and Teaching English to Speakers of Other Languages (TESOL). These programs may logically be assigned to the foreign language department.

Bilingualism is, on the one hand, an attempt to capitalize on the ability of the young child to learn another language with relative ease and, on the other, an effort to derive fuller value from the linguistic treasury of the country's foreign language–speaking population. There are bilingual schools that teach children in two languages: instruction during the early years is offered wholly in the native tongue, and gradually the second language is added until half the instruction is given in each language. In the beginning stages, the material presented in the foreign language frequently repeats the work taught in the native tongue, thereby serving as reinforcement as well as language training. Extensive research has shown that this approach not only does no harm to the ability to assimilate content and express oneself in the native tongue but also provides an invaluable gain in the individual's appreciation of the second culture (14, 26, 30). Volume 2 of the *Britannica Review of Foreign Language Education* (18) indicates that 100,000 teachers of bilingual education will be needed in the 70's (p. 252).

Far more common in most city and suburban schools is a TESOL program. Where a large number of non–English-speaking students attend a school, certain teachers from the school, a county agency, or a central office may be assigned to work separately with them. The elementary school teachers attempt to teach enough basic English to enable the children to keep up with their peers in the regular classes. On the secondary level, the students may attend special classes all day or be withdrawn for tutorial sessions.

Techniques of teaching English as a second language closely parallel those of teaching any other foreign language, with the added advantage of immediate reinforcement by the English-speaking environment and the motivation provided by the constant need to communicate.

In the urgency of improving the English skills of non–English-speaking students, the school often neglects the first language. These children usually come to the United States before their abilities in their native language are solidified. Unless these abilities are further developed, the students may well end their formal training illiterate in both languages. It is, therefore, incumbent on the administrator in charge of curriculum to provide practice in the native language as well as in English for his non–English-speaking students.

Emerging Administrative Procedures

Hiring

The changes of emphasis, direction, and goals in foreign language education demand a review of staffing procedure. The continuing stress on learning to speak the target language as a prime goal underscores the need to interview prospective teachers with an eye to their ability to express themselves fluently in comprehensible, contemporary, educated speech. It has become commonplace for the candidate to be interviewed in the language(s) he is applying to teach. If the department chairman or coordinator is not competent in that language, a teacher from the department may be asked to hold a brief conversation with the candidate. Experience abroad is also preferred; teachers should have first-hand and in-depth acquaintance with the culture of the people whose language they are teaching. They should recognize the values, characteristics, and contrasts embodied in that culture and be prepared to impart an awareness and understanding of these elements to their classes.

Language classes are particularly well suited to differentiated staffing. In accordance with their degree of competence—and state licensing rules—a supplementary staff comprising native aides, college majors, and part-time teachers may be used to monitor laboratory exercises, meet with small conversation groups, operate a resource center, prepare drills, provide extra practice for slower or faster students, serve as a team resource unit, or free master teachers by administering tests and correcting papers. Guidelines for optimal utilization, standards of preparation, and procedures for evaluation of a differentiated staff should be developed. The evaluation should include everyone affected in order to judge the real effectiveness of the staff organization. Clearly delineated but less formal measures are needed to judge the performance and results of peer teachers—the advanced students who work with beginning or intermediate students much as the native aides would do. Instead of being paid, however, the peer teachers may credit the time they spend to course work or to independent study.

Scheduling

Newer modes of scheduling also lend themselves particularly well to foreign language classes. Two methods, back-to-back classes and modular scheduling, provide the flexibility that best suits contemporary foreign language classes whether they are organized about individualized performance or the more traditional group achievement. In the back-to-back classes method, as many sections of the same class as possible are scheduled for the same time slot. This type of scheduling permits the teachers—with the support of the administration, guidance department, parents, and students—to modify speed of teaching, techniques, amount of coverage, and skill priorities over a broad spectrum to conform to the interests, needs, and abilities of each language level. Students may move, voluntarily or at the suggestion of their teacher, with relative freedom from one section to another until they find the class that seems best suited to their preferences and abilities. Because similar sections are offered at the same time, a student wishing to change sections does not need to rework his entire schedule. It is necessary for the principal to plot out the foreign language classes before the others. As described from an administrator's point of view (31, pp. 114-19), this modest step toward individualization of instruction and its resultant low rate of attrition are well worth the effort of building the schedule around the foreign language classes.

Modular scheduling encourages an organization of foreign language classes that makes extensive use of groups of various sizes, progress by small increment instead of semester or year blocks, mini-courses, contract planning, interdisciplinary presentations and projects, and individually paced curriculums. If the schedules are determined on a semester or yearly basis, it is exceedingly important that the time distribution be the result of the department's joint decision as to how the courses are to be developed. For example, if the teacher of a beginning level class wishes to teach grammar, show a film, present a guest speaker, or team up with another department or teacher once a week, a long block of two or three modules should be reserved for that purpose. Different time allotments for testing, reading and vocabulary check, and remedial, regular, and enrichment oral-drill groups should be provided for within the total modular schedule. Upper level classes may allot certain modules to working in the resource center or library, working with native aides, college students, peers, or beginners, using equipment or meeting privately for instruction, guidance, or evaluation, and mutually setting up future assignments.

It is doubtful that the goals of the "new" language programs are best achieved by the traditional five-days-a-week meeting in one classroom. Where the schedule is fixed semiannually or annually, a summer workshop could explore the potential benefits implicit in the modular system; if the school recycles the schedules several times during the year, one or two days before each new schedule is programmed the department should be given the opportunity to meet and evaluate the preceding cycle and remedy its shortcomings or provide for new situations within the cycle.

The trend toward diversification is seen in the scheduling practices in foreign languages. Characteristically the foreign language program has been divided into levels or years of language study. As a result, the school that offers its students four years of four languages would have 16 separate designations, possibly with several sections of each. Students who are tracked (grouped by ability) or who use different texts would be accommodated in extra sections.

The outward appearance of a progressive foreign language program organized about individually prepared objectives would not differ greatly in the first levels. Upper level courses, however, rather than being designated as Language 3, 4, or 5, would very likely have descriptive titles such as Contemporary Spanish Short Story, Advanced French Composition, the History of Germany (taught in German), Scientific Russian, Current Italian Periodicals, or Golden Age Latin Poetry. Some courses might specify prerequisites; many would last only 10 or 20 weeks. The courses would cut across levels of preparation: sophomores, juniors, and seniors would frequently be in the same class.

Administratively, such programming will require (a) flexible use of facilities to accommodate classes of widely varying sizes, including singletons, and (b) encouragement of the staff to prepare themselves to offer specializations that interest their students. The same flexibility will welcome colleagues from other departments with special skills, such as the math teacher who can teach algebra in French. The foreign language staff will have to recognize that the ability to discuss French cookery and the ability to conjugate a verb in the pluperfect subjunctive are *both* viable language skills. Many language teachers, both experienced and newly appointed, retain a strong sense of "traditional" values and must be encouraged to view the whole of language learning from a different viewpoint, as a sum of skills, supplementing each other and put to use as soon as possible and wherever feasible. The result is a language student who is not only linguistically proficient but also more knowledgeable about other ways of life.

Articulation

Still completely unresolved is the matter of proper placement of students. Two considerations operate to make the smooth flow of learning between different schools and different grades a point of dissension. First, not all language teachers agree on the basic methodology to be used in training beginning students. While it probably does not matter which system is ultimately adopted, it is difficult for a student to switch from one approach to another when he changes teachers—for example, from an audiolingual approach to a cognitive code (i.e., grammar-translation) orientation. In each case the succeeding teacher feels that the student is lacking the requisite skills on which to base further learning, while the student experiences a strong sense of disorientation and disillusionment at finding his previous attainments discounted. Many FLES programs were dismissed as unproductive because their graduates, who were highly adept in speaking and understanding the foreign language, were confronted with junior high school programs predicated on reading and writing with strong grammatical bias. Similarly, there are still college foreign language departments dominated by scholars who measure foreign language competence by the student's ability to analyze classical literature, who persist in equating two years of high school language study with one year of college work, and who do not always recognize that approaches to foreign language learning differ.

The second problem is that there is a great disparity in content from one textbook series to another, even among those that espouse the same methodology. Students cannot readily proceed from publisher A's first-level text to publisher B's second-level text without extensive supplementary work on the part of the teacher. One text may have developed its lessons on home situations, another on the American or foreign schools, and still others on historical and geographical elements or familiar incidents relating to the target culture. In each case the basic vocabularly will be very different and, probably, the order of grammatical presentations will vary greatly. If level one of series A presents all work in the present tense, saving its verb manipulations for the subsequent book, and level one of series B stresses early tense development, students switching from series A to series B for their level two work are in for trouble. The teacher will have to resort to double sets of texts, extensive reliance on review workbooks, or the inordinately time-consuming preparation of drills. Fortunately, the coverage of fundamental grammatical elements and elementary vocabulary is completed in most series by the end of level two; a divergence of materials after that point causes fewer problems and may even be welcome as an indication that student preferences are being served.

Coordination

The need for coordination of the total program and all of its components is urgent. Implied in the descriptions above are vital but divergent coordinating tasks that are most effectively delegated to a single individual. This may be an appointed district coordinator, one of several building chairmen, a teacher who has been relieved of some other duties (in a district with no chairmen), or an administrator who has been assigned the supervision of the foreign language staff. This individual will be answerable for the text resources, supplementary media, uniformity of approach, and flow between schools and levels. In view of current trends, he or she will have even more extensive responsibilities than before. Where the whole staff or several members have elected to experiment with new techniques or concepts, especially those leading to an individualized program, the coordinator must be available to help them locate, examine, and evaluate existing programs and adapt them to their own situation where appropriate. He or she must make certain that all students will be able to continue their studies if they drop out of the class or if the new program fails. The coordinator must be prepared to instruct the staff in the implementation of new techniques and, in particular, to help them develop guidelines, objectives, and evaluative procedures. An individualized program may very easily become a free-for-all in which students, while seeming to select programs that reflect their personal goals, are in reality dissipating their energies because of ill-defined and uncertain aims and lack of understanding of how to approach the program and attain the mastery desired. The coordinator must be instrumental in helping the staff evaluate student skills according to acceptable objective measurements, perhaps even using performance objectives. Constant inservice work is required to derive optimum value from relatively unfamiliar approaches.

The coordinator plays an equally important role even where the staff has not selected techniques as radically different as individualization of instruction, contract planning, or programmed learning, but has simply chosen to modify an established procedure. The government no longer provides facilities for the retraining of teachers through NDEA or EPDA summer institutes. As a result, many experienced and even some newly graduated teachers are not properly familiar with progress made in such standard techniques as teaching by means of a dialogue or pattern drill. Without detailed guidance, observation, and demonstration, the dialogue can degenerate too easily from meaningful conversation into the mere parroting of lines. Similarly, a pattern drill taught by a teacher intent on the memorization of the pattern instead of the concept on which the pattern is based may hinder the class from using the information in an unfamiliar language situation. A teacher who does not understand—and agree with—the philosophy underlying the function of the pattern drill may actually defeat the purpose of the lesson. There are few things as boring and irrelevant as a blandly taught, misunderstood pattern drill. Although it was previously felt that an early presentation of printed matter would interfere with proper pronunciation, research in the last few years has indicated the strength that reading and multisensory teaching devices add to the mastery of all skills.

The coordinator has a major inservice function: to promote understanding of accepted techniques, to encourage experimentation and creative adaptation, and to demonstrate and share effective practices among the staff. The administration can help the coordinator by supporting his efforts; by providing inservice workshop time, credits, materials, and expenses after school or in the summer; and especially by understanding the nature of the foreign language education methodologies.

Supervision

Supervision is one facet of coordination. In the sense that supervision ensures the smooth and continuous flow of the program, it is a direct result of coordination. However, in today's foreign language programs, the supervisor has a twofold concern: he must recognize, encourage, and aid his staff's experimentation with new techniques and with programs that accommodate the individual student, but he must be careful not to discourage the effective teacher who is serving his students well despite his adherence to more traditional methods. It is easy to equate change with improvement and excellence, but change for its own sake is of no value. Even where desirable, change may be counterproductive if it is promoted exclusively by administrators rather than adopted by teachers themselves.

The foreign language classroom is a noisy and active place. The supervisor should look for students who are being encouraged to use the foreign language as a normal medium of communication, who are meeting in small groups to discuss some phases of work in the target language, and who are moving from table to carrel to desk as they pursue a particular part of the lesson that they are mastering. Although the teacher in the traditional classroom will exercise more direct control than in the individually organized setup, the supervisor can observe student initiative and self-guidance in the selection of readings, choice of written exercises, and participation in debates and panels. A teacher's straightforward questions seeking set answers should yield to elaborations on the class's reactions to the readings; homework assignments should be diversified. While the chalkboard may still be the principal visual aid, frequent use should be made of the overhead projector, tape recorder, phonograph, and other devices. Bulletin boards should show the range of areas covered and be integrated into the class's activities. A few disparate travel posters are not nearly as effective as calendars, verb charts, scenes depicting the target cultures, letters from pen pals, and other material pertinent to the students' work.

Placement of Students and Choice of Language

For many years, foreign language teachers have been accused of preferring to serve only the intellectual elite or the college-bound students; of necessity, this picture is changing. Foreign languages are entering the mainstream of the total school curriculum for all students, and programs are being tailored to suit the demands of the new clientele. As previously noted, the skills pursued by each student may differ, but each will find some elements that make foreign language study valuable to him. Test results should aid the guidance department in placing each student within the language program but should not serve to exclude anyone from it.

It takes a considerable number of years to develop full proficiency in all facets of a language. A program aimed at total linguistic control would ideally begin in the elementary school in order to take advantage of the abilities peculiar to each grade level. However, not everyone needs or wants to devote a long time to mastering one language. Effectively designed programs permit students of varying talents and interests to derive the fullest possible value from either short or long exposure. Because one does not always know what language one will need 20 years after leaving school, the contemporary class concentrates some effort on the *process* of language learning, which can be of great value in future studies.

Students are often influenced by friends and guidance counselors to seek the "easy" language. There is no easy language, just as there is no hard one. In a language that is inherently different from English, and therefore "hard," the methodology will make allowances by providing for more practice. With today's decreasing emphasis on grammar, the main considerations in recommending a language for study should be the interest it holds for the student, the time available for its study, and the appropriateness of the learning materials to the student's age and ability. The contemporary American student should become more adventurous and less intimidated by languages that have not traditionally been found in our high schools. Proper counseling should encourage students to study languages important in today's world, such as Russian, Japanese, and Chinese.

Latin

Much of the preceding discussion appears to have excluded Latin. It was not meant to, for the values inherent in the study of Latin and the classics are as vital and far-reaching as they have been for centuries. But, instead of emphasizing the "discipline" to be gained by learning Latin, the classicists now point to the relevance of Latin as a source of exciting literature and of glimpses into our cultural past that have meaning for us today.

To implement these changes in direction, new syllabi and new texts have been devised. Institutes jointly sponsored by national, state, and local language organizations have refreshed participants' techniques and reshaped their viewpoints. The result has been to move away from translation into Latin, to rely more on sight translation, to treat grammar as an adjunct to reading, and to adopt many new texts with themes of interest to the contemporary student. Even the audiolingual approach has been adopted in part to help the student develop a feeling for the more formal grammatical aspects of the language. The Latin and Greek cultures are examined in depth in an attempt to understand their role in developing modern values. Viable and successful Latin FLES programs have been developed in Philadelphia and Washington, D.C.

It appears certain that if Latin continues to stress the inherently positive strengths of its materials rather than such secondary benefits as mental discipline and improvement of English vocabulary, its popularity and enrollment will increase.

Testing and Evaluation

In evaluating a foreign language program, student achievement tests, both standardized and teacher-made, are of great importance. Evaluation must also include attitudinal instruments, which determine student opinion about foreign language study and about the people who speak the language natively; clearly, an attempt must be made to determine the degree of cultural receptivity the students have acquired from their foreign language work.

Evaluation of teacher performance is best made by the teacher himself through interaction analysis procedures and videotape recordings and through consultation with the foreign language supervisor. A supervisor should be assigned to the area of foreign languages, as this is a highly specialized subject. An on-the-scene supervisor is essential to ensure smooth articulation, horizontally and vertically; to keep teachers informed about the latest materials, texts, supplementary aids, drills, tests, and professional meetings; to interpret the program to parents, community members, and school board members; and to work cooperatively with administrators on planning the optimum program.

Objective Tests

Standardized test scores predict a student's language ability with greater accuracy than do the opinions or prior notions of teachers of subjects other than foreign languages. The correlation between IQ and language achievement is too low to permit reliance upon the IQ alone as an effective indicator of aptitude. While much still has to be learned about the aptitudes of a good language learner, objective tests that identify potential ability have been devised. The principal reason for ascertaining the student's probable aptitude is to help the guidance department place him. A school that tracks its classes could also make effective use of the information.

Among the more popular tests are the Elementary Modern Language Aptitude Test (6) for lower grades; the Modern Language Aptitude Test (7) for grades 9-12, college, and adults; and the Pimsleur Language Aptitude Battery (25). These tests indicate the student's probable degree of success in assimilating language skills in the standard class. The Pimsleur test is particularly interesting in that components account for the individual's interest in language study as well as his grade point average (GPA).

The objective proficiency examinations most widely administered are the Modern Language Association Cooperative Foreign Language Tests (21). These tests are available on two levels of achievement and two forms for each level in French, German, Italian, Russian, and Spanish. They are composed of four parts that test listening, speaking, reading, and writing achievement separately. The speaking test is recorded on tape and requires a trained evaluator to score it. Although Valette (33, p. 48) has questioned the validity of the test when it is administered to students whose training has been audiolingual, the battery can outline the relative status of portions of the district's or school's program, especially when the test is administered over a period of years. It is relatively simple to establish local norms and, by an examination of the test questions, determine which segments most validly reflect the local program.

The College Entrance Examination Board Achievement Tests now require a listening comprehension portion as well as the traditional written questions. New York State is planning to add an oral skill component to its Regents Examinations in modern foreign languages. These changes reflect the goals sought in contemporary courses.

Classroom Nonobjective Tests

A test representative of the aims of the class's work must incorporate the skills being taught. At present, most foreign language classroom tests are more oriented toward assessing reading and writing proficiency and grammar control than would be indicated by the class time spent on teaching these skills. The reason is that these skills lend themselves more easily to objective testing. In contrast, questions evaluating the student's ability to comprehend material presented aurally are difficult to prepare and time-consuming to administer. If a teacher has several of the same classes, the physical effort of repeating the material is very great unless he can tape the questions. The skill least tested is speaking. The time necessary for each student to speak and be graded is overwhelming, especially if the teacher discusses each student's speech with him or her as a guide for further study—which is the function of testing. Administrators are urged to provide the necessary time and assistance in order to encourage the foreign language staff to evaluate speech. To free the teachers for this vital function, paraprofessionals, native aides, and college students can be trained to grade objectively.

The year-end test—where it is still given—is an excellent opportunity to prepare a well-rounded review of all skill areas covered during the year. The supervisor should verify that test coverage in each skill area is proportionate to the time the work occupies in class. For example, if 25 percent of the class time is devoted to aural-oral drill and only 10 percent to writing, the final test should certainly not demand half its answers in written form.

A Handbook on Foreign Language Classroom Testing (23) and Valette's *Modern Language Testing* (34) can help the teacher prepare meaningful questions in a variety of formats for each skill area and understand the evaluative and teaching function of foreign language tests.

Attitude Questionnaires

In 1970, the Northeast Conference on the Teaching of Foreign Languages commissioned Leon Jakobovits (16), a noted psycholinguist, to prepare an attitude questionnaire for its Reports. The purpose of the questionnaire was to provide the feedback a staff needs in order to see its curriculum methodology and general appearance from a student's point of view. The questionnaire itself has been an aid in assessing numerous programs over the country and spurring improvement and change in foreign language teaching priorities. In conjunction with interaction analysis, it offers the individual teacher a picture of his teaching techniques, attitudes toward his students, and their reaction to him. Other attitude questionnaires explore the students' reaction to other cultures. To test how "alien" an environment is to a foreigner, Seelye (28) composed a questionnaire on Guatemala. Lambert and Klineberg (17) have prepared others to determine whether acquaintance with a person's language makes a student more amenable to that person's culture.

Performance Criteria and Contracts

The growing acceptance of individualized training brings with it a need to express desired pupil performance in exact terms. The use of performance objectives permits each step in the learning procedure to be described in such a way that the student knows precisely what he has mastered and what still lies before him. The teacher no longer states that his students are being trained to "communicate." He now says that they can speak to an educated native at so many words per minute on specified topics with a given number of errors in structure and vocabulary. The specificity of each step makes it comparatively simple to devise increment tests. Programs that take existing materials and break them down by performance criteria with accompanying tests are being used in Tucson, Arizona (4), and Stanislaus County, California (29). Descriptions of these and other programs are available on microfiche through the ERIC (Educational Resources Information Center) system.

To keep students abreast of what is required of them and to assign the work in accessible portions, teachers have been resorting to the contract plan. After a conference with the teacher, each student "contracts" to complete so many steps, units of work, projects, and so on within a specified period of time. Successful completion—the form of which is specified by the contract—gives the student credit toward his grade or certification of mastery.

Grading

Performance criteria, individualized programs, and specialized mini-courses have inspired foreign language educators to reexamine the grading system. If a student enrolls in a course because he enjoys it and is willing or able to attain only semimastery—but that semimastery is of benefit to him—should he be penalized with a low grade? Has a student failed if he completes fewer units of a course than his classmates if he has genuinely assimilated those units? Adhering to the concept that a person who is learning to swim has not failed until he has given up, more and more schools are encouraging their foreign language enrollees by offering pass/fail, pass-honor/pass/fail, or grades of A and B plus "incompletes" until the work reaches the minimum contracted point. Each school that adopts individualization has to determine what kind of grade is earned and when to assign it. Does a student receive A or B when he completes a predetermined series of steps and nothing until then, or is his mark predicated upon the number of steps completed at a definite point in time? To forestall problems of credit evaluations, schools have been converting such grades into scores acceptable to the colleges by means of standardized tests that assure students of proper placement.

Organization

Improvement, reexamination, and curricular change are sparked by many active professional associations. Vigorous leadership is being exercised by the state foreign language bureaus, the individual foreign language teacher groups (e.g., American Association of Teachers of Spanish and Portuguese), and such organizations as the New York State Association of Foreign Language Teachers and the Northeast Conference on the Teaching of Foreign Languages, which represent various languages and levels. Newsletters, conferences, workshops, symposiums, professional journals, and nationwide competitions for students keep the profession united in a common purpose and informed of current matters, research results, and new ideas. Travel groups chartered by the organizations facilitate direct experience with changing cultural phenomena in the different countries.

The newly created American Council on the Teaching of Foreign Languages (ACTFL), sponsored in part by the Modern Language Association, has assumed a major responsibility in advancing the interests of foreign language teachers. ACTFL seeks out and initiates developments in both application and theory in the teaching of all languages at all levels. Its journal, *Foreign Language Annals,* has become a primary source of research data and detailed descriptions of innovative practices. The annual meetings, held in a different part of the country each year, have attracted thousands of foreign language educators and have stimulated and reviewed developments in teaching, philosophy, administration, and all areas affecting programs locally and nationally. ACTFL organizes and commissions workshops, pamphlets, *Focus Reports,* and the *Britannica Review of Foreign Language Education* series. Its activities are closely related to those of the Modern Language Association, the Educational Resources Information Center (ERIC), and other organizations that serve the profession. Administrators are urged to seek ACTFL's aid whenever they need consultative services beyond the resources of their own district and to encourage their staff to take advantage of its services.

A View of the Future of Foreign Language Instruction

What role will foreign languages play in tomorrow's educational program? There will probably be a limitless number of patterns. The availablity of sophisticated equipment, liberated schedules (both in and out of school), and differentiated staffing will all contribute to a wide range of choices. Each student will be able to pursue the study of *any* language for *any* purpose in the manner most suitable for meeting his individual needs and goals. The refinement of technology (CAI, television, videotape cartridges, satellite broadcasts, retrieval centers, etc.) will make it possible for students to use their knowledge and skills in situations that may require direct application.

In the future, foreign languages will be valued as much for their cross-disciplinary function in the study of man as for their intrinsic quality of developing humanistic awareness. Developing creative and exciting methods and materials of instruction that are attuned to the needs of each individual student while keeping pace with technological advances will remain a challenge to the profession.

Glossary *

Audiolingual	The combination of listening and speaking, the two basic language skills; teaching designed to produce and improve these skills.
Audiovisual	(a) Equipment for listening practice using headphones. (b) Listening practice itself, with no oral response expected.
Basic sentences	Those that illustrate the points of structure and the words and phrases that are to be mastered in the dialogues, exercises, and readings of the course.
Chain drill	An exercise, usually oral, in which one student asks a question of another, the second student answers and asks a question of a third, who answers and continues the exercise.
Contrastive linguistics	Comparison of the native language of the learner with the language he is studying, in order to give special attention to areas where the contrast is greatest.
Dictation	A classroom practice requiring the student to write exactly what he hears. Permits the student to examine his ability to comprehend the sound-symbol relationships of the particular language.
Direct method	Foreign language learning during which neither teacher nor student makes any overt use of the student's native language.
Directed composition	A written piece based on a series of directions given to the student; the directions may be in either native or learned language.

* Most of these definitions are taken from Donald D. Walsh (35).

Directed dialogue	A form of oral practice in which the teacher directs a student to make a statement to or ask a question of a second student, who is to react or respond to it. This drill gives unlimited opportunity for practice of forms and patterns. It can also be used for simple recall of basic sentences.
FLES	Foreign Language (in) Elementary Schools.
Intensive reading	Reading of limited pages or lines in such a fashion that the meaning, structure, and references are examined fully.
Intonation	The rise and fall in pitch of the speaking voice.
Kinesics	The systematic study of the non-vocal body motions that play a part in communication, e.g., hand gestures, raised eyebrows, changes in stance.
Linguistics	The systematic study of language or of one or more languages or dialects.
Pattern practice	Drills (generally oral) designed to develop automatic response to verbal or situational stimuli; involve systematic changes in sound, order, form, and vocabulary.
Pitch level	An intonational phoneme that distinguishes meaning.
Rhythm	Recurring stress on certain syllables.
Sound-symbol correspondence	The sound that is associated with a letter or combination of letters in a given language.
Structure	The regularities and patterns of a language viewed as a system in which elements are defined in terms of their relationships to other elements.

Time lag	The length of time allowed to elapse between the presentation of material in oral form and the introduction of the same material in written form.
Warm-up	A practice period at the start of the class period, using familiar materials to reintroduce the sounds and rhythms of the language to the class before new material is introduced.

BIBLIOGRAPHY

1. Allen, Virginia G., compiler, and Paquette, F. Andre, editor. *The Student's World Is the World: New Dimensions in the Teaching of FLES.* Indiana Language Program. New York: American Council on the Teaching of Foreign Languages, 1969.
2. Andersson, Theodore. *Foreign Languages in the Elementary School.* Austin: University of Texas Press, 1969.
3. Birkmaier, Emma M., editor. *Britannica Review of Foreign Language Education.* Vol. 1. Chicago: Encyclopaedia Britannica, 1969.
4. Bockman, John F. *A Three-Year Research Project on Individualized Foreign Language Learning Based in Programmed Instruction and in Management by Consultation—Summary of Rationale and Principal Findings.* Tucson, Ariz.: Tucson Public Schools, 1971.
5. Brooks, Nelson. *Language and Language Learning.* Second edition. New York: Harcourt, Brace and World, 1964.
6. Carroll, John B., and Sapon, Stanley. *Elementary Modern Language Aptitude Test.* New York: Psychological Corporation, 1967.
7. ———. *Modern Language Aptitude Test.* New York: Psychological Corporation, 1959.
8. Dodge, James, editor. *Leadership for Continuing Development.* Reports of the Working Committees of the 1971 Northeast Conference on the Teaching of Foreign Languages. New York: the Conference, 1971.
9. Donoghue, Mildred. *Foreign Language and the Elementary School Child.* Dubuque, Iowa: Brown, 1968.
10. *ERIC Focus Reports on the Teaching of Foreign Languages.* New York: ACTFL/MLA/ERIC, 1968—. [Continuing series of booklets on specific issues in foreign language teaching.]
11. Eurich, Alvin. *High School, 1980.* New York: Pitman, 1970.
12. Fiks, A. I. *Foreign Language Programmed Materials: 1969.* MLA/ERIC Focus Report No. 7. New York: ACTFL/MLA/ERIC, 1969.
13. Finocchiaro, Mary. *Teaching Children Foreign Languages.* New York: McGraw-Hill Book Co., 1964.

14. Gaarder, A. Bruce, and Richardson, Mabel W. "Two Patterns of Bilingual Education in Dade County, Florida." (Edited by Thomas E. Bird.) *Foreign Language Learning: Research and Development.* Reports of the Working Committees of the 1968 Northeast Conference on the Teaching of Foreign Languages. New York: the Conference, 1968. pp. 32-42.

15. Grittner, Frank. *Teaching Foreign Languages.* New York: Harper & Row, 1969.

16. Jakobovits, Leon A. "A Relevant Curriculum." *Foreign Languages and the "New" Student.* (Edited by Joseph A. Tursi.) Reports of the Working Committees of the 1970 Northeast Conference on Teaching Foreign Languages. New York: the Conference, 1970. pp. 15-30.

17. Lambert, Wallace E., and Klineberg, Otto. *Children's Views of Foreign Peoples: A Cross-National Study.* New York: Appleton-Century-Crofts, 1967.

18. Lange, Dale L., editor. *Britannica Review of Foreign Language Education.* Vol. 2. Chicago: Encyclopaedia Britannica, 1970.

19. Lipton, Gladys C., and Bourque, Edward H., editors. *Research, Relevance, Reality: The Three R's of FLES.* Champaign, Ill.: American Association of Teachers of French, 1969.

20. Michel, Joseph, editor. *Foreign Language Teaching.* New York: Macmillan, 1967.

21. Modern Language Association. *Cooperative Foreign Language Tests.* Princeton, N.J.: Educational Testing Service, 1963.

22. Moulton, William. *A Linguistic Guide to Language Learning.* Second edition. New York: Modern Language Association, 1970.

23. Paquette, F. Andre, and Tollinger, Suzanne. *A Handbook on Foreign Language Classroom Testing: French, German, Italian, Russian, Spanish.* New York: Modern Language Association, 1968.

24. Pillet, Roger, editor. *FLES and the Objectives of the Contemporary Elementary School.* Philadelphia: Chilton, 1967.

25. Pimsleur, Paul. *Pimsleur Language Aptitude Battery.* New York: Harcourt, Brace and World, 1966.

26. Potts, Marion H. "The Effect of Second-Language Instruction on the Reading Proficiency and General School Achievement of Primary Grade Children." *American Educational Research Journal* 4: 367-73; May 1967.

27. Rivers, Wilga. *Teaching Foreign Language Skills.* Chicago: University of Chicago Press, 1968.

28. Seelye, H. Ned, editor. *Handbook on Latin America for Teachers: Methodology and Annotated Bibliography.* Springfield, Ill.: State Office of Public Instruction, 1968.

29. Smith, Melvin I. *Teaching Spanish by Being Responsible for Specific Objectives.*

30. Smith, Wayne H. "Linguistic and Academic Achievement of Elementary Students Studying a Foreign Language." *Dissertation Abstracts* 27: 3882A; May 1967.

31. Tursi, Joseph A., editor. *Foreign Languages and the "New" Student.* Reports of the Working Committees of the 1970 Northeast Conference on the Teaching of Foreign Languages. New York: the Conference, 1970.

32. Valdeman, Albert, editor. *Trends in Language Teaching.* New York: McGraw-Hill, 1966.

33. Valette, Rebecca M. *Directions in Foreign Language Testing.* New York: ERIC Clearinghouse on the Teaching of Foreign Languages and of English in Higher Education, 1969.

34. ———. *Modern Language Testing.* New York: Harcourt, Brace and World, 1967.

35. Walsh, Donald D., compiler. *What's What: A List of Useful Terms for the Teacher of Modern Languages.* Third edition. New York: Modern Language Association, 1965.

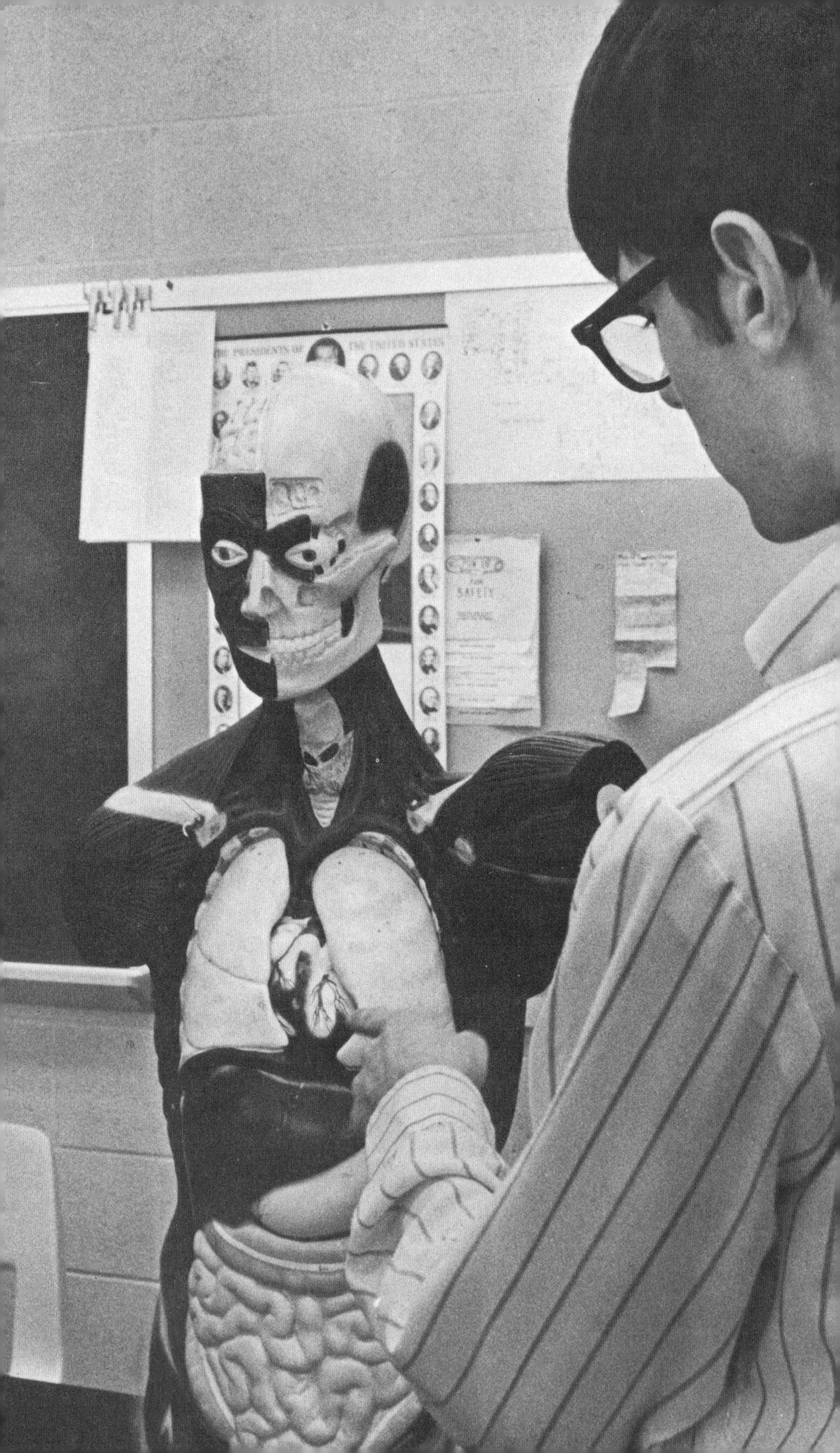
SAFETY

8
Health Education

In the increasingly complex urban society in which most people in the United States live, perhaps the greatest educational imperative for the next several decades will be to help students learn who they are and how to achieve some degree of self-actualization. These are times deeply troubled by racial tension and strife, alienation between young people and adults, and shifting perceptions of acceptable moral codes and values. The challenge to the schools today is to provide curriculums that can help students discover their humanness and how they may live effectively with other human beings. In speaking of this crucial issue the schools must face during the 1970's and 80's, Boulding (7) says—

> It must never be forgotten that what any society is producing is people. . . . the educational system is producing men, not manpower; people, not biologically generated nonlinear computers.

Education, he notes, must be a means, not an end, and must serve man, not technology.

In its "Schools for the 70's" series of books and tapes, the National Education Association called for a series of town meetings across the country to involve teachers, parents, students, administrators, industry, and government in finding ways to humanize the school environment, to develop each student as an individual. The Association for Supervision and Curriculum Development focused on the same problems in its 1970 yearbook, *To Nurture Humaneness—Commitment for the 70's* (4).

Never before has health education had such powerful allies, and perhaps never before has there been such universal awareness of the need for a dynamic curriculum in health education for kindergarten through twelfth grade—not watered-down courses in anatomy and physiology, or lectures on cleanliness and grooming squeezed into physical education, but an educational experience that encourages students to build skills of problem solving, including decision making and critical thinking. What is needed is a curriculum that views health as a dynamic point somewhere on a continuum of well-being, that helps students recognize the interrelationships among the physical, social, and mental-emotional forces that influence their position on that continuum at a given point in time. The ideal curriculum recognizes that health is not an end in itself, but rather a state that enables one to make the most of his potential. Most importantly, perhaps, such a curriculum motivates the student to seek new information as a continuing, life-long commitment.

In sum, health education is an applied science that draws upon the physical, biological, medical, and behavioral sciences for its body of knowledge. It is a discipline that synthesizes concepts and theories from these several areas and interprets them in the context of human needs, human values, and human potential. It is deeply concerned with promotion of personal effectiveness and the quality of human life.

Rationale

Most of the problems that so deeply disturb responsible people at every level of society—family, school, community, state, nation, and the world—are health problems. They are directly involved with health behavior in all its dimensions—physical, social, and mental. What are these problems? The list is as familiar as it is long: drugs, sex, abortion, ecology, pollution. An estimated 10 percent of the total population in urban areas of the United States is afflicted with major mental illness. In a hypothetical community of 500,000 (about the size of Dayton, Ohio), the National Institute of Mental Health predicts there will be 1,980 schizophrenics, thousands of people suffering from depression, nearly 13,000 alcoholics, 9,900 homosexuals, 165 narcotics addicts, and 1,300 mentally ill children (46, p. 4).

In the 1960's, young people between the ages of 16 and 23 represented 12.9 percent of the population but 27 percent of the arrests. They were cited for 26 percent of all murders and non-negligent manslaughter, 50 percent of all forcible rapes, 49 percent of all robberies, to mention just some of the categories of crime (37, p. 120). The latest estimates place the 16-through-23-year-olds at 20 percent of the present population. The adolescent years are critical for these young people who must learn to function effectively in a troubled world. The schools are the only agency specifically organized by society to help them.

Health education is specifically designed to provide the present generation of students with subject matter and teaching methodology geared to their daily needs and problems. Far from being a luxury, health education is very possibly the greatest imperative in education today. "The task of health education is to equip people intellectually and emotionally to make sound decisions on matters affecting their health, safety, and welfare," says Hochbaum (19, p. 1). What is needed is an education that develops competence in applying the best available strategies for survival in a world filled with unprecedented troubles, uncertainties, and opportunities, say Postman and Weingartner (36, p. xv). We need education that produces people who have clear purposes, who know who they are, where they are going, and why, say Raths, Harmin, and Simon (38, p. 12).

The urgency of the need for the kind of curriculum that health education alone offers is implicit in the following description of the present role of education, as viewed by the President's National Goals Research Staff (29, p. 99):

> In the past, the public has equated going to school with education. The role of the school was to transmit information and instill traditional values. The society of today is one changing so rapidly that skills and information become outmoded and traditional values are under challenge. Furthermore, the proportion of information that children receive from the mass media is so large and the range of values to which they are exposed so diverse that it may well be that the schools should be devoted to giving them the cognitive skills for integrating information and a framework within which to sort out the diverse values to which they are exposed.

Health education is essential in the schools because many health needs are not being met either by the family or by community agencies. The family cannot be expected to discover and communicate the ever-changing results of health-related research to its members. As Morrison says (25),

> The family, which is a fine mechanism for transmitting conventional wisdom in a relatively static society, is relatively poor at assimilating and transmitting new knowledge essential to survival in a rapidly moving world.

Health education affords the best medium for bridging the gap between the accumulated new knowledge generated by scientific study and man's application of these discoveries in his everyday world.

The following sections of this chapter will focus on concepts in the body of knowledge special to health instruction *(what is to be learned),* on principles of organization and administration *(how to plan and schedule health education in the curriculum),* on teaching strategies for health instruction *(how to plan teaching-learning activities),* and on valid evaluation procedures *(how to determine the effectiveness of those plans).*

Emerging Concepts in Curriculum Content

In any discipline, the most urgent curriculum problem today is that of deciding what to teach. What content should be selected from the wealth of knowledge that increases even as such decisions are being made? Recent curriculum investigations have concerned means of structuring content so that the student may acquire not only ideas but also the modes of inquiry unique to a field. With these tools, it is reasoned, young people will be equipped to continue learning, to cope with new problems, and to process new information as it is developed at an ever increasing speed.

A Comprehensive, Balanced Health Education Program

The Joint Committee of the American Association of School Administrators and the National School Boards Association, the National Congress of Parents and Teachers, the American Association for Health, Physical Education, and Recreation (AAHPER), and other groups all endorse a comprehensive program of health education in grades K through 12 as the only effective way of meeting the health needs of youth so as to prepare them for their future roles as citizens and parents. Such a comprehensive approach is better than the categorical "bandwagon," crash, or vested-interest approach that leads to one course for sex education, one for nutrition, one for drug abuse, etc. The comprehensive program is based upon an organizational framework designed to meet all the needs, interests, and problems of school-age children.

Two studies at the national level have focused on identifying the most powerful concepts in health education. The first was concerned with providing guidelines for health instruction through identifying concepts and content, while the second was far more comprehensive and productive in the preparation of curriculum materials. Each placed emphasis on identification of important concepts in health education to serve as guides to selection of subject matter for administrators, curriculum specialists, classroom teachers, professional preparation institutions, and researchers. Both studies made contributions to present curriculum trends in health education.

The Health Education Curriculum Commission Project. In 1962 the Curriculum Commission of the Health Education Division, AAHPER, gave priority to the task of identifying (a) the crucial health problems of the 1960's and 1970's relating to school-age children and (b) the related basic health concepts a student should acquire by the completion of 12 years of instruction. Problem areas identified included the following: accidents, venereal diseases, smoking, alcohol, teen-age diets, obesity, poor mental health, lack of adequate family life education (including instruction in teen-age sex problems), periodontal diseases and lack of fluoridation, medical economics, and lack of evaluation of health information. Outstanding authorities in fields relating to these health problems were asked to specify the essential concepts in their fields of specialization. These concepts were then refined and restated, and supporting data were included.

As an example of the kinds of concepts stated by the Curriculum Commission, we quote the following mental health concepts (1):

- Human behavior tends to be ordered and patterned.
- Behavior is complex.
- Behavior is characterized by adaptability.
- Interpersonal relationships are enhanced through an understanding of the factors underlying behavior, including behavior of self and others.
- Extensive research in the behavioral sciences has provided a basis for determining possible causes of certain behavior patterns.
- Understanding behavior involves recognition that there are reasons underlying a given form of behavior.
- Physical and mental disorders may be related.
- Emotional disorders can be treated successfully in many cases.
- Self-acceptance is fundamental to sound mental health.
- Cultural and environmental factors have a considerable influence upon the development of personality and behavior.

For each of these concepts a content outline was developed. For example, under one of the concepts stated above, part of the outline is as follows:

- Self-acceptance is fundamental to sound mental health: Emotional well-being is based on the capacity to appraise oneself realistically, recognizing one's own strengths and weaknesses.

This approach represents a bridge between the traditional health content areas and an overall conceptual framework for a health curriculum. Neither the identified problems nor the concepts inferred from them are intended to represent the total scope of health education.

A project in the planning stage is that of the National Instructional Television Center, in cooperation with AAHPER, to develop a series of 15-minute television programs in health education for children aged eight to nine, with 30-minute inservice programs for the teacher. The health programs will revolve around certain processes and skills.

The School Health Education Study. The nationwide School Health Education Study (SHES), initiated in September 1961 with private funds, began with a status survey of health instruction practices from kindergarten through grade 12 in a stratified random sample of large, medium, and small school districts across the country. The SHES investigations revealed significant weaknesses in instructional and administrative practices in the majority of health education programs investigated. The misconceptions held by students were found to be extensive and potentially dangerous to health. Other problems reported included inadequate professional preparation of staff; indifference to or lack of support for health education on the part of some teachers, parents, administrators, and other influential members of the community; neglect of health instruction when forced upon the physical education program; the lack of a sequential and structured curriculum; ineffectiveness of instruction; and failure to provide instructional materials, classroom facilities, and time for health instruction (42). The frequency with which these and other problems were cited pointed to a need for research and innovation in curriculum design for health instruction.

Accordingly, before the first phase of the study was completed, the second phase, directed toward development of experimental curriculum materials for schools, got under way. The challenge given to the writers selected for this task was to identify priorities for health content areas, to develop a structural framework involving a plan for organizing the scope and sequence for health instruction, and to prepare sample instructional materials based on the curriculum so devised for experimental use in selected school systems. An innovative approach to a curriculum framework that would be useful to schools across the nation seemed essential. The intention was not to create a national curriculum, but to develop a structure that would provide stability yet remain flexible and adaptable enough so that individual schools could modify it to fit local needs.

It was concluded that a new curriculum could best be constructed by identifying and categorizing basic concepts derived from the body of knowledge fundamental to health education. The SHES project viewed the health education curriculum as structured around a hierarchy of concepts. Health itself was placed at the apex, representing the comprehensive, generalized concept to which the lower levels of concepts were subordinate. Health was viewed as a unified concept having three dimensions—physical, mental, and social. These dimensions were further described as follows (40):

> Health is a quality of life involving dynamic interaction and interdependence among the individual's physical well-being, his mental and emotional reactions, and the social complex in which he exists. Any one dimension may play a greater or lesser role than the other two, at a given time, but the interdependence and interaction of the three dimensions still holds true . . . different individuals may be deemed "healthy" without necessarily exhibiting identical proportions of the three dimensions of well-being. At certain times and under particular circumstances, one dimension may be more in need of attention than another in order to maintain and promote a state of optimal health.

At the next level of importance, the three key concepts fundamental to health were identified as *growing and developing, interacting,* and *decision making.* Each represents a life-cycle process typical of all mankind and thus exemplifies the processes underlying health. These key concepts are not separate but interrelated and interdependent.

At a third level, 10 concepts were identified as representing the total scope of health instruction. These concepts, which serve as the components of the curriculum framework, are the following:

> Growth and development influence and are influenced by the structure and functioning of the individual.

Growing and developing follow a predictable sequence, yet are unique for each individual.

Protection and promotion of health is an individual, community, and international responsibility.

The potential for hazards and accidents exists, whatever the environment.

There are reciprocal relationships involving man, disease, and environment.

The family serves to perpetuate man and to fulfill certain health needs.

Personal health practices are affected by complex, often conflicting forces.

Utilization of health information, products, and services is guided by values and perceptions.

Use of substances that modify mood and behavior arises from a variety of motivations.

Food selection and eating patterns are determined by physical, social, mental, economic, and cultural factors.

From these concepts, subconcepts—in the form of facts, principles, generalizations, and values—were developed. In effect, the 10 concepts offer an integrated approach to health curriculum, encompassing the 30 or more separate health topics traditionally covered and providing opportunity for an organized and comprehensive program of instruction.

Among the publications resulting from the School Health Education Study is the basic document, *Health Education: A Conceptual Approach to Curriculum Design, Grades Kindergarten through Twelve* (40), which describes the rationale for and design of the curriculum. Ultimately there will also be 10 sets of teaching-learning guides, extensive compilations of resource and reference materials, and coordinated visual packets of transparencies. The study's conceptual approach to curriculum design has been widely adopted and is proving a valuable asset to curriculum workers in general, and specifically to those responsible for health education. It remains flexible and adaptable to local needs and is being used both in the United States and overseas.

Major Trends in Content and Scope of Health Education

The foregoing two projects at the national level reflect emerging trends in organizing health education curriculums. The notion of concepts as a vehicle for the definition of content has been seized upon with growing enthusiasm by most health textbook authors and by curriculum developers at every level of responsibility, including a growing number in fields other than health education. The word *concepts,* however, is often used to describe content, as supportive to or as an expansion of a topic or area of health instruction. The topics themselves are generally indistinguishable from those representative of a traditional approach to the structure of the body of knowledge. Concepts are thus employed as means of organizing factual information relevant to the topics rather than of providing a framework for that knowledge. Health curriculums developed recently at the state level represent varying degrees of faithfulness to the concept approach.

For example, the 1970 state curriculum handbook *Conceptual Guidelines for School Health Programs in Pennsylvania* (35) addressed itself to the idea and significance of concepts and conceptual learning for health education. The organizing elements of the proposed curriculum are not concepts, however, but 17 of the usual topics: alcohol, anatomy, community health, consumer health, dental health, disease control, drugs and narcotics, family relationships, health careers, heredity and environment, human sexuality, mental health, nutrition, physical fitness, safety, and smoking. The statewide *Framework for Health Instruction in California Public Schools—Kindergarten through Grade Twelve* similarly categorizes concepts, or big ideas, at two levels of specificity by means of 10 content areas (consumer health; mental-emotional health; drug use and misuse; family health; oral health, vision, and hearing; nutrition; exercise, rest, and posture; disease and disorders; environmental health hazards; and community health resources). Since 1967 the State University of New York through the Curriculum Development Center of the state education department has been developing curriculum materials for the elementary and secondary grades based on five strands: physical health, sociological health problems, mental health, environmental and community health, and education for survival. Included in the guides for each strand are major understandings and fundamental concepts, suggested teaching aids, learning activities, references, and supplementary information for the teacher. The State of Washington's *Health Education Guide to Better Health* (working copies) includes concepts for nine health topics and outlines broad, general competencies, sample learning experiences, and resources.

Whatever the plan of organizing content for health education, a comprehensive curriculum is essential. The trend is toward providing sequential and progressive learning experiences from grades K through 12 in broad health content areas including growth and development, accident prevention, use and abuse of mood-modifying substances, consumer health, community health, environmental health, food and nutrition, personal health practices, dental health, communicable and noncommunicable disease, international health, and family life and sex education. To seize upon one area of health behavior and develop it as a separate curriculum is as absurd as it is useless. As Oberteuffer (32) says, "Another thing we don't need is continued fragmentation of the curriculum into little sub-areas relating to health." The two health categories most often offered as separate courses rather than as integrated parts of a total health curriculum are drug abuse education and sex education. It is as though it were reasonable to believe that the drug user has no sexual life, no family responsibilities, no need for nutrition, or that his drug dependence could be viewed as separate from his other health needs. In the case of sex education, it is as though the social, emotional, and physical sexual problems and needs of an individual were unrelated to his behavior and needs in any other area of health-related decision making!

Sliepcevich (42) refers to a "revolving door syndrome," pointing out that crisis-oriented health education programs tend to follow cyclical patterns. Each problem finds its place of top priority in the curriculum during a period of community uproar and is then slowly pushed aside by a new problem with higher priority, only to reappear at the top of the crisis list a few years later; and the cycle continues. The result is that programs—not problems—are eliminated.

A review of curriculum materials in health education indicates that the scope of the instructional program—what is to be taught—is derived from the health needs of the local community, the individual needs of pupils, the legal requirements of the state and local districts, and the objectives set forth for the area and the course.

The emphasis of instruction is moving away from memorization of facts and toward the acquisition of abilities and skills of problem solving. Content is used as a means to motivate thinking, not reciting. Finally, the trend is away from the notion of health as absence of disease or infirmity in their solely physical manifestations and away from the teaching of health as a series of no-no's or finger-wagging admonitions against just exactly what people most enjoy doing. Health is viewed instead as a quality of life, its peak, a means of participating in all life activities with enjoyment and productivity.

Administrative Organization of Health Instruction

The governing board of each school district has the responsibility to provide for a comprehensive, articulated, well planned, and continuously evaluated health education program. To be effective, this program should be systematically and sequentially organized with progression from kindergarten through twelfth grade. Lack of progression can mean deadly repetition. At the college level, education for health is relevant as a contribution to meeting the individual needs of college students on or off campus, as a part of the college health center program, and as a part of the local community health program. Specific programs are needed to provide competence in health teaching for all preservice and inservice teachers as well as for those selecting professional preparation for a career in school, college, or community health education. Planned and vital instruction is essential in teacher education programs for school administrators who need not only understanding of, but preparation for, assuming the administrative responsibility for health programs.

Accountability

Accountability is becoming a prime concern of school administrators as interested citizens, students, board members, and others are requesting (and sometimes demanding) that the quality of education be improved. Accountability means that all the professionals in a school system are held responsible for educational outcomes, so as to provide better student achievement and, in general, better education results.

The essential prerequisites for accountability are definition of behavioral objectives; organization of concepts, content, and educational process; and consideration of the environmental situations in which learning opportunities occur. The output is a body of organized and effectively evaluated results. When a program is well planned, a cost value can be readily applied. More precise instruments are still needed, but the ground has already been broken.

The School Health Council or Committee

Absolutely vital is the organization of a group of representatives from the administration, the faculty, the student body, and the citizenry to carry out health planning, programming, budgeting, problem solving, and coordination. A health coordinator, preferably a qualified health educator, can contribute much toward making this group functional and relevant. Councils have sometimes failed through lack of dynamic leadership. Others have flourished and recommended appropriate action for improving the health program through the use of effective organizational procedures and quality personnel. The Tulare County School Health Advisory Board, Tulare, California, has functioned effectively under leadership of a health coordinator since 1957. New York State programs are now using health coordinators in this way. The State of Florida has encouraged the use of a school health committee plan for each individual elementary or secondary school. Members are appointed by the principal or elected by the faculty. This organizational structure can be used well at the school, district, or county level.

A usual and workable plan for curriculum development is the formation of a health *instruction* committee responsible to the school health council, which in turn reports to the appropriate administrator. Such a committee works closely with the curriculum director and the overall curriculum committee of a school, district, or county.

In some states, several school districts or counties are working cooperatively on the development and implementation of improved health instruction programs, aided by ESEA Title III funds. Some of these projects, such as Project Quest in Los Angeles County, involve experimental use of new materials. In this case, curriculum guides were developed using student health goals and objectives as the organizing elements. Other Title III projects, such as the four-county project in education at Centreville, Maryland, and the three-county project in Florida, have chosen to use and implement the School Health Education Study curriculum materials. The latter project has now been widened to some twenty counties.

Emerging Patterns of Curriculum Organization

A 1964 nationwide status study of prevailing program practices (42) revealed a variety of curriculum organizational plans in operation. The most prevalent one at that time was the incorporation of health content through correlation with other curriculum areas. (A particular subject becomes the vehicle for teaching health units, topics, or other such organizing centers. Correlation with biology, chemistry, social studies, home economics, and physical education has been common.) Evaluation studies have shown that these programs, though attractive on paper, do little toward changing the health behavior of students. Such organization is a fine supplementary procedure for the separate health course; however, as the only method of education for health it falls far short of meeting the needs of children and youth. Evidence indicates that unless a school or school district employs a full-time health coordinator-teacher, health instruction programs organized only on a correlated basis are ineffective.

The current trend in health instruction, as in other areas of the curriculum in the 1960's and early 1970's, is toward organizing health instruction as a separate comprehensive course or courses at the secondary level. Two school districts can serve as examples:

1. In the *Los Angeles City Unified School District,* a principals' committee, with the aid of health education supervisors and curriculum personnel, changed their offerings from a correlated program to one of direct instruction. The present instructional specialist in health education reports that since 1970, one semester of health education has been a district requirement for all pupils enrolled in tenth grade classes in the senior high schools. Since 1969, one semester of health education has been required for all pupils enrolled in seventh grade classes in the junior high schools. In neither instance is time for this instruction taken from that allocated to the physical education program. The health classes are separate and distinct programs, although close relationships are maintained with several related areas. In Los Angeles elementary schools, health is one of the many general requirements in the overcrowded elementary curriculum, but no time allotment is specified. Although the Los Angeles program represents a big step in the right direction, it can be considered minimal in time allotment. In the future, perhaps twice as much time will be necessary if the needs of young people are to be met adequately. Time allotted for health education or health science should be in keeping with that allotted for other essential subject fields in the curriculum.
2. *Alhambra (California) City Schools,* under the excellent guidance of the associate superintendent of instruction, has a well-planned, direct instructional program. Alhambra uses a curriculum committee and a health coordinator. Recently, their curriculum revision has been an interdistrict program, planned with the neighboring districts of Garvey and San Gabriel, which cooperated in developing health education for the 1970's. Writers from each of the districts have collaborated in constructing the teaching guides for an articulated program for prekindergarten through tenth grade, based upon student needs. The curriculum is organized as a cycle

> plan, allowing for important emphases relating to individual, family, and community health to be reviewed over the years in accordance with growth and development characteristics and interests of students. The featured separate course is a two-semester program in the tenth grade. It appears that instruction at the eleventh and twelfth grades is left to natural correlation with other courses and to those teachers who believe in health guidance. The separation of health education and physical education offers promise for increased effectiveness of instruction for both subjects.

As of January 1970, 104 colleges and universities in 31 states reported offering one or more programs with major specialization in health education at the undergraduate and graduate levels (41). Another 30 institutions and 5 more states are in the process of adding such programs. These statistics do not include dual and combined majors such as health *and* physical education. Individuals with specialization in health education are increasingly being sought as health coordinators and teachers, to fill positions in teacher preparation programs for state departments of education, or as health education consultants in health organizations and agencies.

Integration of health instruction remains the predominant curriculum pattern at the elementary level, although elementary programs appear to be using separate blocks of time to a greater degree than formerly. Organizing elements such as health concepts—and also skills, practices, and values—continue to provide centers for specific health learnings. Health instruction units organized around "Mood-Modifiers," "Man Interacting," "Health Has No Boundaries," "Investing in Health," "Food: It Gets to You," and "We the Impressionable Ones" are specific illustrations of central themes.

Today's health education program requires qualified teaching and supervisory staff, adequate facilities, time for organized instruction, and appropriate teaching materials.

Sequence of Instruction

A modern health instruction program should provide progression for students from prekindergarten through the twelfth grade, junior or community colleges, and four-year colleges and universities. Traditional programs have developed a cycle arrangement of health instructional areas or organizing centers, wherein specified problem areas are considered at predetermined grade levels. The Health Education Curriculum Commission made no attempt to develop sequence but left this function to the local school district or school. The School Health Education Study, with its conceptual approach to curriculum design, designated four levels of development in relation to each concept. Related content may be studied at progressive levels of complexity and comprehensiveness. The behavioral objectives for each level prescribe the content. Revisiting of the concept on the successive levels, calling for additional content and different and more complex behavior, provides sequence to the SHES materials. Thus the sequence is a flexible one that leaves exact placement of content to local school systems. Horizontal sequence is incorporated through the medium of the 10 major concepts as reflected by the behavioral objectives identified for each of the four levels. The natural relationship of one concept with another also tends to dictate the horizontal sequence.

Emerging Methods of Instruction in Health Education

If constructs such as concepts, topics, or problem areas give structure to a curriculum, then process defines its essential functions. Health education seeks not to provide answers in the form of prescriptive "content covering" but rather to provoke lifelong habits of questioning. The critical dimension of any method selected for teaching is not so much the subject matter involved as the process through which the learning occurs. Dale (13) points to this new focus on learning ways of *using* information rather than making information itself the instructional goal:

> Much of our thoughtlessly memorized knowledge is inert, undynamic; it isn't going anywhere. A mental miracle will occur when we learn to restructure or rearrange what we already know in response to the solution of real problems. The chief emphasis will be on *reconstruction* of knowledge, not on its *reproduction.*

The methodology of health education is intended to afford students the opportunity to apply what is learned as a means of solving real-life problems. It is from this point of view—recognition of the importance of effective health behavior—that the methods employed in teaching and learning about healthful living must and do emerge. If the learner is to be motivated to change his behavior where this is desirable—whether cognitive, affective, or active—teaching strategies must be selected that, by their very nature, involve his personal participation.

Three factors are fundamental to current methodology in health instruction. First is *selection of material or content* to be taught. The subject matter to be dealt with must be relevant to the life of the learner; if the material is essential to solve a health problem, all of the methods or teaching techniques must be chosen for their contributions to meeting that need. A second factor is *teaching strategies.* These should allow for extensive student involvement in meaningful activities and independent study. The teacher's role should be that of a facilitator of student learning. A third fundamental is *instructional objectives.* These must be formulated precisely. To the extent that they are stated operationally, choice of method is facilitated. For example, compare the following forms of objectives (40):

1. *Understands* disease prevention and control
2. *Integrates* information about disease prevention and control into an effective plan for reducing problems caused by these diseases.

The teacher's interpretation of the first objective is crucial to the decisions involved in devising an appropriate learning activity. Given no more clue than "understands," he might choose any one of many teaching procedures. If, as happens too often with this kind of objective, the student is asked to memorize names of pathogens, the chain of infection, and types of immunizations, there is no assurance that he can or will use these facts as tools in solving a related problem.

The second objective stated above describes the expected cognitive behavior and so provides a clue to method as well as a direction for eventual choice among evaluation procedures. If the method is effective, at the end of his instruction the student will be able to demonstrate the skill and deal with the specified content. (Note that the content is also more explicit in this statement.) Instructional objectives stated with such precision communicate their intent equally well to any teacher who may seek to achieve them. Whatever variation there might be in method or techniques chosen by various individuals to implement the objective, the outcome should be the same—that is, evidence that the specified intended behavior and content have been attained by the student.

To be effective, however, all methods must involve the learner in active participation. Active participation may be of an overt or covert nature and may be in a direct or vicarious situation. A method or instructional device should give the student meaningful experience that can contribute to improvement of his health behavior and the health status of his family and community.

Methods particularly applicable to health teaching—because of the opportunity they provide for individual participation—include discussions, panels, demonstrations, field experiences, committee work, community action and campaigns, role playing, symposiums, buzz groups, computer-assisted instruction, use of resource speakers, research projects, laboratory experimentation, simulation, case studies, and value studies. The techniques most often used for vicarious participation include television (live, kinescoped, closed-circuit, and videotaped); educational films, transparencies, slides, or filmstrips; recordings (reel tapes, records, cartridges, and cassettes); and multimedia.

Problem-solving learning opportunities are particularly effective in health education. While researchers continue to probe the effectiveness of this method as a means of providing greater gains in factual information, investigation supports its superiority as a means of promoting skill development, developing critical thinking, arousing interest, and changing attitudes (15). Such technological innovations as television and the overhead projector have brought new variety to the learning process. Television is increasingly being used both as a source of new information and as a technique in health education (30). Many school systems are using planned ETV broadcasts to supplement and enrich health instruction (11).

There is an increasing concern for values in today's society. Health education provides ample opportunity to guide the student through value-clarifying processes in connection with his reaction to posed issues or problems. Critical thinking, self-analysis, identification of values, and personal commitment help the student take sure steps toward learning who he is (38).

However, no one approach is as productive as a flexible plan employing a variety of techniques and a combination of methods—such as lecture-discussion, discussion, and problem solving. Modern health education uses such a multimethodological approach. A new approach providing a variety of learning experiences while making the most of individual teacher styles and competencies is the team-teaching method. In this approach several teachers form a team with mutual responsibilities for planning, developing, and evaluating the instructional program for a comparatively large number of students. Teachers in any field have differing interests and competencies, but especially in health education, owing to the broad range of disciplines from which its body of knowledge is derived. When teachers pool their resources, each can make more effective preparations and contributions in his field of specialization. Those not involved in the major presentation in an area can give attention to small-group activities. An assumption basic to this approach is that certain aspects of the teaching-learning process occur best on an individual basis, others in small groups of 10 or 15, and still others in very large groups, through lectures, demonstrations, films, or television. While team teaching should not be adopted blindly as an end in itself, it offers many advantages as a method (39).

Fundamental to the effectiveness of any method is selection of materials that reflect the modern concept of health education and meet the needs of today's students. Today's skilled health teacher employs a wide variety of techniques. He selects the one that will do the best job that day, for that topic, for that particular group of students. Any technique can involve the learner emotionally when it is used wisely and well. Increasingly, the trend in all areas of the curriculum is toward acceptance and use of coordinated instructional materials prepared for general use by state or national specialists, often financed through federal grants, and published with the cooperation of textbook publishers. Generally such materials provide a rich array of suggested learning opportunities and evaluation activities based upon research and careful analysis of the sources of the curriculum. Such organizations as the Association for Supervision and Curriculum Development of the National Education Association offer extremely useful guidelines for the selection of new teaching materials.

The development of resource units in specialized areas of the health curriculum continues. Most often these units are prepared by specialized health interest groups. An example is the curriculum guide prepared by the American School Health Association and Pharmaceutical Manufacturers Association *(Teaching About Drugs: A Curriculum Guide, K-12).* Dozens of other guides have been developed in the areas of smoking, nutrition, venereal disease, air pollution—virtually every health-related problem. But where there is no provision for health education in the curriculum, there is no logical vehicle for the effective use of these specialized resource materials, however valuable they may be, nor is there often any real attempt to relate the categorical problem area to the comprehensive notion of health. Such specialized units' chief virtue is their current and authoritative content. They give little consideration to the processes involved in presenting effective behaviorally oriented objectives, learning opportunities, and evaluation techniques that consider the interrelationship and interdependence of *all* areas of health concern.

A comprehensive approach to curriculum planning resulting in a separate time or course dedicated to health instruction provides an opportunity to conserve valuable curriculum time. But efforts to develop health education curriculums are complicated by the vast number of competing national groups organized in the interest of specialized health problem areas and by the availability of public and private funds for particular health problem studies. Resource materials developed for individual health problems must be used as enrichment and supportive materials rather than as a substitute for a sound, overall health program.

Evaluation

Evaluation in health education, as in any other area of education, is the appraisal of the value or worth of a curriculum, a subject, a teaching-learning guide, a unit of work, a teacher, or some other component of a school or college. Evaluation is an appraisal based upon a set of values or criteria, or the assessment of progress made toward established objectives.

Evaluation is an integral part of the health education program. Many administrators and teachers in successful programs give even more emphasis to evaluation than to other aspects of their programs, for very good reasons. Evaluation enables health teachers to measure the worth of their teaching efforts and to inform students of strengths and weaknesses as indicated by their growth or lack of growth in health knowledge, attitudes, and practices. For administrators, board members, parents, and the public, evaluation provides evidence of a program's progress, of teachers' effectiveness, and of students' learning. Evaluation also has public relations value; it can be used by school officials to justify keeping a program or a given number and kind of personnel, or to justify hiring additional personnel.

Trends in Evaluation

Three approaches to evaluation are most prevalent currently. The traditional approach is evaluation by descriptive account. This includes counting the number of students using facilities or participating in a program or the number of hours they have expended on a project. Fortunately, most districts are either abandoning this type of evaluation or using it only in conjunction with other types.

The second approach is evaluation based upon appraisal of the established objectives—in health education, the behavioral objectives formulated to plan teaching and learning activities.

The third approach is cost-time efficiency control, which is becoming more and more useful as the emphasis on accountability has increased. Management techniques such as PPBS (Program Planning and Budgeting System) are often used in this kind of evaluation.

Administrative Use of Evaluation Approaches

An evaluation component of a health education program may be initiated by the administrator, who would request the school health council or committee to submit a plan for evaluating the essential factors of the program as a means of meeting the accountability demands for health education. The plan needs to include all approaches to evaluation. Responsibility should be clearly defined and outlined by the council or committee or by a subcommittee on evaluation. Evaluation should be a continuous part of the program; it might be conducted experimentally to become an ongoing process later.

Too often evaluation groups seeking accountability tend to use a strictly quantitative approach, describing the size of the student population affected by health education, the number of teachers involved, the number and kinds of facilities used, the number of classes offered, the number of contracts with school health services, and other measurements. The whole process is a numbers game, largely involving addition of figures to describe the health education operation. Such an approach tells one nothing about the qualitative aspects of the program.

Comprehensive Evaluation

Emerging evaluation procedures in health education include four types of appraisals:

1. Appraisal of the health education program
2. Appraisal of the changes in health behavior on the part of students
3. Appraisal of the evaluation process, or how effectively those persons making the appraisals have carried out their mission

4. Appraisal of the effectiveness of teachers, supervisors, auxiliary personnel, or administrators.

An evaluation committee incorporating the second approach, appraisal by objectives, needs first to establish goals and objectives for the program. To determine instructional objectives, the investigator must look to three sources for data. First is the learner himself. What are his needs and interests and his present knowledge, attitudes, and practices in regard to his health? What are his developmental needs? What is his socioeconomic background? Answers to these questions have direct implications for curriculum decisions. The second source is the subject matter or content of health instruction. What are the methods of inquiry unique to health instruction? What contributions can the subject make to other educational objectives not primary to this discipline? The third source is the society. What does the learner need to know in order to make sound decisions affecting his own health and that of his family and community? What are the major societal problems that relate to health education? How will health instruction enable the learner to adjust to social forces and trends? What is the cultural background of this student body? What are the resources of the community? What are the legal requirements affecting health instruction?

Perhaps objectives are already formulated in the school health program guide. Perhaps appraisal forms have been established at the state, county, or district level. A number of state departments of education have such appraisal forms. For example, California (8), Michigan, and Ohio have criteria for evaluating elementary, high school, and college health programs. Materials developed by the Los Angeles City Schools and the Tulare County Schools in California are examples of evaluation guides at other levels.

An evaluation plan using the objective approach can be developed by charting the objectives in accordance with the following steps (see evaluation chart, p. 178):

1. Formulate the objectives desired for the school health program or the instructional phase of that program.
2. State the changes desired for people—pupils, teachers, supervisors, administrators.
3. State the kind of changes sought.
4. Select the means of appraisal—checklist, observation, test, or other.
5. Identify situations where changes may take place.

6. Record and interpret the findings.
7. Replan for a more effective program.

A vital part of health education evaluation is appraising changes in student health behavior. This procedure calls for formulating behavioral objectives in health teaching for each content area or health concept and relating the behavioral objectives to the learning opportunities and to evaluation procedures designed to appraise the specific objective. Many times the objectives for the development or change of health practices have long-range implications. Certain health behaviors will not or cannot be practiced until later in adulthood, or until a student is confronted with a problem calling for a specific behavior, or until he is in a position to assume greater responsibility for his own behavior.

Marian Solleder has prepared for AAHPER an annotated bibliography of tests of health knowledge, attitudes, and behavior for elementary, secondary, and college levels, in the booklet *Evaluation Instruments in Health Education* (43). This should be helpful to evaluation committees desiring to use standardized tests to determine the status of their students.

A variety of evaluation techniques can be used to appraise student progress toward established objectives—teacher-made tests directed to the objectives, questionnaires, checklists, surveys, observations, recording of teacher or student logs of experiences pertaining to the objectives, before-and-after photographs depicting changes. Examples of such appraisals are reported by Creswell

Sample Evaluation Plan—School X

1. APPRAISAL OF SCHOOL HEALTH PROGRAM ACTIVITIES

Objectives: School Health Program, School X	Changes in Whom or What	Kind of Changes Sought	Means of Appraisal	Interpretation of Findings	Replanning

and his associates (12) as part of the School Health Education Study evaluation.

Evaluation by Cost-Time Efficiency Control (PPBS)

An administrator facing today's pressures for accountability, if he has not already adopted PPBS—the planning, programming, budgeting system—is probably at least considering it. It is up to him to ensure that this system is applied to the health education curriculum as well as to other curriculum areas and that the focus is kept on curriculum development and on the improvement of instruction and learning opportunities for students. A team approach is called for, involving administrators, teachers, students, board members, parents, and other citizens. Roles need to be spelled out to make the inputs, interactions, outputs, and feedbacks meaningful.

The process of applying PPBS to health education involves—

1. Assessing the significance of the health program by identifying both community and individual health needs.
2. Charting the long-range goals for meeting those needs.
3. Formulating behavioral objectives outlining the health behaviors that can be changed in school—both in the classroom and through other school-sponsored activities.
4. Planning the concepts, content, and methods of the health education program, and including relevant learning activities or opportunities.
5. Formulating and selecting evaluation procedures for appraising progress students have made toward the objectives.
6. Placing a price tag on such a program.
7. Securing the funds for the program and needed personnel.
8. Implementing the program and continuously evaluating its success.

PPBS involves meeting the demands and planning and conducting the health education program on the basis of educational need while paying the cost to provide for a program of significant worth. The Pearl River, New York, experience in improving instruction as well as incorporating a new curriculum in health and family living is an example of applying PPBS and using this approach to evaluation.

Implementation

The logical steps in implementing a new or revised health education curriculum from the blueprint to the action stage are as follows: The curriculum committee, health instruction subcommittee, or other planning group presents the new or revised plan to the assistant superintendent in charge of instruction or to the superintendent himself. The latter discusses the curriculum changes with principals and other administrative personnel, receiving their recommendations. The superintendent, after his acceptance and endorsement, then presents the new or revised plan to the board of education for final approval.

A pilot experimental period may be recommended as a practical step in implementation. Such a tryout period enables faculty to become familiar with and adjust to the needed modifications. It also allows a trial run before sweeping (and expensive) changes are made. A gradual shift to a changed program also provides opportunities for student, parent, and community organization groups to become enthusiastic and to support the recommended program. Well planned and well conducted inservice education for teachers is necessary to ensure success of the program.

Various methods may be used to build support in the press and among community groups. Gaining support from the official and unofficial health groups in the community is paramount to a successful program that meets students' needs in today's society.

Evaluating and implementing any kind of curriculum change is dependent upon the creativity and dedication of the designers. Active administrative support, sustained interest and effort of the faculty members involved, and full parental and community cooperation are essential to the task. The rewards—such things as increases in human vitality and more productive lives—are incalculable.

Health and education are inseparable. The level of health a student attains and maintains is a major determinant of the extent to which he profits from his total educational experience, contributes to society as an effective citizen, and achieves individual family and community goals.

No school system can claim to offer a comprehensive educational program for all students unless it regards education for health as basic to the conservation of its human resources and essential to the attainment of its other educational goals.

BIBLIOGRAPHY

1. American Association for Health, Physical Education, and Recreation, Health Education Curriculum Commission. *Health Concepts: Guides for Health Instruction.* Washington, D.C.: the Association, 1967.
2. American Educational Research Association. "Curriculum Planning and Development." *Review of Educational Research* 36: 339-98; June 1966.
3. Association for Supervision and Curriculum Development. *Evaluation as Feedback and Guide.* Yearbook. Washington, D.C.: the Association, 1967.
4. ———. *To Nurture Humaneness: Commitment for the 70's.* Yearbook. Washington, D.C.: the Association, 1970.
5. Barro, Stephen M. "An Approach to Developing Accountability Measures for the Public Schools." *Phi Delta Kappan* 52: 196-205; December 1970.
6. Beyrer, Mary K.; Nolte, Ann E.; and Solleder, Marian K. *A Directory of Selected References and Resources for Health Instruction.* Second edition. Minneapolis: Burgess Publishing Co., 1969.
7. Boulding, Kenneth E. "Expecting the Unexpected: the Uncertain Future of Knowledge and Technology." *Designing Education for the Future, No. 1: Prospective Changes in Society by 1980.* (Edited by Edgar L. Morphet and Charles O. Ryan.) New York: Citation Press, 1967. pp. 199-215.
8. California State Department of Education. *Criteria for Evaluating Elementary Health Programs. Criteria for Evaluating High School Health Programs. Criteria for Evaluating College Health Programs.* (Three instruments.) Sacramento: the Department, 1962.
9. ———. *Planning, Programming, Budgeting System Manual for the State of California School Districts—an Educational Planning and Evaluation System.* Sacramento: the Department, 1970.
10. Cauffman, Joy. "Effectiveness of Selected Approaches for the Teaching of Health Education." *Synthesis of Research in Selected Areas of Health Instruction.* Washington, D.C.: School Health Education Study, 1966. pp. 158-71.
11. Cox, Helen M. "Sex Education Via Instructional Television." *Journal of Health, Physical Education, and Recreation* 37: 71-72; April 1966.
12. Creswell, William H., Jr.; Hastings, J. Thomas; and Huggman, Warren J. "Results of Experimental Group Testing of the School Health Education Study Materials." *Journal of School Health* 36: 154-64; April 1966.
13. Dale, Edgar. *The News Letter* 35: 3; May 1970. (Columbus: College of Education, Ohio State University.)
14. Goodlad, John I. "Curriculum: The State of the Field." *Review of Educational Research* 30: 185-98; June 1960.
15. Gross, Richard E., and McDonald, Frederick J. "The Problem-Solving Approach." *Phi Delta Kappan* 39: 259-65; March 1958.
16. Grout, Ruth E. *Health Teaching in Schools.* Philadelphia: W. B. Saunders Co., 1968.

17. Hartley, Harry J. *Educational Planning-Programming-Budgeting: A Systems Approach.* Englewood Cliffs, N. J.: Prentice-Hall, 1968.

18. Hastings, J. Thomas. "Evaluation in Health Education." *Journal of School Health* 40: 519-22; December 1970.

19. Hochbaum, Godfrey M. "Measurement of Effectiveness of Health Education Programs." Paper presented at annual meeting of the American College Health Association, Oklahoma City, April 1969.

20. Johns, Edward B.; Sutton, Wilfred C.; and Webster, Lloyd E. *Health for Effective Living.* Fifth edition. New York: McGraw-Hill Book Co., 1970.

21. Joint Committee of the National School Boards Association and the American Association of School Administrators. *Health Education and Sex/Family Life Education.* Washington, D.C.: the Committee, 1968. (Leaflet.)

22. Joint Committee on Health Problems in Education of the National Education Association and the American Medical Association. *Suggested School Health Policies.* Fourth edition. Chicago: the Committee, 1966.

23. ———. *Why Health Education?* Chicago: the Committee, 1965. pp. 1, 3-4.

24. Jones, David M. "PPBS—A Tool for Improving Instruction." *Educational Leadership* 28: 405-409; January 1971.

25. Morrison, Robert S. "Where Is Biology Taking Us?" *Science* 155: 429-33; January 27, 1967.

26. Nagel, Charles. "The Story of Project Quest." *California School Health* 4: 12-23; October 1969.

27. National Association of Secondary School Principals. "Curriculum Change in Health Education." *NASSP Bulletin* 52: 1-138; March 1968.

28. National Education Association, Center for the Study of Instruction. *Schools for the 70's and Beyond: A Call to Action.* Washington, D.C.: the Association, 1971. p. 148.

29. National Goals Research Staff. *Toward Balanced Growth: Quantity with Quality.* Washington, D.C.: Government Printing Office, 1970.

30. National Health Council. *Health Education in Our Schools Today: The Need for Agency Action.* New York: the Council, 1966.

31. National Society for the Study of Education. *Educational Evaluation: New Roles, New Means.* Sixty-Eighth Yearbook, Part II. Chicago: University of Chicago Press, 1969.

32. Oberteuffer, Delbert. "Some Things We Need and Some Things We Don't Need in Sex Education." *Journal of School Health* 40: 54-65; February 1970.

33. ———. "Health and Education—An Appraisal." *Journal of School Health* 34: 184-97; April 1964.

34. ———. "Health and Education—An Appraisal II." *Journal of School Health* 38: 72-84; February 1968.

35. Pennsylvania Department of Education. *Conceptual Guidelines for School Health Programs in Pennsylvania.* Harrisburg: the Department, 1970. p. 4.

36. Postman, Neil, and Weingartner, Charles. *Teaching as a Subversive Activity.* New York: Delacorte Press, 1969.

37. President's Commission on Law Enforcement and Administration of Justice, Task Force on Juvenile Delinquency. *Task Force Report: Juvenile Delinquency and Youth Crime.* Washington, D.C.: Government Printing Office, 1967.

38. Raths, Louis E.; Harmin, Merrill; and Simon, Sidney B. *Values and Teaching.* Columbus, Ohio: Charles E. Merrill, 1966.

39. Schlaadt, Richard G. "Modified Health Team Teaching in Action." *Journal of School Health* 35: 91-94; February 1965.

40. School Health Education Study. *Health Education: A Conceptual Approach to Curriculum Design.* St. Paul: 3M Company, Visual Products Division (Education Press), 1967.

41. ———. *Institutions Offering Programs of Specialization in Health Education.* Washington, D.C.: the Study, 1970.

42. Sliepcevich, Elena M. *Summary Report of the Nationwide Study of Health Instruction in the Public Schools.* Washington, D.C.: School Health Education Study, 1964.

43. Solleder, Marian K. *Evaluation Instruments in Health Education.* Revised edition. Washington, D.C.: American Association for Health, Physical Education, and Recreation, 1969.

44. Stake, Robert E. "Objectives, Priorities, and Other Judgment Data." *Review of Educational Research* 40: 181-212; April 1970.

45. Stovall, Thomas F. "Classroom Methods: Lecture vs Discussions." *Phi Delta Kappan* 39: 255-58; March 1958.

46. U.S. Department of Health, Education, and Welfare, National Institute of Mental Health. *The Mental Health of Urban America.* Washington, D.C.: Government Printing Office, April 1969.

47. Westbury, Jan. "Curriculum Evaluation." *Review of Educational Research* 40: 239-60; April 1970.

9

Home Economics Education

Home economics education curriculums in the schools are changing, influenced by the interest of education decision makers in what home economics has to offer, by legislation giving support to home economics as a part of vocational education, and by changes in society that have affected personal and family living. The central focus of home economics continues to be education for the well-being of individuals and families. Its major purpose in the middle and secondary schools is preparation for homemaking. With the passage of the Vocational Education Act of 1963, home economics also assumed the responsibility for preparing students for gainful employment. Increasing numbers of programs are being offered in grades 11 and 12 that prepare for entry-level occupations that "utilize home economics knowledge and skills." The Vocational Education Amendments of 1968 expanded homemaking education to "consumer and homemaking education," and as a result programs are giving greater emphasis to consumer education, to preparation for the dual role of homemaker and wage-earner, to adaptations in programs relating to social and cultural conditions affecting families, and to the needs of the disadvantaged and the handicapped.

Emerging Concepts in Curriculum Content

Home economics curriculums, if effective, relate closely to the students they serve and to the society for which those students are being prepared. Objectives are drawn from study of a combination of the following:

- The developmental characteristics, interests, and felt needs of students, and their readiness for learning the concepts to be included in the curriculum
- The conditions in society affecting students and their families or affecting the occupational areas students plan to enter.

- The competencies expected by society of the homemaker or of workers in home economics–related occupational areas
- The concepts and generalizations from the subject matter content of home economics.

Developmental Characteristics of Students

Planning home economics curriculums in relation to the developmental characteristics, interests, and felt needs of the students will ensure that what is being taught is appropriate to their grade level and relevant to them and their world. For example, most junior high school students in consumer and homemaking classes are interested in learning how to help with tasks at home, in caring for young children, and in exploring future job possibilities. But girls from disadvantaged backgrounds may reject the idea of helping at home and caring for children because they have too many of these responsibilities already. They may be interested in and need much help with grooming and personal development, however, in order to improve their own self-concept. Boys from disadvantaged backgrounds may be forced to drop out of school and support themselves by junior high school age. These boys need special help in finding part-time jobs and a new image of the man's role in the home (12).

Most eleventh and twelfth graders are beginning to earn money for themselves, so consumer education and budgeting are of interest to them. Many are beginning to think of establishing their own homes, so the study of housing and home furnishings, meal management and nutrition, and preparation for parenthood are appropriate areas to include in a homemaking education curriculum for upper high school students. Those students interested in a home economics–related occupation want concentrated preparation for an entry-level job before graduation.

Conditions in Society Affecting Students, Their Families, and the Work World

Changes in society affect family life in both a positive and a negative way. A relevant curriculum in consumer and homemaking education will help students capitalize on those changes that support stability in families and combat those that tend to undermine family life. The following social, economic, and technical trends should be considered when determining the objectives to be attained in home economics education:

- *Demographic changes.*
- *Threats to stability of family life.*
- *Increased mobility of population,* in particular the shift from rural to urban areas, with an accompanying concentration of health and welfare problems in the cities. (Efforts are being made to stem this trend.)
- *Working wives and mothers,* the number of mothers in the labor force having doubled since 1950.
- *Continued existence of health problems,* among them a steady increase in venereal disease, malnutrition, and drug and narcotics abuse among teen-agers.
- *Unmet educational needs,* with considerable numbers of young people leaving school unprepared to find or hold jobs (8).
- *Increased physical and mental stress,* including tensions from noise and crowding, emotional strain, and changes in body chemistry caused by limitations in man's adaptability to physical extremes.
- *Mounting environmental pollution,* with pure air and water becoming two of the scarcest natural resources.
- *A soaring gross national product,* resulting from improvement in the productivity of the labor force and high consumption.
- *A dilemma of "people problems,"* accentuated by diversity of backgrounds (economic, education, and cultural) coupled with immediate needs and growing aspirations that have reached an explosive intensity.
- *Shortened work time* brought about by large-scale automation, resulting in increased needs for education, cultural development, entertainment, and travel.
- *Unemployment,* advanced technology having left few work opportunities for the unskilled and rendering many skills obsolete (3).

The specific conditions in the local community also need study and analysis when selecting objectives for the curriculum of a particular school. For instance, if in a local community most homemakers work outside the home and trends show a continued increase, it is especially important to prepare girls for managing home and family responsibilities along with a job. Boys also need preparation for assuming their share of responsibility in caring for the home and family. Household work continues to demand time in spite of modern home conveniences. A study in 1968 showed that a total work week of 60 to 70 hours for the homemaker was a common pattern (18). Husbands of working homemakers spent only 5 to 7 hours per week helping with home responsibilities, which consisted mostly of yard work and home repairs. Husbands and fathers need education for helping with such responsibilities as food shopping and care of home and children. Home economics curriculums need to be organized so that high school boys as well as girls may gain the help they need in preparing for their roles in the home.

If many of the working homemakers in a particular community also have preschool children, there may be need for an expansion of day care services and for additional trained paraprofessionals to staff day care centers or to offer day care to individual families. A curriculum for eleventh and twelfth graders in child care and development may be offered to prepare them for day care work. Such a curriculum should be developed to articulate with a postsecondary curriculum in child care development, if students should wish to gain further training for jobs as day care assistants. Articulation with four-year college programs is also needed, for those students who aspire to become professionals in the child development field.

In some communities the home economics curriculum may need to emphasize nutrition, in others the wise use of credit. If there are many teen-age marriages and a high divorce rate among young marrieds in a particular community, the curriculum should focus on education in marriage and personal relationships. A relevant home economics curriculum should help make differences in a community over a period of years, if improvements are needed in the quality of home environments and family life.

Competencies Expected by Society of the Homemaker or Worker on the Home Economics–Related Job

The objectives for consumer and homemaking curriculums will vary somewhat depending upon the competencies expected of a homemaker in a particular community. In a recent study (5) conducted in the southeastern section of the country, the following criteria for an effective homemaker were suggested by husbands, teen-age children, and homemakers themselves:

"Keeps children clean."

"Demonstrates good moral standards."

"Understands and is able to cope with the different characteristics of children of various ages."

"Is a companion to her husband."

"Is a good hostess."

"Is an efficient shopper."

"Considers home and family concerns of more importance than work outside the home."

"Keeps the house clean, neat, and orderly."

"Provides clothing suitable for various occasions."

In some rural communities homemakers are expected to can and freeze food for the family, while in most cities such abilities are not important. In some communities homemakers are expected to make much of the clothing for the family, and sewing is important; in other communities most of the clothing is purchased ready-made, and homemakers are expected to do only simple sewing.

Objectives for curriculums that prepare for home economics–related occupations are planned in relation to the expectations for workers on the job. Each job, or cluster of jobs, is broken down into the tasks to be performed and the competencies needed to accomplish each task. An analysis of three home economics–related occupations—the hotel/motel housekeeping aide, the nursing home housekeeping aide, and the homemaker/home health aide—was made by Beavers and Carpenter (4). Tasks that were similar in all three occupations related to safety, household maintenance, care and operation of equipment, and sanitation. The competencies expected in certain specialized tasks varied for the homemaker/home health aide, depending upon whether the employer was a voluntary, health, or welfare agency. Since the employing agencies for the homemaker/home health aide vary in different communities, curriculum planners would need to know the expectations of particular agencies in the local community. A relevant curriculum reflects local expectations for the students being served.

The Subject Matter Content

After analyzing characteristics and felt needs of the learners, the conditions of society affecting individuals and families or the worker, and the expectations of society for the homemaker or the worker, it is necessary to look at the subject matter available to be taught in home economics. The structure and content of home economics as defined in a series of workshops conducted under the leadership of the Home Economics Branch of the U.S. Office of Education in 1961, 1962, and 1963 still provide a helpful resource for curriculum development (2). New knowledge and facts have been added and generalizations revised, but the following conceptual structure continues to be used in developing curriculums for consumer and homemaking education and for home economics–related occupations:

Human Development and the Family

1. Universality of individuals and families
2. Uniqueness of individuals and families
3. Development and socialization of the individual
4. Challenge and creative possibilities of change

Home Management and Family Economics

1. Environmental influences on individual and family management
   a. Societal
   b. Economic
2. Managerial processes
   a. Decision making
   b. Organization of activities
3. Effective elements in management
   a. Resources and their utilization
   b. Values, goals, and standards

Food and Nutrition

1. Significance of food
   a. As related to cultural and socioeconomic influences
   b. As related to nutrition
   c. As related to physiological and psychological satisfactions
2. Nature of food
   a. Chemical and physical properties
   b. Factors affecting change in properties of food
3. Provision of food
   a. Production
   b. Consumer practices
   c. Protective measures
   d. Management of resources

Housing

1. Influences of housing on people
   a. Physical and psychological
   b. Social
2. Factors influencing the form and use of housing
   a. Human
   b. Environmental

3. Processes in providing housing
    a. Designing
    b. Selecting
    c. Building
    d. Financing
    e. Furnishing and equipping
    f. Managing
    g. Maintaining

Textiles and Clothing

1. Significance of textiles and clothing
    a. Interrelationships of clothing and culture
    b. Social and psychological aspects of clothing
    c. Clothing as a medium for artistic perception, expression, and experience
    d. Textiles and clothing in the economy
    e. Physiological aspects of textiles and clothing
2. Nature of textiles and clothing
3. Acquisition and use of textiles and clothing
    a. Selection
    b. Use and care
    c. Responsibilities of consumers

The overall objectives for a home economics curriculum in a local community are ordered in terms of level, sequence, and continuity relative to the varying amounts of time available for home economics in the school schedule. The objectives are further analyzed and classified according to taxonomies for the cognitive, affective, and psychomotor domains as a basis for selecting appropriate teaching-learning experiences.

Emerging Concepts in Organization and Application of Knowledge

Kimball Wiles once told a regional conference group of home economics educators that home economics programs in the schools should be offered in "large and small packages." The large package would consist of a sequence of courses for those students who need or desire more than one course in home economics; the small package would consist of one-semester or one-year courses available without prerequisite and offered at a time when students who have specialized interests may elect such courses. Since Wiles' suggestion, many variations in curriculum organization have occurred in the consumer and homemaking aspects of programs, and training programs for home economics–related occupations have been added. The programs are so organized as to be available to students with as many varying needs and interests as possible. Recent follow-up studies of young women who enrolled in home economics courses in high school indicate that approximately 95 percent of them recommend that all girls receive preparation for homemaking and for an occupation (7). Boys also need such training.

The following chart shows how curriculum developers in Arizona have identified the knowledge, skills, and attitudes in home economics to be used as a base for developing two curriculums:

HOME ECONOMICS

The Basis for a Variety of Programs

CONSUMER and HOMEMAKING	GAINFUL EMPLOYMENT
Consumer and Homemaking Education assists consumers and helps individuals and families improve home environments and the quality of personal and family life.	Gainful emplyoment means employment in a recognized occupation using the knowledge and skills of home economics, for which persons normally receive a wage, salary, fee, or profit.
Elementary-Secondary-Adult	*Secondary-Adult*
Foods and Nutrition	
Functions of Food World Nutrition Historical and Cultural Aspects Food Preparation Food Money Management Food Buying and Storage Food in the Family Life Cycle	Supervised Food Service Worker—Schools, Hospitals, Institutions, Lunch Counters Assistant to Food Demonstrators Waitress Family Dinner Service Specialist
Home Management and Family Economics	
Decision-Making Process Influences on Consumer Practices Effective Consumer Buying Individual and Family Resources Values, Goals, and Standards	Family Health Assistant Operator of Shopping Service Attendant—Coin-Operated Dry Cleaning Establishment Daily Maintenance Worker—Hospital, Nursing Home, Motel

Housing and Home Furnishings

Housing and Human Fulfillment	Housing Aide
Housing Modifications by Youth	Assistant—Florist's Shop, Gift Shop, Drapery and Slipcover Business
Consumer Decisions	Worker (Department Store)—Home Furnishings, Housewares, China and Glassware
Available Housing Resources	
Social Responsibility for Housing	

Human Development and the Family

Development of the Child	Child Care Assistant—Private Home, Nursery School, Day Care Center, Playground or Recreation Center
Skills in Child Care	Assistant—Children's Home or Hospital, Nursery in Department Store or Industry
Adult Responsibilities	Companion to an Elderly Person
Consumer Information for the Family	
Interpersonal Relationships	
Successful Marriage Qualities	
Family Life in Other Cultures	

Textiles and Clothing

Clothing and Textiles Purchasing	Clothing Maintenance Specialist—Department Store, Dry Cleaning Establishments
Clothing Selection	Seamstress
Clothing Care	Laundry Service Specialist
Construction Processes	Salesperson for Children's and Women's Clothing
Cultural Effects	
Fashion Industry	

—Arizona State Department of Education, April 1969

Consumer and Homemaking Education

The principal goals of consumer and homemaking education are to assist consumers and to help individuals and families improve their home environments and the quality of personal and family life. Offerings in the middle or junior high school are often available to both boys and girls and may be for a semester each year or for a full year at a certain grade level. The curriculum for the pre- or early-adolescent student generally includes the following:

- Understanding and getting along with others
- Enjoying and caring for children
- Improving food habits
- Learning simple food preparation
- Improving personal appearance

- Learning simple sewing
- Making the most of money
- Learning to be a cooperative family member
- Becoming acquainted with job and career opportunities, particularly those related to home economics.

At the senior high school level, home economics programs are organized in different ways. In most schools a comprehensive course in consumer education and homemaking is offered for ninth grade students, for the purpose of giving them a general background in preparation for homemaking. This course may include units in the various areas of home economics, such as the following:

- Learning how to manage school and home activities
- Learning to budget one's money and to spend wisely
- Getting along with family, friends, and employer
- Boy-girl relationships
- Understanding child growth and development
- Understanding the importance of a good diet
- Increasing skill in food preparation
- Increasing skill in selection, basic construction, and care of clothing
- Making the home attractive and comfortable.

In some schools a sequence of two or three comprehensive courses in consumer education and homemaking may be offered, including a course at the ninth grade level. In addition to, or in place of, the advanced comprehensive courses, semester or quarter-long courses in *specialized areas* of home economics may be offered in such areas as child development; home management and consumer education; foods, nutrition, and health; clothing, textiles, and related arts; housing, home furnishings, and household equipment; and personal, family, and community relations. These courses are electives and available to both boys and girls.

Many high schools also offer a semester or year course in "Personal and Family Living" for eleventh and twelfth grade students, focusing on interpersonal relations, the functions of the family, family life in varying cultures, the meaning of maturity and the responsibilities of adulthood, making a wise marital choice, major adjustments within the family life cycle, the multiple roles of the modern adult, responsibilities of parents, understanding children, money management and consumerism, and nutrition and health. In some schools a comprehensive course in consumer and homemaking education may be offered in the eleventh and twelfth grades for girls who have had no home economics and are becoming interested in establishing their own homes. Schools with flexible scheduling and independent study are making it possible for some students to select the aspects of consumer and homemaking education they most need to study in the limited time available in their schedules.

Preparation for Home Economics–Related Occupations

Consumer and homemaking education courses not only prepare for the responsibilities of homemaking and family life, particularly for the dual role of homemaker and wage earner, but also provide the basic preparation for training in home economics–related occupations. Those students interested in an occupation related to home economics may be offered exploratory experiences as part of consumer and homemaking courses in preparation for skill training to be obtained during the upper years of high school or at the postsecondary level.

Home economics–related occupations are expanding because of the increasing need for family services—child care, care of the elderly, meals away from home. An increase in training programs is needed to supply the required personnel. Since the passage of the Vocational Education Act of 1963, which stipulated that home economics be expanded to include preparation for occupations using home economics knowledge and skills, jobs have been identified, curriculums have been developed, teachers have been prepared, and each year an increasing number of high school youth are being trained and placed in jobs. The jobs cluster around the basic subject areas of home economics, including—

- Food management, production, and services: food service worker in school feeding programs, day care centers, nursing homes, hospitals, and commercial food establishments.
- Care and guidance of children: aide in day care centers, nursery schools, centers for retarded children, head start programs, and kindergartens.
- Institutional and home management and community service: homemaker's assistant (household work); institutional, hospital, nursing home, or hotel/motel housekeeping aide; companion to elderly people.
- Clothing management, production, and service: clothing alterer; aide to seamstress or tailor; worker in textile and apparel industries.

- Home furnishing, household equipment, and services: aide to interior designer or decorator; equipment demonstrator; assistant in custom drapery, slipcover, or home accessory production.

Under the leadership of the Division of Vocational and Technical Education in the U.S. Office of Education, a career development project is under way in which the world of work is being analyzed to identify all job cluster possibilities. Based on these analyses, curriculums will be developed to give elementary school students opportunities for orientation to the world of work, and junior high students prevocational and exploratory experiences to help them decide on a cluster of occupations in which they may enroll in senior high school. The goal is to provide students with enough training to get entry-level jobs in their cluster by the end of high school and/or to enter postsecondary training or college. Even students who do not complete high school will have at least some preparation for a job. In the food service field, for example, students may gain some experience with large-scale food preparation and service through helping with the school lunch during elementary and junior high school. In senior high school they may prepare for a cluster of jobs in food service and then continue to specialize at the postsecondary level.

Programs for Ethnic and Cultural Groups, the Disadvantaged, and the Handicapped

Adaptations in home economics programs are made to add relevance for students from varying cultural backgrounds. In the Southwest, for example, education in family meal management is adapted to include Mexican and Indian foods but is also designed to encourage the use of fresh fruits, vegetables, and milk. In the inner cities, where many families from the South have migrated, the teaching of nutrition includes continued use of greens in the diet, but it also attempts to encourage students and their families to use methods other than frying in preparing meats, in order to limit the oversupply of fat often found in the diets.

A home economics curriculum to prepare disadvantaged students for the dual role of homemaker and wage earner has been developed for inner-city schools (6). This suggested one-year course emphasizes "Skills for Living" during the first quarter. During the middle two quarters the students are helped to secure part-time jobs. They bring all their on-the-job problems to class, where they receive guidance in how to cope with them. Students also work on their salable skills—in this case, in the food service area. The last quarter of the course focuses on how to manage the home when the homemaker carries the dual role. Boys enrolled in the courses often come from homes without a husband-father figure. They need help in developing a new concept of what husbands and fathers can do to improve the quality of family life. Students who have enrolled in this "dual-role" course are ready to profit from skill training for a cluster of occupations offered at the upper high school level.

Home economics programs have also been adapted to students with various handicaps. Mentally retarded students may learn to do the routine types of jobs in housecleaning occupations. Hard-of-hearing students may acquire the skills necessary for a number of occupations where they can read instructions and follow demonstrations. Home economics classes may be offered for groups of students with similar handicaps, or small numbers of handicapped students may be given special help in classes for regular students. Some home economics teachers have studied in the field of special education to gain the understandings and competencies needed to work with handicapped children.

Emerging Methods of Instruction

Reality-centered teaching has been the goal of most home economics teachers. Learning experiences are offered to accomplish relevant objectives through various avenues—in class through discussions, demonstrations, and laboratory experiences; in the home through planned carry-over experiences; both in and out of class through individualized experiences and through participation in the activities of Future Homemakers of America. For students preparing for home economics–related occupations, simulated experiences may be offered in the classroom, or they may participate in supervised or cooperative work experiences.

In-Class Learning Experiences

A variety of class learning experiences are used. The development of attitudes, appreciations, and interests is an important part of the teaching in home economics. Round-table discussions, panel discussions, symposiums, role-playing situations, and games may offer appropriate learning experiences for developing objectives in the affective domain. Objectives in the cognitive domain may be achieved through problem-solving situations from which generalizations may be drawn, through reading, through having experts in the field talk to the classes (with accompanying discussion to be sure the students have gained an understanding), or through demonstrations by the teacher, other students, or resource persons. Objectives in the psychomotor domain are developed most effectively through laboratory—or some type of "in-hands"—experiences. Many of the objectives to be achieved, especially in programs preparing for home economics–related occupations, are of high ability or skill level. Students must have many opportunities for supervised practice to achieve skill-level objectives.

Individualized Experiences

In schools with flexible scheduling, students have time for independent study and work. If a teacher seeks to individualize instruction within an organized class, she provides opportunities for students to work at their own pace or to go beyond the class if possible. Under the leadership of Ray and Shear (13) at Pennsylvania State University, a series of individualized home economics learning packages ("HELPS") is being made available. Other packages ("LAPS" and "UNIPACKS") are also in production. These packages will be useful to teachers who lack the time or creative ability to develop their own. If individualized instruction is to be effective, many good self-teaching materials are needed.

Planned Carry-Over Experiences in the Home

Home economics students have always been encouraged to bring their home problems to class for solution and to apply what they have learned in class to their home situations. This was one of the first forms of individualized instruction and continues to be an effective method today.

Home economics teachers believe they must know the students' families and home situations in order to be effective. Many teachers continue to visit the home of each student, particularly those teaching in small towns and rural communities. In some states, home economics teachers are hired on a 10- or 11-month basis, giving them time in the summer to visit the homes of students enrolled in home economics classes for the fall term. Becoming acquainted with urban students' families is difficult, but contacts may be made through the help of visiting teachers and school or community social workers. Students' parents may also be invited to attend planned occasions in the class. When students are placed in part-time jobs as part of their training for a home economics–related occupation, parents should be informed about the nature of the work-study program. Many approaches are needed to build the bridge between school and homes that is fundamental to a relevant home economics program.

Activities of Future Homemakers of America

The Future Homemakers of America (FHA) is the national organization for students who are enrolled, or have been enrolled, in home economics classes in school. It is the nation's largest organization for junior and senior high school students. Its overall goal is to help individuals improve personal, family, and community living. Another goal has recently been added through the creation of HERO (Home Economics Related Occupations) chapters, to provide opportunities and projects that help students gain competency for an occupation. FHA's method of teaching is highly effective because the members select their own objectives and plan their own activities and projects, with the home economics teacher(s) serving as their adviser(s). FHA's 1969-73 program of work offers many opportunities for enriching class learning experiences by correlating activities with classwork:

Objective: To strengthen bonds within the family and between the family and the community.

Projects: Our Future as Homemakers
Stable Home—Stable Life
Make Time Work for You
Decisions That Count

Objective: To help youth comprehend the problems of society and contribute to their solutions.

Projects: To Dare Is To Care
Our World—A Growing Heritage
Preparedness—The Key to Opportunity

Supervised or Cooperative Work Experiences

In order for a student enrolled in a course preparing for home economics–related occupations to gain the skills necessary for securing and holding a job, some supervised experience on the job is essential. Sometimes the student works under the supervision of both the teacher and the employer. If the student is able to perform the job well enough that the employer feels he is worthy of pay, the student earns while he works. The student should develop a carefully outlined plan for these cooperative work experiences, with the help of the employer and the coordinator or teacher of the program.

The Teacher of Home Economics

Each state has developed its own certification requirements for teachers of the consumer and homemaking education aspect of the home economics program. In most states, teachers are required to have a general education foundation, competence in each of the home economics subject areas (and, in some states, strength in one subject area), and professional education including student teaching.

Certification requirements for teachers of courses that prepare for home economics–related occupations are in the developmental stage in a number of states. Usual requirements include—

1. Depth in subject matter background in the area to be taught. For instance, the teacher of child care and guidance must have at least a minor in child development, and even greater depth of background would be important for many teachers.
2. Work experience background in situations similar to those for which students are being prepared. The teacher's own experience allows for realistic teaching as well as practical guidance in arranging for students' work experiences and in placing students.

Home Economics at the Postsecondary Level and for Adults

Offerings in consumer and homemaking education are expanding in the postsecondary vocational-technical schools and in community colleges. For many of the young people enrolled, it is the "teachable moment" for education in establishing and maintaining a home. A series of semester or quarter courses in such areas as home management and consumer education, housing and home furnishings, nutrition and meal management, and child development and family relationships may be of particular help to these students. If there is limited time in students' schedules, a comprehensive course in "Consumer and Family Life Skills" may be offered, or models of instruction on different topics may be available for individualized learning.

Also offered at the postsecondary level are programs to prepare for supervisory assistant or technical positions in home economics–related occupations—such positions as food service supervisor, dietary technician, child development associate, family welfare associate, and textile technician.

Many schools offer series of lessons on various aspects of consumer and homemaking education for adults in the community. Often these learning opportunities are offered in the neighborhoods where people live, particularly in low-income areas of the cities. Classes are held in public housing centers, neighborhood centers, churches, or storefront buildings in the community. Adults may also return to school to prepare for a home economics–related occupation. Special courses may be offered for adults, or they may be able to enroll in training programs offered in the postsecondary vocational-technical schools or community colleges.

Summary

Home economics curriculums should remain flexible and open to change in order to be relevant to the students they serve. But there are also some constants for individual, family, and community living that need to be preserved. Continuous evaluation and revision of programs will make it possible to strike an acceptable balance.

The major goal to be achieved in home economics programs is an increasing number of stable homes—homes where the homemaker and other family members assume their roles to the satisfaction of all, where children are assured of a good start, where those in the work force have acquired the basic attitudes and habits needed for success, and where family members gain the support and security needed to live in this complex world. Home economics contributes to this goal by (a) focusing on the strengthening of homes and families through education and (b) providing quality trained personnel to deliver services needed by individuals and families to help them maintain strength and stability.

BIBLIOGRAPHY

1. Allen, Alice A., and King, K. F. "Family Relations Courses Taught in High Schools in the United States." *Journal of Home Economics* 62: 19-22; January 1970.
2. American Home Economics Association. *Concepts and Generalizations: Their Place in High School Home Economics Curriculum Development.* Washington, D.C.: the Association, 1967.
3. Byrd, Flossie M. "A Definition of Home Economics for the 70's." *Journal of Home Economics* 62: 411-15; June 1970.
4. Carpenter, Karen Fox, and Beavers, Irene. *Competencies Needed for Common Tasks in Three Home Related Occupations.* Thesis conducted as part of Project No. 29, under grant from Iowa Department of Public Instruction, Division of Vocational Education, Des Moines, Iowa.
5. Cross, Aleene, and others. *Evaluation of Vocational Home Economics Programs in Terms of the Effectiveness of Full-Time Homemakers and Homemakers Who Are Also Full-Time Employees.* Research Project No. 071204, funded under contract with the U.S. Office of Education, Washington, D.C., 1971.
6. Dabrymple, Julia I.; Lowe, Phyllis; and Nelson, Helen Y. *The Efficiency of Home Economics Courses Designed to Prepare Disadvantaged Pupils for Their Homemaker-Family Member Role and the Dual Roles of Homemaker and Wage Earner.* Research Projects Nos. 6-3049, 6-3050, 7-0006, funded under contract with the U.S. Office of Education, Washington, D.C., 1970.
7. Division of Educational Research. *Young Women in Virginia—A 10-Year Follow-Up Study of Girls.* Richmond, Va.: State Department of Education, 1966.
8. Egan, Mary C. "To Serve Is to Know." *Journal of Home Economics* 61: 13-16; January 1969.
9. Hurt, Mary Lee, and Alexander, Margaret. "New Challenges for Home Economics Educators." *Journal of Home Economics* 61: 771-75; December 1969.
10. Kaffer, Philip G., and Sevenson, Gardner. "Individualizing Instruction for Self-Paced Learning." *Clearing House* 42: 405-10; March 1968.
11. Kohlman, Eleanor L.; Smith, Frances; and Christmann, Phyllis. "Problems of the Working Girl." *American Vocational Journal* 45: 26-27; December 1970.
12. Phillips, Romeo Eldridge. "First-Born in the North." *Educational Leadership* 26: 21-23; October 1968.
13. Shear, Twyla, and Ray, Elizabeth. "Home Economics Learning Packages." *Journal of Home Economics* 61: 768-70; December 1969.
14. Simpson, Elizabeth J. "Challenges in Curriculum Development in Home Economics." *Journal of Home Economics* 60: 767-73; December 1968.
15. Spitze, Hazel T. "Needs of the Students as a Basis for Curriculum Decisions." *Illinois Teacher of Home Economics* 9: 101-26; 1965-66. (Urbana: Division of Home Economics Education, University of Illinois.)

16. ———. "Some Keys to Teaching the Neediest." *Illinois Teacher of Home Economics* 8: 209-13; 1970.

17. Time. "The American Family: Future Uncertain." *Time* 96: 34-39; December 28, 1970.

18. Walker, Kathryn E. "Homemaking Still Takes Time." *Journal of Home Economics* 61: 621-24; October 1969.

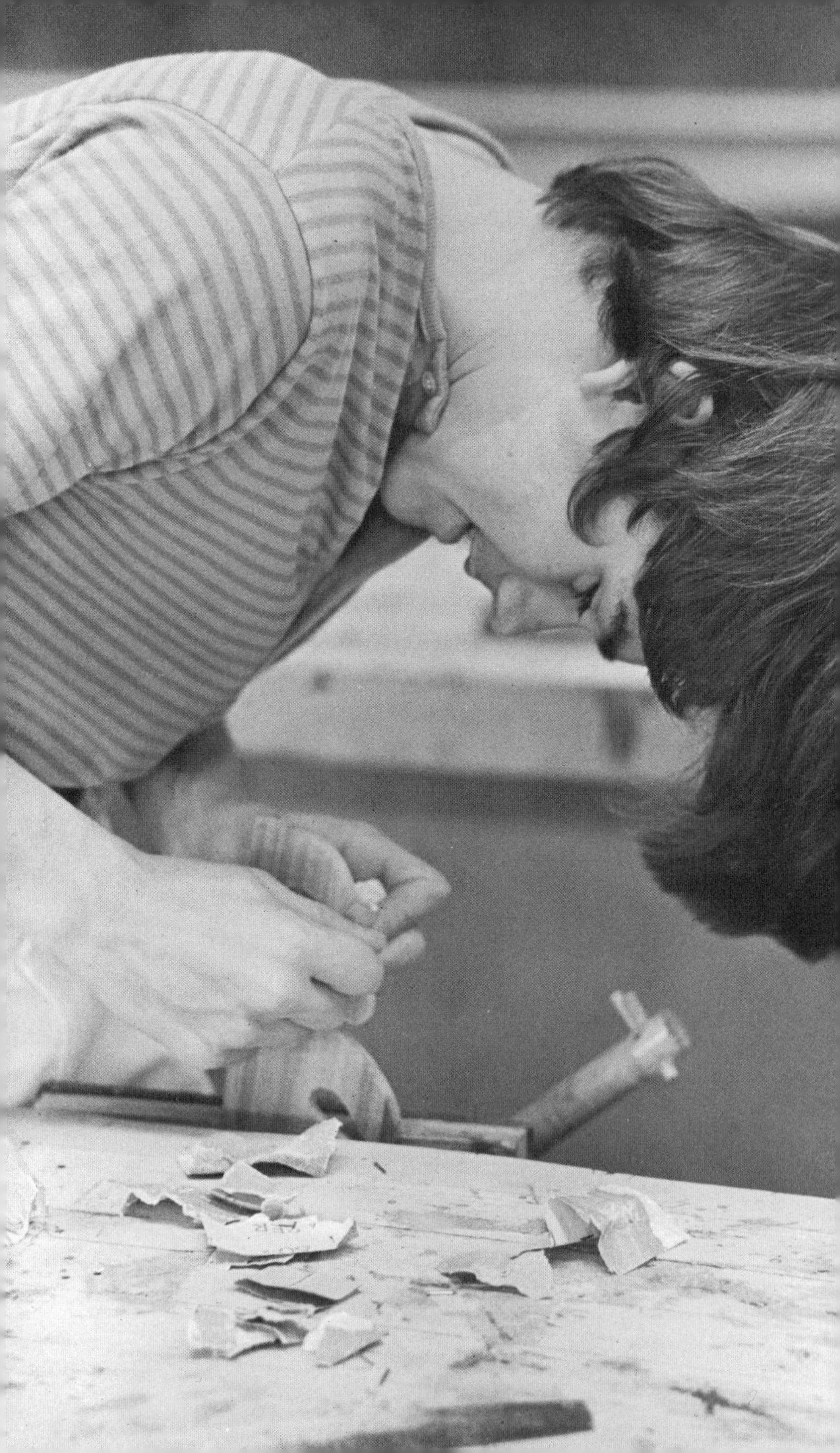

10

Industrial Arts Education

Industrial arts is an integral part of the American comprehensive educational system, which is designed to develop the complete human being. Its body of knowledge is the technology used by industry in the production of goods and materials. Among its many goals are the development of (a) human skills necessary if one is to become a productive citizen in our industrial society and (b) personal flexibility and adaptability to changing technology.

The study of industrial arts is as basic to our culture as is the study of the sciences and humanities. The ability to create and control technology is dependent upon one's ability to think and perform. The need for improved technological literacy and competence on the part of every citizen becomes increasingly critical as man compounds his accumulated knowledge. Industrial arts contributes relevant experiences that broaden technological understanding and help the student eventually to be able to master technology rather than to become its slave. Its interdisciplinary nature helps him to find new motivation for learning and to develop sharper perceptions of himself in contrast to his man-made world.

The schools have the responsibility to provide students with a realistic orientation to the complex interrelationships of their total environment and to cultivate a continuing commitment to improving the quality of life. The systematic study of technology must be seen as an essential part of each person's education, enabling him to improve and control his environment.

Each new generation needs guidance in developing the ability to adapt to changing technological conditions and practices. Industrial arts contributes significantly to the transmission of our cumulative technological culture. Each generation can proceed from existing technology without being required to rediscover knowledge or practice.

Industrial arts provides knowledge, comprehension, and opportunity for application leading to technological literacy; awareness, response, and values relating to personal stability;

and tactile control, association, and correction necessary for productivity in meeting the needs and responsibilities of the individual and society.

Emerging Concepts of Instruction

Activity-oriented instruction is the basis for most of the "new" developments that have been proposed for the improvement of education. But since its inception, industrial arts education has made student activity the predominant element in its instructional program. "Learning by doing" is the original form of scholarship and remains the primary technique for the transmission of accumulated knowledge.

Many young adults are indicating that they are neither satisfied with nor confident in their ability to cope with the intricacies of the machine and its concomitant effects. They are saying, "We will neither compete with nor participate in the technology that has produced the highest standard of living on earth while dehumanizing society with critical environmental problems." Charged with the responsibility of transmitting and improving culture, education finds its record of accomplishments questioned. Responding to societal pressures, leaders in education, politics, and local communities are now calling for a rebirth of the whole educational enterprise, from nursery schools through higher education. Our schools need not be confining or sterile; they must become flexible and open.

Industrial arts has passed through several phases of curricular development in arriving at its general education orientation. Originally the "trade and job analysis" approach was used. In the late 1920's and early 1930's the concept of the "general shop" emerged, which allowed for generalization of content and the study of several different types of activities. The general shop permitted small as well as large schools to provide a greater variety of experiences than could be achieved through the unit shop.

Industrial arts education must increasingly focus its attention upon the long-term needs of an educated person in a technological society. Deciding what to teach in a program designed to provide flexibility and adaptability for future careers of an unknown nature has led to the realization that technology demands new approaches to preparing people for productive lifetimes in a constantly changing society.

Elementary Level

Over a hundred years ago, Superintendent Edward Sheldon of Oswego, New York, implemented industrial arts activities for elementary children. The recurring emphasis on manipulation of tools and materials is an indication of the continuing value of industrial arts for young children. The Montessori approach to the education of young children and the more recent approach of the British infant schools clearly indicate that the open classroom, organized around "doing," is productive.

The real world of children is made up of things—things they wear, things they eat, things they see, things they play with, things their families use. Verbalization comes into the picture long after personality has been shaped by the visual and tactile experiences that a child's environment provides. An environment offering few sensory experiences produces a disadvantaged child. Evidence exists that multisensory experiences without the background of psychomotor experience fail to produce significant change.

A student's need for success, contribution, and identity is critical. A concept of self and the maintenance of self-esteem are necessary for the normal development of personality. The possibility of promoting a feeling of success is of such importance that industrial arts education might be justified on this basis alone.

Several approaches to the study of industrial arts at the elementary level have been developed by various curriculum projects and educators. These include in-class work areas supervised by the classroom teacher, mobile carts of tools and equipment, and a centrally located work area staffed by a specialist. The preferred arrangement is a separate classroom-size work center staffed by a consultant, to which groups of children are scheduled through conferences with the classroom teachers. The industrial arts consultant can be either an elementary teacher with special preparation to teach industrial arts activities or an industrial arts teacher who specialized in early childhood education.

The degree of correlation of industrial arts activities with ongoing classroom studies varies with the interests of the teacher. Establishing the identity of the subject as an integral part of the total curriculum seems critical to the implementation and continuation of a program of industrial arts at the elementary level.

There are many aspects of technology that are well within the abilities of young children, and it is the responsibility of the school system to provide a foundation for a lifetime of productive citizenship. Industrial arts is the only discipline prepared to organize psychomotor activities relating to technology for elementary children.

Middle Schools

The "school in the middle" seems to be an organization that has evolved from school housing factors as much as from philosophical rationale. Middle schools can include children from grade 5 through grade 8. Although a spread of age groupings exists, the middle school is not a "junior" anything. It does not need a watered-down secondary academic, social, or extracurricular orientation to provide an instructional program that prepares for entrance into high school.

With the return of an organizational breakpoint between grades 8 and 9 and an increasing move toward more flexible curriculums for secondary schools, it seems appropriate to think of the middle school program as foundational, much as the former junior high school philosophy proposed. Industrial arts can provide foundational experiences with tools, materials, and processes during study of the man-made world, just as other disciplines provide such experiences during study of the natural world.

The increasing tendency of the populace to change jobs, averaging five times per working lifetime, makes it increasingly relevant to provide a common program at the foundational level. Since the choice of electives at the secondary level may lead to a variety of careers in the service, production, technical, or professional fields, industrial arts education at the middle school level must build a common background by providing sufficient practical guidance to allow students to make a responsible career choice at the appropriate time.

Secondary Schools

Secondary level industrial arts continues the development of concepts and meaningful experiences begun in the foundational program in earlier grades. Individual courses extend and enrich the curricular content by providing an opportunity for research and development problems in special interest areas. Psychomotor ability supplements skills of analysis in providing a solution to problems in many diverse fields. Medicine, engineering, communications, and almost all human activities relate to the design, production, consumption, and disposal of the products of technology.

The "machine," in fact, pervades every aspect of our lives, including consumer, cultural, vocational, and recreational endeavors. Experiences in industrial technology enhance the ability of students to be adaptable and literate for a lifetime of productive citizenship.

No longer does the production of goods occupy the majority of employed persons. Service occupations have grown faster than goods-producing occupations. This changing cultural pattern places a responsibility on the schools to provide higher levels of basic education. There is now a dichotomy between those wishing to provide for general programs of industrial arts, with their long-term goal of adaptability, and those favoring occupational education programs, with their short-term goal of employment. In some states the term "industrial education" is used for programs combining these two functions, primarily to enable school systems to be eligible for federal funding.

Manpower needs of the future seem to indicate that while a degree of specialization will be required, so will a high degree of flexibility. As the variety of the types of employment expands, there also must be a comparable extension in the breadth of experiences to which a student is exposed. To be of maximum benefit to students, education must prepare them for a future of applying new knowledge to constantly changing technology.

Emerging Organizational Patterns

Research in the last few years has identified many different approaches to the organization of instruction. Dudley (8) identified five basic approaches that have been used in industrial arts education:

> *Trade Analysis*—The traditional approach to the production of articles with an implied tool skill development. Often substitutes for occupational education in locations that preclude access to relevant training.
>
> *Materials and Forces*—Basically a survey of raw materials and their conversion into products and services. This approach is characteristic of programs in many urban centers.
>
> *Technical Orientation*—Usually a pretechnical program making heavy use of research, development, and experimentation.
>
> *Interdisciplinary*—Uses activity, and sometimes a common facility, to reinforce learning in other subjects at the elementary level.

Conceptual—May analyze man's role as a builder-communicator-producer, may study the impact of tools and machines on mankind, or may use a sociological approach to the analysis of industrial organization systems.

The pages that follow provide a condensed sampling of the various approaches. Most plans are directed at a particular grade level. Some present new approaches to basic instruction; others build upon previous traditional programs to provide alternate ways of achieving productive citizenship.

The Elementary Industrial Arts Project, Bertie County, North Carolina

The Elementary Industrial Arts Project, which began with a federal grant in June 1968, effects a reinstatement of industrial arts in the elementary schools of North Carolina and hopes to develop into a workable model for other school systems. Elementary students in Bertie County have an opportunity to learn how technology influences the world around them through films, field trips to industries, and classroom activity related to industrial technology.

Industrial arts has been combined with the basic curriculum through a child-centered approach that is presented at the child's level of understanding and capability. Materials are being developed to correlate with all areas of the elementary curriculum. Physical activities appropriate to each child's ability and comprehension are used to stimulate and motivate the child. The student learns to apply knowledge and problem-solving abilities to practical situations that are personally important.

This project uses the talents and abilities of elementary teachers to implement industrial arts in the ongoing curriculum. Teacher workshops are being developed to provide the training necessary for correlating industrial arts with other subjects. A supervisor and curriculum coordinators are employed to work in the classroom, assisting the teacher. Commercial mobile tool carts are provided in each of the schools in the project. Junior-size workbenches provide work surface and storage. Hand tools and several power tools are provided.

The five basic areas of industrial technology—power, communications, transportation, construction, and manufacturing—serve as a vehicle for the learning experiences. Students at any grade level may be involved in any one of the five basic areas, depending upon interest and correlation with other subjects. Activities include projects on paper and papermaking, circuit boards to assist in science, rocketry, mapmaking, telegraph systems, mass-produced projects, safety signs, pottery, the printing industry, textiles and clothing, crystal radios, and photography.

By combining industrial arts with the basic curriculum in a child-centered approach, the Elementary Industrial Arts Project attempts to prepare young children to deal successfully with their physical and social environment. Industrial arts activities provide an opportunity for a child to discover and develop competency in dealing with the technological world and its relationship to daily living.

The Industrial Arts Curriculum Project (IACP), The Ohio State University

The Industrial Arts Curriculum Project defines industrial arts and technology as the study of the efficient actions of men in attaining material goods, principally those available through construction and manufacuring activities. It has developed two secondary school courses, *The World of Construction* and *The World of Manufacturing,* to provide an understanding of these industrial technologies. Curriculum materials for both courses include textbooks, laboratory manuals, teacher's guides, achievement tests, and related visual aids and instructional hardware.

Through study of *The World of Construction,* students learn how bridges, dams, roads, tunnels, and buildings are produced by a managed personnel production system. The importance of construction management is emphasized in activities ranging from preparation of drawings and estimation of construction costs to testing of soil and hiring of construction personnel. Students become familiar with production and service practices by building parts of structures, placing concrete, assembling steel beams, laying bricks, installing electrical circuits, plastering walls, and many other representative activities. Students also plan and build a model house and engage in city and regional planning.

The World of Manufacturing is concerned primarily with developing an understanding of how the managed personnel production system produces and services manufactured goods. Students become familiar with the processes common to all manufactured goods by studying the planning, organizing, and controlling of representative production systems. Activities include researching, designing, and engineering materials and processes to produce manufactured goods. Students become familiar with occupations, materials, tools, and various production procedures. They experience custom, job, and continuous producing techniques. For example, as a result of manufacturing a variety of different items, students would know how a managed production system affects human and material resources in generating products. Students' activities represent the industrial technologies (practices) common to manufacturing.

The two courses are the result of six years of intensive research, development, field testing, and revision. Each IACP course includes daily behavioral objectives to guide the teaching-learning process. Both courses have been developed for classes meeting for one 45-minute period each day of the school year (about 36 weeks) or the equivalent. The program may be implemented in standard facilities. (For information write the Director, Industrial Arts Curriculum Project, The Ohio State University, Columbus, Ohio 43210.)

American Industry Project (AIP), Stout State University

This project defines industry as an institution in our society which, intending to make a monetary profit, applies knowledge and utilizes human and natural resources to produce goods or services to meet the needs of man. It attempts to achieve two broad goals: (a) to develop an understanding of industry, and (b) to develop the ability to solve industry-related problems.

Thirteen basic concepts provide the body of knowledge for *American Industry*: communication, transportation, finance, property, research, procurement, relationships, marketing, management, production, materials, processes, and energy—all of which function in a unique environment of government, private property, resources, competition, and public interest.

Three one-year courses or levels have been identified for use in the secondary schools. Level I provides a broad view of industry and involves the solving of simple industry-related problems. It is written to be introduced to eighth grade students. The other two levels may be offered at any time after Level I has been completed, although Level III seems better suited to the eleventh and twelfth grades. By the time a student reaches Level III, he is involved in independent study related to concept areas of his own interest.

American Industry can be introduced into both general shop and unit shop laboratories, but it is better suited to a general shop arrangement. It has been taught successfully at all academic and socioeconomic levels, in schools enrolling the urban culturally disadvantaged as well as in small rural schools.

A teacher of *American Industry* should participate in special orientation courses because the AIP uses (a) a conceptual rather than factual approach, (b) a different approach to activity than has been traditional in industrial arts, and (c) industry rather than technology as its source. (For more information, contact the American Industry Project, Stout State University, Menomonie, Wisconsin 54751.)

The Maryland Plan, University of Maryland

Student-centered experiences at the junior high level form the basis of an approach that relates objectives, program, and student outcomes to one another. It was developed to use knowledge from the fields of philosophy, psychology, and sociology along the lines of current trends in curriculum and instruction. Behaviorial analysis provides the means to ensure that goals and outcomes have a high level of precision and consistency.

The Maryland Plan calls for a learner-centered classroom environment. The teacher must be willing to function as a manager or facilitator of education—one who inspires, encourages, and evaluates.

This approach tends to be more academically oriented than some of the others. Some people might challenge it on the basis that it provides only a superficial look at the broad concepts of industry. One of its strongest features is cognitive understanding of the role and process of industry in society; psychomotor skill development with tools and machines is only a secondary objective.

The Maryland Plan necessarily requires (and contributes to) a revised and unique laboratory environment. It offers such activities as individualized construction with many materials, line production of a product, seminar sessions, research, experimentation, testing of materials, detailed planning, and industrial role playing.

The uniqueness of this plan as an ultimate application of knowledge gained in English, mathematics, science, history, business, and other subject areas of the school deserves careful consideration by educators at all levels. If one's philosophy is based on the merits of a child-centered exploratory experience, the Maryland Plan has much to commend it. The program is backed by a considerable amount of field testing.

Grade 7 is an anthropological approach to basic elements common to all civilized mankind, requiring 90 class periods (45 minutes each) over 9 or 18 weeks. Content includes the development of tools and machines, power and energy, communications and transportation, and the contribution of these elements to the growth of civilization.

Grade 8 is a contemporary approach to the study of American industry, requiring 90 class periods (45 minutes each) over 18 weeks. Content includes an in-depth study of (a) a major basic industry using the group project method and (b) an industry using the line production method.

Grade 9 includes a personal emphasis on individual psychological needs and resourcefulness, requiring 90 class periods (45 minutes each) over 18 weeks. Content includes contemporary units of study, advanced major industry study (groups), research and experimentation, technical development, and advanced line production. All grades are taught in a general shop with audiovisual facilities, library, seminar, and planning areas. (Address inquiries to the Director, Department of Industrial Education, The University of Maryland, College Park, Maryland 20740.)

Industrial Arts Technology, State of Maine

Industrial Arts Technology is one of several innovative methods of implementing content already developed. This plan grew from a need for a new approach, one that would be simple yet adequate and easily adaptable to change.

This approach classifies American industries into the following categories: Manufacturing, Construction, Power and Transportation, Electronics, and Service. In a comprehensive general laboratory, all students are engaged in the same unit at the same time, not only to permit integration of content but also to minimize the confusion sometimes associated with other methods. These units in proper order provide a progressive and spiraling curriculum.

Within the framework of the unit, concepts can be introduced to help the student gain a better insight into our industrial and technological society. The unit permits the use of virtually every method for teaching industrial arts. It is exceptionally flexible and easily adaptable to any industrial arts curriculum.

The selection of unit titles is based on both student interests and industries representative of the technological culture. Basic functions of an industry are included in each unit so that a student starting at any level can gain a measure of understanding of industry or technology.

Units generally concern themselves with research and development, personnel administration, production and service, finance, and marketing. The total program attempts to achieve the following objectives:

1. Understanding of industry and technology and their impact on society
2. Skill in the use of tools, machines, and equipment, and their related processes and problems
3. Desirable attitudes toward work, workers, and the products of industry.

(For information write the Supervisor of Industrial Arts, State Education Department, Augusta, Maine 04330.)

The Developmental Approach, New York State

Industrial arts education interprets industrial technology to provide personal adaptability for the long-term needs of productive citizens in an industrial society. It develops the capacity to participate successfully in a technological world.

The developmental approach provides coordinated experiences related to industry and technology in a form relevant to the individual's level of development, as well as an opportunity for the development of basic manipulative and verbal skills. It cultivates socioeconomic values and promotes development of attitudes that will assist students in formulating and attaining individual goals. It incorporates activity and content that will serve future citizens in the interpretation of the technological society. This plan uses the project method of instruction, involving both individuals and groups.

The developmental approach organizes technological learnings into different levels, programmed according to the age, grade, and/or maturation of individual students:

- At the primary level, *Introduction to the Nature of Work* includes information and activity relating to man and his tasks as an integral part of the instructional program. Girls and boys should be scheduled into a work center whenever a supportive activity can be correlated with an ongoing instructional unit.
- At the intermediate level, *Exploration with Tools and Processes* relates the broad technologies to activities and learning. The shop/laboratory should be scheduled on a regular basis as an educational resource.

- At the early secondary level, *Utilization of Materials and Forces* represents a foundation for the development of basic skills, appreciations, and knowledge. The shop/laboratory is an essential part of the organization for instruction.
- The advanced secondary level presents in-depth *Experiences in Industrial Technology* to capitalize on the interests and maturity of the students. Selected technologies are used to provide an identity and meaning for content organization and to serve as a base for course development. Basic Series courses are designed for average students, the Technology Series for high-ability students. Courses may be organized on a modular, semester, or term plan.

All grade level themes relate to the broad technologies of production, communications, and power, and all provide for curriculum, facility, and staff organization.

Nature of Work

K-Work Environment
1-Service
2-Manufacturing
3-Communications
4-Power

Exploration with Tools and Processes

5-Construction
6-Transportation

Utilization of Materials and Forces

7-Wood, Ceramics, Drawing, Plastics
8-Metals, Graphic Arts, Electricity, Power Mechanics

Experiences in Industrial Technology

9-12 *Basic Series*
Ceramics, Electricity, Graphic Arts, Mechanical Drawing, Metals, Plastics, Power Mechanics, Woods

9-12 *Technology Series*
Graphics Technology, Power Technology, Production Technology

Industriology, Wisconsin State University

Development started in 1965 on an improved means of aiding boys and girls to learn about industry in our developing society through an updated industrial arts curriculum. Two federally funded programs—a Prospective Teacher Fellowship Program (1966-67) and an Experienced Teacher Fellowship Program (1967-68)—provided financial support for the efforts.

The industriology program is designed to provide a basic understanding and interpretation of industry for all students. It is intended to supplement, revise, and modify existing industrial arts programs within existing facilities. It is not intended to replace industrial arts as a curriculum, although the term *industriology* is intended to replace *industrial arts*.

Concepts and materials are being developed by university staff personnel, graduate students, and teachers in field test centers. Materials are being printed and distributed through Wisconsin State project personnel. Twelve schools in the Platteville area are cooperating and providing laboratory facilities and field test support.

This innovation has been planned as a four-phase process. Phase I, Development and Structure of Industry, for all boys and girls in grades 7, 8, or 9, has been completed. Materials available for use in this phase include a Study Guide, Information and Job Sheets, Teaching Plan and Activity Sheets, Instructional Aids, and a slide set. Phase II, Basic Elements and Processes of Industry, for grades 9, 10, or 11, is still under development. Some "module" instructional materials presently available for experimental use include Single-Family Dwelling Design, Time and Motion Study, Industrial Advertising, Process Planning, and Product Development. Phase III, Modern Industries, for grades 10, 11, or 12, and Phase IV, Vocational and Occupational Guidance, for grades 11 or 12, are still in the planning and development stage.

Industriology is not intended to require special facilities; existing industrial arts laboratories should prove adequate. It requires only single-period daily blocks of time and readily adapts to the semester plan. Relatively speaking, this need not be an expensive program to implement. Major expenditures would be for printed materials, inservice training, audiovisual equipment and materials, and probably some professional consultation services in the beginning. Teacher willingness and desire to implement this program would be fundamental to its success. It would require quite a good deal of extra effort and preparation by the teacher. (Requests for further information and assistance in implementing industriology in your school system should be addressed to Director, Industriology Project, Department of Industrial Education, Wisconsin State University at Platteville, Platteville, Wisconsin 53818.)

Galaxy Plan, Detroit Public Schools

The galaxy approach to educating young people for the world of work results from the impact of the Detroit Public Schools' report, "Preparing Pupils for the World of Work" (1962), the deliberations of the Research Council of the Greater Cities Program for School Improvement, and the contributions of many educators, business and industry personnel, and lay people. The challenge of preparing a student for the correct one of over 40,000 kinds of jobs is tremendous.

This plan is one element in the three-pronged approach to a total educational system: career preparation (exploration of occupation galaxies or clusters, selection of a family of occupations, and depth training in a specific occupation), basic education (language, mathematics, social studies, and sciences), and personal development (psychology, health, creative arts, and cultural arts).

Three objectives have been established to undergird this approach to career preparation:

1. To provide each student with a more efficient opportunity to learn about the world of work
2. To provide each student with a better opportunity through actual laboratory experiences to choose the career he would like to follow
3. To provide every student (including full-time general and college preparatory students) with a manipulative skill that would be of immediate value to an employer.

The basic premise for the galaxy approach to career preparation is that occupational families may be grouped into four major clusters: materials and processes, visual communication, energy and propulsion, and personal services. The grouping of knowledge and manipulative and attitudinal skills into the four major clusters accounts for calling the plan the galaxy approach, since instruction is based on exposing the student to a variety of skills and knowledge common to a galaxy of occupations within each major group.

To provide an articulated educational program from grades 7 through 12, the galaxy approach is structured to consist of three phases. Exploratory experiences are provided in Phase I (junior high). These experiences occur in each of the four clusters or families as students rotate on a semester basis. In Phase II (grade 10) the student is given a chance to explore a reduced field of occupational possibilities. In Phase III (grades 11 and 12) the student—with the assistance of teachers, counselors, and parents—

may select a specific cluster in which to specialize. These two-year programs are designed to equip every student with a salable skill.

(Further information may be secured from the Department of World of Work Education, Vocational Education, Detroit Public Schools, Detroit, Michigan.)

Interdisciplinary Programs

Correlated programs are not new to the field of industrial arts. Their history can be easily traced to programs in other fields, core-curriculum efforts of the 30's, and attempts to make learning more relevant by using experiences and expertise from other fields. In the early and middle 1960's, considerable impetus for programs of this type came from the Ford Foundation and subsequently from other groups and agencies.

The primary rationale for such programs is the premise that education should be a unifying experience rather than a series of unrelated and self-contained classes. Two basic types of plans can be grouped under the general heading of integrative programs: (a) correlation with other subject areas and (b) identification of commonalities within an area. The many programs that stress correlation between industrial arts and other subject areas, especially three sponsored by the Ford Foundation, are of particular interest.

The Correlated Curriculum Project in New York City, centered around the areas of business, health, and industry, has been in operation since 1966. It is designed as a laboratory-centered, career experience program with interrelated activities in mathematics, science, and English, providing a correlated instructional program during each of the three semesters of study in business, health, and industry. Courses in such areas as social sciences, music, and literature are not correlated, but every effort is made to draw up the natural relationships. When they have determined their basic occupational direction, students proceed to specialize in one of the broad areas. Experimental data suggests a high level of success in terms of dropout rates, attendance rates, and graduate performances.

The Richmond Plan in Richmond, California, developed in 1961 in cooperation with San Francisco State College, is based on the same rationale, but focuses on four integrated and correlated courses (English, science, mathematics, and technical) beginning in the eleventh grade. Pretechnical students in this plan study appropriate lessons in each of the areas, using content from the other areas for constant reinforcement.

The Partnership Vocational Education Project is a demonstration project that focuses on interpreting contemporary industry. While based at Central Michigan University in an industrial teacher preparation program, it is in operation in several Michigan secondary schools. Since 1965, the Project has maintained a program in which industrial education is the focal point, supported by correlated experiences in English, mathematics, physics, and chemistry. It also draws on a partnership between secondary schools, industry, community colleges, and the university.

Further information on these programs can be obtained from—

Director
Correlated and Pre-technical Programs
Board of Education, City of New York
480 Pacific Street
Brooklyn, New York 11217.

Director
Center for Technological Education
San Francisco State College
15 Southgate Avenue
Daly City, California 94015.

Chairman
Department of Industrial Education and Technology
Central Michigan University
Mt. Pleasant, Michigan 48858.

Summary

There are many approaches to the teaching of industrial arts. Whatever their organization and purposes, all instructional programs recognize the inherent value of providing activity-oriented learning experiences for the student.

Our investment of local, state, and federal funds in the furniture, equipment, and supplies to support an exposure to industrial arts programs is enormous and unmatched anywhere else in the world. It represents a commitment to maintaining the highest standard of living known to man.

The protection of our environment is one of the greatest challenges facing us today. To improve social and cultural conditions, there is a need for continuing review of the patterns of school organization, curriculums, and teacher education.

Local administrative and supervisory personnel must share responsibility for effective implementation of instruction in industrial arts. Philosophy, rationale, approaches, and organization may provide the framework for an instructional program, but successful implementation is dependent upon teacher performance and the support the teacher receives from his administration.

BIBLIOGRAPHY

1. American Industrial Arts Association. *Developing Human Potential Through Industrial Arts.* Proceedings of the Twenty-Seventh Annual Convention (Tulsa). Washington, D.C.: the Association, 1965.
2. ———. *Frontiers in Industrial Arts Education.* Proceedings of the Twenty-Eighth Annual Convention (San Francisco). Washington, D.C.: the Association, 1966.
3. ———. *Industrial Arts and Technology—Past, Present and Future.* Proceedings of the Twenty-Ninth Annual Convention (Philadelphia). Washington, D.C.: the Association, 1967.
4. ———. *Man-Science-Technology.* Proceedings of the Thirty-Second Annual Convention (Louisville). Washington, D.C.: the Association, 1970.
5. ———. *New Concepts in Industrial Arts.* Proceedings of the Thirtieth Annual Convention (Minneapolis). Washington, D.C.: the Association, 1968.
6. ———. *Where the Action Is.* Proceedings of the Thirty-First Annual Convention (Las Vegas). Washington, D.C.: the Association, 1969.
7. Cochran, Leslie H. *Innovative Programs in Industrial Education.* New York: McKnight & McKnight, 1970.
8. Dudley, Arthur J. "Periscoping Contemporary Industrial Arts Programs." *School Shop* 28: 33-35; November 1968. (Condensed in *Education Digest* 34: 41-43; January 1969.)
9. Maine State Department of Education. *Industrial Arts Technology: A Study of American Industry.* Augusta: the Department, 1965.
10. New York State Department of Education. *Early Secondary Industrial Arts, An Instructional Guide.* Albany: the Department, 1967.
11. ———. *The Secondary School Curriculum of New York State, A Handbook for Administrators.* Albany: the Department, 1970.

11

Mathematics Education

It is a truism that mathematics education—like education in any discipline and, indeed, education in general—is an ongoing process. At any given time there may be either a state of relative equilibrium between what should be going on and what actually is going on or a state of considerable activity marked by serious reconsiderations. An excellent study of this phenomenon as it relates to mathematics education appears in the 1970 yearbook of the National Council of Teachers of Mathematics (NCTM), *A History of Mathematics Education in the United States and Canada* (37).

While in the first third of the century the hope was somehow to reach the ideal (the definitive program as to content, organization, and methods), in recent decades there has been increasing acceptance of the concept of the permanently evolving program. There have been relatively long periods during which the changes taking place were small and minor. However, these periods have been becoming increasingly shorter, and the needs for more fundamental changes and for a greater number of them have been becoming more urgent. The major cause, of course, is the tremendous knowledge explosion and the fantastic (even terrifying) increase in the rates of change of all the processes in the world that affect all education—including mathematics education.

Emerging Trends in Curriculum Content

Background

Practically everybody is familiar with the phrase "revolution in school mathematics" as it has been used for the last 15 years. The phrase represents almost colossal efforts to update, improve, and change significantly mathematics teaching and content at all levels in American schools. The period immediately after World War II was the time at which momentum for change began to build. With the publishing of the *Report of the Commission on Mathematics* (10) in the late 1950's, the "revolution" got into full swing.

The Commission's *Report* stressed a nine-point program for college-capable students:

1. Strong preparation, in *both* concepts and skills, for college mathematics at the level of calculus and analytic geometry.
2. Understanding of the nature and role of deductive reasoning—in algebra, as well as in geometry.
3. Appreciation of mathematical structure ("patterns")—for example, properties of natural, rational, real, and complex numbers.
4. Judicious use of unifying ideas—sets, variables, functions, and relations.
5. Treatment of inequalities along with equations.
6. Incorporation with plane geometry of some coordinate geometry, and essentials of solid geometry and space perception.
7. Introduction in grade 11 of fundamental trigonometry—centered on coordinates, vectors, and complex numbers.
8. Emphasis in grade 12 on elementary functions (polynomial, exponential, circular).
9. Recommendation of additional alternative units for grade 12: either introductory probability with statistical applications, or an introduction to modern algebra.

The teacher will recognize this prescription for a mathematics curriculum as far different from the one he encountered as a secondary student. The Commission *Report* was a clear attempt to influence change through the work of mathematicians, mathematics teachers, and teacher trainers (10, p. xii). The work of various experimental curriculum development projects had the same objective. Such projects as the University of Maryland Project, the School Mathematics Study Group, the University of Illinois Committee on School Mathematics, the Madison Project, and others attempted to develop models of curriculums and teaching approaches to serve as guideposts for school administrators and teachers in their planning. The philosophy guiding the various projects embraced the following ideas, in addition to those referred to in the Commission's nine-point program (2, pp. 116-17):

1. Promote mathematical ideas.
2. Emphasize the importance of strong teacher training programs.
3. Emphasize the *structure* of mathematics and *precision* in use of language.

4. Emphasize teaching by discovery and teaching for meaning and understanding.
5. Emphasize the applications of mathematics.
6. Build curricula around various unifying concepts from kindergarten through grade 12, using a spiraling approach.
7. Abandon drill for drill's sake, and select drill carefully to reinforce learning and enhance understanding.
8. Emphasize psychological research in the teaching and learning of mathematics.

The typical program used in American classrooms at present is, in large part, a derivative of these curriculum models.

The Present and the Future

But what new content is emerging in the curriculum now, and what content will appear in the next decade? Present curriculum work aims at incorporating roughly the following mathematical content (4, 15):

1. *Arithmetic Number Systems*
    - Understanding numbers, with *set* as the key idea.
    - Counting numbers, with the associated ideas of matching (correspondence), equivalence, comparison of sets, and various properties of sets.
    - Naming numbers, including work in nondecimal numeration systems.
    - Addition as an operation, using the operation of union of sets; properties of the operation.
    - Subtraction as an operation, using the idea of a remainder set, the idea of an inverse operation, or operation on a number line; properties of the operation.
    - Algorithms of addition and subtraction, using nondecimal numeration systems.
    - Multiplication as an operation, using the idea of repeated addition, Cartesian product defined on sets, and properties of the operation.
    - Division as an operation, using the idea of an inverse operation, splitting a set into subsets, or repeated subtraction; properties of the operation.
    - Algorithms of multiplication and division.
    - Prime numbers and factorization of composite numbers into primes.
    - Modular or clock arithmetic and properties of operations.
    - Extending the system of natural numbers to the systems of integers and rationals; the properties of operations defined on these sets.

- Decimals and related exponent notation.
- Extending the rational numbers to the system of real numbers; properties of operations defined on this set.

2. *Algebraic Systems*
   - The concept of a mathematical group, with many and varied examples (e.g., addition of integers, rigid transformations of the plane, symmetries of a square, addition in clock arithmetic, etc.).
   - The concept of a field, with many and varied examples (e.g., addition and multiplication in clock arithmetic, addition and multiplication of real numbers, etc.).
   - Sequences and series.
   - Extending the real numbers to the system of complex numbers, and the properties of operations defined on this set.
   - Vectors, operations defined on vectors, and vector spaces; examples of these ideas.
   - Linear transformations and matrices.

3. *Geometry and Measurement*
   - Geometric shapes such as cubes, cylinders, etc., and the ideas of point, line, plane, and space.
   - Incidence properties such as intersecting and nonintersecting lines and planes.
   - Curves and polygonal figures.
   - Angles.
   - Congruence, thought of first as one figure fitting onto another; classification of geometric figures.
   - Measurement of length—assignment of numbers to compare characteristics of objects, including such things as transitivity of length, precision, and error of measurement.
   - Angle measurement.
   - Area of closed regions of a plane.
   - Volume of solids.
   - Congruence and rigid motions, using the ideas and terminology of mappings and transformations: translations, reflections, and rotations.
   - Vectors and properties of operations defined on vectors.*
   - Measures, including measures of line segments and angles.
   - Triangle congruence.
   - Perpendicularity and parallelism of lines.
   - Synthetic, vector, coordinate, and transformational approaches to geometry at the high school level.

4. *Functions*
   - Using the idea of a set as the fundamental notion, covering relations, mappings, and functions in depth, giving symbolic, verbal, and graphical treatments of the ideas.*
5. *Applications*
   - Applying mathematical ideas and reasoning in mathematics, sciences, and everyday situations. Emphasis is placed on problem formulation, analyses of problem situations, and methods of solutions.*

Not all the elements of the above skeletal outline have achieved equally uniform, extended, and universal acceptance. Those that have been accepted least are marked by an asterisk (*). These topics are receiving attention in only a small number of schools, even though textbooks are giving them increasing space and treatment. However, they are likely to gain increasing attention during the next decade.

Moreover, the basic ideas and methods of mathematical logic, probability, statistics, and calculus are making their way into school programs. This trend is expected to continue in the immediate future, with perhaps more far-reaching changes in the distant future. More emphasis will also be placed on mathematics as a basis for understanding computers and the related technology.

A number of comments seem in order regarding the above outline. First, the reader may observe that some of the content was part of his undergraduate training in mathematics. It is indeed true that much "college-level" mathematics has been moved to the secondary level, with subsequent movement of "secondary-level" mathematics to earlier grade levels. These shifts have been made possible by removing some "old" content, cutting back on drill for drill's sake, and making use of unifying concepts and the spiraling technique in curriculum development. Thus, many abstract notions are now introduced at the elementary level in very concrete form, with subsequent treatment of the same ideas later at higher grade levels. The treatment becomes more extensive and sophisticated as the student progresses through the curriculum; we now find students successfully studying mathematics from a quite formal and rigorous point of view in the late secondary years.

Use of unifying concepts and the spiraling technique has also made it possible to break down the traditional compartmentalization of the mathematics curriculum. It is now common to find algebraic and geometric ideas introduced in an integrated fashion at all levels of the curriculum. Similarly, ideas from probability and statistics are built into the curriculum starting at the elementary levels. The latest example, in the form of an experimental project using these curriculum development ideas, is the Secondary School Mathematics Curriculum Improvement Study. This project is striving to develop a completely integrated curriculum for grades 7 to 12 and is succeeding in bringing even more undergraduate-level mathematics to college-bound students at the secondary level.

Contrary to what might be expected, the period of experimentation in curriculum organization in mathematics that has continued for the past 15 years has not resulted in a single dominant pattern. Instead, we appear to be entering a period of ever-increasing diversity of patterns in the organization and application of knowledge in mathematics education. For each emerging concept there is an identifiable counterproposition. To each generalization about curriculum patterns there are obvious exceptions. For these reasons school administrators should have some familiarity with the great number of ideas they will encounter in connection with the mathematics curriculum, for in the last analysis, the administrators will have to depend on subjective judgment along with objective evidence in deciding which mathematics curriculum may be good for their school.

Less importance is now attached to work in other bases than was the case in the early days of modern mathematics. Other bases yield different numeration systems only, and these are not as important as different number systems. While sets are still important and will continue to be important, there is a growing awareness on the part of mathematics teachers that the major emphasis should be on sets as useful tools in terms of language and symbolism to teach other concepts, rather than on sets for their own sake. Set theory is not taught in lower grade levels, but the student is introduced to a useful language that should help him learn mathematics more easily.

The major trend today in the search for unifying ideas is toward using the concepts of relation and function (and their graphs) as unifying elements throughout almost the entire mathematics curriculum, starting as early as the primary grades. A rather formal definition of function is introduced as early as the fifth grade. High school algebra texts are being rewritten with the relation and function concepts as the prevailing and unifying ideas. Plane geometry texts are including more coordinate geometry. The use of the function concept in this basic way is the direct result of a quarter century of urging on the part of prominent mathematicians and mathematics educators and is probably long overdue.

The mathematics programs of foreign countries are having an influence on the mathematics curriculum that is as yet extremely difficult to assess. In some ways, American mathematics education seems "behind" that of many foreign countries (not all Western European), because some foreign students study very sophisticated concepts at very early grade levels. Also, some countries have experimental programs using laboratory techniques and eliminating some of the boring formalism. School leaders should realize that American principles of education are different from those of foreign countries. In mathematics education, teachers are working with a large, heterogeneous group, from which many students would be dropped at an early grade in other countries. At least two current experimental programs, however, are based rather directly on foreign models.

Specific concepts in curriculum development at least partially traceable to increasing foreign influence include the following:

1. The introduction of vectors and transformations, especially at the junior high school level.
2. Experimentation with the laboratory approach in elementary and junior high school.
3. The use of Cuisenaire rods and other attribute blocks.
4. Consideration of introducing linear algebra before calculus.

The concepts that are emerging today may be classified into two general categories. They relate either to changes in subject matter or to changes in methodology or educational philosophy.

New Ideas in Content and Organization

New ideas emerging in the content and organization of mathematics education include the study of mathematics history, mathematics rather than arithmetic in elementary school, use of the metric system, algebra in grade 8, introduction of statistics and probability, varied patterns for plane geometry, advanced placement, a two-year algebra program, and alternatives to the traditional high school sequence.

In general, elementary and secondary mathematics is not arranged in the historical order in which it was developed. But units on mathematical history provide motivation, alternate ways of working problems, cultural information, and recreational value. In the coming years, applications of the history of mathematics will become even more important as a part of the emerging pattern of content. This trend is highlighted by the 1969 NCTM yearbook,

Historical Topics for the Mathematics Classroom (36). There is the likelihood that more courses will be organized from a historical point of view, based on the theme that mathematics is a cultural achievement of the human race and that any educated person needs to have some appreciation of it.

One continuing trend is the broadening of the meaning of the term *elementary school mathematics,* which has almost completely replaced *arithmetic* as a description of the subject matter. The elementary school student is exposed not only to the principles and practices of arithmetic, but also to many of the basic concepts from other areas of mathematics: solution of equations, intuitive geometry, measurements, coordinate systems, functions and relation, the language of sets, probability, number theory. Much of the work in percent, three-dimensional geometry, and square root, formerly taught in junior high school, has also become part of the elementary program. Since few or no concepts have been removed from the program, it should be evident that more is now expected from the pupil and that to teach all of this material to the average student in six years without sacrificing arithmetic skill is very difficult.

The increasing use of the metric system in this country, which may soon culminate in the complete adoption of the system for all everyday uses, is beginning to have a strong influence on the mathematics curriculum. Metric concepts are found in elementary textbooks, and several weeks of instruction are generally devoted to them on the junior high level. Some applied mathematics problems in high school use metric units. For the future, it is optimistic to hope that students will be "bilingual" in measurement—able to use the English and the metric systems equally well.

The increasing tendency to offer a regular algebra course to qualified students in the eighth grade is a noticeable development in curriculum organization. This course does not differ in any way from the usual ninth-grade programs, except that the students are a year younger and the course is sometimes taught by teachers with an elementary rather than secondary orientation. It is often assumed that students who take algebra in grade 8 will continue to take a total of five years of high school mathematics, including a year of analytic geometry and calculus. Exactly which students should take algebra in the eighth grade rather than the ninth is still debatable.

One of the modern branches of mathematics currently being introduced in secondary school (and sometimes in elementary school) is probability and statistics. It is uncommon to devote a year, or even a semester, to the study of statistics and probability; the material is usually inserted in algebra courses as an application. It also appears in some general and applied mathematics courses. It is often used for enrichment activities, sometimes in connection with a computer. It is possible that in the next five years some regular sequence of topics in statistics and probability will be developed and will come to constitute a recognized and integral part of the secondary mathematics curriculum, but such a trend is not yet certain.

No one can safely predict what is going to happen to the traditional tenth grade geometry course, but many mathematics educators feel that great changes will take place in the near future. The dominant course pattern today is still the formal course in Euclidean geometry, with an introduction to the geometry of three dimensions and to coordinate geometry. One emerging trend already in evidence is toward including brief introductions to such other geometries as projective geometry, finite geometries, non-Euclidean geometries, and topology. A second emerging pattern is the introduction of the concept of transformations. In the next few years, it is expected that geometry courses with transformations as the unifying theme will become more common at the high school level, and it is possible that these will eventually replace traditional geometry as the prevailing pattern. Another possibility is to increase the importance of coordinate geometry until it becomes the major theme in the tenth grade course. Still another possibility is to teach intuitive or informal geometry courses, even for the college-bound, with less emphasis on proof and postulates and more stress on practical applications. In any event, it seems reasonable to predict that fewer and fewer students will be spending an entire year in a development restricted to plane Euclidean geometry. What the typical pattern of high school geometry will be in ten years is far from settled at the moment.

Closely connected with the teaching of algebra in grade 8 is the trend toward advanced placement, whereby students may receive college credit for up to a year of calculus taken at the high school level. Advanced placement requires taking a formal test through an established procedure; however, not all colleges will give credit under these circumstances. In some cases, students may receive credit for a college calculus course if they have had the same material in high school, even if they have not taken the advanced placement test. There are a great variety of twelfth grade courses for the superior student, and it appears likely that they will become increasingly popular as advanced placement becomes more widespread.

With the enrollment of almost every student in algebra classes in some schools, it has been necessary to provide for those who cannot complete the regular course in a year. Some students take two years to complete the regular first year of algebra. In some schools, a course called "introduction to algebra" is taught for one or both of these years. Because of the large numbers of inadequately prepared students who want to take an algebra course rather than a general mathematics course, the two-year algebra program has been very useful in some schools, and some of the students have continued on to geometry.

Similarly, in some districts new mathematics sequences, some as long as four years, have been devised. Sometimes these alternate sequences integrate much of the traditional material, rather than segmenting it into yearly blocks. Sometimes they place more emphasis on intuition and applications and less emphasis on postulation development or proof. Although designed primarily for students not going to college, these courses can be taken by many who do plan to attend college. Colleges seem to be becoming less concerned than they once were with the specific high school mathematics courses taken. In particular, relatively large numbers of economically deprived students with little previous mathematical background are taking college mathematics courses.

Changing Philosophy

To a large extent the emerging mathematical content is being embedded in curriculums for college-bound students. School administrators and curriculum coordinators are now faced with the question of content for students who are not college-bound. Ferguson (17, pp. 166-67) has some suggestions to offer. Essentially, he calls for offering the same mathematical content at a different pace. Average mathematics students would cover somewhat less mathematics (in varying amounts) than would accelerated students.

Perhaps the greatest challenge facing mathematics educators today is to provide mathematical instruction that is *relevant* to the needs of students and society. For those students who are interested and highly motivated in mathematics, the programs now in existence are very good and appropriate. However, some students are not interested in mathematics for use in further study of mathematics, physics, engineering, statistics, and so on; their primary interests are in the fine arts or nonphysical sciences. For these students we need to develop curriculums that emphasize the historic, cultural, biographic, philosophic, artistic, and social aspects of mathematics. Such emphases in the mathematics curriculum can make a contribution not only to a student's knowledge of mathematics, but also to his appreciation of the relations between mathematics and other discipline areas. They may also pay dividends in shaping more positive attitudes toward mathematics. Shaping such attitudes is as important as imparting specific mathematical knowledge (3, 16). If school administrators, teachers, and mathematics educators are to provide the best possible mathematical studies in the school programs, then we must make available different kinds of curriculums that provide not only for differing levels of ability but also for different levels of *interest* in mathematics.

Providing mathematics curriculums for all types of students requires curriculum materials and teaching techniques that illustrate how mathematical ideas are related to and can be used in various other discipline areas, and how mathematical studies are relevant to both individual and occupational needs. Experimentation is now under way, primarily dealing with liberal arts approaches to mathematics at the undergraduate level; the trend will continue and will extend down into the secondary level in the near future.

Emerging Trends in Organization and Method

Organization Based on the Way Students Learn

The current philosophy of teaching for meaning shows no sign of giving way to any other emerging philosophy. Encouraging intuition and discovery and making sure of understanding before developing skills are the basis for the current pattern: intuitive material followed by generalizations followed by practice. Fortunately, more forceful statements by mathematics educators are correcting a common misconception about the role of practice. The introduction of modern mathematics was not meant to lead to the elimination of practice. Mathematical skills are as important as ever. Indeed, the truth of the matter is that curriculum designers expected the introduction of modern mathematics to *raise* skill levels, because the understanding would come first. But teachers often spent too much time in concept development at the expense of time that might have been devoted to skills. In other words, the concepts of modern mathematics were not at fault so much as the way these ideas were implemented. Now the emerging trend is to try to achieve the correct balance between concepts and skills. There is reason to believe that *less* practice, applied at the right time and in the right way, can accomplish as much as extended practice without understanding or motivation. It is hoped that students in the future will have even greater use of mathematical skills, without any sacrifice of concepts or understanding. Administrators and the public have a right to expect adequate performance on tests of mathematical skills.

The Spiral Approach

Most current textbook series in mathematics and most mathematics educators seem to advocate the spiral approach. In simple terms, this approach calls for a topic to be taught several times, each time at a slightly more sophisticated level. For example, sets are taught in every grade from 1 through 9 and beyond, but the program is not the same in any year. The third grade teacher, for example, is not finishing the job of teaching sets, but is reviewing what the students know and extending this knowledge. Topics are not taught to completion in any one grade level, nor are skills always mastered at an adult level the first time a topic is introduced. A thorough understanding of the spiral concept is necessary to gauge the amount of practice necessary before leaving a topic.

The Mathematics Laboratory

One of the most interesting of all the emerging trends in the mathematics curriculum is the use of laboratory techniques. Some schools have set aside rooms called mathematics laboratories, featuring visual aids, measuring devices, computing equipment, and other resources. The learning activities emphasize experimentation, the use of intuition and discovery, applications, and problem solving, in contrast to formal classroom procedures based on sequential textbook content. To some extent, the inspiration for the mathematics laboratory is found in such primary school programs as the Nuffield Project in England, but its most widespread use in the United States so far seems to be in the junior high school. There will be future attempts to apply the relatively unstructured approach of the mathematics laboratory to the teaching of the structured college preparatory sequence in mathematics.

Use of Computers and Desk Calculators

It is necessary to mention the increased use of small, desk-size computers in secondary schools. While they have not yet influenced the organization of the basic curriculum, they are providing extensions and enrichment experiences, and there is the growing possibility that some secondary school courses may be rewritten with a greater stress on computer-oriented mathematics. The use of flow charts in junior high school texts is one example of such an orientation.

Individualized Programs

Normally the organization of the mathematics curriculum is such that groups of students study the same basic content. An emerging concept is that the basic organization should be made flexible enough to provide an individual "prescription" for an individual student. At both the elementary and the secondary levels, individualized programs are being used in ways that indicate they are no longer experimental. Instead of the textbook or even a structured sequence of material providing the basis for the organization, it is the needs of the individual that determine which materials will be provided. In general, under this plan, the classroom situation emphasizes supervised study rather than guided discussion or lecture. The quality of individualized programs is subject to question, and the evidence that all students can benefit is scanty, but there seems little doubt that the programs offer promise, especially for students who have not been making sufficient progress under the more traditional organization of content.

Emerging Trends in Evaluation

The current emphasis on behavioral objectives on the part of some educators has caused mathematics teachers to give attention to what is expected in the way of student performance for each specific section, page, or idea introduced. The achievement of these objectives must be measured in terms of performance on an objective test. Starting with behavioral objectives and organizing the curriculum accordingly may eventually result in the need for considerable restructuring of the sequence of mathematics topics.

A dominant trend seems to be to place less and less emphasis on standardized tests. There have been serious charges that they do not test minority students fairly, that they do not test for the objectives of the course, and that they are not appropriate for predicting the ability or future potential of students. However, college entrance tests and the advanced placement tests are still an important aspect of qualifying for college, and the organization of the high school mathematics curriculum is still dominated to a remarkable extent by what the colleges expect. Also, the emerging concept of performance contracting, if modified to meet many valid objectives, may cause those schools involved to restructure the mathematics curriculum so that goals are always measureable in terms of objective tests.

Summary

To repeat an earlier statement, the administrator will find a great diversity of patterns, with some conflicting and opposing trends. While the prevailing trend still appears to be toward greater abstraction and more mathematics at a lower level for many students, an opposite trend toward a lower level of sophistication, less emphasis on college-preparatory courses of a formal nature, and more emphasis on intuitive arguments is rapidly emerging. It is probable that in the next few years both trends will continue at once. The result may well be patterns of organization of material that can be adapted to the needs of individual classes and students, rather than the single traditional curriculum pattern once popular in mathematics.

A final word of warning on evaluation is in order. With national assessment and performance contracting the order of the day, administrators and mathematics educators will have to be alert and careful in their evaluation of such external measurements. Because of traditional and still widespread misunderstandings of what the outcomes of mathematical instruction should be, mathematics is peculiarly susceptible to abuse in attempts to measure outcomes. The ease with which the attainment of some skills—often useless ones and in meaningless contexts—can be tested makes mathematics an ideal subject for manipulation by unprofessional and unscrupulous operators.

BIBLIOGRAPHY

1. Ashlock, Robert B., and Herman, Wayne L., Jr. *Current Research in Elementary School Mathematics.* New York: Macmillan Co., 1970.
2. Becker, Jerry P. *The Scope of Mathematical Changes in Curriculum and Concept Since 1894.* New Brunswick, N.J.: Graduate School of Education, Rutgers University, 1968.
3. ———, and Traugot, Irving. *How Can We Justify the Teacher of Mathematics in the Secondary School?* New Brunswick, N.J.: Graduate School of Education, Rutgers University, 1971.
4. Begle, Edward G., and Richey, Herman G., editors. *Mathematics Education.* Sixty-Ninth Yearbook, National Society for the Study of Education. Chicago: University of Chicago Press, 1970.
5. Bidwell, James K., and Clason, Robert G. *Readings in the History of Mathematics Education.* Washington, D.C.: National Council of Teachers of Mathematics, 1970.
6. Biggs, Edith E., and MacLean, James R. *Freedom to Learn: An Active Learning Approach to Mathematics.* Don Mills, Ontario: Addison-Wesley Publishing Co., 1969.
7. Brown, Robert O., Jr. "New Mathematics for a New College." *Mathematics Teacher* 64: 123-26; February 1971.
8. Brydegaard, Marguerite, and Innskeep, James E., Jr., editors. *Readings in Geometry from The Arithmetic Teacher.* Washington, D.C.: National Council of Teachers of Mathematics, 1970.
9. Buffie, Edward G.; Welch, Ronald C.; and Paige, Donald D. *Mathematics: Strategies of Teaching.* Englewood Cliffs, N.J.: Prentice-Hall, 1968.
10. College Entrance Examination Board. *Report of the Commission on Mathematics: Program for College Preparatory Mathematics.* New York: the Board, 1959.
11. Conner, Forrest E., and Ellena, William J., editors. *Curriculum Handbook for School Administrators.* Washington, D.C.: American Association of School Administrators, 1967.
12. Copeland, Richard W. *How Children Learn Mathematics—Teaching Implications of Piaget's Research.* New York: Macmillan Co., 1970.
13. Davis, Robert B. *The Changing Curriculum: Mathematics.* Washington, D.C.: Association for Supervision and Curriculum Development, 1967.
14. Education Development Center. *Goals for the Correlation of Elementary Science and Mathematics: The Report of the Cambridge Conference on the Correlation of Science and Mathematics in the Schools.* Boston: Houghton Mifflin Co., 1969.
15. Educational Services Incorporated. *Goals for School Mathematics: The Report of the Cambridge Conference on School Mathematics.* Boston: Houghton Mifflin Co., 1963.
16. Eilber, Charles R. "College Preparatory Mathematics: Preparation for What?" *Mathematics Teacher* 61: 46-49; January 1968.

17. Ferguson, W. Eugene. "Current Reforms in the Mathematics Curricula—A Passing Phase or Progress?" *Mathematics Teacher* 57: 143-48; March 1964.

18. ———. "The Junior High School Mathematics Program—Past, Present, and Future." *Mathematics Teacher* 63: 383-90; May 1970.

19. Glennon, Vincent J., and Callahan, Leroy G. *Elementary School Mathematics: A Guide to Current Research.* Washington, D.C.: National Council of Teachers of Mathematics, 1968.

20. Grossman, Anne S. "Mid-nineteenth Century Methods for the 1970s." *Arithmetic Teacher* 18: 230-33; April 1971.

21. Henderson, Kenneth B. *Teaching Secondary School Mathematics.* "What Research Says to the Teacher," No. 9. Washington, D.C.: National Education Association and Association of Classroom Teachers, 1969.

22. Howes, Virgil M. *Individualizing Instruction in Science and Mathematics.* New York: Macmillan Co., 1970.

23. Johnson, Donovan A., and Rising, Gerald R. *Guidelines for Teaching Mathematics.* Belmont, Calif.: Wadsworth Publishing Co., 1967.

24. Joint Project on the Administration of Mathematics Programs. *Administrative Responsibility for Improving Mathematics Programs.* Washington, D.C.: American Association of School Administrators, Association for Supervision and Curriculum Development, National Association of Secondary School Principals, National Council of Teachers of Mathematics, 1965.

25. Kramer, Claas, editor. *Problems in the Teaching of Elementary School Mathematics: A Book of Readings.* Boston: Allyn & Bacon, 1970.

26. Kramer, Edna E. *The Nature and Growth of Modern Mathematics.* New York: Hawthorn Books, 1970.

27. Lockard, J. David, editor. *Seventh Report of the International Clearinghouse on Science and Mathematics Curricular Developments, 1970.* College Park, Md.: Teaching Center, University of Maryland, 1970.

28. Mayor, John R. "Science and Mathematics: 1970s—A Decade of Change." *Arithmetic Teacher* 17: 293-97; April 1970.

29. McIntosh, Jerry A., editor. *Perspectives on Secondary Mathematics Education.* Englewood Cliffs, N.J.: Prentice-Hall, 1971.

30. National Association of Elementary School Principals and National Council of Teachers of Mathematics. *Teaching Mathematics in the Elementary School—What's Needed? What's Happening?* Washington, D.C.: the Association and the Council, 1970.

31. National Conference of State Supervisors of Mathematics. *Programs in Mathematics for Low Achievers.* Report to the National Conference of State Supervisors of Mathematics, University of Virginia, Charlottesville, Virginia, June 27-July 9, 1969. Washington, D.C.: National Science Foundation, U.S. Office of Education, 1970.

32. National Council of Teachers of Mathematics. *Computer-Assisted Instruction and the Teaching of Mathematics.* Washington, D.C.: the Council, 1969.

33. ———. *The Continuing Revolution in Mathematics.* Washington, D.C.: the Council, 1968.

34. ———. *Experiences in Mathematical Ideas.* Vol. 1, with Teaching Package. Washington, D.C.: the Council, 1970.

35. ———. *Experiences in Mathematical Ideas.* Vol. 2, with Teaching Package. Washington, D.C.: the Council, 1970.

36. ———. *Historical Topics for the Mathematics Classroom.* Thirty-First Yearbook. Washington, D.C.: the Council, 1969.

37. ———. *History of Mathematics Education in the United States and Canada.* Thirty-Second Yearbook. Washington, D.C.: the Council, 1970.

38. ———. *The Teaching of Secondary School Mathematics.* Thirty-Third Yearbook. Washington, D.C.: the Council, 1970.

39. National Science Foundation. *Curriculum Activities in Mathematics for Elementary and Secondary Schools.* Washington, D.C.: the Foundation, 1970.

40. Nuffield Mathematics Teaching Project. *Computation and Structure.* New York: John Wiley & Sons, 1968.

41. ———. *Computation and Structure, 3.* New York: John Wiley & Sons, 1968.

42. ———. *Mathematics Begins.* New York: John Wiley & Sons, 1968.

43. ———. *Shape and Size.* New York: John Wiley & Sons, 1968.

44. ———. *Shape and Size, 3.* New York: John Wiley & Sons, 1968.

45. Oettinger, Anthony G. *Run, Computer, Run: The Mythology of Educational Innovation, An Essay.* Cambridge, Mass.: Harvard University Press, 1969.

46. Picard, Anthony J. "Piaget's Theory of Development with Implications for Teaching Elementary School Mathematics." *School Science and Mathematics* 69: 275-80; April 1969.

47. Spitzer, Herbert F. *Teaching Elementary School Mathematics.* "What Research Says to the Teacher," No. 2. Washington, D.C.: National Education Association and Association of Classroom Teachers, 1970.

48. Suydam, Marilyn N. "Continuing the Math Revolution." *American Education* 6:26-35; January/February, 1970.

49. Williams, Irene S. "A Progress Report on the Implementation of the Recommendations of the Commission on Mathematics." *Mathematics Teacher* 63: 461-68; October 1970.

50. Willoughby, Stephen S. *Contemporary Teaching of Secondary School Mathematics.* New York: John Wiley & Sons, 1967.

51. Zoet, Charles J. "Computers in Mathematics Education." *Mathematics Teacher* 62: 563-67; November 1969.

12

Music Education

Emerging Curriculum Concepts

"Comprehensive music programs in all schools" is a major goal announced by the Music Educators National Conference (MENC) in 1970 after a year-long, nationwide project to identify the objectives of this group of professionals (9). School superintendents, too, probably would state this as one of their goals, for they have demonstrated over the years that they are convinced of the value of music as a subject for study in the schools. How can a superintendent tell whether his schools have a comprehensive music program that is abreast of the times? What is the nature of the curriculum for such a program?

The MENC goals and objectives project produced 35 specific objectives for the profession of music education. Three of these, selected for priority attention, describe the characteristics of a comprehensive music program for today's schools. MENC proposes to—

- Lead in efforts to develop programs of music instruction challenging to all students, whatever their sociocultural condition, and directed toward the needs of citizens in a pluralistic society.
- Lead in the development of programs of study that correlate performing, creating, and listening to music and encompass a diversity of musical behaviors.
- Advance the teaching of music of all periods, styles, forms and cultures.

A comprehensive music program, then, is "challenging to all students," recognizes "a diversity of musical behaviors," and involves "music of all periods, styles, forms and cultures." The purpose of such a program is to establish for every student a sound and permanent relationship with music. It is aimed at making all students aware of the many-faceted nature of the subject and helping each of them to build a relationship with music that gives satisfaction and personal growth during the school years and throughout life. Can the schools reasonably accept any less responsibility for musical art, when by giving some types of music a place of prime importance in their life-style, students so forcefully demonstrate readiness for participation and study?

Music for All

Elementary Schools. Experiences in music have traditionally been provided for all students in elementary schools of the United States. Ideally, childhood is a time to experience music through singing, listening, playing instruments, moving and dancing, composing, and experimenting with musical patterns. Such a curriculum involves children in performing, analyzing, and creating music; through these activities they derive the pleasures and insights of esthetic experience and develop musical skills (3). Music reading has been stressed in various degrees, depending mostly on the time available and the teacher's belief in the value of reading in relation to the values of other musical pursuits. Recent evidence that skill in reading musical notation transfers to skill in reading words may have an effect on the degree of emphasis (4).

Dissatisfaction with the level of understanding of music in most American schools led to the appointment of an Elementary Music Study Commission of the Music Educators National Conference. This group prepared a book, *The Study of Music in the Elementary School—A Conceptual Approach* (13), to help teachers bring about intellectual apprehension of music as a result of the student's participation in musical experiences. More and more elementary schools are turning to conceptual learning of music in the belief that the benefits will be longer lasting. The intellectual concepts of musical content—of sound sources, pitch, rhythm, timbre, and design—form the basis for the curriculum (17). Participative activities are the means of learning. It is believed that this fundamental approach to musical study can ensure a positive relationship to music for virtually all children.

These directions have obvious implications for organizing the elementary school program. In a majority of school systems, music has been the responsibility of the classroom teacher in a self-contained classroom. Music specialists, when provided, have helped in the preparation of instructional materials and with inservice education, but they have had only minimal contact with the children. If the curriculum is to deal with basic concepts of the discipline, the teacher must indeed know something more about the art than can be learned in a few methods classes.

MENC's Commission on Teacher Education has recommended—

> . . . that music in the elementary school be taught by music specialists. It recognizes, however, that this may not be feasible for every school at present. Moreover, even when there is a specialist assigned to a school, there will be times when the classroom teacher must take some responsibility for classroom musical experiences.

The Commission has developed a list of minimal musical competencies for classroom teachers (10). Some combination of the music specialist and classroom teachers who have these competencies is required to provide the desirable daily musical development of children.

The foundation of a comprehensive music program is a solidly based curriculum with concepts of musical content developed through ever-enlarging experiences. James Mursell's theory of "cyclical sequence" in which "any concept will occur many times with added meaning" (5) and Jerome Bruner's "spiral curriculum" in which "it is possible to introduce the child at an early age to the ideas and styles that make an educated man" (2) require that basic principles remain constant in ever-widening circles of understanding. Observation, analysis, and creative manipulation of sound sources, pitch, rhythm, timbre, and design continue to be the basic musical explorations. A primary child singing "Pop Goes the Weasel" develops a concept of rhythmic pulse as he claps or skips and of the rhythmic pattern as he sings the words and plays the pattern on a percussion instrument. An older child, developing more complex rhythmic concepts, may hear, perform, or create two rhythmic patterns simultaneously. A young child listening to "Carillon" from *L'Arlesienne Suite,* by Bizet, may discover the three large sections of the musical design and learn to refer to them as "A, B, A." An older child will learn to recognize subsections within each large section and many of the musical relations of the parts to the whole.

Secondary Schools. Providing music for all students in the secondary schools offers a special challenge to music educators and administrators. Music is not likely to be a required subject in secondary schools, although many junior high schools do have some requirement and a few senior high schools require some esthetic experience for graduation. In order to interest a great number of students, the musical offerings in the secondary school must be varied. Success of a music program might better be judged by the percentage of the student body involved than by the performing ability of any select group.

In the secondary school, students should continue exploration of the nature of music and the development of skills begun earlier. Emphasis should be placed on developing critical abilities. Students should learn to go beyond "like" or "dislike" and "good" or "bad," to consider a musical work on the basis of its own content and purposes. There are standards for considering the effectiveness of composition and performance of the rock, soul, and country music so familiar and appealing to the students. But the basis for analysis is different from that for analyzing a Brahms symphony. Electronic music, chance music, jazz, and many other idioms of the twentieth century each require consideration in their own terms rather than in terms of a nineteenth-century work. The development of "a sense of responsibility for exercising . . . critical judgment for the improvement of the musical environment of [the student's] community" was one of the goals set forth in "The Arts in the Comprehensive Secondary School" (15).

Diversity of Musical Behaviors

Performance. Performance has always played an important part in music education in America and should continue to do so, since music is essentially a performing art. The traditional performing groups—choirs, bands, and orchestras—will continue to occupy a significant place in the school music curriculum, since they provide a means of studying examples of music literature of the past and present. Small ensembles, both vocal and instrumental, should provide other opportunities for studying music. These are increasing as part of the school offerings because of their value in developing individual musicianship.

In performance classes, emphasis should be placed on further development of musical concepts—on learnings that will be valuable long after the final performance of the particular composition. A band class learning to play a score or a chorus preparing to sing a choral composition should learn to perform the composition well and in the style the composer intended. In addition to the skills needed for a good performance, the students should know the general and historical setting of the composition; they should notice and understand the rhythmic, melodic, harmonic, and design principles used by the composer; they should relate the style of the composition to that of other works they hear on recordings. In other words, even in "Band" or "Chorus," students should study

"Music." Music teachers are encouraged to limit public performances to the number that allows in-depth musical study in performing classes.

Other types of performance have recently become a part of the curriculum. Stage bands playing big-band jazz have won increasing acceptance. Instruction in improvisation, as part of the stage band program and in other classes, has added a new dimension to music education.

Rock is part of the school scene in many communities, and through it music educators are reaching groups of students never before interested in school music performance. Guitar classes are often a part of the school music program, and class instruction in piano and organ has taken on a new vigor. Instruments such as the dulcimer and banjo and even the sitar are to be found in music rooms of schools that have recognized the importance of serving a diversity of musical interests. No secondary school student with a sincere interest in any type of music should have difficulty finding opportunity in a school system with a comprehensive music program.

Listening. Skill in listening should be taught young people no matter what their musical preferences or other musical pursuits may be. This important skill is needed whether a person is a casual consumer or an advanced performer of music. Only through listening to music can a person become acquainted with a reasonably large repertoire. The finest pianist can learn to play only a very small part of the music available for his instrument. This avenue of study makes it possible for a teacher to introduce many types of music and music for many performance media. He can teach the design principle of variations on a theme through the second movement of the Haydn *String Quartet in C Major* or through the work of a pop musician, such as Chad Stuart's "Pantheistic Study for Guitar and Large Bird." He can give students enjoyment and esthetic experience through the distinctive sounds of an organ prelude, a cello concerto, or an electronic work—in fact, through the whole rainbow of tone color available in recorded performance of music. Listening should be an integral part of every course in music. A comprehensive music program will provide opportunity for all students to develop discriminative listening skill.

Music is playing an important role in humanities and allied arts courses in many secondary schools (12). Administrators show great interest in these courses, because they realize that it is important for all citizens to have insight into the broad culture of human beings. Aware that music, properly understood, can deepen the understanding of history, literature, religion, and the other arts, music educators are generally ready to cooperate by helping students enlarge their listening repertoire and become more skilled listeners. Conversely, music educators know that the study of humanities and other arts can only deepen a student's empathy for music and for art in general. Music teachers are justified in insisting, however, that significant musical learnings should result from these academic unions. There must be sufficient time allotted in the course to make possible a satisfactory level of music learning. A properly trained music educator must be among those assigned to teach such courses.

Composing. Music is a creative as well as a performing art, and today's schools increasingly recognize the creative aspects of the school experience. The addition to the curriculum of improvisation, which is merely instantaneous composing, has been mentioned. The importance of original material to rock groups is one of the refreshing aspects of this phenomenon. Arranging is part of the stage band experience for many of the students.

Electronic music is a recent addition to the literature. Students composing in this medium are challenged to organize electronically produced sounds into something meaningful (8). In so doing they gain insight into compositional principles and processes that apply to all musical composition.

The comprehensive music program will provide opportunities for a student to engage in any musical behavior that interests him. A major thrust of MENC's Contemporary Music Project is development of courses in comprehensive musicianship, which integrate and synthesize principles of performance, composition, and analysis (6).

All Periods, Styles, Forms, and Cultures

Just as the music curriculum is no longer restricted to General Music, Band, Orchestra, and Chorus, the music being performed and studied through listening is not limited to Western art music. The study of the music of the "high culture" of the Western world is still a legitimate aim, of course; in fact, there has been an improvement in the quality of music taught in recent years. These changes in curricular content are significant because music of high quality is apt to be more satisfying esthetically and more stimulating intellectually.

But the teaching of Western music of high quality is now paralleled by the teaching of a greater *variety* of music in terms of eras and geographic sources. Performing groups are no longer limited to the music of the eighteenth and nineteenth centuries but are singing and playing music from ancient times and all other periods including the present. The different musics of Asia, the Pacific Islands, and South America are all a part of the good curriculum (16). A few high schools even have ethno-musicologists on their staffs. There is a healthy concern for the products of today's composers, inspired in part by MENC's Contemporary Music Project (7).

The music curriculum has been broadened also to include less sophisticated, less formal types of music. There is interest in the study of folk music and its relation to history, and in the development of American popular music. Jazz is an accepted part of the curriculum in many schools. The lyrics of currently popular songs are forcing the schools to give more serious attention to music's social significance.

Enjoyment

A comprehensive music program should make a difference in students' enjoyment of music. Superintendents complain that all too frequently music educators are so absorbed in maintaining what they consider to be standards of musical quality that the life is squeezed out of the program. In community studies conducted recently by an MENC staff member, superintendents stressed the importance of demonstrating the joy that music can bring. "There are not enough teachers who can communicate with the 'other 80 percent' so that kids get real enjoyment out of music." "We must not kill enthusiasm." "I want students who will say, 'Oh boy! Music!' "

A music educator who thinks his job depends on bringing home an A rating in a festival or pleasing the football crowd needs the superintendent's counsel in directing his energies to a more comprehensive program that will lead to genuine enjoyment for a greater number of students (1).

Emerging Administrative Considerations

Evaluation

In recent years music educators—like most other teachers—have been engaged in stating curricular objectives in behavioral terms. Using concepts of musical content as the basis of the curriculum provides a means of evaluating the learning that is taking place. Many music departments have developed 12-year goals for the program (14), along with specific objectives for each level of instruction and for each course. As a discipline, music can benefit by such treatment so long as the joy of music is not overlooked.

Credit

If music is indeed to become more a part of the high school curriculum, the matter of credit must be considered. As one superintendent has observed, "the pressures of the college-bound schedule are a deterrent to more music in the school." The development in 1971 of an Advanced Placement Music Test may be some indication that music credit is being more readily accepted by colleges. It also points up the important fact that credit in music should indicate that some significant musical learning has been accomplished. Notwithstanding the plea for enjoyment in school music, the experiences should result in musical learnings that last a lifetime. If such knowledge results, there is no reason to consider credit in music as different from credit in other subjects, even in determining class rank. The Joint Committee on School-College Relations of the National Association of Secondary School Principals and the American Association of Collegiate Registrars and Admissions Officers has for some time recommended that all credit subjects be included in computing class rank.

Faculty

The Teacher Education Commission of the Music Educators National Conference has set as its objective the development of teacher education programs in music that will provide "music educators who are competent, flexible, creative, curious, and prepared to survive and flourish in a world of change" (11). Such teachers are necessary if a comprehensive music program is to be successful. Superintendents are encouraged to join the Music Educators National Conference in calling for a new type of teacher education in music.

Summary

Educational inertia is as likely to be found in a music department as anywhere else. Hence it is not to be expected that schools will develop comprehensive music programs immediately upon the announcement of this as a goal. Superintendents can encourage the movement and look for evidence of it, however. Affirmative answers to the following questions would indicate that staff are aware of what contemporary music education is and are attempting to develop a comprehensive music program:

1. Are most students touched directly in some way by the music program of the schools?
2. Are performing groups, without sacrificing an adequate standard of performance, studying the music they play or sing and gaining a genuine understanding of it?
3. Is music of all periods from the middle ages to the present taught in the schools? Are students hearing and performing music of other cultures, jazz, and the informal music of their own culture?
4. Is there a strong interest in experimenting with musical sound, improvising, and composing? Are these activities used in many musical learning experiences?
5. Does school music study develop discriminating listeners?
6. Is there concern for development of skills that students can use after they leave school? Is this concern demonstrated in work with small performing ensembles as well as large groups?
7. Is there a renewed seriousness of purpose in achieving some definite goals for music learning in the elementary school? Is this reflected in the increased call upon music specialists?
8. Is there a spelled-out, written-down curriculum for all music courses? Are the curricular goals stated in behavioral terms where possible?
9. Are the music teachers receptive to all student musical interests, no matter how naive and unsophisticated?
10. Is there evidence of true enjoyment of musical experiences on the part of at least the majority of the students?

BIBLIOGRAPHY

1. Boyle, J. David, and Lathrop, Robert. "The Impact Experience: An Evaluation." *Music Educators Journal* 59: 42-47; January 1973.

2. Bruner, Jerome S. *The Process of Education.* Cambridge, Mass.: Harvard University Press, 1965. Chapter 3, "Readiness for Learning," pp. 33-54.

3. Landis, Beth, and Carder, Polly. *The Eclectic Curriculum in American Music: Contributions of Dalcroze, Kodaly, and Orff.* Washington, D.C.: Music Educators National Conference, 1972.

4. Movsesian, Edwin A. "Reading Music and Reading Words." *Today's Education* 58: 42-43; January 1969.

5. Mursell, James L. "Growth Processes in Music Education." *Basic Concepts in Music Education.* Fifty-Seventh Yearbook, Part I, National Society for the Study of Education. Chicago: University of Chicago Press, 1958. Chapter VI, pp. 140-62.

6. Music Educators National Conference. *Comprehensive Musicianship: An Anthology of Evolving Thought.* Contemporary Music Project, No. 5. Washington, D.C.: the Conference, 1971.

7. ———. *Contemporary Music for Schools.* Contemporary Music Project, No. 1. Washington, D.C.: the Conference, 1965.

8. ———. *Electronic Music.* Washington, D.C.: the Conference, 1968.

9. ———. "Goals and Objectives for Music Education." *Music Educators Journal* 57: 23-26; December 1970.

10. ———. "Musical Competencies for Classroom Teachers: An Initial Report from Task Group IV of the MENC Commission on Teacher Education." *Music Educators Journal* 57: 40-41; May 1971.

11. ———. *Teacher Education in Music: Final Report of the MENC Commission on Teacher Education.* Washington, D.C.: the Conference, 1973.

12. ———. *Toward an Aesthetic Education.* Washington, D.C.: the Conference and the Central Midwest Regional Educational Laboratory, Inc., 1971.

13. ———, Elementary Music Study Commission. *The Study of Music in the Elementary School—A Conceptual Approach.* Washington, D.C.: the Conference, 1967.

14. ———, Committee on Music in General Education. *Music in General Education.* Washington, D.C.: the Conference, 1965.

15. National Association of Secondary School Principals. "The Arts in the Comprehensive Secondary School." *Bulletin of the National Association of Secondary School Principals* 46: 1-19; September 1962.

16. Smith, Barbara B. "Music in World Cultures." *Music Educators Journal* 59; October 1972 (entire issue).

17. Zimmerman, Marilyn Pflederer, and Sechrest, Lee. *How Children Conceptually Organize Musical Sounds.* Cooperative Research Project No. 5-0256, Northwestern University, 1968.

MOHAWKS
612
MOHAWKS
1068

13

Physical Education

Physical education is the school subject concerned with the development and use of the individual's movement potential. Some of its most enthusiastic advocates have claimed all-pervasive benefits from a required curriculum in movement experiences, K through 12 and continuing into higher education. Its severest critics have made it a primary target for effecting economies in instructional time and educational budgets. Teachers and administrators who are genuinely seeking more relevant learning experiences for children and youth are asking how the untapped potential of the physical education curriculum can be more fully realized.

What does the discipline have to offer to the human search for knowledge? What movement understandings and skills, and which attitudes relating to movement behavior, are essential to the pursuit of happiness? These are questions that must be answered if physical education is to serve the learners for whom educational programs are organized.

The purposes of physical education have been stated at many levels of sophistication. In the simplest terms, those responsible for school programs in human movement have been concerned with health, play, and movement skill. Physical educators with differing convictions and in changing circumstances have viewed these concerns in varying relationships to each other, in individual and social contexts, and with greater or lesser attention to scientific knowledge, particular neuromuscular coordinations, or specific attitudinal changes. But physical education curriculums have consistently sought to develop some degree of physical fitness, recreational competence, and skillful movement.

In the past decade, professional leaders in American physical education have accorded high priority to the clarification of the theoretical structure for physical education. This effort, currently sponsored by the American Association for Health, Physical Education, and Recreation, is directed toward identifying and describing a framework for analyzing physical education as an area of scholarly study and research and as a professional field of work. The attempt to clarify the academic discipline focused on phenomena of human movement, project research activities needed to extend this field of knowledge, and apply established knowledge to advance physical education curriculum development has been fraught with difficulties; much confusion currently exists.

Certain relationships are clear, however. Extensive research and scholarly study are needed to further the discipline of human movement. At the same time, the present state of the arts and sciences of human movement is sufficiently advanced to enable substantial improvements in physical education curriculums and sound curricular research leading to future breakthroughs.

A consensus exists for using a conceptual framework for curricular decision making in physical education. However, the specific framework that can be used most advantageously has not yet been empirically tested. Hence, physical educators are using many different procedures at the local level, and the conceptual framework to be described in the following paragraphs must be regarded as tentative.

A Purpose-Process Conceptual Framework for Curricular Decision Making

The school child needs movement learnings to function meaningfully in the real world; the youth needs physical education to help him or her become a fully functioning adult. Curriculum content in physical education must offer students movement experiences related to the common purposes of moving, planned so that they learn how movement functions in human life. These experiences must (a) fulfill personal developmental potential, (b) develop movement skills to adapt to and control the physical environment, and (c) help the student relate to other persons. These are key purposes of movement, which delineate important curricular content of physical education. Key purpose concepts for describing the scope of the physical education curriculum may be identified and defined as follows.*

---

* The purpose concept framework is a result of group study during the past year at the University of Wisconsin. Major contributors were Peggy Chapman, Sheryl Gotts, L. Sue Jones, Douglas Knox, Sandra Knox, Marie Mullan, Leroy Smith, R. Peter Bauer, James Francis, Wilma Harrington, Marilyn LaPlante, David Uhrlaub, Emily Watson, Donald Brault, Philip Pabich, M. JoAnne Safrit, and Sarah Robinson.

MAN MASTER OF HIMSELF: Man moves to fulfill his human developmental potential.

Physiological Efficiency: Man moves to maintain his functional capabilities.

Circulorespiratory Efficiency. Man moves to develop and maintain his circulatory and respiratory functions.

Mechanical Efficiency. Man moves to increase and maintain his range and effectiveness of motion.

Neuromuscular Efficiency. Man moves to maintain or improve his muscular function.

Psychic Equilibrium: Man moves to achieve personal integration.

Joy of Movement. Man moves to derive pleasure intrinsic to human motion.

Self-Knowledge. Man moves to gain self-understanding and appreciation.

Catharsis. Man moves to release tensions and frustrations precipitated by the pressures of modern living.

Challenge. Man moves to test his prowess and courage through physical activity.

MAN IN SPACE: Man moves to adapt to and control his physical environment.

Spatial Orientation: Man moves to relate himself in three-dimensional space.

Awareness. Man moves to construct a conception of his body and how it moves in space.

Relocation. Man moves to propel or project himself from one place to another in a variety of settings.

Relationships. Man moves to regulate his body position in relation to stationary and moving objects and persons in the environment.

Object Manipulation: Man moves to give impetus to and to absorb the force of objects.

Maneuvering Weight. Man moves to support, resist, or transport mass.

Object Projection. Man moves to impart momentum and direction to a variety of objects.

Object Reception: Man moves to intercept a variety of objects by reducing or arresting their momentum.

MAN IN A SOCIAL WORLD: Man moves to relate to others.

Communication: Man moves to share ideas and feelings with others.

Expression. Man moves to convey his ideas and feelings.

Clarification. Man moves to enhance the meaning of other communication forms.

Masking. Man moves to obscure his intent or emotion.

Group Interaction: Man moves to function in harmony with others.

Teamwork. Man moves to share in common movement goals.

Competition. Man moves to vie for individual or group goals.

Leadership. Man moves to motivate and influence group members to achieve common goals.

Cultural Involvement: Man moves to take part in movement activities that constitute an important part of his society.

Participation. Man moves to develop his capabilities for taking part in movement activities popular in his society.

Movement Appreciation. Man moves to understand and become an appreciative observer of sports and expressive movement forms.

Cultural Preservation. Man moves to understand and extend his cultural heritage.

The purpose concepts describe the functions of movement in achieving human goals and thus define the scope of the physical education curriculum. The *processes* by which one learns to move must also be an integral part of curricular planning. The purpose-process conceptual framework promotes an action-oriented system focusing on the individual learning to move. Movement processes represent one large category of human behavior. Process learnings are, therefore, essential curricular outcomes. Sequence in physical education can best be facilitated by organizing curricular content in terms of a hierarchy of desired movement process outcomes. The following classification scheme conceptualizes a hierarchy of movement learning processes and offers a taxonomy for the selection and statement of educational objectives in the motor domain, applicable in any curricular area dealing with this domain.

LEARNING BEHAVIOR	DEFINITION
1.0 Generic Movement	Movement operations or processes that facilitate the development of human movement patterns
1.1 Perceiving	Recognition of movement positions, postures, patterns, and skills by means of the sense organs
1.2 Imitating	Duplication of a movement pattern or skill as a result of perceiving

1.3 Patterning	Arrangement and use of body parts in successive and harmonious ways to achieve a movement pattern or skill
2.0 Ordinative Movement	Meeting the requirements of specific movement tasks through processes of organizing, performing, and refining movement patterns and skills
2.1 Adapting	Modification of a patterned movement or skill to meet specific task demands
2.2 Refining	Acquisition of smooth, efficient control in performing a movement pattern or skill as a result of an improvement process, e.g.— a. Elimination of extraneous movements b. Mastery of spatial and temporal relations c. Habitual performance under more complex conditions
3.0 Creative Movement	Processes of inventing or creating skillful movements that will serve the unique purposes of the learner
3.1 Varying	Invention or construction of unique or novel options in performing a movement pattern or skill
3.2 Improvising	Extemporaneous origination or initiation of novel movements or combinations of movements
3.3 Composing	Creation of unique movement designs or patterns

The key concepts in the field of human movement are (a) those related to the functions of movement in prolonging and enriching the quality of life, which define the scope of the curriculum in physical education, and (b) those concerned with the processes by which an individual learns to facilitate, extend, and use fully his unique movement capabilities, which provide a basis for sequencing potential learning experiences in physical education. Learning movement processes is combined with learning key purpose concepts, as teachers develop instructional objectives using elements of human movement as the content focus and movement processes to identify the level of instruction. This procedure can be used to generate educational objectives for individual learners and for instructional groups in any learning environment, employing a wide variety of such learning media as traditional and popular games, stunts, sports and dance activities, innovative challenges in movement education, new and intriguing physical recreation opportunities, and unfamiliar but potentially stimulating movement experiences.

For example, a group of elementary school pupils may engage in a series of learning activities directed toward the development of concepts of spatial awareness. The teacher may structure learning environments to include open and confined spaces, indoor play areas and different types of natural terrain, and learning media selected from locomotor, ball-handling, kicking, striking, gymnastic, and aquatic activities. Children could be challenged at different levels by series of educational objectives developed progressively in each activity area. On the other hand, a secondary school student who has selected an instructional module in tennis may direct his energies toward elaborating and refining his concepts of object manipulation and communication, as well as spatial awareness, while progressively developing competence in movement processes, as illustrated in the following series of motor objectives that call for him to be able to—

- Recognize the ready position (perceive).
- Replicate the ready position (imitate).
- Execute the ready position (pattern).
- Adjust position to oncoming ball (adapt).
- Control position and movement to strike ball (refine).
- Alter striking pattern for different court placement (vary).
- Anticipate return of ball (improvise).
- Unbalance opponent (compose).

Since the physical education curriculum is concerned with cognitive and affective learning as well as motor learning, curriculum designers will provide for the identification and achievement of education objectives in these domains as well, but sequencing in the physical education curriculum is primarily in terms of motor development and motor learning.

The purpose-process framework serves as a conceptual structure for designing curricular alternatives according to the needs and interests of differing groups of learners in varying school and community settings. The following description of contemporary physical education in a hypothetical community is offered to illustrate the implementation of this framework.

Physical Education in Update Public Schools

"Update" is a rapidly growing community of approximately 50,000. A recently established industrial plant with substantial federal contracts and a newly designated state university, originally planned as a two-year community college, contribute to a varied population and an expanding economy. The school district operates 10 elementary schools, three middle schools replacing grades 6 through 9 in an earlier organizational pattern, and a comprehensive three-year high school.

Elementary School Physical Education

Each elementary school has two indoor areas suitable for group movement activities. One area (circular in the newer buildings) is equipped with a variety of hanging and climbing equipment, including stall bars, ladders, ropes, stegels, wall peg boards, and numerous boxes, benches, bars, and ladders that can be quickly assembled in various combinations to design interesting movement tricks and sequences.

The larger of the two physical education areas is rectangular or square, outfitted with plastic partitioning walls that can be rolled up from the floor to form intersecting solid panels. These transparent walls divide the area into four smaller spaces and provide firm rebounding surfaces. They can also be converted into mirrors. The TV monitors, videotape recorders, and sound projection equipment are located in cabinets in the four outside walls where they offer no safety hazard and are protected from damage.

Outdoor areas are planned to take advantage of different natural settings. Trees have been spared where possible, and most schools are provided with a grassy area of uneven terrain as well as a flat all-weather surfaced area. Municipal storehouses and local businessmen have contributed large pieces of equipment for installation on the playgrounds to supplement standard commercial climbing and hanging apparatus. The children have enjoyed participating in contests to decorate the equipment and landscape the areas. Such portable equipment as balls, ropes, beanbags, canes, tires, nets, and the like are available for both indoor and outdoor use.

Local educational philosophy supports environmental designs for learning, which are value-oriented to increase the pupil's sensitivity and receptivity to needed social programs, to improve his skills in group relations, and to enhance his creative use of leisure. Communication is now viewed as a legitimate core around which to plan the elementary school curriculum, so that the various areas of study may contribute to the child's ability to cope with his world on his own terms. Movement experiences in schools have come into their own in the last decade as educators have recognized the crucial role played by movement in self-expression and communication. Individualization of learning is a continuing goal implemented with the assistance of sophisticated technological equipment. Computers compile diagnostic appraisals of the relevant backgrounds, abilities, interests, and learning styles of each child, making it possible for the teacher to propose tentative goals for each student and a program of learning experiences designed to achieve them.

The activity content of the elementary physical education curriculum includes learning modules or short capsules of movement experiences planned to develop fundamental concepts and progressively increasing abilities. Much of the child's movement curriculum is organized to focus on "man in space." Much emphasis is given to general body awareness, basic locomotor patterns of walking, running, hopping, sliding, jumping, galloping, skipping, and leaping, and body management skills of dodging and guarding stationary and moving objects, chasing, tagging, stunts, tumbling, and apparatus. Ball- and object-handling activities involving throwing, catching, kicking, and striking also receive major attention.

Elementary learnings in using movement to relate to others are achieved through creative rhythms, folk dance, and games. Every child has at least occasional opportunities in physical education to express his personal ideas and feelings through self-directed movement. Games are selected and designed to provide practice in the particular movement skills already identified and to stimulate the development of elementary concepts of rule-functioning in group activities, cooperation, competition, and leadership.

Physical education experiences throughout the elementary school are designed (a) to assist the individual child in self-mastery, through development of an acceptable body image and a positive concept of himself in movement settings; (b) to provide ample opportunities for knowing personal joy in movement; and (c) to further the progressive development of strength, flexibility, balance, and cardiorespiratory endurance. Physical activities already discussed (movement exploration, fundamental locomotor movements, body management activities, ball- and object-handling practice, rhythms and dances, traditional and creative games) provide the learning media for reaching these goals.

The roles of the physical educator in elementary education have shifted since most teachers completed their professional certification requirements. Today's teacher works with groups of children to focus on problems, stimulate movement learning activities, and help establish criteria for solutions to problems. He also serves as a tutor-challenger, working with individual children to help them discover their interests, strengths, and weaknesses. He is expected to contribute, according to his personal talents, television teaching, learning programs, videotapes, innovative learning aids, and self-evaluative games and devices that enable children to assess their own levels of skill achievement, fitness, creativity, and communications effectiveness. He is a learner about learning as he struggles to make increasingly successful decisions about how to present material to children or how to encourage children to seek new personalized movement answers.

Middle School Physical Education

The middle school offers a unique challenge to the physical educator. All three middle schools use modular scheduling and team teaching. In some instances teaching teams cut across attendance-district lines to permit optimum use of teacher specializations. For physical education learning, children are grouped according to skill achievement levels in the various areas. Many classes are coeducational, although instruction in team sports, aquatics, and track and field is usually given separately to boys and girls. Both large- and small-group instruction is scheduled regularly, with the typical pattern providing the middle school student seven 30-minute modules of physical education weekly, two in groups of 26-75 students, and five in groups of 25 students or less.

Each middle school has an outdoor field area; one full-sized standard gymnasium with large adjacent storage areas for gymnastic equipment; a smaller gymnasium for dance, wrestling, self-defense, body mechanics, and certain gymnastic activities; and a pool designed especially for flexible instructional use. In addition, one middle school has an indoor track and field area that can be converted to an ice rink. Another has eight tennis courts that are flooded in winter for skating. The newest middle school is located near a hilly wooded area, which has been developed as an outdoor education and camping area for year-round use and as a site for beginning skiing instruction in winter. Students are transported by school bus in order to share these specialized instructional facilities. All middle school physical education facilities are operated by the city recreation department for evening, weekend, and summer neighborhood programs.

The Update curriculum in middle school physical education has two major elements: (a) expanding students' understanding of movement through the refinement of personal skills and (b) deepening their social understanding through experiences in movement activities of their own and other societies. Concepts of self-mastery are strengthened by achieving higher levels of skill in familiar activities and by successfully meeting the challenges of learning new skills. Venturesome activities requiring personal courage are included. Dynamic posture is studied directly, but most students receive no formal instruction directed primarily toward strength, flexibility, and circulorespiratory endurance unless individually prescribed exercise programs are indicated.

Students work toward a growing understanding of movement principles in situations emphasizing modifications of environmental media. Aquatic experiences comprise from 20 to 35 percent of individual programs. All students learn principles of buoyancy and adaptations of biomechanics, balance, and breathing appropriate to propulsion in the water. Instruction includes specific water survival techniques, elementary forms of rescue, standard stroke patterns, diving, water stunts, and alternate elective modules for those students qualified for more advanced aquatic activities.

Tumbling, gymnastics, and trampolining are emphasized to extend concepts of spatial awareness, locomotion, and balance and to encourage the development of body projection skills using limited ground contact. Basic gymnastic skills acquired during elementary school years serve as a foundation for learning standard stunts required in competition on all pieces of apparatus. Capsule programs have been developed to help students at a wide range of individual performance levels to work independently in large-group instructional settings with minimum supervision. Creative exercise routines offer opportunities for fun and novelty as well as for the satisfaction of skill achievement.

Track and field activities are stressed and extended to include outdoor challenges in locomotion, balance, and skillful performance on land surfaces modified by sand, snow, or ice. All students are introduced to ice skating and skiing. Unique forms of body projection and locomotion, more advanced skills in object projection, and concepts associated with physical activity, such as recreation, catharsis, and risk taking, can be experienced meaningfully in such contexts.

Middle school organization offers unparalleled opportunities for socialization through the development of team sports and social dance skills. Skill development and team strategy are stressed in the familiar team games popular in the community: soccer, touch football, basketball, volleyball, hockey, and softball. Group games reflecting the recreational interests of young people in other societies are also introduced. Students from differing subcultures within the larger Update community share such aspects of their heritage with each other. Exchange students from other countries and local citizens or foreign visitors who have lived in regions where other games are popular provide key resources. Social dance offerings include traditional dances, American square dance, folk dances of many lands, and currently popular dance forms. Opportunities for healthful competitive sport and for recreational dance are varied and extensive in middle school extraclass programs.

Physical education teachers in the middle schools need to have a commitment to the unique requirements of this age group, to be enthusiastic about guiding students in after-school programs, to feel challenged by participation in team teaching, to be well-skilled in several specialized areas, and to be competent in planning instructional materials using modern technology to facilitate movement-concept learning.

High School Physical Education

Update High School is an exciting place to work. Facilities are unusually flexible. The emphasis is on the "pod"—or module—with simple basic units easily convertible to teaching stations of varying shapes and sizes. A series of small activity areas can be used for as many as 24 individual practice spaces or, by combining two or more such areas, to accommodate groups of two to six learners. Students have frequent access to the instructional materials center, which is equipped with facilities for viewing films and videotapes, carrels for independent study assisted by teaching machines, and a growing collection of books, charts, slides, films, recordings, videotapes, and learning programs, selected or developed by members of the physical education staff.

Special-purpose areas include handball courts, a wrestling room, golf cages, and an adaptive physical education area. A single classroom, located in the physical education wing, is available for departmental use. Generally, large-group instruction is scheduled in the four gymnasiums lined with standard court markings and equipped with movable dividing doors. Outdoor areas are modest in size and covered with all-weather surfacing or synthetic turfs. Public and private recreational facilities outside the school are used extensively. Students have limited use of the middle school swimming pools for competitive teams, aquatics clubs, special events, and remedial instruction.

Update High School established modular scheduling several years ago. Current schedules are built on a 20-minute module. Physical education is using two-, three-, and four-module blocks most frequently. Limited use is made of single modules, for learning activities that do not require changing clothes or for particular purposes that can be accommodated by intradepartmental scheduling. Occasionally, longer time blocks are used for elective physical education to facilitate such learning opportunities as golfing at the local country club, intermediate or advanced skiing at the public ski area in the state park 10 miles north of Update, or curling at the new facility recently developed by a small group of private citizens.

Five years ago, Update High School survived a series of student protests. It was difficult to identify the real issues among the various demands for black coaches, interscholastic competition for girls, varsity teams in lacrosse and volleyball, more sports opportunities for under-130-pound boys, free bowling, more basketballs for check-out for recreational use, discontinuance of regulation uniforms, and soft drink and candy machines in the locker rooms. But when the furor subsided, it turned out that what the students really were seeking was physical education relevant to their needs in a world significantly different from that in which their teachers attended high school. Fortunately, it was mid-May when the student demonstrations reached their peak. School was closed early and student-faculty-parent groups were formed for summer study. The need for major changes was recognized. Civic and educational leaders decided to remodel the entire curriculum on the basis of thoughtful restatements of educational objectives. Consultants were employed to work with small committees in developing objectives for the total program and for the individual curricular areas. Each committee included students and parents as well as faculty members. Administrators and consultants assisted the different committees as requested. Each area committee was charged with the responsibility of stating objectives to describe the desired outcomes for each student at graduation and to facilitate continuing student evaluation and guidance.

The physical education committee recommended three major goals for the graduate of Update High School: (a) understanding and appreciation of human movement, (b) physical fitness, and (c) lifetime sports competence. These goals were implemented in a systems approach to individualizing instruction. Today's curriculum is the result of ongoing experimentation with many variations in curricular patterns and a wide diversity of instructional techniques. In physical education, as in other subjects, the curriculum now undergoes continual development and change. The present physical education curriculum has three elements, each corresponding to one of the major goals. Students are expected to demonstrate achievements in each of these areas. At the initial curriculum input point, the student participates in an assessment unit to determine his or her status in each area.

Understanding and Appreciation of Human Movement. The first element, understanding and appreciation of human movement, consists of three modules: movement fundamentals, movement as expression and communication, and movement in society. If it is determined through the evaluation procedures applied in the assessment unit that the student needs to review the fundamentals of movement emphasized in elementary and middle school physical education, he is scheduled for this module first. If he already meets the minimum standards with regard to posture, body mechanics, and intermediate knowledge of movement principles, he may bypass the movement fundamentals review unit or module and move directly to another of the program modules in this element.

In the module designed to focus on movement as expression and communication, each student may select from among several submodules in choreography or the development of new games or movement forms. Experiences in choreography are not restricted to modern dance, but also include creating a water ballet, free exercise routing, or living statuary tableaus; designing movement sequences for musical and theatrical productions; staging a physical education demonstration; or programming movement for film or television showings. A student who is intrigued with the analysis of sports skills may select some performance problem and try his hand at working out a new skill technique. Some students, singly or in small groups, have invented novelty events for local track and field days, archery meets, or aquatic fun nights. Occasionally students motivated to invent something personally relevant have produced new games, original dances, or unique movement activities that might become the successors to the hula hoop, Frisbee, and skateboard.

The movement in society module includes an introductory sport appreciation submodule programmed for all students and additional submodules for further individual choice. The sport appreciation submodule provides a brief overview of the historical role of sport in various cultures, explores the critical role of movement in child development, highlights basic concepts of sociology of sport and of sport psychology, and identifies contemporary social problems relating to sports participation locally, nationally, and internationally. This submodule is a prerequisite to others in the movement in society module. The student chooses at least one additional submodule in guiding movement activities of children, leading neighborhood activity programs, planning family recreation activities, or studying movement activities of other societies or particular subcultures.

Physical Fitness. The second element of the physical education curriculum consists of three modules: muscular strength, circulorespiratory endurance, and survival aquatics. The student who demonstrates adequate strength and endurance in the assessment unit may bypass the first two modules completely. The student who needs further development of strength or endurance may select submodules in weight training, gymnastics, jogging, circuit training, or track and field. Or he may prefer to move into other sport or activity modules, such as orienteering, basketball, or handball, to increase his strength or endurance. Most students complete survival aquatics as ninth graders, but 20 to 30 percent of the high school students need additional work in this area. Many can demonstrate proficiency in the entire fitness element without enrolling in any of the fitness instructional modules.

Lifetime Sports Competence. In the third element, competence in at least two lifetime sports is required of all students for graduation. A short sports orientation module is scheduled for all sophomores, emphasizing the advantages of voluntary participation throughout life, suggesting procedures for planning personal activity programs, and providing information about available curricular choices and competence standards in each sport. Competence standards are practical tests of ability to participate at an intermediate skill level, as, for example, a particular bowling handicap, a standardized minimum archery score, a given performance classification in skiing, a judge's rating in gymnastics, or an appropriate competitive classification in tennis. The student is free to select any of the many lifetime sports activities offered at beginning, intermediate, or advanced levels, depending upon his ability level. The graduation requirement ensures that he will have met designated standards in at least two sports.

Classes. All students are individually programmed. Except for the initial assessment module, one expressive movement module, the sports appreciation module, one additional movement in society module, and the lifetime sports orientation module, they may select any activities for which they meet the entry qualifications. Physical education is a required sophomore subject; juniors and seniors who have demonstrated the required competencies are not required to continue in the physical education curriculum, but most students elect additional units. Elective study in physical education includes, in addition to the curricular content already discussed, such offerings as history of sport, sociology of sport, sport psychology, and physiology of exercise, scheduled as semester courses or units within courses developed cooperatively with faculty of other departments.

All classes are coeducational, except for wrestling and a few of the team sport sections. Approximately 80 percent of the students participate in either intramural or interscholastic sports. Boys' teams compete in 12 interscholastic sports, girls' teams in seven. Mixed teams are organized for interscholastic competition in tennis, golf, badminton, and bowling.

Update High School's class instruction in physical education uses a great deal of problem solving. Students are encouraged to test different techniques for performing sport skills in order to select those that they can use most effectively. Concepts of biomechanics and exercise physiology are refined through experiences in applying fundamental movement principles and elementary knowledge of human physiology to new sports activities and specific training challenges. A high premium is placed on the esthetic aspects of movement experience, on expressive applications of movement abilities, and on creative solutions to movement problems. Numerous instructional models and individual learning programs have been developed for local use, especially for the required modules or units. Videotape recorders and many types of teaching machines are used for frequent individualization of instruction and student self-testing. Many open laboratories are scheduled for free choice activities and for conducting individual projects.

Staff. High school physical education staff members are necessarily highly specialized in particular sport, dance, or gymnastic activities. Some have joint appointments as part-time athletic coaches, but all staff members assigned teaching responsibilities in physical education are selected on the basis of their qualifications as physical educators. These qualifications include, in addition to the appropriate certification, skill in individualizing instruction, interest in action research, openness to student self-direction, knowledge of evaluation and assessment techniques, depth of preparation in biological and behavioral sciences, appreciation of movement arts, and willingness to become an advocate of innovation in physical education.

Emerging Concepts in Physical Education Curriculum Development

Physical education has a unique role in the school curriculum. While its long-range goals have much in common with those of other curricular areas, its primary learning media are sport, dance, and gymnastic movement forms. Realization by every student of his individual movement potential requires flexible facilities rather than standardized contest gymnasiums, which tend to prescribe program content. Effective physical education programs depend upon the commitment of sufficient student time and enough qualified educational specialists to the accomplishment of objectives carefully selected and enthusiastically pursued at the local level.

The physical education programs in the Update Public Schools illustrate the selection of particular curricular alternatives based on a purpose-process conceptual framework for curricular decision making in physical education. Many different choices are available. Sound contemporary physical education curriculums, while diverse, reflect the same general concepts.

Emerging Concepts in Content

1. The key concepts in the field of human movement are those related to the functions of movement in prolonging and enriching the quality of life. Curricular content is selected to fulfill personal developmental potential, to maintain fitness, to develop individual movement skills, and to help the student relate to other persons.

2. In selecting content from the body of knowledge relating to human movement, physical education curriculum planners are concerned with providing for esthetic and ethical meanings as well as with communicating the findings of the empirical sciences. Contemporary physical educators recognize the need to integrate the rapidly expanding knowledge in the behavioral sciences with the substantial knowledge in biological science that is the foundation for the curriculum. They acknowledge the potentials of both the arts and the sciences of human movement.
3. Human movement necessarily involves interaction of the individual with his environment. The individual learner aims to raise his level of fitness and to increase his proficiency in movement skills; he is also concerned with using movement as a medium for achieving other goals, including desired modifications of his physical and social environment. Physical education curriculums must, therefore, be dynamic. Content is seen to be continually changing, rather than a repetitive cycle of seasonal games.

Emerging Organizational Concepts

4. Curricular experiences in physical education are organized in terms of a conceptual framework. Concepts of human movement, rather than specific games and movement activities, guide the structuring of learning environments.
5. Sequence in physical education is based on the hierarchy of learning processes by which an individual learns to move. The movement processes by which an individual learns to facilitate, extend, and use fully his unique movement capabilities provide the basis for sequencing potential physical education learnings.
6. Student groupings are determined by assessing individual status with regard to program goals, experiences needed to accomplish individual student purposes, and personal interest in particular movement activities among the myriad available. Grouping according to these criteria leads to more coeducational classes, more ability grouping, and more flexibility in physical education class size than have been the traditional practice.
7. Satisfying learning experiences in physical education vary in the length of time required for completion of a curricular unit. Today's physical education is organized in units of related movement concepts—modules that can be sequenced in varying combinations of differing lengths according to local, individual, and group priorities.
8. The total time allotment needed for physical education varies with individual students and is based on competence

in achieving program goals. Students with special developmental needs and unusual learning problems require additional instruction and guidance in movement activities and should have access to special education programs. Several curricular alternatives should be available to all students for developing required competencies. Elective physical education should be offered to students who have demonstrated minimum satisfactory competencies but desire further learning opportunities in the field of human movement.

Emerging Concepts in Instructional Procedures

9. Learning media for physical education are widely diverse. Popular sports, dances, and gymnastic activities are viewed as media for learning rather than as ends in themselves. They are supplemented in a complete physical education curriculum by interesting movement activities of unlimited scope. The sophisticated technology of the space age has provided innumerable learning aids for individualizing instruction. It has been amply demonstrated that more learners can successfully complete more movement tasks at higher levels of skill if learning environments are structured to permit individuals to achieve their own purposes at rates appropriate to their own abilities.
10. Desirable learning environments in physical education are designed to provide for affective growth and development. They are carefully structured so that motor skill proficiency is not sought at the expense of strengthening the integrity of personal value systems or reinforcing needed social values. Attention is given to supporting cognitive knowledge with relevant opportunities for acquiring attitudes predisposing to positive behavior.
11. Recognition of physical education's potential and responsibility for encouraging the development of human creativity is relatively recent. Learning situations can and should be planned to explore the entire range of possible human movements, to elicit new alternatives in movement behavior, and to encourage individuals to create unique modes of self-expression in movement.
12. Since the ultimate goal of the physical education curriculum is the education of self-directing, responsible individuals, instructional procedures focus on the growth of persons and the autonomy of individuals committed to improving the quality of life for all members of society. It follows that techniques of self-evaluation, self-testing, student goal setting, and individual and group problem solving are emphasized.

BIBLIOGRAPHY

1. American Association for Health, Physical Education, and Recreation. *Knowledges and Understandings in Physical Education.* Washington, D.C.: the Association, 1969.
2. ———. *Promising Practices in Elementary School Physical Education.* Washington, D.C.: the Association, 1969.
3. ———. *This Is Physical Education.* Washington, D.C.: the Association, 1965.
4. ———. "Toward Program Excellence—The Physical Education Position Papers." *Journal of Health, Physical Education, and Recreation* 42: 41-53; April 1971.
5. Brown, Camille. "Physical Education." *Curriculum Handbook for School Administrators.* (Edited by Forrest E. Conner and William J. Ellena.) Washington, D.C.: American Association of School Administrators, 1967.
6. ———, and Cassidy, Rosalind. *Theory in Physical Education—A Guide to Program Change.* Philadelphia: Lea and Febiger, 1963.
7. Cassidy, Rosalind. "Changing Perspectives . . . A Personal Journey." *The Fourth Amy Morris Homans Lecture.* St. Louis: National Association for Physical Education of College Women, 1970.
8. Eyler, Marvin H., editor. "The Nature of a Discipline." Monograph. *Quest IX* (National Association for Physical Education of College Women and National College Physical Education Association for Men.) December 1967.
9. Fraleigh, Warren P. "A Prologue to the Study of Theory Building in Physical Education." *Quest XII:* 26-33; May 1969.
10. Johnson, Perry B., and others. *Physical Education—A Problem-Solving Approach to Health and Fitness.* New York: Holt, Rinehart and Winston, 1966.
11. Mackenzie, Marlin M. *Toward a New Curriculum in Physical Education.* New York: McGraw-Hill, 1969.
12. Mordy, Margaret A., editor. "Educational Change in the Teaching of Physical Education." Monograph. *Quest XV,* January 1971.
13. Mosston, Muska. *From Command to Discovery—Teaching Physical Education.* Columbus, Ohio: Charles E. Merrill, 1966.
14. Nixon, John E., and Jewett, Ann E. *The Physical Education Curriculum.* New York: Ronald Press Co., 1964.

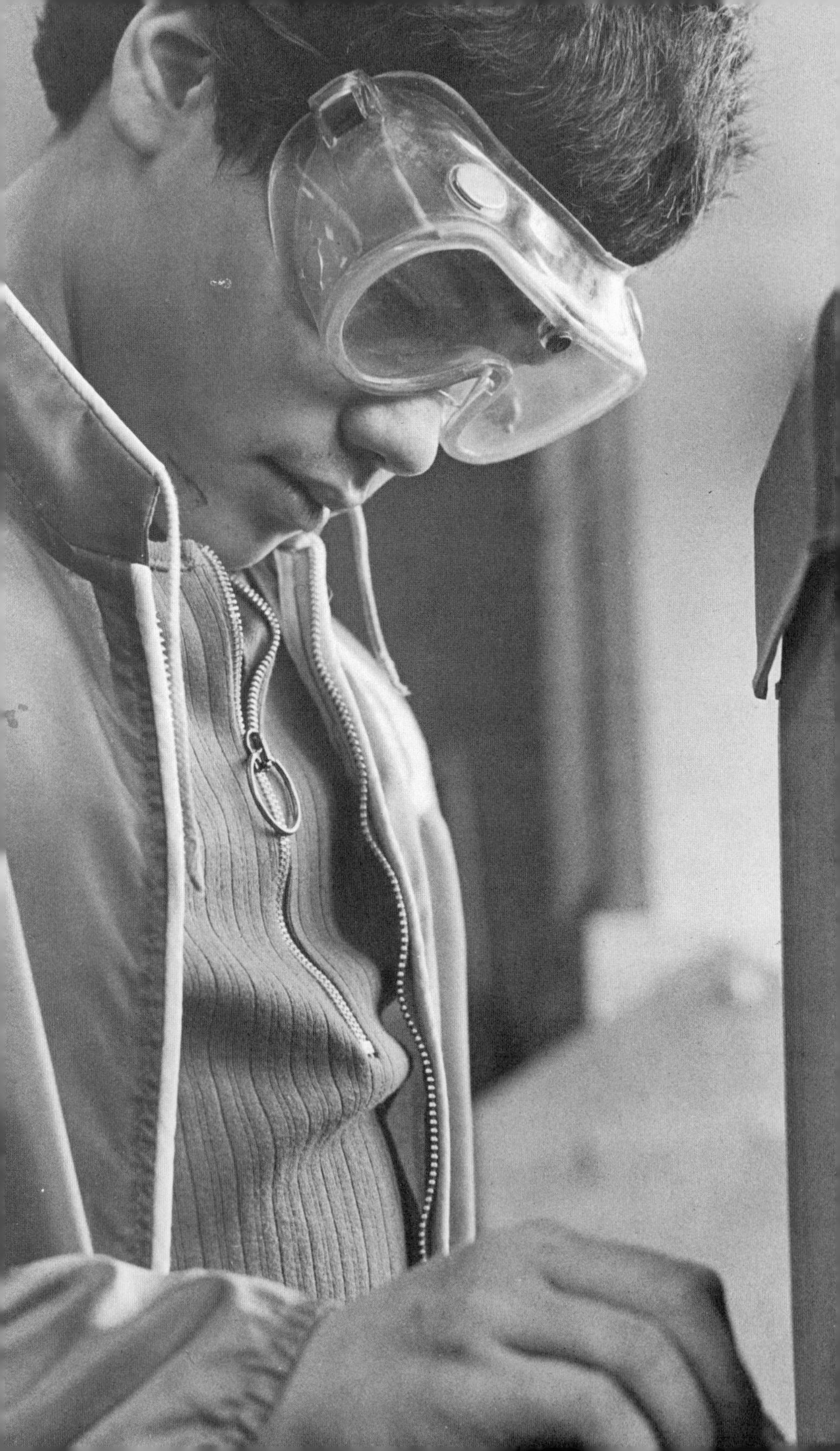

14

Safety Education

My interest is in the future, because I'm going to spend the rest of my life there.
—Charles F. Kettering

Federal and state governments' increased participation in accident prevention has placed the spotlight on the school administrator's responsibility to provide increasing leadership in the field of safety education. The Highway Safety Acts of 1966, the Occupational Safety and Health Act of 1970, and the proposed Safe Schools Bill are but three examples of government action on this growing national problem.

The Role of Safety Education

Safety education as a discipline stands at the crossroads. Surely it is an indifferent society that, while stressing the significance of life, fails to educate its citizens in the means of preserving it. Education for safe living is an inherent right of every human being.

The school administrator's concern with effecting substantial improvements in school accident prevention programs is based on several vital factors:

1. Accidents are responsible for more than 100,000 deaths and 12 million injuries annually, at a known cost of 20 billion dollars, plus unknown costs estimated at four times that amount.
2. The continuing technological development and increasing mobility of society involve progressively greater exposure to a wider range of hazards for children, youth, and adults.
3. Education is a valid and important process in conserving human and environmental resources.
4. Administrators fulfill their obligations to society by including in the curriculum the development of knowledge, skills, habits, and behaviorial traits to enable children, youth, and adults to recognize and deal effectively with potentially hazardous situations.

5. Safety education is multidisciplinary, extends across all subject fields, and is in harmony with total educational goals.
6. Safety education is only as effective as the people who administer and teach it.

It has been said that the education community will gradually eliminate social class discrimination. Indeed, much progress has been made in the last decade. However, as Robert M. Hutchens suggests in *The Learning Society* (9), we still think there are two kinds of people—those who can be educated and those who can only be trained—despite research evidence that the IQ is a function of the environment, including the school environment. Is it too farfetched to consider "safety IQ" within this context?

Some schools in the United States still operate on the principle that in order to learn, one must be able to read. For those who find reading too difficult, no matter for what reason, education (including safety education) becomes not a matter of internalizing other basic skills, but a frustrating experience directed toward reading for reading's sake while delaying—perhaps even psychologically destroying—other learnings important to the individual. Many nonreaders have been taught to be safe and efficient operators of complex industrial machinery, heavy construction equipment, and motor vehicles on streets and highways. This kind of success in learning often enables them to overcome blocks to reading and other formal learnings and subsequently to move ahead in the broader academic fields of education.

Some scholars foresee a continued shift away from largely superficial courses (e.g., dead languages) toward more relevant, real-world instruction. In this context, safety education surely will become universal in our schools as one of those subjects practical for all citizens.

Emerging Concepts in Safety Education Programs

The leadership of the school administrator is the key to an effective safety education program (11). He must provide the necessary thrust for coordinating the essential elements of the school-community program in accident prevention through administration, instruction, and protection.

The School-Community Action Program

With the administrator's guidance and inspiration, the school can fulfill its important goal as the community center for maintaining optimum safety. Citizens should be able to identify freely with school-centered efforts toward cooperative action for a safer place in which to live. The student, the teacher, the parent, the farmer, the merchant, the physician, the policeman, the engineer —to name a few—have significant contributions to make. All can help to identify hazardous behavior and environmental conditions and perform an important role in a communitywide plan—their own plan—for improvement. Any safety education program should be the result of a democratic decision-making process.

The wise administrator knows that an important part of his job is to stimulate action in the community and to give appropriate credit for sincere effort without singling out one or a few for disproportionate publicity. Plans will vary among communities, and experience will likely indicate the need for modifying plans in a given community as the program progresses. While it is impossible to present a blueprint for a safety education program, some general guiding principles for such school-community action can be stated:

1. *Define and measure the community problem.* A logical beginning is to make a survey of the school and community needs for education and services in safe living, including consideration of behavioral and environmental hazards. It need not be an elaborate and highly technical survey, but it should involve representatives of the community and the school. The people need to answer for themselves such questions as, What do we need to improve traffic conditions? How can we protect schools and homes from fire and other hazards? What can be done to cope with occupational hazards? What facilities do we have and how can we make full use of them? Step-by-step solution of the smaller problems with unanimity of purpose will lead to understanding and willingness to attack the larger problems.
2. *Organize for action.* Different phases of the various problems will need to be attacked at different times and in different ways. Participants in the project should organize into groups according to their interests, but there should be an overall organizational structure to ensure adequate exchange of information and activity among the various groups throughout the community. A steering committee might operate to great advantage in coordinating the safety activities to provide maximum benefits for all citizens.
3. *Include specialized services.* Most state departments of education and some colleges and universities employ safety education specialists who, together with general curriculum specialists, may be most helpful in providing the necessary services to the local school system and perhaps to some individual school-community safety projects. Some local

school systems are also able to provide safety services to the school-community program. The suggested roles for state and local school system safety education specialists are outlined in the 1967 *Curriculum Handbook for School Administrators* (11, pp. 233-37).

4. *Provide for continuing leadership.* The school-community safety program will require continuous guidance by the school administrator. He or she should exercise leadership in such areas as the following:
   - Obtaining financial support to provide for the needs of those enrolled in school and for community activities involving adults in the school-centered safety program
   - Organizing schedules and instructional approaches to accommodate as nearly as possible the entire school-community population
   - Arranging realistic programs to help inservice teachers integrate safety education into the curriculum and become more proficient with innovative hardware and software
   - Finding ways to incorporate related content such as (a) alcohol and its influence upon human behavior and (b) emergencies arising out of such changes in the community as new building projects, the development of new industry, or the opening of new highways
   - Building support for safety education through effective media communication and through contact with the public.

5. *Select services offered by community groups.* Schools need access to the knowledge of the world, whether that knowledge comes from libraries, industrial laboratories, or government files. Safety organizations, business and industry, and other organized groups can make constructive contributions to school-community safety. It is appropriate for such groups to call attention to instructional needs and to offer their special skills as needed by the school. Many of these groups are in a position to conduct research applicable to school safety. Often they can cultivate goodwill and build unity and cooperation.

   It is the responsibility of the school administrator to select from the services and materials available outside the school. Many of these are good, but some are better than others; in a program designed for the greatest life-saving benefit only the best should be selected. Services and activities offered to the school must be evaluated in terms of the following considerations:
   - How much do they contribute toward the ultimate goal of developing safe behavior and a safer environment today and tomorrow?

- How much student time does the outside project or safety service take?
- How much teacher time does such activity take?
- How nearly does the proposed activity come to reaching all of the students who should benefit?
- How much does it cost?
- Can all student participants experience success, or are some eliminated along the way while a few are singled out as safety "star players"?
- What is the school's liability in case of injury in the conduct of the outside-sponsored activity?
- What are the chances for positive or negative community reaction? What is the activity's potential public relations value to the school?
- Is the program under the auspices of the school and directed by the school administration?
- Are trained and carefully selected school personnel in full charge of the program offered?
- How many of the teachers and other school personnel are involved in the interest of accident prevention as represented by the activity?
- Is it a "separate package" activity, or is it closely related to the basic program of the school?
- Does it include cooperative contributions from all interested forces throughout the community?

These guidelines should help the school administrator and the leaders of the school-community safety program make certain that they are participating in all worthy activities offered, while safeguarding against those that are only a waste of time or an exploitation of the students or the program.

Accountability

The term *accountability* is now much in vogue. In providing administrative leadership for accident prevention, accountability should be viewed as neither a burden nor a rein on administrators and teachers but as a privilege. This "privilege" point of view, as it applies to general education, has been set forth by Harlacher and Roberts (8). They identify the following articles of belief in support of accountability as an administrative privilege (p. 30):

1. Both administrators and teachers should be held accountable for student failures.
2. An individual educational plan should be developed for each student, using a wide variety of learning experiences.
3. An educational institution ought to be judged on the basis of what it does for and with students.

4. Learning should be aimed at mastery by all students, not just a chosen few.
5. Individualization of instruction requires provision of optional paths to learning and the utilization of a highly diversified teaching-learning team including part-time teachers, peer tutors, and community volunteers.
6. Education must be learner- and learning-centered, measured by performance criteria.
7. Teachers ought to be managers of the learning process—change agents, guides, monitors, questioners—not feeders of information.
8. Each learner ought to be able to start where he is and become all that he is capable of becoming.

The administrator cannot adequately apply these principles without both providing safety education and creating the safest possible environment. Successful programs already in progress in many school systems show that administrators are concerned about the appropriate application of these principles to safety education, but such programs are by no means universal.

Unsafe practices continue in many schools. To cite two examples, an administrator in one school system planned to convert an extra room for temporary use, despite the lack of windows or adequate fire-escape facilities and despite a limited budget that would allow only unsafe placement of electrical outlets; in another system, an elementary child fell from school playground equipment when there was no professional supervision, suffering a brain concussion. Few books on curriculum make any mention of safety. It is unfortunate that an author of general curriculum materials can be so uninformed about the booby traps built into modern American roads that he refers to the nation's superhighways as a testimony to the genius of American technology, industry, and labor.

Communities also continue to engage in unsafe practices. The Washington, D.C., Beltway and the approaches to it are only one example of inadequate highway planning and engineering that fail to allow for the time and distance requirements of limited human reflexes (16, p. 156).

Historically, architects and engineers have not allowed sufficiently for the vagaries of human interaction with the environment. Gradually it is becoming recognized that a systems approach to design and construction—employing expert knowledge of the relation among man, machine, and environment—is essential to safety, conservation, and efficiency. Education, including higher education, has a responsibility for instructional and protective decision making that will provide maximum levels of structural and environmental safety. Accountability for this kind of concern begins in the schools, where youngsters early in life are developing the basic concepts for safe conduct and the assumption of responsibility for maintaining a safe environment.

More Than the Sum of Its Parts

Safety education and accident prevention are a synergy—the effect of the whole is greater than the sum of its parts. Accidents must be treated within the context of the larger culture if they are to be kept to a reasonable minimum. As suggested earlier, the multidisciplinary approach to the study of accidents and to the design of effective programs of instruction holds far greater promise than piecemeal approaches by people working separately in different disciplines. Administrators, curriculum specialists, and researchers need to work together toward improvement of accident prevention efforts in schools and communities.

More Than the Sum of Its Parts

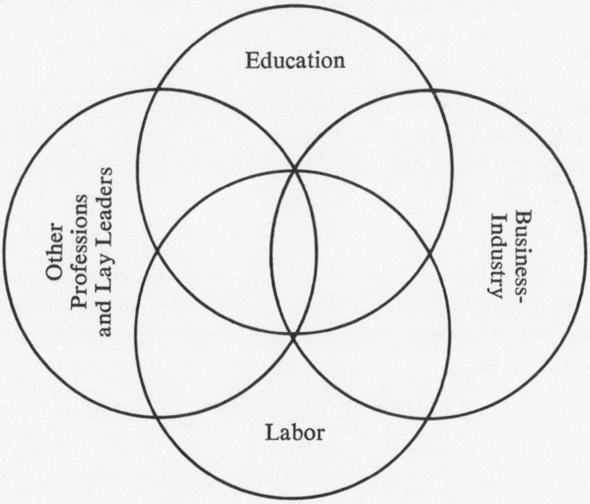

So that a program in safety education and accident prevention may be greater than the sum of its isolated parts, the school administrator, his professional staff (including specialists in all disciplines), and students should join together in an overall effort to develop scientific controls of behavior and environmental conditions. Here are a few examples of questions that need to be answered through the interdisciplinary approach:

- What constitutes safe performance?
- What appeals are most effective in creating positive safety motivation?
- To what extent can the individual be conditioned through learning experiences to respond safely under emergency conditions?
- How can we design equipment to account for human shortcomings?
- Can equipment be designed not only to provide minimum safeguards against human error through shields, covers, and the like, but also to detect mistakes in human performance and signal this information in time for corrective action?
- Can we prescribe environmental standards for safe working conditions?

In a recent survey, the U.S. Office of Education found that more than 13 million adults are participating in some kind of educational activity *not* centered in a formal post–high school institution. Henry Sill (22) predicts that by the end of this century the average person may live to be 100 years old or more. The school administrator may draw his own conclusions with respect to the current curriculum and the need for greater emphasis on education for survival in the future.

Accidents in industry are now at a 14-year high and still rising. School-community outreach projects can readily lend themselves to overcoming conditions that cause accidents. It is estimated that half the people living in large cities are undereducated and incompetent in terms of today's social and economic standards. Some studies indicate disproportionately high accident frequency among low socioeconomic groups. Outreach programs can be important vehicles for extending accident prevention activities directly to the people in their neighborhoods. Many activities, including safety programs, can be offered for adults at little cost. Some are supported by federal funds.

Older persons are highly susceptible to accidents, especially those who do not have an opportunity to learn how to adjust to a rapidly changing environment and to their own growing frailties. It is becoming increasingly important for schools to serve the needs of older people in their own neighborhoods. According to the latest Census report, 38 million people in the United States are over 54 years old, and the number is projected to 44 million by 1980. Through accident prevention services to them the schools may gain invaluable support, for older persons vote in larger numbers than any other age group.

Emerging Methods of Instruction

The primary aim of safety education is to prevent destruction caused by accidents. Though safety education has already demonstrated its worth, school administrators and the public are concerned about improvement. We must fashion new approaches, better teaching strategies, and better protective countermeasures.

Elements of Quality in Teaching for Safe Living

Creative planning and teaching for safe living are based on principles of learning and of human growth and development. In a spirit of inquiry and growth, we can inspire the learner to learn sound, low-risk behavior. Choosing safe courses of action requires continuous decision making: teaching safe behavior means teaching for sound decision making.

Teaching safety requires a person-to-person relationship. Merely to lecture to students about safety or to require them to memorize a set of safety rules would be extremely naive. Teaching safe behavior involves knowing how the learner feels about himself, about people, and about things around him, in order to help him relate to them in safe ways.

For example, a young boy was upset when his dog was run over by a truck. Fortunately, he verbalized his feeling that if he too ran in front of a truck he could go to heaven and see his dog. Prompt counseling helped him to realize that a dog can be replaced. Circumstantial indications, though seldom legal evidence, in many accident reports suggest a suicide motive. The child with "school phobia" to the level of headaches and stomach cramps could well be an accident about to happen.

To create a setting in which the learner develops patterns for safe living, a teacher needs a strong sense of human worth and dignity. He must consistently demonstrate his understanding of and appreciation for safe conduct. It takes a number of situational learning experiences to develop inferences, concepts, or general ideas that influence subsequent behavior. Competency in teaching includes expertise in recording facts about a learner, hypothesizing about the learner only as these facts emerge, and later putting such accumulated facts together to derive guidelines for stimulating the learner to assess and deal safely with the risk in a situation.

Most students want to learn safety, once they understand the importance of such learning. Mere training in fixed habits does not make allowance for the adjustments and flexibilities demanded by modern life. It is not enough to drill the student on safe use of tools, on the use of seat belts in automobiles, or on closing the drawer of a file desk, for he will adopt these practices only to the extent that he comes to accept them as being important to living. It is important to keep in mind that the individual learner teaches himself safety to the extent that he becomes motivated and recognizes his own need for learning. The administrator and teacher create the situation and the climate for this self-appropriated, self-valued learning for safe living (10, pp. 220-21).

Social concern for the safety of others can be developed and learned best in the process of group living. To be an accepted member of a group is important to the individual, even in connection with his choice of low-risk conduct in a given situation. Failing to be accepted, he may choose to have an accident to get the attention he so desperately needs.

Caution needs to be matched by courage, lest life and learning become anxious, fear-bound, and inhibited. It is important to ensure that individuals not venture into situations before they have gained enough experience to operate safely in them. This warning contains strong implications for overall administrative, protective, and instructional responsibilities for the safety of the individual. The physical and emotional differences among pupils determine the differences in the types of activities they can undertake safely and the rate at which they can adjust to conditions and advance toward maturity in choosing low-risk behavior. Situational task analysis should be made by the administrator and the teacher and ultimately by the learner as he gains the necessary competencies (12).

Environment and Host-Agent Concept of Accidents

Although accidents are not a disease, what physicians have called the accident syndrome is remarkably similar to disease in terms of causal relationships and possible countermeasures. Accidents are usually a combination of three forces: the host, usually the human; the agent, an errant object or other cause of injury; and the environment in which the host and agent are operating. This host-agent-environment concept of accidents has been used primarily in research (7, pp. 231-32), but it can also be used by school administrators and teachers and applied in real-life situations.

Past studies have too often been limited to accumulating large amounts of statistical data, which alone are not sufficiently revealing of the real nature of accidents. Interrelationships among the factors involved are usually missing. Whether in research or in the real-life situation, consideration must be given to place and time of environmental exposure and to the victim's age, sex, and physical and mental state at the time of the accident. Inevitably, consideration of the many variables will produce more realistic substance for teaching safe behavior and more adequate protective countermeasures. The critical-incident approach employed in other areas of education and in behavioral studies is also being used in accident research, with a resultant emphasis on behavioral aspects in teaching and learning safety.

Defining and Testing the End Product—Behavior

Safety education includes teaching knowledge and skills of safe behavior, both of which can be measured by tests. But another component of behavior is attitude, which can be defined in various ways. There are no accurate measurements of attitude. The student taking an attitude test tends to respond with the answers he knows we want; the attitude evaluation becomes a knowledge test only. But from behavioral science, as well as from practical experience, we know that an educational effort that stops with knowledge and skills is incomplete. We often witness unsafe behavior by those who have both knowledge and skills. The usual attitude tests do not predict the learner's future action in situations in which he has relatively free choices. Safety education can be evaluated only by measuring the end product—behavior.

Ultimately, with the aid of research, we must gain greater sophistication in assessing long-term teaching-learning outcomes as they relate to safe behavior. Life is a series of problem-solving situations, to which the individual responds by acting in some definite and observable manner. We must learn to make objective, on-the-spot checks of situational response, as industry now does with some success. If our teaching has been effective, then the student may be expected to be an effective problem-solver in situations involving risk:

1. He will recognize potential accident problems and demonstrate *desire* to deal with them safely.
2. He will display *confidence* and *ability* to deal with the situations safely, instead of depending on guesses or hunches.
3. His *actions* in each situation will be accurate and safe.

Some efforts are being made to advance beyond the knowledge-skill testing level in this field. The "semantic differential," a means of measuring meaning and recognized relation of specific terms to safe behavior, has had limited use. The educator can use this approach at the practical level to assess safety value concepts held by individuals. These concepts, including behavioral reflections of attitude, may be observed over a period of time and scored as a composite representation of a learner's commitment to safe behavior.

Another approach is the projective technique, designed to catch the essence of the learner's image of himself in relation to safe or hazardous behavior and environment. A sentence-completion exercise can be used. Some sentences may be in the first person form, some in the third. The situation may be indicated and an emotional reaction to it required, or vice versa. For example,

1. When the electric power goes off I ______________________.
2. Nothing enrages George more when driving than ____________.
3. It was late and breakfast wasn't ready, so ________________.

Attempts to develop tests to measure hazard judgment and to predict personal accident tendencies are now being made. Such instruments, if effective, could be useful in teaching-learning situations.

Mobility

There is an increasing trend today to draw on teaching-learning services outside the school building; educators talk of converting the whole city into a school. This cannot be done without safe and efficient school-operated (or at least school-controlled) transportation. School transportation has been a significant part of rural education programs for many years. Now it has become just as essential in providing the necessary mobility for education programs in cities. Mass public transportation is not the answer. Metropolitan areas will be increasingly choked by lack of adequate transportation in the foreseeable future. Rapid transit systems will not keep pace with the needs of the general public, much less with the unique needs of students and faculty who seek to use the total community for learning. Public transportation, at best, will carry students only to those potential learning laboratories located on or near main routes. Few students who do not have their own transportation will have access to off-route community laboratories unless it is provided by the school system. The accident problem, which has already reached major proportions in the city, could become catastrophic without carefully planned and safely operated school transportation services.

Beyond the immediate concern of providing transportation for students, there are even broader implications for the schools in the continuing technological development and increasing mobility of our society, which are exposing all citizens to an ever wider range of hazards. International groups are at work developing plans for more efficient and safer mobility among nations. At the rate our world is shrinking, uniformity of traffic regulations cannot come too soon. A discouraging note is that both within the United States and in the international community, action has often been limited only to traffic safety, despite the need for a more comprehensive approach to the conservation of people and their environment.

Technology is capable of making cities highly adaptable to change, capable of accommodating shifts in substantial segments of population. Of great importance to such adaptability will be the flexibility of whole communities, including education. Diversified systems of small-unit flexible transport catering to all types of individuals and groups will be needed. Safe public vehicles for children, the infirm, and the elderly must get greater attention (13). Industry, operating under the Occupational Safety and Health Act of 1971, will adapt more rapidly than in the past for safer working conditions.

Reports to the United Nations indicate that the human accident toll of the world exceeds 750,000 deaths per year. A rising death rate from accidents in most European countries has been evident over the last 10 years. Although there is widespread distress about the rapidly increasing population of the world, there are also disturbing indications that we can easily destroy the human race by failing to plan and educate for orderly existence and the preservation of life and the environment. Alvin Toffler discusses a strange new race of nomads and the modular man, who will exist entirely detached from other people. He describes the period into which we are now moving as that of the "super-industrial revolution," in which the only semblance of equilibrium we can hope to maintain will come through the design of new social regulations.

The individual needs new principles for facing the onslaught of novelty in life; in short, he needs a new kind of education (23, pp. 357-63). Educators would do well to consider the following questions:

1. How can we renovate the curriculum to incorporate more effective learnings for conservation of life and environment?
2. Recognizing education as a lifelong process, the task of which is to shape an "adaptable" rather than a "finished" human being, can we develop programs, including safety programs, that will involve adults who never finished high school?
3. Can we offer programs in the community, starting with practical accident prevention projects for all ages, through satellite learning stations, mobile classrooms, radio, television, computer consoles, and two-way cable television linked with the school system's learning resources center?
4. Can the school develop integrally related safety curriculums designed to prepare people for the world of work?
5. Are present curriculum offerings appropriately related to the problems of living in a shrinking world?
6. Can all school systems develop and maintain optimum placement of safety materials in the curriculum for learners at all growth and developmental levels?
7. How can the entire school population, which in itself constitutes a social system, organize for ongoing, schoolwide accident prevention? (Even professional staff members are often victims of costly accidents.)

Emerging Trends in Implementing Elementary School Safety Education

Elementary school safety education provides a foundation for learning experiences in safe living. Safety concepts learned early are applicable immediately as well as in future situations. The need for sound curriculum development in elementary school safety education is vast. Misconceptions about what is valid in teaching safety pervade the teaching profession.

Accidents occur in a variety of settings and situations. Backyard swimming pools, for example, particularly the small, plastic-lined variety, can be treacherous hazards. Left uncovered when not in use, they are death traps. Used by unsupervised children, they spell tragedy. Even a refreshing cool drink, if served in a glass container, can turn a pleasant party into the scene of cruel lacerations. Elementary school children, through careful planning and involvement, can be sensitized to the dangers in their environment and can help parents to care for toddlers.

The rotary lawnmower might be one focus of an elementary school safety education effort. Alert teachers, recognizing the dangers—sharp blades, wet grassy slopes, and bullet-like flight of glass, stone, and metal—would introduce the problems to their students. After careful exploration involving teachers, maintenance personnel, lawnmower sales and service establishments, hospitals, and physicians, students could conduct a community education program.

Action is needed at local, state, and national levels (a) to involve a wide range of educators in planning for safety instruction and (b) to involve children in realistic and meaningful experiences that lead to safe behavioral patterns.

An ideal safety education effort would bring a representative group of educators and other leaders together for a planning symposium to develop useful content and a variety of approaches for effective instruction. The representatives working in the symposium would suggest ideas and techniques to help teachers teach safety. They would identify and design program directions and services. They might also—

1. Select local school situations for demonstration projects.
2. Select representatives for community participation and leadership.
3. Select safety elements, with pupil involvement.
4. Determine approaches and procedures for effective activities (e.g., demonstrations for orientation and sharing information).
5. Have specific schools or communities concentrate on different aspects of the problem.
6. Develop a plan for communication during the project, in cooperation with media, students, and lay leaders.
7. Develop presentations of successful activities to other students, teachers, local associations, and school systems.
8. Develop a report and guidelines for wide use.

The above strategies for wide involvement of personnel were employed in a demonstration project in Prince George's County, Md., in 1969. Its success was attested to by the administrators, teachers, and students involved. Among the valuable outcomes were the conclusions reached that (a) safety is a natural part of other subjects, (b) it usually enriches other learnings, (c) it should not be something offered only at certain designated times, and (d) it need not require extra time and effort on the part of teachers and pupils. Here is a statement from the project report prepared by the group (14):

> Many teachers may feel that including safety in their curriculum would necessitate the teaching of an extra subject and the setting aside of time each week to devote to the safety "curriculum." No one need tell a teacher that this is impractical from the standpoint of "finding the time." What, then, can be done to incorporate this vital content into all areas of the curriculum?
>
> The teachers who prepared this material answer this question from their own experiences. Each of them sought opportunities during their day-to-day class activities to introduce safety concepts. In reviewing their efforts they said that natural or appropriate incorporation of safety content was vital to success.

Emerging Trends in Secondary School Safety Education

The administrator is the key to the direction secondary school safety education will take in the future. He will determine whether it expands and improves, remains on the plateau where it seems to be today, or defers to other federal, state, and local agencies to provide the needed thrust for accident prevention. There are clear indications that, without aggressive leadership by top officials in the education community, other agencies, both public and private, will become increasingly active in safety education, stimulated by the availability of federal (and in some instances state) funds for conducting safety programs.

The limitations of such fragmented programs are evident. Many will be piecemeal projects dealing with one narrow area, such as shop safety, fire safety, aviation safety, driver education, or pupil transportation. All will compete with schools and colleges for the time of children, youth, and adults. These "separate package" projects, even if offered as adjuncts to school-centered curriculums, have a poor chance of being more than the sum of their parts in terms of long-range accident prevention. Some of these nonschool efforts will be worthwhile, of course, and there will continue to be a need in our society for worthwhile accident prevention efforts beyond the reaches of the school. Nevertheless, the schools, with intelligent, aggressive administrative leadership, are in the best position to provide a full spectrum of effective safety education.

Future safety education and accident prevention should be incorporated into the widest possible range of curriculums from kindergarten through grade 12 and should include comprehensive protection countermeasures. The learning can be enriched by articulation of the subject matter throughout elementary and secondary curriculums. A recent national project produced a set of "Teaching-Learning Guides" for a conceptual approach to safety curriculum design for grades K-12 (21). The Guides present four safety learning progression levels, but are not identified with traditional grades. They thus support the movement toward nongraded, individualized instruction.

Secondary school efforts need to be expanded and improved. Often only a few separate programs are offered. Driver education is the most common one, but in many school systems even this program is inadequate. Unfortunately for the nation as a whole, driver education, more than 35 years after its introduction, is still reaching little more than half the students approaching legal driving age. And all too frequently, limited time and sketchy treatment of the substance produce young drivers who are not qualified for the road.

Since driver and traffic safety is the predominant secondary school accident prevention offering, it will be used on the "from" side of the following model of a program in transition:

FROM	TO
Driver and Traffic Education, which . . .	*Comprehensive Safety Education,* which . . .
1. Exposes students to a concentrated offering in a single high school course	1. Provides general safety learning experiences to K-12 students, adults, and college and university students.
2. Offers limited "outside" instructional activity	2. Offers learning experiences that go beyond the four walls of the classroom and include home, mobile classrooms, satellite learning stations, more extensive field trips
3. Provides limited curricular offerings	3. Provides an enriched curriculum that runs the gamut of safety, including appropriate concepts from the broader areas of conservation of human and natural resources

4. Puts primary emphasis on driving knowledge, skills, attitudes, and traffic citizenship	4. Emphasizes conceptualization needed to recognize hazards in various situations, with appropriate attention to basic skills and responsibility for safety
5. Involves limited number of school personnel — often high school driver education teacher only	5. Involves all teachers (K-12 and beyond), parents, counselors, school administrators, school board members, and other decision makers
6. Is only an adjunct to the mainstream of education	6. Permeates all facets of education
7. Becomes stigmatized ("Now it's time for safety.")	7. Blends naturally and appropriately into many other curriculum experiences
8. Is basically a "tell 'em and test 'em" experience.	8. Accomplishes broad behavioral objectives through fresh, realistic approaches involving learners at all levels and using a wide range of instructional media —television (conventional and cable), radio, newspapers, computers (at school, in satellite learning stations, or on receiving consoles at home), other technology as available.

Safety education must be extended both vertically and horizontally: teachers at all levels and in many subject areas must collaborate with safety specialists (e.g., the driver education teacher) in creating articulated safety learning experiences. Such experiences need not require the expenditure of extra time by the safety specialists or by the other teachers, provided the safety substance is appropriately integrated into each teacher's ongoing work. In other words, the specialists should assist other teachers in planning and teaching safety as an integral part of their respective fields, instead of attempting the whole job themselves in a separate course.

The safety specialists will have an important additional role. Given this articulated teaching-learning process, students will master the basic safety concepts more fully and be more committed to safety citizenship than they would under the separate-course approach. The safety specialists, along with a cadre of instructional aides, will be able to work with students to develop neuromuscular skills, necessary in such activities as operating bicycles, motorcycles, automobiles, school buses, tractors, home appliances, shop equipment, farm and/or industrial machinery, and heavy construction machinery. Simulated devices for developing skills in some of these areas are available to schools now, and as school services extend into the community cooperatively with agriculture, business, and industry, interested students will have opportunity for actual guided experience in learning safe operations.

One way to begin the transition to such a safety education program would be through a pilot effort, limited at first to selected, cooperating elementary and secondary schools. The transition could extend to other schools as its feasibility could be tested and demonstrated.

Emerging Concepts in Curriculum Content

It is widely recognized that there is an ever-changing body of safety knowledge essential to the development of competent citizens.

More than the Sum of Its Parts
(Personnel Interrelated Roles)

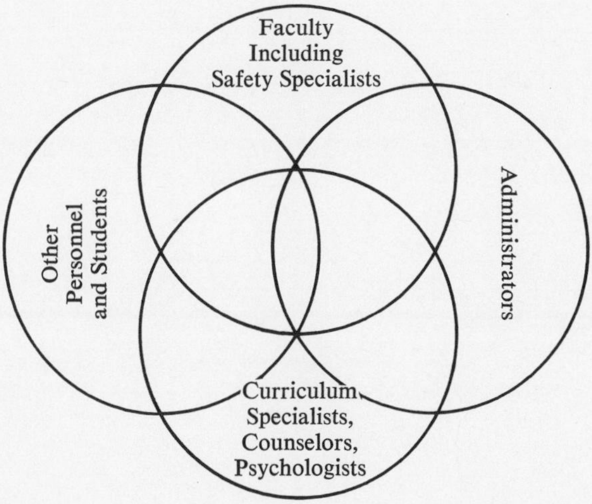

Safety education specialists will need to be involved with other teachers, administrators, researchers, curriculum supervisors, counselors, and psychologists in the logical incorporation of this body of knowledge throughout the curriculum. Such cooperative involvement will ensure that the knowledge is conceived as integral content needed by all to develop capability for selecting low-risk alternatives in the symbiosis of man, machine, and environment. Cooperative involvement will also provide the climate in which learners can develop a commitment to accident-prevention citizenship. Although detailed treatment would be impractical here, a number of general content areas can be identified.

Behavioral and Environmental Elements

The following are the major elements to be considered in safety instruction and protection. The list is neither exhaustive nor indicative of priorities.

1. Accident Reporting and Analysis
   a. Systematic plan for reporting and recording
   b. Periodic review and analysis
   c. Adjustment of curriculum and protection procedures as indicated by accident information
2. Building Engineer Training
   a. Fire control
   b. Equipment maintenance
   c. Housekeeping
   d. General safety (slippery floors, glass doors, handrails)
3. Cycle Safety (bicycle or motorcycle)
   a. Instruction and testing for safe operation
   b. Inspection
   c. Operation and parking regulations
   d. Licensing
4. Disaster Preparedness (tornados, floods, bombs in buildings, fires in homes and forests, civil defense)
   a. Safest areas inside and outside buildings, depending upon type of disaster
   b. Methods of signaling the threat of disaster and type of refuge to be taken
   c. Building inspections (at regular intervals and following emergencies)
   d. Drills, alternate routes
   e. Teacher preparation for emergencies, including first aid
5. Home Living Conditions and Safety
   a. Maintenance and safe use of appliances, toys, power mowers, and other urban or rural home equipment

   b. Inspection and maintenance of property (stairs, railings, porches, wiring; lead content of peeling paint)
   c. Knowledge of self-operating apartment elevators
   d. Dealing with crowded, noisy, and poor housekeeping conditions

6. Interpersonal Human Factors
   a. Aggressive, hazardous play
   b. Bullies and gangs
   c. Dealing with pupil's lack of self-esteem and potential for accidents
   d. Dealing with pupil's lack of involvement with others in play and work, including participation in maintaining property in safe condition
   e. Consideration of fear and frustration within the context of accident causation
   f. Relationship with parents and siblings and accident potential

7. Play Areas (school, home, community)
   a. Maintained in safe condition
   b. Adequately fenced when necessary
   c. School play areas continuously supervised by faculty
   d. Guidance of children into play activities appropriate to their skills and readiness for safe participation
   e. Safety inspection of facilities
   f. Development of pupil knowledge and awareness about safe areas and play activities at home and in the community
   g. Control of dogs and other animals

8. Seasonal and Vacation Safety
   a. Boating
   b. Water skiing
   c. Swimming
   d. Picnicking

9. Traffic Safety
   a. Selecting and training safety patrols
   b. Designating safest routes
   c. Developing knowledge of regulations and of traffic control devices
   d. Pedestrian safety
   e. Use of school bus and public transportation
   f. Driver education (automobile, motorcycle, and, where appropriate, snowmobile)
   g. Training for school bus drivers, commercial fleet operators, and industrial machinery operators in connection with vocational training

Special Areas of Safety

The following areas are treated in greater detail because of their unique elements and/or because of a certain urgency about them for schools and administrators now and most likely in the immediate future. Singling them out is *not* meant to imply that they should be isolated from the overall, comprehensive program of safety and accident prevention in schools and communities.

Safety for the Physically Impaired. While safety education for the physically handicapped is by no means universal in American schools, there are some outstanding programs for nonambulatory, semiambulatory, sight-handicapped, and aging persons. Some school systems are using funds from the Vocational Rehabilitation Administration of the U.S. Department of Health, Education, and Welfare to provide instruction for the physically handicapped. The U.S. Office of Education is also providing training grants for teachers of impaired persons.

Adequate, coordinated planning can open worlds to the handicapped by helping them to compensate for their impairments. They can learn to move about the home, the school, the office, and elsewhere and to participate in vocational and leisure time activities. They can acquire competence in a range of day-to-day activities, including operating an automobile. One of the important tasks of education is to help the so-called normal person to understand that physical impairment is usually only a matter of degree, not total disability.

Our society has discriminated against the handicapped by failing to make all buildings accessible to and usable by them. Modifications can be made at little or no extra cost, and they often render a building or other facility more convenient for the average person as well. Replacing curbs and steps with ramps to accommodate wheelchair students may be resisted by some school people on the theory that it will cost more to maintain them. But experience has shown that ramps greatly reduce the time required to sweep sidewalks in summer and remove snow in winter. The ramps also prove safe for the impaired persons, for other pedestrians, and even for vehicular traffic, because of the smoother flow and easier mobility they provide.

Pupil Transportation. Tremendous improvement in pupil transportation has been made over the years, thanks to the cooperation of educators, manufacturers, and other interested groups. This improvement has been brought about largely through national conferences held from time to time, state legislation designed to improve transportation programs, and local supervision and guidance of a national transportation system that has been called the largest and safest in the world. In the past 25 years, all states have prescribed standards for school buses, and almost all of them enforce these standards. About half the states have reasonably adequate instruction programs for school bus drivers, and local transportation programs in general are operated fairly efficiently.

Despite the progress, however, the standards and procedures for operation—including selection, training, and supervision of drivers—are not adequate to meet increasingly complex problems. It is imperative that continuing efforts be made toward safer and more efficient pupil transportation operation. In the future, continuing vigorous efforts must be made at national, state, and local levels to deal with the technical problems of building, maintaining, and operating school buses and with the changing nature of traffic in which they must operate. The federal government, through its Highway Safety Administration, is actively developing standards and programs in this field. Yet the education community bears great responsibility for dynamic leadership and direction in the area of pupil transportation.

Under administrator guidance, the education community can help determine the kind and extent of safety features that should be built into school buses and the scientific means by which bus performance can be measured. School administrators can also lead in the determination of how school transportation safety can be furthered by periodic state inspections of motor vehicles—not only school buses but all the other vehicles that school buses encounter in their daily operation. We need to develop a system of school bus accident reporting that will provide information useful for program improvement. Both the education community and the general public need to know more about the effectiveness of the school bus stop law.

Much more sophisticated programs for selection, training, and supervision of school bus operators are needed. Although most states require some type of special license to drive a school bus, these requirements, as well as the state agencies that issue the licenses, differ. On the surface, the requirements for prospective school bus drivers may appear to be reasonably complete in virtually all states. Local school districts or independent operators of school bus services, however, often interpret the requirements broadly, relegating the state standards to the level of general guidelines at best. A systematic procedure should be developed for local school districts and other employing groups to use in choosing from available candidates for the position of school bus driver.

Today more than one out of three students enrolled in school is a school bus passenger, and the ratio will jump drastically as students in urban areas increasingly make use of transportation facilities to reach learning resources outside the school. Schools need to make instruction in safe use of buses a regular part of the curriculum.

The yellow school bus, its driver, and its passengers are more visible to the general public than any other part of the school operation. The driver is important not only for the safe transport of his passengers but also as a public relations representative for the school system.

To All School Bus Drivers

He takes to school the children small,
A service done for us
And watches over one and all—
The man who drives the bus.

He shares the children's chatter gay,
To them his name is known
He guards them safely day by day
As though they were his own.

Not lightly can his task be faced
Fair days, or snow or rain
In him the parent's trust is placed
To bring them home again.

Oh, School Bus Drivers one and all,
Be heartening it must
To have the care of children small
And know so great a trust.

—Edgar A. Guest

Eye Protection. Eye protection has long been a concern of American education and of school administrators. As activities in which students are expected to participate have increased in complexity and in danger to the eyes, safeguards against eye injury and instruction for their appropriate use have taken on paramount importance. At least 20 states have passed laws or issued administrative rulings requiring students and teachers to wear eye protection devices in specified school programs—mainly in vocational and industrial arts shops and science laboratories. But these laws, like laws limiting the speed on highways, do not necessarily prevent accidents.

Several organizations, including the American National Standards Institute, the National Safety Council, and the National Society for the Prevention of Blindness, have issued statements in support of legislative or administrative rulings on the use of eye protection equipment and, in so doing, have identified some of the problem areas:

- Signs quoting pertinent protection provisions of the law, even though posted and plainly visible to those using shops and laboratories, are often disregarded by students and faculty alike.
- The availability of protective devices is often a problem; while some state laws authorize their purchase from school funds, in other states they must be purchased by students and teachers.
- Some types of devices, such as the "splash goggles" used in chemistry laboratories, are not compatible with contemporary hair styles.
- A student participating in more than one shop or laboratory may use the same device for all, even where it is not adequate.

School administrators must work for the development of regulations and practices that will not inhibit student capabilities, will provide maximum protection, and will make allowance for human adjustment. Administrators should ask themselves the following questions:

- Considering that valid practices must be adapted to local needs and will logically change with conditions from time to time, are state and local school board regulations more practical than those prescribed by state legislation?
- If so, how can school systems, both state and local, participate most effectively in the development of practical regulations and procedures?
- Are all groups that may be concerned—e.g., state education departments, school administrators, school boards, parent-teacher associations, other citizen groups, and safety education specialists—involved in the development of the plan? Has provision been made to determine how any rules and policies may be affected by already existing laws and regulations?
- Is professional advice, including consultation from physicians specializing in eye problems, available to ensure that what is desired is set forth appropriately?
- Is the plan structured so as to provide realistic funding and other necessary support?

- Are overall principles and purposes of teaching and learning clearly identified to avoid ill-conceived regulations and procedures?
- Are provisions made to ensure that responsibility will be placed with people who can implement the program most effectively?

In a program for eye protection, just as in any other program of education, budgeting is of utmost importance. Financial support must be provided not only for the acquisition of equipment but also for the necessary periodic repairs and maintenance. Funding is also necessary for the instructional phases of the program, which are appropriately integrated into the general program along with other safety content.

Disaster Preparedness. There are few major national issues on which we find a greater divergence of opinion than that of civil defense or disaster preparedness. The emotional factors that lie behind opinions on this issue often make people impervious to change.

Disaster preparedness includes protection against the hazards of natural disasters as well as those of nuclear war. It is logical to treat the two as related entities. People in areas where the tornado, the hurricane, the earthquake, or some other natural disaster is a rather common experience understand the hazards and generally tend to have protective programs. But there are few programs for protection of the school population against the radiation effects of nuclear weapons. Until the world is truly at peace, this kind of preparedness is just as essential.

The public and a substantial number of school officials are poorly informed on the subject. Providing the greatest possible physical protection and civil defense education for the school population includes informing the public about civil defense. In so doing, the school develops support for its own program.

The most practical approach to civil defense is to build the maximum protection factor into schools and other public structures and to provide consistent, realistic instruction for dealing with radioactive fallout from nuclear blasts. Time is on the side of man's survival, for the radioactivity of fallout begins to weaken at once. Similarly, distance from the radioactive fallout means weaker radiation. Finally, shielding—placing the greatest possible density of material between persons and fallout—reduces the intensity. Every building provides some protection.

Through use of "slanting" (offsetting structures to break direct passage of air through entryways and corridors) and other techniques, the protection offered by new school buildings can be increased with little or no cost. There are also many expedient measures that can be taken to improve the protection factor of existing buildings without sacrificing esthetic quality.

Accidental Injury and Death from the Effects of Alcohol. Alcoholic beverages continue to play a significant role in human social relationships throughout most of the world. Among nations where the problem has been studied, cultural norms and social expectations relating to the use of alcohol seem to be shifting toward greater permissiveness.

Because even a low level of alcohol in the bloodstream adversely affects human performance, the use of alcohol plays a major role in accidents in industry, among seamen, in private aviation operations, in recreational boating, and most frequently on streets and highways.

So serious is the alcohol problem in the nation's traffic accident picture that the federal government has placed it first among those to be dealt with through nationwide programs for traffic safety. The National Safety Administration predicts that of the 60,000 people who will die in traffic accidents each year during the 1970's, almost half will be under the influence of alcohol (15). There are some 8 million alcoholics in the United States.

At least four cultural or ethnic attitudes with respect to drinking practices can be identified (20): (a) abstinent culture (negative and prohibitive); (b) ambivalent culture (conflict between different coexisting value structures); (c) permissive culture (permissive, but negative toward drunkenness); and (d) permissive dysfunctional culture (permissive about drinking and about behavior of the intoxicated). It is evident that alcohol abuse—frequently a deep-seated cultural problem—is not likely to be remedied through a lecture or preaching approach. A long-term educational approach starting early in the learner's school experience, coupled with therapy when needed, would seem to have the greatest chance for success. Such an approach further supports the concept that accident prevention experiences should extend from childhood throughout life.

*Providing Safe School Buildings.** Thousands of obsolete and unsafe school buildings across the country, as well as the many private schools springing up in old garages and abondoned stores,

---

* This material is adapted from materials developed by a special committee and staff of the former Safety Education Commission of the National Education Association.

Some Dimensions of Inadequate or Unsafe School Facilities

School Site

Situation	Problem	Countermeasures: Preconstruction	Countermeasures: Postconstruction
1. School built too near highway or railroad track	a. Speed	a. Build elsewhere.	a. Provide municipal protection of teachers and students from traffic dangers; construct overpasses; gear signals to school needs.
	b. Noise	b. Build elsewhere.	b. Buffer with appropriate plantings or masonry baffles.
	c. Air pollution	c. Build elsewhere. (Teachers, students, and lay leaders should be involved in school site selection.)	c. Air-condition for climate control.
2. School in takeoff and landing path of airport	a. Noise	a. As in (a) above.	a. Seek legal action to limit noise or change pathway.
	b. Crash danger	b. As in (a) above. (Check Federal Aviation Agency regarding planned airports.)	b. Seek legal action to change pathway.
3. Space around building for parking and loading areas for private cars, school buses, and cycles	Inadequate space, congestion, danger to teachers and students from moving vehicles	Design facilities to separate functions; e.g., pedestrian walkways to parking area should be physically separated from moving vehicles. Plan separate areas for cycle parking.	Facilities must be studied and a plan designed to separate functions either physically or by staggered scheduling.

4. Walkways around building	a. Obstructions projecting from building, e.g., casement window	a. Require six foot clearance between walkway and projection.	a. Eliminate projections; relocate walkway to avoid projections.
	b. Heavy snow slide from roof	b. Require six foot clearance (or more, depending on height of building) between walkway and building.	b. Relocate walkway.
5. Blending of school with site, grading, etc.	a. Poorly designed steps from floor level to ground level at doorway	a. Construct walkway or platform leading to doorway on same level as floor inside.	a. Rebuild outside walkway to bring it to floor level; gradual ramp may be adequate.
	b. Lack of ramps for physically handicapped persons	b. Include these facilities in building design and construction.	b. Add facilities as necessary.
		Building Interior	
1. Walking surface	a. Stairways	a. Build standard, uniform treads and risers throughout building; ramps rather than stairways; handrails on both sides (middle, too, on wide stairways); nonslip treads.	a. Add handrails on both sides and in middle if necessary; add nonslip treads or carpeting
	b. Texture	b. Install carpeting or nonslip surface.	b. Use nonslip waxes; add abrasive surface overlay
2. Interior doors	a. Swinging into areas of heavy traffic	a. Plan to swing away from heavy traffic.	a. Rehang doors to swing in safe direction.

		Countermeasures	
Situation	*Problem*	*Preconstruction*	*Postconstruction*
	b. Glass partitions	b. Install protective glass.	b. Replace unsafe glass with protective variety.
3. Drinking fountains	a. Obstructing traffic	a. Build alcoves for fountains.	a. Remove and relocate; construct gradual buffer.
	b. Poorly designed spigots that do not safeguard against damaging mouth and teeth on impact	b. Install spigots of safe design.	b. Replace old spigots with safe ones.
4. Casement window	Swinging into classrooms or work spaces	Use another style; provide for clearance (no closer than six feet from floor).	Replace with double-hung or sliding pane; seal closed where opening could endanger teacher or children.

point to the need for providing a safer environment for teachers and children. Even in new and relatively safe schools, school buses, science laboratories, kitchens, and shops often operate far below reasonable standards for teacher-student safety. Other unsafe school facilities are listed, with suggested countermeasures, on pages 300-302.

Protection Against Violence and Vandalism. The targets of school violence and vandalism include people, equipment, buildings, school buses, and other motor vehicles. Dealing with violence and vandalism involves treating delinquent behavior on the part of certain students in an effort to achieve social stability. The following initial steps are suggested to administrators, teachers, parents, students, and others interested in doing something about this problem:

1. Send a questionnaire to selected school districts to find out the nature and scope of their vandalism and violence problems and to learn of programs used to prevent them.
2. Survey state education agencies to determine what relevant recommendations and materials they may have issued for statewide use by schools and communities.
3. Using the results of the first two steps, plus firsthand observation in a few communities where schools are active in countermeasures, develop a plan for prevention and put it into effect.
4. Identify the conditions that may turn out to be root causes for future disorders, giving special consideration to—
   - School administrative personnel and their relations with students, teachers, and classified school employees.
   - Teachers and their relations with students and with each other.
   - School regulations affecting students.
   - Daily school routines affecting students.
   - Nature and extent of available opportunities for student participation in revising school rules, routines, and conditions.
5. Survey students periodically (both through samplings of individuals and through representatives of various classes or other groups) to determine their special concerns in terms of administrative personnel, teachers, rules, regulations, or other factors. Identification of such concerns and action on them may prevent violence in the future.
6. Seek to identify leaders among student groups who might be consulted about the trends in what students are saying and who could offer advice as to how to bring about what they believe are needed changes.

7. Set up situations for role playing among school personnel (some of whom could play student types) in order to develop understanding and sensitivity regarding human relationships in the school environment.
8. Plan, with care and persistence, effective parental roles related to potential school disorders.
9. Develop year-round extended day program of effectively supervised safety, recreation, and study geared to the needs and interests of all youth and adults.

Summary

Safety education stands on the verge of a real breakthrough. Federal aid to education, state funding, the Highway Safety Act, and the Occupational Safety and Health Act are providing a new impetus in this area.

The promise is here, and so is the challenge. Our rapidly changing, increasingly complex society is placing new and complex demands upon administrators and schools. The educational system must enable students to cope successfully with hazards to life, property, and environment. More often than not, this kind of safety learning can be integrated into other basic learnings without significant additional cost and effort.

The alternative is an educational effort worthless to the thousands who will not survive to benefit from it. We value human life and the contribution of general education to it. How much is an expensive education worth when it is buried, especially if there has been no opportunity to put it to use? Schools must better develop the knowledge, skills, and behaviors that enable people to recognize and overcome accident potential.

A comprehensive program of protection and safety education must be implemented as an intrinsic part of the total school program. Such programs must attain specific objectives in harmony with total educational goals. Safety education is citizenship education of the highest order. It is performance on a profit-sharing basis.

A program of this nature is aimed at reaching the total population, including students, administrators, counselors, teachers, librarians, custodians, cafeteria workers, bus drivers, other service personnel, and the community. It is concerned with enabling individuals to apply intelligence in determining their own safe behavior and to use their own reasoning powers for selecting productive actions. Maintaining a safe environment is an integral part of the total program.

Public education is concerned with promoting the welfare of our total society as well as of the individuals within it. Since accidents affect the welfare of both society and the individual, what could be more directly related to the concerns of public education than accident prevention? Like Kettering, the administrator is interested in the future, because his students are going to spend the rest of their lives there.

BIBLIOGRAPHY

1. American Association of School Administrators. *Profiles of the Administrative Team.* Washington, D.C.: the Association, 1971.

2. American Association of School Administrators and National Commission on Safety Education. *A Realistic Approach to Civil Defense: A Handbook for School Administrators.* Produced in cooperation with the Office of Civil Defense, Department of Defense. Washington, D.C.: Government Printing Office, 1966.

3. American National Standards Institute. *Specifications for Making Buildings and Facilities Accessible to and Usable by the Physically Handicapped.* New York: American Standards Association, 1961.

4. Bureau of Labor Standards, U.S. Department of Labor. *Proceedings of the President's Conference on Occupational Safety.* Bulletin No. 263. Washington, D.C.: Government Printing Office, 1965.

5. Drucker, Peter F. *The Age of Discontinuity: Guidelines to Our Changing Society.* New York: Harper & Row, 1968.

6. Florida Department of Education. *Minimum Standards for School Buses: Standards for School Bus Operation.* Tallahassee: the Department, 1970.

7. Haddon, William, Jr. "The Interrelationship of Host, Agent, and Environmental Variables." *Accident Research: Methods and Approaches.* (Edited by William Haddon, Jr., Edward A. Suchman, and David Klein.) New York: Harper & Row, 1964.

8. Harlacher, Ervin L., and Roberts, Eleanor. "Accountability for Student Learning." *Junior College Journal* 41: 26-30; March 1971.

9. Hutchens, Robert M. *The Learning Society.* New York: Frederick A. Praeger, 1968.

10. Key, Norman. "The Role of Safety Education." *Education for Safe Living.* Fourth edition. Englewood Cliffs, N.J.: Prentice-Hall, 1966. pp. 220-21.

11. ———. "Safety Education." *Curriculum Handbook for School Administrators.* (Edited by Forrest E. Conner and William J. Ellena.) Washington, D.C.: American Association of School Administrators, 1967.

12. ———. "Safety Education." *Encyclopedia of Educational Research.* Fourth edition. London: Macmillan Co., 1969. p. 1163.

13. McHale, John. *The Future of the Future.* New York: George Braziller, 1969.

14. National Commission on Safety Education, National Education Association. *Where the Learning Is.* Washington, D.C.: the Association, 1969.

15. National Highway Safety Administration, U.S. Department of Transportation. *The Alcohol Safety Countermeasures Program.* Washington, D.C.: the Administration, 1970.

16. ———. *Proceedings: National Driver Education and Training Symposia.* Washington, D.C.: the Administration, 1969.

17. National Safety Council. *Highway Safety Manpower and Training.* Chicago: the Council, 1968.

18. National Study of Secondary School Evaluation. *Evaluative Criteria.* Washington, D.C.: the Study, 1970.

19. ———. *Evaluative Criteria for Junior High Schools.* Washington, D.C.: the Study, 1970.

20. Pittman, David J. "Alcoholic Beverages in Culture and Society." *Alcohol and Accidental Injury.* Proceedings of a Conference. Washington, D.C.: Government Printing Office, 1966.

21. School Health Education Study. *The Potential for Hazards and Accidents Exists, Whatever the Environment.* Washington, D.C.: the Study, 1971.

22. Sill, Henry. *Man: The Next Thirty Years.* New York: Hawthorn Books, 1968.

23. Toffler, Alvin. *Future Shock.* New York: Random House, 1970.

24. Venn, Grant. *Man, Education, and Manpower.* Washington, D.C.: American Association of School Administrators, 1970.

15

Science Education

The Emerging Science Education Program

Changes in society, in the environment, in our culture, and in the psychology of learning make changes in education, and more specifically in science education, imperative. During the past 15 years, the science program (K-12) has undergone major curriculum reform in terms of philosophy, objectives, content, methodology, and techniques used in evaluation. But this reform, while substantial, must still be considered only one phase of a continual program in revision and development—a program that began soon after World War II, rather than after Sputnik, as many believe. Sputnik did help by arousing American educators, scientists, and political leaders to make available large sums of money through the National Science Foundation and other agencies both public and private, to prepare science curriculum materials, and to assist in the preservice and inservice preparation of teachers.

The first efforts in curriculum reform have only partially answered the questions of *what* and *how* to teach science and have failed to answer the more basic question of *why* we teach what science we do. The successes and failures of the new K-12 science programs have alerted educators and psychologists to study and evaluate critically their basic assumptions about teaching and learning as they apply to *all* pupils. It is more apparent now than ever before that improvement of curriculum objectives, content, and methodolgy must begin with a thorough analysis of (a) the nature of science, (b) the nature of society, and (c) the nature of the learner.

Objectives of Science Education

The overarching objective of science education must be the preparation of a scientifically literate adult—one who perceives and believes in the logical processes of science, who understands the natural world in which he lives, who has some understanding and appreciation of the interaction of science and technology, who understands the impact of science on society and of society on science, and who has the interests and attitudes necessary to study and explore science as an aid in solving personal and environmental problems.

Each committee or group preparing science curriculum materials for a particular grade level or subject area acted independently with respect to objectives and content. One might ask, What would be the nature of the science curriculum had efforts been made to design and develop a K-12 program beginning with the *same* concepts of science, society, and the learner? The science curriculum reform movement may, in all honesty, be described as a patchwork program. Nevertheless, a review of the new programs in science education reveals certain general objectives. These were stated by the Education Commission of the States in the science section of the National Assessment of Educational Progress (2) as follows:

Objective I.	Know the fundamental facts and principles of science
Objective II.	Possess the abilities and skills needed to engage in the processes of science
Objective III.	Understand the investigative nature of science
Objective IV.	Have attitudes about and appreciation of scientists, science, and the consequences of science that stem from adequate understandings.

The new programs, then, stress scientific knowledge, abilities and skills, processes, and attitudes. These general objectives give direction for the formulation of course objectives, which in turn are reflected in the classroom teacher's daily behavioral objectives. The classroom teacher must formulate specific objectives in three domains: (a) the cognitive (mental and intellectual processes of the learner), (b) the affective (appreciation, attitudes, emotions, and interests of the learner), and (c) the psychomotor (neuromuscular and physical skills).

Emerging Concept of Content

The traditional content of the science curriculum has consisted of the major facts, concepts, and principles of the discipline. The new programs in science have added another dimension: they attempt to develop an understanding of how scientific information is obtained and how it is used to solve problems. Recent research in the psychology of learning has revealed that the child learns best when he is actively involved (physically as well as mentally), when he is experiencing inquiry processes in investigating problems of interest to him. The learning theories of Bruner (knowledge of dynamic process, importance of conceptual structure), Gagne (sequence of learning materials), Piaget (level of maturity), and others have played an important role in the development of recent science programs.

New programs for the elementary school range from the hierarchical concept of organization (e.g., "Science: A Process Approach" by the American Academy for the Advancement of Science) to a completely flexible, teacher-determined program (e.g., the "Elementary Science Study"). Secondary school programs, for the most part, are oriented toward inquiry processes but retain major emphasis on the facts, concepts, and principles of the discipline. In general, the new programs place little or no emphasis on the social or esthetic context of science, the application of science to leisure-time activities, or the use of science to solve persistent personal or societal problems.

The explosion of scientific knowledge is reflected in the new programs: emphasis is placed on identifying conceptual themes and treating each in depth, instead of attempting to cover the whole gamut of knowledge in a given field. This shift is a difficult one for some classroom teachers to adapt to. Some of the new programs seem to emphasize the kind of science that is good for science and the scientists rather than the kind that is good for students in our schools today. Content, writing style, and types of laboratory experience seem clearly designed for the middle and upper levels of student ability. Efforts have been made in some programs to prepare materials for low ability levels, but without complete success. In the hands of a skillful, dedicated teacher, most of the programs can be adapted for a broad range of student ability.

Emerging Concept of Methodology

One characteristic of all the new programs is a focus on inquiry, investigation, and self-discovery—the involvement of the learner in the learning process. The emphasis has changed from *content* per se to the *processes* by which science is studied. The role of the teacher has changed from "a purveyor of information" to "a director of learning activities"—one who establishes a classroom climate in which learning takes place. The teaching strategies are not fixed but rather vary with the objective, the concept, the pupils in the group, and the teachers.

Science programs designed for student involvement demand a wide range of equipment and a degree of flexibility in the physical plant. They require ample room for storage of materials and projects and for student investigation, exploration, and experimentation. Many of the new programs come as packages including teacher and student manuals and the materials necessary for laboratory work. These self-contained programs are convenient, but they may be slightly more costly for the school. In most cases, it is money well spent.

The modern concept of methodology is vastly different from the methodology in more conventional programs. The change is greatest at the elementary school level, where science has usually been taught as another reading subject. Having inservice workshops conducted by individuals who are well versed in use of the new materials will help teachers make the change smoothly.

The programs developed during the past 15 years have not solved all the problems in science education, but they have made many important contributions. For the first time, the federal government has provided funds for curriculum reform, large numbers of individuals outside the field of education have become interested, and the need for change has become apparent in all areas of the curriculum. Educators are critically evaluating the real role and objectives of American education in an attempt to meet the ever-changing needs of the school population and the larger society.

Table 1 reveals some of the major efforts in the science curriculum reform movement that have been funded by grants from the National Science Foundation and other public and private agencies. These programs have been influential in producing changes in other individual and commercially prepared science curriculum materials. Before selecting a science program, it is well to review them all—those in Table 1 and those prepared without special grants or funding. Programs must be selected on the basis of the educational philosophy of the district, its objectives, the nature of the community and the aspirations of its people, the interests and needs of its school population, and the attitudes and preparation of its teachers.

Selecting the proper program may be a long and difficult task, but it will save many hours of frustration for teachers, students, parents, and administrators in the long run. The new program will not necessarily make a strong teacher out of a weak one. The products of curriculum reform are not "teacher-proof"; they are not easier to teach and demand more planning time than traditional science curriculums do. A new program, because of its nature and its involvement of the learner, will probably require some additional facilities and equipment. It will not meet the needs of all students as written, but in the hands of a skillful teacher it can be adapted to a broad segment of the school population. A good inservice program is essential to ensure maximum teacher effectiveness in using the new materials. Teachers should be encouraged to include some of their own ideas in the curriculum and to search continually for innovative ideas in curriculum and instruction.

We live in an age of science—of space exploration, atomic energy, biotic drugs, and ever improving systems of transportation and communication. Science influences the world of human affairs—economic, political, and social. Students must experience some science education in order to understand their culture and environment. It is essential that they have the best science program possible if they are to solve the many problems in the years ahead.

Elementary Science Education

Emerging Trends in Curriculum

A little over ten years ago, scientists and science educators began looking at science education at the elementary level with a renewed interest. They were not pleased with what they saw: programs built largely around one or more textbook series with a major emphasis on factual knowledge, technological information, and the physical sciences. The programs were mostly teacher-centered and provided little or no opportunity for the student to do anything but read and talk about science, which was presented both by the teachers and by the textbooks in a very authoritarian manner. Appalled by the discrepancy between what was being taught as science and what they felt science as a human enterprise should be, the scientists and science educators initiated a large number of attempts to produce curriculums that more nearly reflected the true nature of science.

Some of the new curriculums were organized around conceptual schemes, some around the processes of science, and some as just a large number of discrete units. Some attempted to integrate science and mathematics, or to use one topic, such as astronomy,

TABLE 1

Funded Programs in Science Education

Curriculum Project	K	1	2	3	4	5	6	7	8	9	10	11	12
Elementary Science													
AAAS Science: A Process Approach	←	—	—	—	—	—	→						
COPES Conceptually Oriented Programs Elementary Science	←	—	—	—	—	—	→						
ESS Elementary Science Study	←	—	—	—	—	—	—	—	→				
IDP Inquiry Development Program					←	—	→						
MINNEMAST Minnesota Mathematics and Science Teaching Project	←	—	—	→									
SCIS Science Curriculum Improvement Study	←	—	—	—	—	—	→						

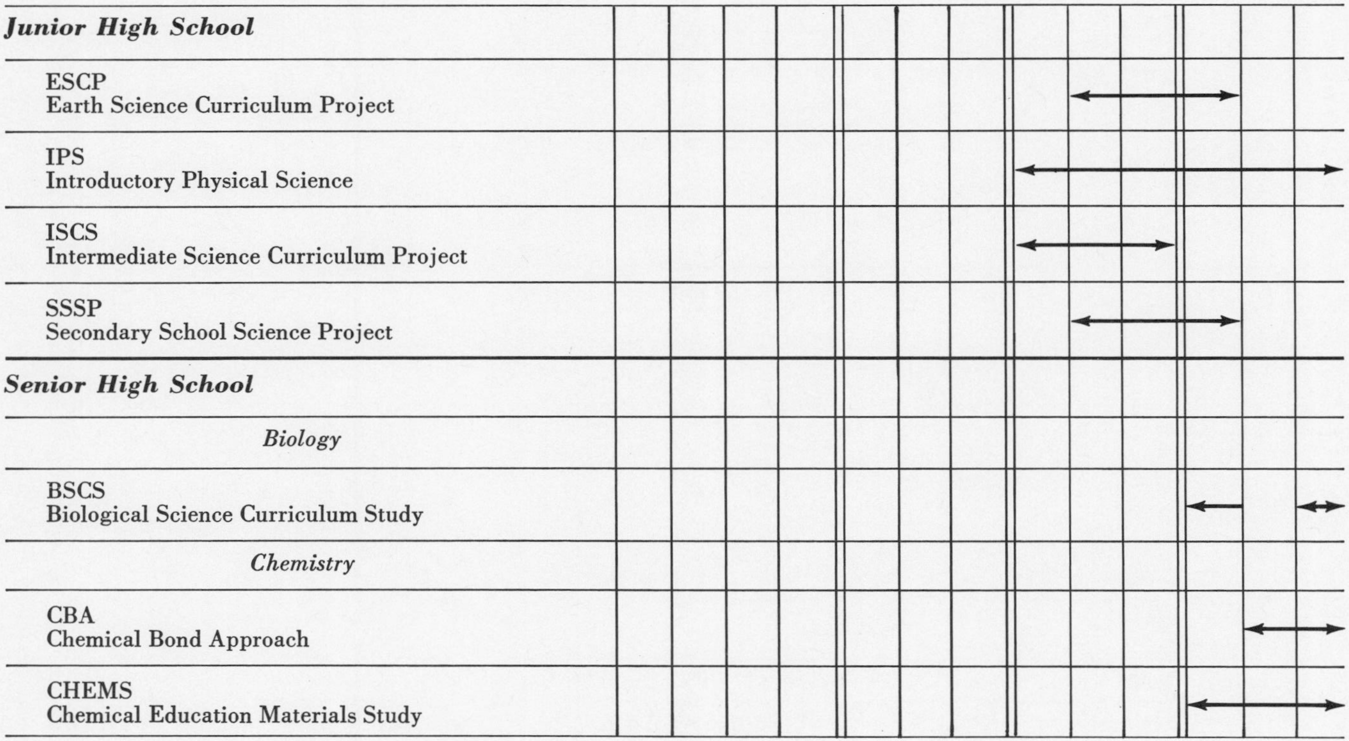
Junior High School
ESCP
Earth Science Curriculum Project
IPS
Introductory Physical Science
ISCS
Intermediate Science Curriculum Project
SSSP
Secondary School Science Project
Senior High School
Biology
BSCS
Biological Science Curriculum Study
Chemistry
CBA
Chemical Bond Approach
CHEMS
Chemical Education Materials Study

GRADES

Curriculum Project	K	1	2	3	4	5	6	7	8	9	10	11	12
Physics													
Harvard Project Physics											↔	↔	↔
PSSC Physical Science Study Committee												↔	↔
Portland Integrated Sciences											↔	↔	↔
Technology													
ECCP The Man-Made World											↔	↔	↔

as a unifying thread around which the entire elementary science program could be built. The various new programs had a number of common elements that made them completely different from all previous ones: they placed major emphasis on discovery techniques and inquiry learning, and they called for student involvement on a much larger scale. Most of the programs also required a redefinition of the elementary teacher's role.

Science: A Process Approach (AAAS—American Academy for the Advancement of Science)

History: Initiated in Washington, D.C., in 1962, the AAAS program was being used by more than 50,000 teachers in 1970-71.

Objectives: The program is based on the philosophy that the processes of science and the scientific approach to gaining knowledge have a fundamental importance in the general education of every child.

Content and approach: Probably the most structured of all the new elementary programs, the AAAS program is based entirely on behavioral objectives. The program is material-centered, with the students manipulating equipment and gathering their own data for each lesson. The AAAS program is based on the psychology of Robert Gagne.

Teaching materials: Equipment and printed materials for grades K-4 are available from the Xerox Corporation.

Conceptually Oriented Program in Elementary Science (COPES)

History: COPES was started in September 1965 at New York University by Morris H. Shamos and J. Darrell Barnard, who sought to develop a program based on the "great ideas" in science.

Objectives: COPES is to be an action-centered program based on a spiral scheme, which stresses the major concepts of science as identified by the writers of the program.

Content and approach: The COPES program uses a student-centered approach with strong emphasis on laboratory investigations. It draws most of its activities from the physical sciences.

Teaching materials: Only one of the five planned teacher's guides is available. There are no plans to provide a kit of materials for this program; the task of collecting materials is left to either the individual teacher or the science consultant.

Elementary Science Study (ESS)

History: ESS originated with the Educational Development Center, Cambridge, Massachusetts, in 1960. A large group of scientists, science educators, and classroom teachers were brought together to develop this program.

Objectives: The group sought to produce a highly individual, experimental program in which the children have access to the materials for open-ended rather than teacher- or textbook-directed investigations.

Content and approach: The content of this program includes a wide variety of topics, drawn about equally from the physical and life sciences. The method of instruction is independent study, including laboratory investigations with discussion groups.

Teaching materials: There are 56 units now available from the Webster Division of the McGraw-Hill Book Company, covering grades K-8. The local school must use these units to put together its own science program. For most of the units a materials kit is offered.

Inquiry Development Program (IDP)

History: J. Richard Suchman has developed this program as a result of his interest in inquiry techniques. The program was started in 1959 with a grant from the U.S. Office of Education.

Objectives: The major goals of the IDP program are to foster and promote inquiry techniques and to encourage students to view the world as a scientist does.

Content and approach: An IDP session begins with the presentation of an inquiry problem or discrepant event; the students then discuss the problem and usually generate a number of theories. After the discussion session they are free to experiment, review the event, and consult other resources.

Teaching materials: There are a number of materials available for this program—film loops, teacher's guides, teacher's demonstration kit, student experiment kit, and a resource book from Science Research Associates (SRA). Dr. Suchman claims the program can be used in grades 4 through 10; SRA recommends it for grades 6 through 9.

Minnesota Mathematics and Science Teaching Project (MINNEMAST)

History: The MINNEMAST program was started in 1961 at the University of Minnesota by Paul C. Rosenbloom.

Objectives: The aim of this coordinated mathematics and science program is to provide for process acquisition, attitudinal changes, and scientific literacy in elementary school students.

Content and approach: Content is drawn from both mathematics and science and is to be taught through independent study, laboratory investigations, seminars, and discussion groups.

Teaching materials: Units 1 through 30 for grades K-3 are available by writing the director, Roger Jones. A textbook, *Ideas in Mathematics,* is available from the W. B. Saunders Company.

Science Curriculum Improvement Study (SCIS)

History: This program was established in 1962 by Robert Karphis at the University of California, Berkeley.

Objectives: The major objective of the Science Curriculum Improvement Study is to provide a conceptual scheme for science instruction in grades 1-6 and to offer a materials-centered, laboratory, investigative approach for students to develop this scheme.

Content and approach: The program consists of six units in life science and six in physical science, to be taught through discovery learning and inquiry.

Teaching materials: All of the units for grades 1-6—teacher's guides, student manuals, and materials kits—are available from Rand McNally and Company.

All three of the currently available programs—Elementary Science Study, Science Curriculum Improvement, and Science: A Process Approach—are materials-centered and make the materials available in kit form along with the printed units. Accessibility of materials removes a sizable burden from the teacher, who no longer has to gather, borrow, or construct equipment. It also helps ensure that science will be a regular part of the elementary school curriculum.

With these programs on the shelf, developed and ready to use, the next task to accomplish in elementary science education is implementation. Having once selected a program, how does one go about seeing that it will be correctly used? There are a number of techniques for implementation, but basically they can be grouped into two classes—summer workshops and inservice training. Whether to use one or the other or a combination of both is a local administrative decision made on the basis of many factors. Principals should be included as participants in any summer workshop or inservice training program, to ensure teachers that their administrators understand what they are trying to do with the new program, and to give the administrators a knowledge of the problems involved and the new methods being used.

If possible, start the program with only volunteer teachers from each building. After the first year other teachers will be eager to become involved, and there will be a trained core of experienced teachers on hand to help them. It is then possible to effect a very smooth transition from a traditional program to one of the new science programs. Without a carefully conceived plan for implementation, the chances for success of any of the new elementary science programs are greatly reduced. It is also important to plan some sort of follow-up help for the classroom teacher to ensure full development of the new mode of instruction needed for the new elementary science program.

Future Trends in Elementary School Science Education

What is the future direction for elementary school science? Unless this future is given some thought, it will just happen and the results will probably not please anyone.

A renewed interest in nature study is seen for the near future, but it will be different from the nature study we have known in the past, which tended to be anthropocentric and without structure. Nature study in the near future may take another name, such as environmental studies. It should have a uniting thread (e.g., evolution) to give it structure, and it must be biocentric. The new nature study programs will most likely incorporate the methodology used in such programs as the Elementary Science Study and the Science Curriculum Improvement Study. They will also use many of the psychological findings on which these same programs are based.

It seems probable that along with the development of nature studies programs, there will be a continuation of the current trend toward outdoor education. Outdoor education programs are particularly important for urban schools, where opportunity for exposure to the out-of-doors is limited or nonexistent.

Secondary Science Education

The new programs in secondary science education have a number of similarities: (a) they do not attempt to cover science broadly, but instead select representative science concepts from the rapidly expanding fields; (b) they emphasize learning activities designed to give students a flavor of the method by which scientists enlarge their special fields of knowledge; (c) they offer field-tested materials prepared by teams of specialists and practitioners; and (d) they received extensive financial support from public resources, primarily the National Science Foundation. The result has been a revolution in curriculum materials and teaching methodology.

Earth Science Curriculum Project (ESCP)

History: In 1962 the American Geological Institute (AGI) joined the stream of secondary science project developers and focused on the earth for study. With National Science Foundation support, the AGI selected geologists, oceanographers, meteorologists, astronomers, and other scientists to produce materials. After four years of testing and rewriting, a finished product was ready.

Objectives: The course presents the basic principles of the earth as man's home and as part of the solar system and universe. Through extensive directed experiences, students learn the ways by which scientists have increased man's knowledge of his home in space. Students learn the tentative and speculative nature of conclusions about the earth and understand that there are many unsolved problems remaining for exploration.

Content and Approach: There are four basic units: the dynamic, constantly changing earth; earth cycles (air, water, land, energy); the earth's biography; and the earth's environment in space. Conceptual themes include flow of energy in the universe, adjustment to environmental change, conservation of mass and energy in the universe, earth systems in space and time, uniformity of process, and historical developments in the earth sciences. The planners consider the course to be an experience-centered presentation, emphasizing concept development, general methods of inquiry, and the specific means by which earth scientists carry on their investigations. The course is normally intended to be taught before biology, replacing the general science course that frequently repeats science presented in the elementary grades.

Teaching Materials: Materials include a text, laboratory manual, teacher's guide, laboratory equipment, films, pamphlet series, and transparencies.

Cost: The total cost of ESCP Class Kits for a class of 30 students is $800 to $900.

Comments: The course is widely used, and teacher institutes for ESCP teachers continue. Earth science as a topic is commonly accepted as appropriate for the prebiology level of science teaching and for both the science-terminal and science-prone student.

Introductory Physical Science (IPS)

History: The first materials for *Introductory Physical Science* were produced in 1963 by Educational Services Incorporated (now Education Development Center), an organization that had grown out of the earlier efforts that produced *PSSC* (Physical Science Study Committee) *Physics*. Trial materials for students and teachers were produced and tested over several years before the course was finally published in 1967. The National Science Foundation funded much of the project. Recently *Physical Science II* has been developed as an extension of the first course.

Objectives: Introductory Physical Science intends to give "a beginning knowledge of physical science" and the manner by which scientific knowledge is acquired. It is an introductory course for all students for whom biology probably will be the last contact with science at the secondary level. *Physical Science II* is intended for those who will take advanced sciences, including physics and chemistry, or for those who have had biology and want additional opportunities to study physical science.

Content and Approach: The major theme of *Introductory Physical Science* is the evidence for the atomic model of matter through study of carefully selected materials rather than through survey: quantity of matter (mass), properties of matter, solubility and solvents, separation of substances, compounds and elements, radioactivity, atomic model of matter, sizes and masses of particles, molecular motion, and heat. *Physical Science II* extends the basic concepts developed in the first course. Attainment of objectives depends upon careful laboratory work, guided reasoning, and careful reading. (Experiments can be carried out in rooms with individual flat desk tops and only one sink.)

Teaching Materials: Materials include textbooks, teacher's guide, laboratory equipment and apparatus (laboratory activities are included in texts), tests, and films.

Costs: The assortment of materials (including chemicals) for 24 students costs about $600.

Comments: IPS has been used in grades 8 and 9 with students of wide ability range. It has also been used for the terminal science student who has had biology. Consultant services are available to teachers who use the materials.

Intermediate Science Curriculum Study (ISCS)

History: The pilot study for ISCS began in 1964. Funding for materials development and classroom trials came from the U.S. Office of Education and the National Science Foundation. Scholars in science, professional educators, classroom teachers, and specialists in educational media and procedures were called upon throughout the project. Continuous testing and revision have made possible commercial production of materials for grade 7 by Silver Burdett.

Objectives: The published materials state that students should develop the capacity to interpret natural phenomena and the technological world in which they find themselves. They should gain a "valid understanding" of the nature of science and of the way scientists have accumulated scientific knowledge. The writers feel that science at the junior high school level should be primarily for general education purposes and secondarily for future science courses or for future vocational purposes.

Content and Approach: A key tenet of this program is that process skills should be developed *simultaneously* with understanding. Student investigation is constant; classwork is mostly "thing-centered." Students handle objects, observe them, measure, test, try, do. For the first year the science concepts center on electrical energy, work, friction, heat, and the like; the concepts build upon one another almost always on the basis of things experienced. Text materials provide extensively for "excursions," which permit students to go off independently to interesting studies related to the main themes. Sufficient flexibility is built into the development to enable students of varying ability to profit from the study and to proceed at varying rates.

Teaching Materials: The seventh grade program, now in commercial form, includes a hardback text in two parts ("core" and excursions), teacher's guide, and student record book. Laboratory materials have also been produced. Comparable materials for grades 8 and 9 have been developed and will be released in commercial form in the future. Program developers are working on self-assessment procedures and computer-aided instruction materials.

Time, Space and Matter (Secondary School Science Project)

History: Often called the Princeton Project, this project began in 1963. The National Science Foundation has been the principal funding agency. Scientists, teachers, and materials specialists prepared trial classroom materials, which were extensively tested and revised. All materials are now commercially available.

Objectives: The main objective is for the student to learn the nature and history of his physical world through direct observation and inferences. The student learns how knowledge may be built through a sequence of investigations involving both mental and manipulative skills.

Content and Approach: Nine basic investigations are the heart of the program. They deal with motion and substance; a slice of the earth; from microcosm to macrocosm; levels of approximation—the need for precision; measuring time, space, and matter; the ceaseless change on the surface of the earth; a study of earth change—the Grand Canyon; the surface of the moon; the worlds in space—dimensions of a vast scale.

Discussions supplement the laboratory investigations, field trips, and independent study.

Teaching Materials: There is no text. Rather, there are nine student investigation books, teacher folios, a series of reading booklets, and recommended laboratory equipment and supplies. Consultant services are available for teachers using the materials, and activities for preservice or inservice programs may be obtained.

BSCS Biology (Biological Science Curriculum Study)

History: Biological Science Curriculum Study Biology is one of the most extensive programs to come out of the past 15 years of curriculum experimentation. Under the general direction of the American Institute of Biological Sciences and funded primarily by the National Science Foundation, scholars in biological fields and competent classroom teachers started developing the several versions in 1958. Writing conferences and trial editions finally produced three completely separate biology courses, popularly known as the Green Version *(High School Biology: BSCS Green Version)*, the Yellow Version *(Biological Science: An Inquiry Into Life)*, and the Blue Version *(Biological Science: Molecules to Man)*. Additional materials have been produced for those students often unsuccessful in academic achievement and for those who successfully complete an introductory course in biology. All materials are now commercially published.

Objectives: The all-embracing concept woven throughout all BSCS materials is scientific inquiry and the structure of science. Students learn basic concepts about their living world through much the same kind of examination of that world as scientists themselves employ. Each version presents themes, principles, and applications of biology with a different focus: ecology and living communities (Green), cell and developmental biology (Yellow), and molecular biology (Blue).

Content and Approach: The three basic versions and extensive special materials make it possible for teachers to find suitable BSCS materials to meet the general needs and interests of virtually any group of students. The course approaches are as varied as the materials. Inquiry in the scientific manner is fundamental to these programs. Very extensive laboratory and field study activities have been developed, along with visual aids and supplemental reading materials. Enriched teaching is potentially very great in these programs. Eighty percent of the content is common to all three versions.

Teaching Materials: Materials include three versions of basic texts; a second course, BSCS Special Materials (for academically unsuccessful students); tests; laboratory blocks; special research problems; pamphlets; self-instructional programs;

teacher's handbook; single-topic inquiry films; inquiry slides; special paperbacks; and bulletins.

Comments: The various versions have received widespread approval. Through appropriate selection, the needs of teachers and students may be met quite well. Extensive and excellent laboratory activities constitute a main strength of the programs. Special institutes for teachers are available.

Chemical Education Materials Study (CHEM)

History: This program, one of the early nationwide science curriculum projects (1959), brought chemistry professors and able high school chemistry teachers together to prepare a strong introductory course. Original materials were rewritten several times by teams and were tried extensively in representative schools across the country before the final edition was published in 1964 (Webster, McGraw-Hill). The writing and trial projects were funded by the National Science Foundation.

Objectives: The authors intend a basic and intensive introductory course presenting those principles and concepts "found by chemists to be useful in understanding chemistry." Laboratory activities from *Investigating Chemical Systems* support the text, *Chemical Systems,* by helping the student to experience chemistry as a practicing chemist would see it.

Content and Approach: The course is built on chemical systems and mental models, the working concepts of chemists themselves. Underlying themes include atomic structure; interaction of atoms, with special reference to electric energy; charge cloud and atomic orbital models; kinetic-molecular theory and enthalpy; covalent, metallic, and ionic substances; chemical equilibrium; and reaction rates. Lectures, discussions, demonstrations, and laboratory work constitute the main classroom approaches, with laboratory work intended to provide experiences of the kind scientists have.

Teaching Materials: Materials include text, laboratory manual, teacher's guide, tests, and supplementary readings from the *Journal of Chemical Education.*

Comments: The course is intended to be an introductory course suited to high school juniors and seniors. Some large schools use it as the "advanced" course in chemistry; it offers a good foundation for the college-bound and particularly the science-oriented student.

Chemical Education Materials Study (CHEM)

History: The steering committee, starting in 1960 and headed by Nobel Laureate Glenn T. Seaborg, obtained the services of outstanding university chemists and leading high school chemistry teachers for the development of this course. Funds were provided by the National Science Foundation. After several years of trial materials and pilot studies in selected high schools, hardback editions of *Chemistry—An Experimental Science* were published in 1963 by W. H. Freeman.

Objectives: Considered to be an introductory course, the content presents basic chemistry principles that interrelate and unify diverse natural phenomena. The text and laboratory work reveal the steps by which scientists gain knowledge of the physical world. Principles and concepts represent the most modern developments in the field compatible with the comprehension level of secondary school students.

Content and Approach: Several major concepts are developed, including atomic theory, phases of matter, mole concept, energy, rate and equilibrium characteristics of chemical reactions, chemical periodicity, bonding, and descriptive chemistry. Laboratory work is intended to support the contention that chemistry is an "experimental" science. There is an emphasis on discovery of basic concepts. Lectures and discussions are enriched with carefully prepared films, film loops, and demonstration materials.

Teaching Materials: Materials include the text, laboratory manual, teacher's guide, tests, films, programmed instruction booklets *(Slide Rule, Exponential Notation)*, teacher's guide to CHEM films, and teacher training films.

Comments: Students need reasonable facility with algebra to handle many of the problems. The course is considered to be suitable for the average student in grades 11 and 12 and provides a "strong foundation for college-bound students." The basic CHEMS course is now published in several different forms by various publishers. Summer institutes are available for teachers.

Harvard Project Physics

History: Initial planning for this course was funded by a grant from the Carnegie Corporation. As work progressed during 1962-63, additional funds were provided by the Alfred P. Sloan Foundation, the National Science Foundation, and the U.S. Office of Education. Writers of the program included physicists, historians and philosophers of science, chemists, and secondary school teachers. Pilot materials were prepared and tested across the nation before the authorized interim version was published by Holt, Rinehart and Winston in 1968-69.

Objectives: By presenting coherent ideas selected from the vast amount of content existing in the field today, the course intends to help the student (a) understand the workings of nature—good "physics"; (b) see the relation of physics to other sciences, particularly chemistry and astronomy; and (c) understand that physics has a cultural component with wide social consequences and that physicists are human beings who have their triumphs, trials, and tribulations. Students should get a sense of these aspects of science through their own investigations in the field.

Content and Approach: The course is built on six basic units: concepts of motion, motion in the heavens, the triumph of mechanics, light and electromagnetism, models of the atom, and the nucleus. The approach for the course may be described as multimedia and multilevel. Students are fully encouraged and expected to learn from text, readers, programmed materials, visual aids, laboratory activities, and handbooks. Through appropriate selection of content and materials, students with varying levels of interest in science can make satisfying progress in a variety of ways. The teacher may choose from varying styles the one most suitable to him.

Teaching Materials: Materials include student text, student handbook (presenting laboratory and other student activities), readers, teacher's guides, test booklets, and transparency sets. Each of the foregoing is prepared as separately bound material for each of the six content units. In addition, there are programmed instruction booklets, supplemental units, film loops, sound films, and teacher training films. The readers are unique among secondary science materials in their presentation of original articles, passages from books, and the productions of artists, all of which represent scientists in action or the history, philosophy, and cultural consequences of science.

Costs: Holt, Rinehart and Winston indicate that a "starter" set of laboratory apparatus is approximately $1,800, and a "recommended" set (for 32 students) is approximately $3,000. Overhead projection transparency sets for the various teaching units range from approximately $40 to $65, and film loops are about $25 each. Sound films may be purchased or rented.

Comments: Course developers intend the Harvard Project Physics to be a course with a humanistic emphasis, connecting physics to man's other intellectual, social, and artistic endeavors. Great flexibility in treatment is intended, and a real effort is made to attract students of diverse interests and abilities. Teachers benefit from special assistance in teaching the course, and summer institutes are offered.

Physical Science Study Committee Physics

History: PSSC Physics was developed through grants by the National Science Foundation and the Ford Foundation. Starting in the fall of 1956 a group of university physics professors and secondary school physics teachers began preliminary drafts. Trial texts, teachers' guides, laboratory guides, visual aids, and laboratory and demonstration apparatus were developed with the aid of many collaborators. The materials were used in pilot schools and were revised almost annually; a final package was first published by J. C. Heath and Company in 1960. Since that time, there have been two revisions of the basic text.

Objectives: The primary objective of PSSC Physics is to develop an understanding of the physical world. In addition, the students should become aware that physics, unifying the concepts of time, space, matter, and energy, is a never-ending subject of study. The authors believe it is important for students to understand that physics develops through the imaginative work of men and women quite like themselves, and that in physics, as in all sciences, the laboratory is the primary source of learning.

Content and Approach: The text and laboratory activities no longer follow an "encyclopedic" approach to physics but rather limit themselves to three main themes: light and optics, kinematics and dynamics, and electricity and atomic structure. There is minimal stress on application of physics to man's problems. The teaching approach is intended to lean heavily on laboratory activities, performed so that "the experiences lead to text reading" rather than to have laboratory activities confirm or support what has previously been read or discussed. Excellent films, other visuals, and laboratory and demonstration equipment are available to the teacher.

Teaching Materials: Materials include student text, laboratory guide, teacher's resource book, advanced topic materials, tests, films, projectuals, and equipment.

Comments: The PSSC program offers excellent, modern physics. The student needs skill in mathematics to develop the basic understandings. Originally it was hoped that the course could be adapted to students at many levels of ability, but experience indicates that it is most suitable for able students. The course is often considered to be "college-prep physics." There is little emphasis in the text on applications of physics to home, community, industry, or man's basic social science-oriented problems. The "lab first" classroom approach is difficult to put into practice. Summer institutes are offered for PSSC teachers.

The Portland Project

History: More and more attempts are being made to integrate or fuse several separate subjects (within the sciences or among science and other disciplines) at the secondary level. One such effort, to combine physics and chemistry in a two-year course, began in Portland, Oregon, in 1963. In 1967 the writing teams began to expand the course into a three-year program including biology and behavioral sciences. The first year of the course is now available in "semicommercial" form, and in the near future the entire three-year sequence is expected to be available commercially. The entire program is now being used in Portland schools and in some neighboring districts.

Objectives: The primary objective is to help students understand themselves and their natural world and to comprehend the processes by which scientists add to the human store of knowledge. The students should see in a comprehensive way their relation to the universe and should sense the underlying unity among the traditionally separate sciences.

Content and Approach: Basic concepts that are generally fundamental to behavioral sciences, biology, chemistry, and physics are threaded throughout the three years. The first part of the first year emphasizes the student himself, with principles drawn from the behavioral sciences. The first-year course is written rather tersely, providing sufficient background for students to go to the laboratory to experience the important general principles in science. Each year places great emphasis on the processes of science.

Teaching Materials: Materials include texts (one for each year), teacher's guides, student manuals, 16 tests for the three years, and general orientation materials for teachers. Some simple specialized equipment is needed for activities early in the first year (the behavioral sciences emphasis), but it can be constructed by teachers and students. Virtually all the rest of the program can be carried out using materials commonly found in science laboratories.

Comments: While the course is designed for grades 10, 11, and 12, it has been used in grades 9, 10, and 11. The first year provides a general education emphasis for students who plan no further science study. The first year also is introductory to the next two years. Some schools report high sequential enrollments because of the continuing nature of the work. Individual science teachers with general preparation can teach the first-year course. The second and third years should be team-taught, using the special abilities of teachers with specific backgrounds.

The Man Made World (ECCP—Engineering Concepts Curriculum Project)

History: The project, with offices at the Polytechnic Institute of Brooklyn, originated under the sponsorship of the Commission on Engineering Education. Project planning began in 1965. Trial editions of curriculum materials written by scientists, engineers, and educators were tested in schools across the nation in subsequent years, and commercial editions have been announced.

Objectives: The course is designed to help all students meet their future responsibility for guiding the direction of our society. It intends to show that the current world is essentially man-made—shaped by technical accomplishments, natural resources and principles, and various modes of thinking, as well as by arts, skills, and inspiration. The developed concepts are relevant to the natural and social sciences, business, the arts, communication, and the humanities.

Content and Approach: The subject matter for this course is different from that of any other commonly known science or technical course. It starts with man and his technical devices and moves on to decision-making processes (where technical devices play a role), optimization and modeling as concepts in problem solving, and the use of the computer. After extensive treatment of the computer as the most representative device in the man-made world, the course turns to dynamic systems, feedback, and stability, and finally returns to a general discussion of man and the machine. Procedures include independent study, laboratory investigations, seminars, discussions, and computer simulations using analog and digital computers when they are available.

Teaching Materials: Materials include text, laboratory manual, teacher's manual, discussion "games," and tests.

Comments: This course is quite different from virtually anything offered in schools today, but it covers an aspect of life seriously needing attention in education. Developers state that students at the top two-thirds of the ability scale in grades 10, 11, and 12 can profit from the course. Consultant services for teachers are available, as are preservice and inservice teacher training activities.

The courses described above are representative of curriculum development in recent years. These specific courses are being widely used, and the materials are also being adapted by independent writers, planners, and publishers. Thus an increasing number of commercially available texts reflect the influence of the foundation-supported work. In addition, a wide range of teaching materials can be found, including laboratory and demonstration materials, visuals of many kinds, teacher's guides, supplemental readings specially prepared, independent research activities, and the like. In most cases, special assistance to teachers is available in the form of inservice activities or institutes.

Another encouraging advance is the special preparation of curricular materials for the extreme ends of the educational spectrum: the low achiever and the student not oriented to science at one end, and the very able student at the other end. It is generally agreed that more needs to be done at these points, particularly for the less able students.

The Future of Science Education

What will be the nature of science education in the future? Will it differ drastically from today's teaching-learning situations? What instructional materials will be available? Will the objectives change, or will new emphasis be placed on existing ones? In what kind of setting will the science teacher and student find themselves? What kind of society will exist in the future? What can be done to shape the future of science education in a purposeful way? These are but a few of the questions to which we must address overselves. They help us to identify educational alternatives and provide data for making deliberate and careful decisions concerning science education. The decisions of today will largely determine the nature of science education in the future.

Science Education Today

An analysis of science education as it presently exists ought to be the basis for developing and implementing science curriculums. The present patchwork method of developing science curriculums and fitting them unquestioningly into the existing school structure cannot result in the kind of science education that the 21st century will require.

It might appear from a cursory examination of the last decade's projects to improve science courses that an adequate science program in the public schools could become a reality if science teachers and administrators implemented these "new" programs in the manner in which they were intended. After all, it is apparent that the projects had strengths, among them the following: (a) scientists and teachers were brought together to develop the programs; (b) a variety of instructional materials were developed; (c) emphasis was placed on basic science and scientific processes; (d) the content of textual materials was updated; (e) the investigative laboratory was suggested as a focal point for classroom instruction; and (f) the importance of understanding the structure of the discipline was stressed.

However, a closer examination reveals that the new programs had major weaknesses: (a) they failed to provide continuity from course to course; (b) previous learnings were assumed which in fact had not taken place; (c) the nature of the learner and the process of learning were frequently ignored; (d) the reading levels were too difficult for large numbers of students; (e) student interests and problems were not incorporated into the instructional materials; (f) objectives for students were stated vaguely or not at all; (g) adequate evaluation programs were never developed; (h) the science content did not directly relate to the major problems facing mankind; (i) large numbers of teachers were never adequately prepared to teach the courses as they were intended to be taught; (j) the general education function of science was given little or no attention; (k) it was assumed that the existing school organization and grade level divisions were appropriate for implementing the programs; and (l) the science content was selected by looking more to the past than to the future.

Toffler (5) has suggested that our schools are similar in many ways to the factories of the 19th century. They are divided into arbitrary segments. Attendance is mandatory. Bells ring, and students respond. Students sit in assigned seats in crowded rooms. Certain students receive preferential treatment. Track systems and self-fulfilling prophesies are widespread. Interaction is only between teacher and student and is initiated only by the teacher. Lecture predominates. Individuality and creativity are stated as objectives but are subdued by instruction and evaluation. Articulation is nonexistent. Certain subjects and concepts are taught to all students at stipulated times. Our schools are actually preparing students for an industrial-revolution society, rather than for a technological-revolution society. Students are not being prepared for the present or the future; they are being prepared for a past that no longer exists.

Possible Alternatives

Simply to criticize schools and the teaching of science without offering a means for possible improvement is counterproductive. The problem is not to sensitize educators to the fact that the schools need improving. Most people have realized for some time that the teaching and learning of science could and should be improved. The problem is to determine what improvements are needed and how they can be implemented.

Shane (6) and Cornish (1) have suggested that the answer to improving the teaching and learning of science lies in *future-planning*. This procedure is not to be confused with future planning. The latter is linear, passive, and based on intuitive guesses as to what the future may be like; it involves planning to meet the future rather than planning the future. Future-planning, on the other hand, is active. It assumes that the future can be at least partially determined by systematic conjecture based on the projection and analysis of what the future has to offer. Thus, future-planners describe or forecast future alternatives based on data presented by experts in such areas as human population, science, technology, sociology, education, and anthropology, using mathematical models and simulation by computers to analyze the data. Once future alternatives are identified, future-planners choose a plan of action from among the alternatives, based on such questions as, What kind of society do we wish to have, and what kind of human beings do we want in that society?

Science educators, following the example of industrialists, economists, social scientists, and militarists, should establish future-planning groups in every school and community. The groups should include science educators, students, administrators, parents, futurists, and specialists from the various academic disciplines. After all, no one individual or group of individuals holds a monopoly on insight into the future. A mass movement of future-planning groups ("Councils of the Future") has been suggested by Toffler (4). The groups devoted to probing the future of science education should project assumed futures, open the alternatives to public debate, and begin to shape the future rather than be its passive witness.

Some of the groundwork for future-planning groups has already been done. People like Van Til, Shane, and Rogers (6), Cornish (1), and Goodlad (3) are using systematic conjecture to predict what society may be like in the future. The following are some of their predictions for the next three decades:

- The population of the United States will be between 340 and 400 million by the turn of the century.
- Most of the population will live in urban areas.
- The gross national product will be two to three-and-one-half times greater than the present one.
- Technological development will continue at a rapid rate and will become more sophisticated.
- Social problems will persist.
- The knowledge explosion will accelerate.
- The workweek will shorten, leaving more time for leisure.
- Change will become even more rapid.

- The work force will begin to move out of factories and offices into the home and community.
- A national and possibly world community will emerge.
- Goods and services will become available to a greater proportion of the general population.
- The use of computers will become more widespread.
- The invasion of privacy will continue on a larger scale.
- A greater emphasis will be placed on the importance of education.
- Man will gain a greater understanding of environmental relationships.
- Space conquest will increase.
- People will become even more transient.
- Nationwide personal data banks will be established.
- It will be possible to modify personality by drugs.
- Physical handicaps will be reduced or eliminated.
- The life span will be appreciably increased.

These predictions for the future are based on an assumption that a system break will not occur. System breaks are sudden unexpected changes, such as thermonuclear war or world famine, which drastically alter the system.

The kind of society that has been predicted offers schools and science education a large number of alternatives, limited only by the extent of educators' imagination, knowledge of future developments, and ability to divorce themselves from the past. Some of these alternatives are the following:

1. Education—including the teaching and learning of science—will probably begin at a very early age and continue on a plug-in/plug-out basis throughout a person's life. Continuous, life-long learning would reduce the need for the artificial divisions and regimentation of public schools. In fact, it might reduce the need for public schools altogether. In their place could be community learning centers that make use of the unique contributions of museums, hospitals, parks, theaters, factories, and other private and public institutions. With advances in technology, electronic consoles could become commonplace, and the home could become the center for extensive supplementary schooling.
2. Personal fulfillment (rather than preparation for the world of work) might become an objective for learning science. The teaching of science could be directed toward self-realization and learning for the joy of learning.
3. The emphasis in science teaching may shift from the memorization of content to how to locate and use scientific informa-

tion. The knowledge explosion will continue to make it difficult if not impossible to determine what scientific information is of most worth, and science content will be stored in memory banks and be available upon request.

4. Personalized self-instruction may become a reality, resulting in a less homogenous science curriculum. A wealth of individual instructional media and time will be available, so that students of all ages will be able to proceed through individual programs in science at a comfortable, self-determined rate. The materials will be available at times convenient to the learner and begin at a point appropriate to his background and experience. Personalized self-instruction implies more choices over a wide range of science content and materials. It should result in reducing the number of required science courses and the schism that exists between science teaching and real life.
5. It should not be assumed that an individual will be competent in all facets of science teaching. Differentiated staffing may become a reality, using the special abilities, interests, and skills of individual science teachers, students, and persons from industry and the community.
6. Differentiated staffing and machines may free the science teacher from present-day routine and allow him to develop instructional materials and to interact on a humanistic level with individuals and small groups of students.
7. Instructional innovations such as experiential programming, role playing, computer-mediated seminars, televiewers, three-dimensional television and photography, rapid transmission of facsimile materials, computer games, and low teacher-student ratios may eliminate the science lecture.
8. Biochemical aids and controlled nutrition may be used to maximize the learning of science.
9. Overstaffing of schools or learning centers may result from differentiated staffing, personalized instruction, and a shorter workweek. Deliberate overstaffing would allow science teachers to engage in a numbers of activities, including teacher exchanges with foreign countries, continued professional training, and various nonteaching activities.
10. Personal data banks and personalized science curriculums may allow students and teachers to change from school to school or community to community with a minimum of difficulty.
11. Science teachers and students may become more future conscious, perhaps through reading science fiction and descriptions of great utopias, playing games dealing with future speculation, participating in fun and fantasy, discussing the future in situations free from censorship, writing future autobiographies, and studying probability and methods of prediction.

12. Science has been artificially fragmented by man into various units such as biology, physics, chemistry, geology, and so on. When a student investigates a scientific phenomenon, he may find that one isolated unit of science will not provide suitable answers. Therefore, science for the future could be taught and learned as it really exists, i.e., as integrated science.

Conclusion

A number of practices that appear to be directed toward the future are identifiable at the present time. "Mini-courses" are becoming available in science, organized around problems of concern to students. More freedom is being given to students to choose their course requirements from among a variety of science courses. Open and outdoor science classrooms are beginning to appear. At least one high school has abandoned the traditional school building in favor of museums, research laboratories, storefronts, and homes (4). Programmed science materials are becoming available more rapidly, although many of them are extremely crude and cover only the lower cognitive levels. Science educators are beginning to place more emphasis on humanistic and affective goals for the teaching of science. Many schools are offering courses that integrate the fields within the sciences and integrate the sciences with other disciplines. More emphasis is being placed on environmental science, and several school systems are experimenting with differentiated staffing.

Although these practices are promising, their adoption may or may not result in the kind of science education that the future requires. Simply adopting new practices and placing them in the existing philosophical and methodological framework would be an additional patchwork attempt to improve the teaching and learning of science. Science teachers and administrators need to anticipate the future and influence it in predetermined ways. Future alternatives should be identified, and selection from among them should be based on the quality of life we want in the future.

BIBLIOGRAPHY

1. Cornish, Edward. "The Science Teacher Futurist." *Science Teacher* 36: 21-24; January 1969.
2. Education Commission of the States, National Assessment of Educational Progress. *Science Objectives.* Ann Arbor, Mich.: the Commission, 1969.
3. Goodlad, John. "The Future of Learning: Into the 21st Century." *AACTE Bulletin* 24: 1, 4-5; March 1971.
4. Silberman, Charles E. *Crisis in the Classroom.* New York: Random House, 1970.
5. Toffler, Alvin. *Future Shock.* New York: Random House, 1970.
6. Van Til, William, editor. *Curriculum: Quest for Relevance.* New York: Houghton Mifflin Co., 1971.

16

Social Studies Education

The curriculum reform movement of the 1960's began with great enthusiasm and high hopes. Many educators felt that of all the changes needed in the schools, curriculum reform deserved the greatest emphasis and the speediest implementation.

By 1970, however, curriculum reform had begun to lose its aura of importance and urgency. To be sure, curriculum development projects are still credited with improving school programs, and the need for new and revised curriculums is still widely recognized. But the social crisis engulfing our society and challenging our institutions, including the schools, has altered the entire context within which curriculum change is viewed and evaluated. Curriculum reform is increasingly seen as peripheral to the critical situation facing the schools, and "survival manuals" are taking the place of "curriculum project manuals" as guidelines for education reform.

From the vantage point of the early 70's, the rise and fall of curriculum reform appears to have been truly meteoric. Ten years ago there was, practically speaking, no such thing as a curriculum project in the social studies. Five years ago projects were flourishing all over the country in a colorful profusion of sizes, forms, structures, purposes, and philosophies. Today many of the projects have gone out of existence.

Yet while the "development decade" may have come to an end, many of the innovations generated by curriculum projects are still very much alive. Their influence can be identified in many places, and they have left their stamp on a number of the changes proposed for the social studies in the coming decade. Before considering the social studies as they are developing in the 70's, it is worthwhile to reconsider the nature and scope of the curriculum reforms that emerged through the efforts of the curriculum projects.

On the surface, the most striking feature of the curriculum projects is their variety. They range from ambitious K-12 programs to intensive units of only a few weeks. Some stay rigorously within the bounds of a particular discipline, while others borrow freely from any of the social sciences—anthropology, history, economics, sociology, geography, psychology, and political science. Their teaching procedures and materials vary from the relatively traditional to the highly experimental and include simulations and nonverbal games, artifacts, models and "original" documents, multimedia kits and audiovisual resources, as well as pamphlets, source books, and readings.

Despite the diversity of their educational aims and methods, however, virtually all the curriculum projects share one common trait—a commitment to a new view of the social studies in which students are encouraged to acquire skills and insights as well as information. Rote learning and expository teaching have been deemphasized, if not excluded. In their place has evolved an educational program based on teaching students how to learn, exposing them to general principles and concepts, and, above all, structuring the classroom experience in such a way that students are led to discover ideas for and by themselves.

In terms of scope and orientation, four general categories of curriculum projects can be distinguished.

1. *Comprehensive* projects aim at providing a complete social studies education for one or more grades, and at least two of the comprehensive projects have already developed programs extending from kindergarten through senior high school. What distinguishes these comprehensive programs from more traditional curriculum guides is partly their conscious attempt to produce intellectual consistency and coherence and partly their explicit awareness of the academic disciplines within which they are operating. The net result is, at its best, an integrated curriculum in which a body of related ideas unfolds with increasing depth at each level of the student's educational career.

   This cumulative and sequential structure can be seen in a number of comprehensive projects. The Providence Social Science Curriculum Project (K-12) and the Taba Curriculum Development Project (1-8) both structure the curriculum around the idea of the child's expanding awareness, so that the earliest grades center on family and neighborhood, the middle grades on regions and cultures, and the upper grades on civilizations or nation-states. Project Social Studies at the University of Minnesota (K-12) builds its program by introducing concepts in a relatively simple form in the early grades and adding levels of meaning and sophistication later on. The point is that whatever organizing principle is used, there is always some explicit principle or philosophy that underlies and unifies the project.

2. The projects structured around a *specific discipline* tend to display a somewhat different emphasis from that of the comprehensive projects. Although there are many points of similarity, projects fostered by economics, anthropology, geography, or sociology are more likely to be preoccupied with the methods and problems peculiar to those disciplines. These curriculum projects, in other words, often attempt to convey not only the updated content of their discipline but the methodology as well.

   In the Anthropology Curriculum Study Project, for example, students examine reproductions of tools and attempt to make inferences about the cultures represented. The Committee on the Study of History has produced a unit entitled "What Happened on Lexington Green? An Inquiry into the Nature and Methods of History," which confronts students with a mass of conflicting data and asks them, in effect, to act as historians in interpreting it. Units in the Sociological Resources for the Social Studies on stereotypes (Images of People) and on race relations (Class and Race in the United States) recommend that teachers help their students confront and analyze their own feelings of prejudice and unconscious acceptance of discrimination. And the High School Geography Project has devised an activity in which students apply geographical concepts in predicting the development of the city of "Portsville" (Seattle) from 1850 to the present.
3. *Area studies,* the third type of curriculum project, generally take a wide-ranging, multidisciplinary approach to their subject matter. The aim of these projects, such as Project Africa and the Asian Studies Inquiry Program, is to help students experience the totality of another culture by studying its social structure, religion, economic system, history, and folklore.
4. *Special purpose* projects include all those that have some special aim or orientation not found in any of the other projects. Among the special projects are Law in American Society, an investigation of such legal issues as free speech, criminal procedures, and public order; the Intergroup Relations Curriculum, a program designed to sensitize children to the existence of group allegiance and intergroup hostility; the Diablo Valley Education Project, a project of the Center for War/Peace Studies, designed to help students investigate alternatives other than war for resolving conflicts; and MATCH (Materials and Activities for Teachers and Children), a series of multimedia kits that emphasize learning about the students' immediate environment from objects, artifacts, models, and direct observation.

What is most important about these and other curriculum projects is not so much their novelty per se, but rather their willingness to depart from certain hallowed classroom roles, procedures, and traditions. Many projects, for example, put a premium on student creativity and discovery to the point of denying teachers their role as dispensers of knowledge. As a result, teachers must become catalysts for learning rather than sources of information, while students must discover how to form and evaluate their own ideas rather than simply assimilate the ideas of others. New social studies projects often insist, moreover, on the absence of "correct" answers to many questions, which may prove disconcerting for those teachers (and students) who take comfort in finding "the" answer at the end of the lesson.

Curriculum developers are also becoming more courageous in inserting controversial, emotional, or value-laden topics into their new courses and programs. A question from the World Studies Inquiry Series, for example, opens the door to once-forbidden speculation by asking students whether, as poor Chinese peasants in 1949, they would have favored or opposed the Communist government. A sequence of readings in the Sociological Resources for the Social Studies unit on poverty encourages an examination of values through a series of questions: Do the poor pay more? Is poverty decreasing? What is being done about poverty? What's best? Other projects deal with such sensitive issues as race relations ("Negro Views of America" in the Harvard Social Studies Project Public Issues Series) and the morality of using atomic weapons ("Hiroshima: A Study in Science, Politics, and the Ethics of War" by the Committee on the Study of History). The new projects are providing a refreshing realism in their treatment of social and political issues, thereby displacing the idealized but stale descriptions that plague many traditional social studies courses.

Curriculum projects, in short, represent an original, sometimes even iconoclastic, departure from standard social studies fare. Combined with the teacher training programs of the 60's—Master of Arts in Teaching (MAT) and NDEA and NSF Summer Institutes and Academic Year Fellowships—they have contributed substantially to efforts seeking to improve the quality of social studies instruction in the schools.

Ironically, however, the gains of the past decade now serve to underscore the inadequacies persisting in the schools. Changes in curriculum, for example, point up the need for reform in other areas such as school governance. Students taught to value independent thinking in social studies classrooms often demonstrate their attitudes and skills in areas outside the formal curriculum, much to the anguish of school officials.

It is now clear that while better trained teachers and improved instructional materials are necessary elements of the change process, they alone are not sufficient to accomplish fundamental reform. Unless teacher training and curriculum development are linked to other components of the education process—grounded in school experience on the one hand and sensitive to the concerns of the outside community on the other—they seem certain to fail. One real contribution of the curriculum reform efforts of the last decade may have been that they called attention to the difficulties and complexities involved in bringing about educational change.

Social Studies for Survival

Our educational system is never free from the conflicts and tensions that divide society at large. In periods of explosive social change schools, like other social institutions, are likely to be under conflicting pressures to reform and to preserve traditional roles at the same time.

The frustrations of the curriculum reformers in the 1960's have helped us understand how complicated it is to produce educational change and how politically sophisticated our reforms must be if they are to succeed. Many reformers, for example, took a simplistic view of the schools as passive, largely identical organizations willing and able to change according to some logical plan devised by outsiders. Now we are beginning to realize that a vast array of interlocking roles and responsibilities is involved. Schools are complex organizations, populated by individuals occupying varying positions, responding to various clients, playing different roles, and clinging to different perceptions of what the enterprise is all about. In this setting, the adoption of a new, experimental course or the entry of a better trained teacher may set off a "rise in expectations" that is beyond the capacity of the schools to satisfy, thereby arousing deeper dissatisfaction with present programs and goals.

Furthermore, the speed with which American society changes often makes educational remedies obsolete by the time they are adopted. Most curriculum projects spend three to five years developing a particular approach or set of materials, by which time the results of their labors may appear trivial or uninteresting. Recent discontent with the schools, as evidenced by student unrest, community protests, taxpayer revolts, and the search for alternative modes of education, may be more a consequence of the schools' inability to keep pace with the growing list of demands than of their unwillingness to change at all.

Of all the events and upheavals occurring in the late 60's, perhaps three have the profoundest implications for educational reform:

1. *The widespread unrest created by the war in Vietnam.* Resistance to the war was often initiated by students. In a few short years the calm of high school and college campuses was broken by frequent disruption and demonstrations. The gap between generations was greatly exacerbated by the war. While this issue sparked the initial unrest, the young quickly added environmental health, racial discrimination, educational reform, and the use of resources to the list of grievances demanding radical social change.
2. *The intolerable conditions in the inner cities of America.* Widespread racial turbulence suddenly made visible to the nation the bitterness and despair of the millions of Americans trapped in urban ghettos. The pace of change in this instance was such that within a few years educational programs regarded as adequate were seen as obsolete and even dangerous.
3. *The drastic shift in the outlook of the younger generation about its role in American society and the educational system.* Sparked in part by a mass communications system that simultaneously and immediately reaches young and old, rich and poor, the young have been spurred on by identification with the struggle of blacks, Chicanos, Puerto Ricans, women, and other groups for recognition and acceptance.

It is imperative that the educational system respond to this revolution in the attitudes and demands of Americans, especially those who until recently have been largely neglected by society. The speed of change and of disintegration will continue to outrun the provisions for accommodating change unless we do things in the 70's that we would never have dreamed we could do a few short years ago. A growing awareness of the need to understand and to come to grips with such interrelated social issues as the generation gap, credibility crises, communications management, environmental health, disarmament, peace, violence, and racial and social justice seem destined to force changes in American schools, including basic revisions in the way children are taught to think about the social world. The demand for results, the impatience of the public, the need for efficiency, and the increased availability of technology are likely to bring about changes in school governance, organization, curriculums, and the roles of school personnel.

Predictions about the exact nature of new programs are impossible. We can, however, identify some of the trends that may shape the future of social studies:

1. The classroom will probably cease to be the exclusive setting for education. Participation in community projects; direct observation of governmental, business, and professional activities and processes; and foreign and domestic travel will become a part of most students' "school" experiences. Responsibility for education will be more widely shared among community agencies and groups, requiring a redefinition of the role schools play in the whole socialization process.
2. Interdisciplinary studies, cybernetics, games and simulations, data banks, storage and retrieval systems, teaching machines, dial-access programs, and television and videotape equipment will be more widely used.
3. More efforts will be made to apply learning theories as a means of speeding the learning process.
4. The teaching staff will have differentiated responsibilities and salaries.
5. Students are likely to become more impatient with irrelevancies and incompetence in school programs and personnel. Living in a society that provides numerous opportunities to acquire information, skills, and insights, students will become more critical of school programs that seem to be overly academic or unrelated to their lives.
6. The availability of an ever greater variety of texts, pamphlets, and other instructional materials will increase opportunities for individualized instruction.

Many of these developments are already influencing school operations.

Goals and Objectives

Intertwined with the problems of curricular change is the question of goals for the social studies. There has always been and probably always will be disagreement about the purpose of a social studies education. But for those interested in educational reform, the matter of objectives assumes special relevance. We need to know what we are changing for and what changes will produce the kind of social studies program that fulfills our expectations. Hence the debate continues over the questions, Is the preparation of good citizens the primary objective, or should training in the social sciences be emphasized? Is a value-centered or a value-free approach most appropriate?

Most educators probably would agree on the necessity of teaching students to deal with cognitive problems, but today's students—who are often participants in, as well as observers of, contemporary social issues—need to know how to handle value questions as well. Complicating the whole situation is the desire on the part of most social studies educators to help students develop humanistic and democratic values.

The net result is a kind of ideological polarization in which some critics of the educational system are advocating the transformation of social studies classes into strategy sessions for the coming social revolution, while others at the opposite end of the spectrum cling to the notion that indoctrinating students in indisputable values or policies is the only hope of salvaging our institutions. In actual practice, of course, the various approaches are not necessarily mutually exclusive. Value-free instructional materials can, for example, be used in the process of reflecting on social values, just as training in the social sciences can clearly contribute to the development of good citizens.

More and more, however, programs and curriculum guidelines are being built around particular emphases. A look at a few of these may not only help clarify the issue of goals and objectives but provide useful models for change as well.

Emerging Approaches to Curriculum Organization

Social Studies and Social Science

Social studies, which draws on all of the social sciences, must somehow have a focus or pattern if it is to be articulated. While many secondary teachers may have little intellectual interest in the academic reorganization of the social studies or in the relations of academic disciplines in a theoretical context, most will have a deep interest in the problems of selectivity and organization in the school program. The pressures of time in which to work contrasted with the vast quantities and great variety of materials to deal with, to say nothing of the emotional nature of many of the issues, argue for careful consideration of focus or pattern if only from the standpoint of efficiency. The need to reorganize our concept of the academic disciplines and of social studies to deal more adequately with social education has been increasingly recognized at all educational levels.

Perhaps the most ambitious recent effort to provide social studies guidelines is the proposed "Social Sciences Education

Framework for California Public Schools," released by the California Statewide Social Sciences Study Committee in 1970 (3). This large-scale effort, involving more than two hundred social scientists, draws on the various social science disciplines to formulate a model emphasizing inquiry processes. These are grouped according to three different modes of thinking: analysis, integration, and valuing.

The proposal asserts that an effective curriculum in the social sciences has three major components: (a) processes of investigating (observation, classification, definition, comparison and contrast, generalization, inference, and communication) and modes of learning (analysis, integration, and valuing); (b) concepts and generalizations (a concept being a set of ideas enabling one to recognize and classify something that may be either abstract or concrete, and a generalization being a statement applying to all members of a designated class); and (c) settings and topics, which serve as selected examples of human experience (places, events, times, peoples, issues, problems) providing the subject matter within which the processes of inquiry are applied and from which concepts and generalizations are drawn.

The program design is as follows:

Grades K-2. Mankind: Man's Distinctive Characteristics

Topics

1. What is man?
2. How do men and animals adapt to and change the land they live on?
3. How do men and animals communicate?
4. How do people live together?
5. How are people alike and how are they different?

Grades 3-4. Man and Land: Cultural and Geographical Relationships

Topics

1. What is the relationship between the natural environment and animals on the one hand and man on the other?
2. How have different groups of men developed different ways of living in the same or similar environments?
3. How has urbanization altered man's relation to the natural environment?
4. How are problems of living being met in the modern urban environment?
5. What is human about human beings?

Grades 5-6. Mankind and Men: Interaction, Diversity, Individuality

Topics

1. What happens when different groups of men come in contact?
2. How have ethnic groups and individuals affected American development?
3. How do different groups interact in the contemporary United States?
4. How do human groups interact in different cultures?
5. How is any man like no other man?

Grades 7-9. Man and Systems: Political and Economic: Urban Environments

Topics

1. How do societies decide what is to be done and who is to do it?
2. How do societies decide who gets what?
3. How do market economies develop and function?
4. How do democratic political systems develop and function?
5. How are decisions made in the command political economy?
6. How are decisions made in the mixed political economy of the present-day United States?
7. How can underdeveloped societies cope with the demand for rapid modernization?
8. How did the emergence of cities change the life of man?
9. How have cities varied in their functions and characteristics?
10. How has modern urbanization changed the life of man?
11. How can the quality of urban life be improved?

Grades 10-11. Man: Past and Present (Historical Integration)

Topics

1. How did the United States come to be the way it is, and how is it changing?
   - 1a. How did the social structure that the colonists brought from Europe change in the course of their life in America?
   - 1b. How did Americans develop a sense of nationality?
   - 1c. How did Americans develop a more democratic political system?
   - 1d. What impact has the introduction of enslaved Africans had on American life?

1e. How have Americans adjusted to the diversity of peoples and cultures?
1f. How has the United States responded to industrialization and large-scale business organization?
1g. How have Americans been affected by their relations with the rest of the world?
1h. Where is American society headed today?

2. How have national groupings and conflicts affected the life of man?
   2a. What makes a "State" a "State"?
   2b. Why have societies sought to impose their wills on other societies?
   2c. Why do military establishments so universally exist, and how do they affect the societies of which they are a part?
   2d. Can man's technological abilities for destruction be offset by his imagination and the desire to maintain the peace?

3. How has India maintained its cultural unity over such a long period and such a diversity of peoples?
   3a. How did the principal features of traditional Indian culture take shape and persist?
   3b. How has Hindu India interacted with its invaders?
   3c. How did traditional Indian culture affect the struggle for independence?
   3d. How are traditional and modern elements interacting in present-day India?

Alternate Topic 3. How did China develop mankind's most durable sociopolitical system and why has it been replaced?
   3a. How did the principal features of traditional Chinese culture take shape and persist?
   3b. How has Confucian China interacted with its invaders?
   3c. How did the Chinese establish their modern independent nationality?
   3d. How are traditional and modern elements interacting in present-day China?

Alternate Topic 3. Why has Japan become Asia's only technologically advanced society?

Grade 12A. Man as a Decision Maker: Social Policy in the United States

Topics

1. How do ordinary citizens influence the decisions that affect them?

2. How are ordinary citizens influenced in making and accepting policy decisions?
3. How are decision makers influenced by persons with special status and by special interest groups?
4. What range of decisions is possible *within* organizations?
5. What is the effect on social policy decisions of relationships *between* organizations?

Grade 12B. Man, His Goals and Aspirations: Selected Studies

Illustrative Topics

1. Ethnic groups and social policy
2. The Selective Service System
3. Immigrant and Black experience in the United States
4. Islam, Buddhism, and Hinduism in comparative settings
5. The influence of religion on art and architecture
6. New African nations and world affairs.

In brief, the program deals with the simplest analytic processes in grades K-5. Behavioral definition is introduced in grades 5-6. The integrative mode is the main emphasis beginning in grades 5-6 and continuing through grades 7-9. The value mode is introduced in grade 9. Hence, by the end of grade 9 all of the inquiry processes involved have been clarified and practiced.

A Citizenship Approach

Given the goal of effective participation in a democracy, the questions of what schools ought to teach and how they should be organized and managed cannot be neatly separated. Schools must recognize the growing insistence by both parents and students on citizen rights. They must respond to demands for more meaningful participation in a manner designed to strengthen reasoned allegiance to a democratic political system. The alternative is to contribute to the deterioration of the democratic ideal.

Those who advocate this approach are faced with some fundamental questions about the citizenship aspects of social studies: How does—and should—our educational system transmit our political heritage? How can it transmit democratic values without imposing a straitjacket of conformity inimical to democratic processes? What democratic processes are most important—the ones portrayed in civics books? in city hall? on the streets of inner cities? How are these processes reflected in the way our schools actually operate?

A recent major study of civics education (4) shows that many students see their schools as essentially undemocratic institutions and are increasingly frustrated and angered by the manner in which schools make decisions affecting their lives. The study's major goal was "to develop behavioral objectives and guidelines for a civics curriculum able to prepare students for effective civic participation in the 1970's." The objectives, designed to develop citizens who are competent in the complexities of democratic decision making, are formulated in terms of citizen behavior:

> *Objective One: The citizen participates in the decision-making process of his society.* The data show that high school students rarely participate in the resolution of conflicts in which they aré participants. Less than one-fifth of the students reported having any say in the resolution of their problems. Resolution processes which would involve student participation are not operative in the overwhelming number of cases. The great majority of students also expressed dissatisfaction with the outcome of their conflicts. Students demonstrate a lack of ability to deal with democratic problems effectively; they also complain about the lack of democratic realities in their lives. We conclude that only a truly participative system of decision making within the school itself will help students develop both the skills of democratic decision making and the consequent faith that it can be successful.
>
> *Objective Two: The citizen makes use of alternative courses of action. If he finds no viable options open, he creates new alternatives for democratic action.* The existence and use of meaningful alternatives for action are essential to a democratic society. Students at all levels and in all types of schools expressed no alternatives to the course of action in almost three-fourths of all reported incidents. Present civics education is not developing citizens who see and use democratic processes as means to obtain their goals.
>
> *Objective Three: The citizen analyzes courses of action for their democratic bases, feasibility, and anticipated and actual consequences.* Few students were even able to identify alternative courses of action. The process of analyzing alternatives, vital to effective citizenship, includes determining the democratic basis, feasibility, and anticipated consequences of each alternative.
>
> *Objective Four: The citizen employs negotiation, mediation, and arbitration in resolving conflicts.* The effective use of negotiation and mediation are essential democratic means for resolving problems. However, in the majority of student-reported incidents, conflicts were solved by a unilateral decision by an authority. The reported incidents involved no

student participation at either the basic level of decision making or the level of conflict resolution.

Objective Five: The citizen understands and analyzes issues from viewpoints other than his own. Democratic problem solving requires the ability to understand the viewpoints of one's adversaries. The data suggest that for the most part secondary school students lack this ability. Not only did the overwhelming majority fail to perceive alternatives, but the techniques attempted in the alternate questionnaire forms (specifically to elicit alternative views) likewise failed to produce rounded viewpoints.

Objective Six: The citizen sees democratic issues in problems of others, as well as in his own life. Concern for the rights of others is a basic element of participation. The democratic citizen must be concerned with democracy as it functions in the lives of others. The protocols indicate that democratic concerns of the students tend to revolve around themselves rather than around others.

Objective Seven: The citizen recognizes the value and utilizes the power of group action. In our society, the formation of groups and organizations is the traditional means of mobilizing power to effect social policy. Readings of the protocols reveal that students do not grasp the power of group action, although half the protagonists are groups rather than individuals.

Objective Eight: The citizen distinguishes personal issues and conflicts from institutional issues and conflicts, and attacks the two accordingly. The data show that students see the majority of conflicts as occurring with persons or groups rather than with institutions. However, the great percentage of issues concern school governance. The students largely perceive these issues in personal rather than institutional terms, thereby diminishing their ability to resolve immediate conflicts or effect long-term change.

Objective Nine: The citizen grasps and acts on the principles involved. Democratic decision making requires the ability to conceptualize the problem and to act on principles rather than on feelings or personal desires. The evidence gathered in the study leads to the conclusion that students are not abstracting their concrete problems above a personal level.

Objective Ten: The citizen relates his principles to relevant incidents. Democratic action requires both principles and concrete experiences. Some students appeared bothered by abstract problems when they were unable to perceive them concretely (reverse of Objective Four). One-seventh of the protocols talked about abstract problems without mentioning specific incidents. In teaching civics, values and beliefs must be joined with concrete daily experiences in democracy if a citizenry capable of democratic action is to be developed.

As shown by the analysis of the psychological process codes in light of Piaget's "decentering" concept, there appear to exist stages or degrees of civic development in children. The objectives just specified defined goals for civic education. The following developmental guidelines indicate the present level of interviewed students in relation to goals of civic education. They describe for educators the degree of civic-mindedness of junior and senior high school students. They are not to be seen as goals but as developmental stages of civic competence. Understanding of such stages should serve to identify the most useful points at which to begin teaching civic awareness to students.

Guideline One: Junior high school students' problems are focused more on the students themselves than are those of senior high school students. Junior high students for the most part write about personal problems. Conflicts are seen as conflicts with individuals. The developmental trend toward increasing involvement with nonpersonal problems has been identified in all comparisons.

Guideline Two: Senior high school students are more concerned with group problems than are junior high school students. The four junior-senior high school comparisons show decisively that the group factor increases from junior to senior high school. Involvement with group problems definitely increases with age.

Guideline Three: Junior high students have more conflicts with their peers than do high school students, while the latter report more conflicts with authority figures. The cross-sectional comparisons show that, without exception, incidents involving peers decrease with age, and incidents concerning authorities increase with age.

Guideline Four: Problems with institutions occur much more frequently in the senior high than in the junior high. Except in the school for gifted girls, all comparisons showed that high school students reported a greater percentage of institutional conflicts than did junior high students. Junior high students reported a greater share of problems with "persons." The school for gifted girls showed no difference between the percentage of personal incidents described by junior and senior high students.

Guideline Five: High school students have a more highly developed abstractive capacity than junior high students do. The preceding four guidelines all distinguish junior and senior high school students on the basis of an abstractive faculty, i.e., a capability for extending one's field of action from personal and immediate to more impersonal and distant concerns. Depersonalization is the process that differentiates junior and senior high students on each dimension of civic-mindedness. The ability to extend oneself beyond the personal element and the immediate situation is the key to development from the first (junior high level) to the second (senior high level) stage of civic-mindedness.

This study provides some interesting perspectives for those who bear responsibility for developing new curricular and institutional structures. In particular, it suggests that—

1. The content of civics courses should not consist of abstract problems and principles that have no bearing on a student's life in school. The curriculum should focus on concrete situations in school and community life.
2. The traditional teacher-student relationship and administration-student relationship must change. Students must be given the opportunity to make decisions within the classroom and school environment.
3. The school must become a civic community in which diverse groups take part in policies and decisions, and in the process learn to become effective participants.

The experience of the last decade seems to support these propositions, reinforcing the idea that what is needed is not merely a restructuring of social studies but of the school itself. A further discussion of this position can be found in *The Schools and the Democratic Environment* (5). It is also implicit in some of the work of the High School Government Project at Indiana University. In this context the improvement of instructional materials and teaching strategies in the 1960's is seen as but one stage in a development process that includes restructuring the schools as well.

A World View

Much of secondary school social studies, backed up by a lot of home conditioning, still tends to convey the impression that the West is and has always been superior to all other civilizations. The nineteenth century position of dominance by the Western cultures over the rest of the world is presented as natural and its continuance into the future as indefinite. Some of the most widely used textbooks convey the impression that while civilization may have started in places like Mesopotamia, it failed to improve man's lot until the Israelites and Greeks took over. They in turn passed it on through the Romans and Christians to Northern Europeans, with whom it moved to North America and achieved the ultimate.

In the past decade there have been many attempts to correct this parochial and dangerous outlook. Current events, the study of other nations, and world problems units or courses have long been used to insert international content into the curriculum. More recently, using area studies has become a popular method of expanding international perspectives. There is a growing feeling that students need to know more about various parts of an increasingly interdependent world. Furthermore, intergroup tensions in the United States have sparked numerous efforts and programs designed to help students develop the capacity for understanding and working with people whose lives and backgrounds may be very different from their own. The study of a number of areas or cultures in depth has replaced or been added to the more traditional, generally chronological study of world or American history.

While the area studies approach is often an improvement over traditional chronological approaches, it has so far been only partially successful in providing insights into the manner in which all major cultural heritages and their national subdivisions have grown and developed within their own traditions throughout history. Even more important, it generally fails to provide a context within which to consider the fact that acceleration of human mobility and communication greatly increases cross-cultural and cross-national contacts, thereby speeding up the process of cultural change and making it more complex. To make matters worse, the study of current events still tends to provide a view of the world in the context of U.S. foreign policy issues—thus perpetuating the big-nation syndrome and the crisis approach.

While area studies allow "equal time" for non-Western cultures, they usually reinforce the image of the world as separate patches of real estate. Likewise, the proliferation of culture studies or units examining the traditional relations of nation-states may prevent students from seeing the world as an increasingly interdependent unit.

A Global Approach

The global approach that was developed during the 60's may drastically change this situation. In this approach the world is studied as a unit and man as a single species. *An Examination of Objectives, Needs and Priorities in International Education in U.S. Secondary and Elementary Schools* (1), a study supported by the U.S. Office of Education, describes the approach and lists in detail the goals and objectives for reshaping the social studies with an international emphasis. Among the goals are the following:

1. Overcoming the Western orientation found in most textbooks and curriculums and helping students achieve a more

objective and global perspective on cultural, economic, and political diversity.

2. Developing empathy toward other cultures and values both in the United States and in the world, along with an appreciation of the similarities and differences in human life around the world.
3. Increasing student awareness of the natural tendency toward an ethnocentric bias in the way people see each other, and helping them to reduce this bias.
4. Helping students develop techniques and methods of inquiry and independent thinking in order to cope emotionally and intellectually with the continuing change, complexity, and ambiguity in human affairs.
5. Helping students develop an understanding of the process of decision making in regard to local, national, international, and global issues.
6. Emphasizing the global perspective and the future in a way that helps students imagine and objectively make choices.

The major objectives for international education delineated by the study are the following (adapted from "Securing Man's Survival: Toward a Basic Course of Study," a working paper for the U.S. Commission for UNESCO):

I. *The K-12 curriculum should develop students' knowledge about and understanding of the world system.*

A. The curriculum should develop students' knowledge of the earth as a planet. This implies—

1. Developing some comprehension of the place of the world system in cosmic space and time, including some understanding of—
    a. The location of the earth in the cosmic system.
    b. The differences and similarities between the earth and other planets.
2. Developing some understanding of the earth as a set physical system that both conditions and is conditioned by living systems—particularly man.

B. The curriculum should develop students' understanding of mankind as a species. This implies—

1. Developing a comparative understanding of man as one of many living systems, including insight into—
    a. The similarities and differences between living and nonliving systems and between man and other living systems.
    b. Man's common biological and psychological needs.

2. Developing an understanding of the sources of differences in human actions and life styles, that is, some understanding of human behavior as being socially learned and culturally conditioned.

3. Developing some understanding of the major structural characteristics of the human species, summarized by such generalizations as: The human species is—

   a. Racially, linguistically, culturally, and institutionally diverse.

   b. Generally economically depressed with vast disparities in the wealth, education, and health of its members.

   c. Rapidly expanding in numbers and becoming increasingly urbanized and industrialized.

   d. Increasingly interdependent.

C. The curriculum should develop students' understanding of the global social system as one level of human social organization. This implies—

1. Developing some understanding of the major entities that comprise the contemporary international system, including—

   a. Some comparative understanding of the approximately 130 nation-states in the modern world.

   b. Some functionally oriented understanding of cross-national organizations, both governmental and nongovernmental.

   c. Some understanding of the international status of the planet's polar regions, its oceans, and outer space.

2. Developing some historical understanding of the nation-state system as one of many possible forms of politically organizing the human species.

3. Developing an understanding of major social processes within the international system, including some grasp of—

   a. Internation war, conflict, and conflict resolution.

   b. Internation collaboration and integration.

   c. Internation communications, trade, investment, and foreign aid.

   d. Cultural diffusion and migration.

4. Developing some understanding of major international social problems, including some insight into the problems of—

   a. Controlling or managing intergroup, and particularly internation, violence and creating institutions for the peaceful resolution of conflict.

b. Controlling population growth.
c. Controlling the social and psychological costs of rapid sociocultural change, particularly technological change, urbanization, and the bureaucratization of social organizations.
d. Controlling further deterioration in man's natural environment while using the world's oceans and outer space for the welfare of all mankind.

II. *The K-12 curriculum should develop the capacity of students to view the world system as a whole, and particular phenomena within it conceptually, comparatively, and globally.*

A. The curriculum should develop within students a capacity to think of empirically concrete or historically specific phenomena (events, institutions, actions, etc.) as particular instances or cases within a larger class of analytically comparable phenomena.

B. The curriculum should develop within students an ability to compare two or more phenomena in a conceptually sophisticated way. This implies—

1. An ability to conceive of the objects being compared in terms of both similarities and differences.
2. An ability to recognize that one's relative perception of similarities and differences is influenced by the size and nature of the sample of objects being compared.
3. An ability to think of differences as matters of degree rather than kind.

C. The curriculum should develop within students a capacity to envision the world as a totality and to perceive particular phenomena within a global frame of reference. This implies developing a comprehension of—

1. The interrelatedness of man as a system of life and the planet earth as a set of linked physical systems.
2. The world system as one subsystem within the total cosmic system.

III. *The K-12 curriculum should develop the capacity of students to make logically valid and empirically grounded analytical judgments.*

A. The curriculum should develop within students a "realistic" attitude toward knowledge. This implies developing within students—

1. An understanding of knowledge as a set of man-created hypotheses or images.

2. A capacity to conceptualize phenomena in alternative ways.
3. An awareness of the influence of cultural setting and social situation on human knowledge in general and on their own perception and interpretation of the world in particular.

B. The curriculum should develop within students an understanding of and some skill in the process of social scientific inquiry.

IV. *The curriculum should develop the capacity of students to make rational, analytical, explicit, and human normative judgments. In order to create these capacities the curriculum should—*

A. Seek to develop within individuals the psychological freedom to hold attitudes independent of personality needs and group norms.

B. Seek to develop in students an ability to analyze normative disagreements in terms of semantic, perceptual, and valuational sources of conflict.

C. Develop in students an ability—
1. To articulate explicitly the values in terms of which they believe given phenomena should be judged.
2. To consider explicitly the operational or behavioral meanings of values in terms of which judgments are to be made.
3. To consider explicitly the information that is needed to reach sound judgments about whether or not a given object possesses the desired value qualities.

D. Develop within students modes of thinking that are—
1. Relatively free from the influence of egocentric, ethnocentric, and stereotypic perceptions.
2. Characterized by moral or ethical complexity.
3. Characterized by a capacity for empathetic understanding and a "world-minded" value orientation.

V. *The curriculum should develop the capacity of students to understand, analyze, and judge foreign policy decisions.*

A. The curriculum should develop students' knowledge about and conceptual understanding of how foreign policy decisions are made, particularly within the American system.

B. The curriculum should develop students' ability to analyze foreign policy decisions in terms of the major factors operating within the decision-making process.

VI. *The curriculum should develop students' capacity to observe intelligently and critically the current history of the world system.*

A. The curriculum should develop within students the motivation, vocabulary, and conceptual understanding needed to follow current events through the mass media.

B. The curriculum should develop within students an understanding of the structure and functioning of the international communication system.

VII. *The K-12 curriculum should develop the capacity of students to adapt constructively to the "realities of the human condition." This means endowing students with—*

A. Sensitivity to and emotional acceptance of diversity in human actions, perceptions, cognitions, values, and social institutions.

B. An acceptance of—and a set of socially responsible attitudes toward—technological and sociocultural changes.

C. Sensitivity to and acceptance of the political and ethical implications of mankind's increasing interdependence.

D. An ability to perceive and feel themselves to be responsible members of subnational, national, and cross-national groups.

E. An ability to tolerate emotionally the tensions of continued intergroup conflict and hostility.

Now that pictures of the earth as seen from the moon are part of every visual medium from television to teachers' bulletin boards, a global perspective has become truly inescapable. Political and economic interdependence, instantaneous communication, issues of global ecology, and rapid intercontinental travel have all worked to change our awareness, but none has quite had the impact of seeing our fragile green globe floating in space. This startling glimpse of the earth as a unit, combined with a growing sense of urgency about environmental deterioration, suddenly makes it both more possible and more necessary than ever before to reorganize our knowledge from a global perspective. Henceforth, international studies must be designed for the riders-on-the-earth-together generations: there must be education about global society as a whole, as well as about its parts.

Globalizing American education will not always be easy. Students who come from our own poverty cultures, for example, may find little to excite them in studies of world cultures and problems—problems that are far more remote and far less real than the immediate struggles and misfortunes in their own lives. The ghetto child and his rural counterpart in Appalachia are not likely to be intrigued by poverty in India or tribal struggles in Nigeria unless they are demonstrably and undeniably relevant to them.

Developing a world view may therefore mean bringing America's "underdeveloped" areas into the classroom alongside similar situations from Asia or Latin America. Sensitizing students to American poverty and how it is related to parallel conditions in other areas helps to break down the notion that only distant countries and people have development problems. As a result, students come to recognize man's interdependence, the universality of his needs, and the necessity of coping with threats to human survival on a global basis.

Poverty, pollution, population, and the lack of the necessary international cooperation to tackle these issues effectively might well become the basis for an international curriculum. Space exploration and the environmental crisis seem to provide the immediacy needed to arouse student and community interests. A rationale for such an approach can be found in *International Education for Spaceship Earth* (6), and evidence of the appeal of the "spaceship earth" approach in international studies can be found in—

- The Glenns Falls (New York) City Schools' working paper for Project Survival, "We Are a Single Human Community," as well as their "Teachers' Survival Kit."
- The Cedar Rapids, Iowa, "Spaceship Earth Curriculum."
- The Teacher Workshop and Curriculum Program on Spaceship Earth at Harwood Union High School, Moretown, Vermont.
- The global approach being developed in the San Ramon Valley (California) Unified School District, using Ehrlich's *How To Be a Survivor,* a plan to save spaceship earth, as one text.

The increasing quantity and variety of materials taking a global approach and suitable for use in high school classrooms is further evidence of the increasing interest in this approach among teachers.

Summary

Today everybody seems to be convinced that the schools should be changed; the question is how and to what ends. The experience of the 60's and early 70's indicates that basic changes in the school environment are essential. Neither improving the social studies curriculum nor training better teachers is likely to result in meaningful change unless the school itself is drastically restructured. The schools should reflect more clearly the nature of the communities within which they reside and at the same time provide more opportunities for students to learn to become effective citizens by participating in school policies and decisions.

There is, however, no single formula by which schools everywhere can be changed and improved. The same is true for social studies. The patterns, approaches, and goals outlined in this chapter represent only a few of many possible schemes for reorganizing social studies instruction. All decisions regarding curriculum design necessarily involve judgments in a number of sensitive areas that limit or in other ways influence those decisions. The theoretician may be able to disregard such elements as teacher competence and commitment, enthusiasm, intransigence, public pressures, available funds, and access to instructional materials, but curriculum workers do so at great peril. These limitations, together with the lack of agreement among social scientists, the changing nature of knowledge, the lack of widespread understanding of the implications of learning theory, and the nature of community concerns, argue strongly for a flexible pattern of organization that can be adapted to local conditions.

If the rich resources produced by the research and development efforts of the 60's can be adapted to changing school needs, the prospect for change in the 70's may be very good. Adaptation probably requires, among other things, that the big packages representing year-long courses in a single discipline be broken up and restructured. This procedure will not please many scholars, nor are many educators willing to accept the responsibility for repackaging the products of curriculum development, but it may be the best way to salvage the often high-quality materials produced in the 60's. Perhaps the time is ripe to try mixing the traditional and the new in the same school in order to reflect more accurately the community and society at large. In so doing, the school might also help work out new and desperately needed patterns of cooperation, tolerance, and mutual respect among the diverse groups that constitute American society.

BIBLIOGRAPHY

1. Becker, James M. *An Examination of Objectives, Needs and Priorities in International Education in U.S. Secondary and Elementary Schools, Final Report.* ERIC Document ED 031 612. Washington, D.C.: U.S. Office of Education, 1969. (The Summary and Recommendations of the study are available from the Foreign Policy Association, 345 E. 46th St., New York, N.Y. 10017.)

2. Beyer, Barry K., and Penna, Anthony N., editors. *Concepts in the Social Studies.* Bulletin No. 45. Washington, D.C.: National Council for the Social Studies, 1971.

3. California Statewide Social Sciences Study Committee. *Social Sciences Education Framework for California Public Schools: Kindergarten and Grades One through Twelve.* (Proposed) An abstract, revised draft. Sacramento: California Department of Education, 1970.

4. Center for Research and Education in American Liberties. *Civic Education in a Crisis Age: An Alternative to Repression and Revolution.* New York: Teachers College, Columbia University, September 1970.

5. The Danforth Foundation and the Ford Foundation. *The Schools and the Democratic Environment.* New York: Columbia University Press, 1970.

6. King, David. *International Education for Spaceship Earth.* New York: Thomas Y. Crowell Co.

7. Lester, G. Sidney. *The New Social Studies: A Selected Bibliography and Review.* Corte Madera, Calif.: Marin Social Studies Project.

8. Marin Social Studies Project. *Directory of Research and Curriculum Development Projects in Social Studies Education.* Corte Madera, Calif.: the Project, 1971.

9. Pennsylvania Department of Education. *Social Studies Today: Guidelines for Curriculum Improvement.* Harrisburg: the Department, 1970.

10. Sanders, Norris M., and Tanck, Marlin L. "A Critical Appraisal of Twenty-Six National Social Studies Projects." *Social Education* 34: 383-93; April 1970.

Professional autonomy
of the local association

17

Planning and Organizing for Improved Instruction

The 1960's

During the 1960's the schools were exhorted, loudly and strongly, to innovate, to change, to be creative. The changes so vigorously recommended were predominantly changes in content, "new" subject matter to be taught. Proponents of the "new"—directors and staffs of the national curriculum projects, who were for the most part college and university professors of academic subjects—were calling on teachers, especially elementary teachers, to teach subjects for which methods were not available and for which teachers accustomed to the self-contained classroom lacked the required skills. Most teachers were not psychologically ready for the changes required. The success of any new curriculum was tied to the ability of the teachers.

College and university subject matter specialists proclaimed their supreme ability to decide what should be taught and also to produce instructional materials they considered appropriate. The academicians had discovered curriculum development, but they were ignorant of the classroom and children's learning. Therefore, they took their disciplines out of the context of human nature. For the most part they were concerned exclusively with subject matter and ignored the basic need, long accepted by specialists in curriculum, for the learner to be dealt with as a complete person—a social, emotional, esthetic, physical person—as well as an intellectual being.

When curriculum workers—who, whatever their varied titles, were charged with responsibility for curriculum development and improving instruction—opposed and denounced isolated, purely cognitive learning, the academicians called them antiintellectuals and pushed on, ignoring warnings of the consequences of overemphasizing the cognitive to the exclusion of other learner needs. Being politically astute, they also ignored the institutional levels of curriculum decision making, bypassed the specialists in this realm of the school's operation, and went directly to private publishers and other large sources of finance (where there was no public control of funds) to publish and market their instructional materials. These materials are now in hardcover textbooks; teachers are using them in the way they have traditionally used the textbook—as the largest single determiner of what is taught.

The role of the curriculum worker became unclear. The curriculum project staffs went directly to the teachers, inviting them to summer workshops to learn the new materials to be taught; however, they failed to involve teachers in any continuous thought and study, so the teachers taught the new materials in the same old ways.

The curriculum reformers of the 60's did not present new, sophisticated models for the curriculum development process; in fact, their models were quite traditional, perhaps without their even knowing it. Because they ignored the curriculum literature, they accepted as "new" models that had actually prevailed for nearly a century. However, as Lawrence Cremin (5) has noted, "They did increase the number of options available within selected subject areas; and they did break the increasingly exclusive hold of professionalized curriculum-makers on the direction and control of the process" (p. 216).

The Rebellion

Then came the rebellion of some of our finest youth, who demanded meaningful, relevant education. Their disenchantment was met with surprise and shock. It was too late to turn back the calendar, to heed the warnings of the curriculum workers who had been stating in a steady but unheeded voice the need for education to be meaningful for each learner, whatever his level of schooling, in terms of his motivations, interests, and abilities. Academic reform had ignored the importance of the learner-centered philosophy espoused by the curriculum specialists.

The youth rebellion made education decision makers realize that schooling as it had been conducted—to satisfy the needs of society, that is, to fit the young for citizenship in society—had miserably failed the individual student in his search for self-fulfillment. Attempts to meet external societal needs via schooling had in no way produced youth who were more fully human individuals. Schools in the 1960's had not been successful in creating an environment in which a child could grow into an adult, could grow into his own best self. The personal meaning of curriculum and instruction had been overlooked by the curriculum decision makers.

Next came the disenchantment of blacks with their local schools, which they perceived as keeping them down by giving them inferior preparation for life. They pointed out the unconscious racism of most basic readers and social studies texts. Because curriculum workers were often either the authors of these texts or members of textbook selection committees, they were charged with being major perpetrators of institutional racism. This charge was a real blow to curriculum workers, who had been generally recognized as the most liberal and radical thinkers on the education scene and whose long-time philosophy had been a humanistic one.

Now in the 1970's the rest of the education community is climbing on the *humaneness* bandwagon. The word appears in the titles of many current education publications. Thus another movement in curriculum and instruction dawns.

Even during the 1960's several well-received publications had been concerned with the human learner. *Perceiving, Behaving, Becoming,* the 1962 yearbook of the Association for Supervision and Curriculum Development (ASCD), emphasized self-actualization. *Imperatives in Education,* published by the American Association of School Administrators (AASA) in 1966 (1), outlined the following urgent needs (note the emphasis on human qualities):

- To make urban life rewarding and satisfying
- To strengthen the moral fabric of society
- To deal constructively with psychological tensions
- To make the best use of leisure time
- To work with other peoples of the world for human betterment.

Movements in the curriculum field are commonly recognized as swinging between the child-centered and the content-disciplines philosophies. In the 1920's the scientific method approach to organizing the curriculum was predominant; in the late 20's and the "progressive" 30's, the focus shifted to the child; subject areas were emphasized in the 50's and 60's; and now there has been a return to the human learner (12, 15).

The New Curriculum Movement

Schools in the 1970's are confronted with a new set of matters demanding educators' immediate attention:

accountability	master contracts
alternative schools	master plans
assessment	negotiations
behavioral objectives	performance contracts
decentralization	PPBS (Program, Planning,
differentiated staffing	Budgeting System).

For the most part these are organizational matters of a bureaucratic nature. In no way do they involve basic curriculum concerns, nor do they necessarily have any effect on curriculum decision making as we now understand the process. Exhortations will not suffice to handle these matters. Some are buttressed by legal requirements that make it mandatory for administrators to take prescribed actions by a given date. Others are supported by community demands, especially the demands of black and third world parents. Private firms are offering instruction and guaranteeing results, with remuneration dependent on measurable improvements in learners' skills. Teachers' demands for a major role in all decisions about curriculum are included in the master contracts that have recently been negotiated.

Amid all this, where are curriculum and instruction? Where is the responsibility for curriculum decisions? What ever happened to the learners? Are there to be no curriculum concerns in the 1970's? Even a casual examination of some recent surveys of educators' opinions and major concerns makes one apprehensive about the curriculum development process.

The California Teachers Association and the California Association of School Administrators conducted a survey in April 1971(4) that asked California schools to identify their innovative programs. The predominant innovations were *not* matters of curriculum and instruction. Of the elementary schools responding, 60.4 percent listed teacher aides; 53.5 percent listed team teaching; 47.9 percent cited individually prescribed instruction; and 44.4 percent mentioned instructional television (pp. 15-16). Among intermediate and junior high schools the most common innovative programs were the teaching of reading (66.9 percent), classes for gifted students (59.7 percent), teacher aides (55.6 percent), and team teaching (54 percent) (p. 34). Senior high schools reported work experience programs (85.1 percent), teaching of reading

(79.4 percent), teacher aides (55.4 percent), and ethnic studies (54.3 percent) (pp. 53-54). Recent California legislation requiring an eighth grade reading level for high school graduation may be in part responsible for the frequency of reading programs. Minority demands were the impetus for the addition of ethnic studies.

Based on a spring 1971 survey of teacher opinions, the National Education Association's *Research Bulletin* for December 1971 reported the major problems encountered by public school teachers to be large classes, insufficient time for rest or preparation, lack of public support for schools, inadequate salary, and insufficient clerical help (14). Here also the list of major problems includes no curricular or instructional matters.

Similarly, an informal survey conducted for Louisiana ASCD in January 1971 among 200 teachers, K-12, in 15 Louisiana school systems revealed greatest teacher concern about lack of discipline due to failure of parents, wide range of abilities, high pupil-teacher ratio, and excessive record keeping (11).

In September 1970, Edmund J. Farrell asked 20 key members of the National Council of Teachers of English for information about general pressures on teachers in their local areas, as well as pressures unique to English teachers. A number of the pressures cited by respondents clustered around the terms *too much, too little,* or *too many,* e.g., too much paperwork, too little time, too many students, too many classes (8).

If the survey results cited may be considered representative of concerns of the early 1970's, the overwhelming preoccupation of school personnel seems to be with finding ways to cope with quantities via such procedures as team teaching and the use of teacher aides.

Late in 1971, ASCD published *Curricular Concerns in a Revolutionary Era* (10), a collection of articles from its well-known journal, *Educational Leadership.* Sections include "Values: The Challenge, the Dilemma," "Individualization: The Pupil as Person," "Social Involvement: The Issues, the Ideals," "The Search for Theory," "Ethnic Studies: The Richness of Pluralism," "Whorls in a Revolutionary Society," and "In a World Setting." These sections contain excellent statements of the issues facing our pluralistic society, but one must ask of ASCD (the professional organization geared primarily to the needs of curriculum workers), Where are the support and assistance for the supervisors, the consultants, the curriculum workers, of whatever title? Is it possible that the curriculum workers were bypassed so effectively by the subject-matter specialists of the 1960's that they are no longer raising audible voices about planning curriculum change? Who is speaking today for curriculum and instruction?

A clear voice is found in *The American School Superintendent,* an AASA research study based on a survey of superintendents in 1969-70 (9). One item on the survey questionnaire asked what current educational issues or challenges they perceived as most crucial. Predictably, adequate financial support was the number one issue identified by superintendents in all categories of school district size. But the number two issue, not so easily predicted, was "demands for new ways of teaching or operating programs." This concern was ranked high (never any lower than fourth) by all categories of superintendents (pp. 57-58). Here at last is an indication of concern for instruction!

The AASA questionnaire also asked the superintendents what kinds of specialists should be added to their school system staffs to increase performance and output levels. The greatest percentage of respondents (52.5 percent) called for more specialists in curriculum and instruction; thus "superintendents continue to have the traditional instructional orientation" (p. 60). A superintendent's comment in another 1971 AASA book, *Profiles of the Administrative Team* (2), further demonstrates this orientation (p. 70):

> Leadership in the development of the curriculum is the prime responsibility of the superintendent. Operation of a school system without strong leadership in curriculum is potentially a detriment to the quality of education each child receives. A competent business administrator should only be considered for the superintendency if he has extensive preparation in the area of curriculum or is able to devise an organizational pattern which will provide this leadership.

The contrast between publications addressed to curriculum specialists and to superintendents is clear. The latter reveal the persistent administrative concern for instruction and the recognition of need for administrative leadership in this area. The former focus on the changing social values and the concerns of the multiple publics served by the American schools.

As Tucker (7) has pointed out (p. 189):

> The curriculum profession is caught on the horns of a dilemma. On the one hand, we value the basic principles of the common school, but we know that we must begin to probe its basic assumptions in the light of changing social values. On the other hand, if we actively promote alternatives, this may

> further fragment and splinter a profession which has struggled mightily to achieve a modicum of conceptual and professional coherence.

Educators must be aware of pluralistic values and the resultant demands for "alternatives" to the schools. Actions must be taken. The pluralistic publics will not wait. Meeting their demands is consistent with the curriculum philosophy of providing for individual needs and involving the learner in his learning experiences. However, the responsibility for action does not rest with curriculum specialists. Their positions are supportive and consultative; they provide excellent leadership on what *should be* but do not generally plan strategies or devise management techniques. Who has the authority to act? Obviously it is the chief administrator, whose leadership function is rapidly taking on certain aspects of management.

The concerns listed at the beginning of this section call for increased bureaucratic activities. A different kind of planning for curriculum change seems to be required. Bruce Joyce (12) has written of bureaucracy in this way (p. 320):

> As organizations become bureaucratic, it becomes very difficult to make changes, *except* by imposing them through systematic modification of routine operations performed by many individuals—a bureaucratic method through which bureaucracy co-opts the innovator.
>
> The schools have not been equipped to make changes even in this manner (probably only the most progressive industries of the most authoritarian governments are so equipped) and they became bureaucratic, therefore, and bureaucracy produced obsolescence. For the bureaucratization tended to freeze the operation of the school around behaviors which had been created for former generations, and which, while they *might* have had applicability to those generations, promised less and less as time went on. . . .
>
> Bureaucratization has brought the schools into a serious conflict with most of the prescriptive curriculum theories. (Prescriptive theory describes what *should* be done, while descriptive theory describes what will probably happen if certain conditions obtain.) Nearly all prescriptive theorists have advocated that the learner understand what he is trying to learn, that he share in the making of at least some of the rules of his education, and that the teacher be sensitive and personal in his dealings with the student. These are exactly the opposite of bureaucratic behavior. The bureaucrat becomes insensitive, puts the organization ahead of the individual, and sees authority as external to the participants in the situation.

A Historical Perspective

Perhaps a brief look at how the curriculum field developed will clarify the present state of affairs. Curriculum as commonly used dates from the 19th century. William Torrey Harris, superintendent in St. Louis during the 1870's, developed a solution for problems brought on by universal schooling: he adapted to the school system many bureaucratic industrial procedures. Concern for curriculum accompanied the progressive movement of the 1930's, when schools were faced with teaching an increasingly heterogeneous group of students a great variety of subjects. The progressive movement followed Harris's lead.

Influential committees of the National Education Association and the professional organizations of teachers and scholars began making recommendations about curriculum. Individual school systems devised such innovations as the Dalton Plan and the Winnetka Plan. Bobbitt, Charters, Dewey, Judd, and other individuals formulated curriculum theories. All this activity produced much literature on curriculum reform and recommendations, which became the base for a new field of specialization: the curriculum. It had become obvious that the superintendent could not do all the curriculum work required and that specialists would be needed to manage this part of the education process. Thus the study of curriculum gradually came to be a separate field of graduate study for "preparation of knowledgeable practitioners to assume an emergent role within school systems committed to curricular innovations" (5, pp. 213-14). These specialists were trained in the education departments of universities, rather than in the subject matter departments—a separation that was to culminate in the divisiveness of the 1960's.

The field of curriculum grew without any generally accepted agreement on its parameters and without even any generally agreed-upon definition of the term. Definitions remain so broad, vague, and ambiguous that they have failed to give direction to the specialists themselves or to the curriculum centers that have been set up with federal funds in recent years.

Furthermore, there has never been any agreement on what the curriculum specialist should be called or on what his or her specific role should be. Curriculum specialists have traditionally shunned the "administrator" label, preferring to occupy staff positions in order to identify more closely with classroom teachers and to foster a more cooperative atmosphere. But teachers have always perceived them to be administrators. In one western state, the curriculum workers organization has recently abandoned the pretense and merged into a federation of all school administrator groups.

Historically, teachers have objected to the process of supervision: all too often they have seen curriculum workers as constraints. When asked to move into curriculum or supervisory positions, however, few teachers refuse.

Curriculum workers cannot resolve the chief teacher concerns listed earlier—the need for fewer students, fewer classes, fewer clerical duties, more free time for planning. As Larry Cuban has observed (6),

> Subject supervisors are also trapped by the Operating System's endemic distrust and regulations. They are powerless to effect changes and therefore are irrelevant to those they are pledged to help. . . . Charged with responsibility, yet empty of authority, supervisors can only advise, cajole, and supplicate. Confronted by powerlessness, supervisors turn inward. They conduct workshops, collect information, visit classes, and prepare sample lesson plans. . . . They give class to the operation but they are expendable.

It should be pointed out that not only the supervisors but the administrators and teachers as well are caught in the school system's operating procedures and its definition of their roles; they are not free agents.

There is some evidence that subject matter supervisors are disappearing from the roster or organizational structure of school systems. Increasingly, school districts have not been filling the vacancies created by retirement or other normal causes. Financial difficulties and decentralization are no doubt contributing factors, but there seems to be no great outcry from administrators, teachers, or the public for restoring these services. In some school systems, subject matter specialists have been shifted abruptly to different functions with demotions in title and salary.

Financial justification for changing responsibilities for curriculum development is becoming more frequent. The Oakland (Calif.) *Tribune* for November 11, 1971, quotes President Englehardt of Englehardt and Englehardt, Inc., education consultants: "Examine the hierarchy of coordinators and specialists at the administrative level. Is it fiscally sound to have them sitting around thinking about what they will introduce into the science or English program?" Englehardt favors releasing teachers who have specialized in a subject field and giving them time to move around the schools and get new programs started. "The financial savings can be considerable and the changes will occur in a much more stimulating situation." Such advocacy of released time for teachers and of the resulting financial savings gives support to the teachers' demands for a greater role in curriculum decisions, just at the time when these demands are increasing. Teacher militancy has spread to curriculum development.

Negotiations and Curriculum Decisions

A major fact of life in today's negotiated agreements is teacher involvement in curriculum decisions. The NEA *Research Bulletin* reports that "of the 978 comprehensive agreements effective during the 1968-69 school year in school systems with a pupil enrollment of 1,000 or more, 451 (46.1 percent) contained one or more provisions directly or indirectly affecting the curriculum decision-making process" (13). Teachers have been successful in their power struggle in welfare matters and now demand a major role in curriculum development. They make no distinctions between matters that should be negotiated and those that should be left to other processes.

Negotiating machinery, which is based on the industrial model representing a power struggle, has regrettable effects on curriculum decisions. In such a procedure administrators and teachers are clearly polarized, while curriculum workers, students, and often principals are not represented. Decision making at the bargaining table ignores the usual requirement for curriculum making: a process of study and research drawing on learning theories, human growth and development, and knowledge from the separate subject matter areas. Deliberate study prior to reaching a decision was long the domain of the curriculum specialist. Quite different is the negotiating process, which may end in compromise based on factors other than professional judgment. Compromises are inevitable consequences of negotiations between competing power structures. What is best for students does not enter into the power struggle.

Look, for example, at the following items from teacher contracts in Michigan (16, pp. 10-11):

> Meetings—only one meeting per month of any kind may be called by the administration, and it shall be limited to no more than one hour in length.
>
> Curriculum Work—any teacher who is asked to attend a meeting after his stipulated contractual hours to do curriculum planning must be monetarily compensated. Further, if he is

asked to develop curriculum materials, he must be compensated for this.

Pre-School Workshops—this must not exceed one day, unless otherwise negotiated by the association and with additional compensation.

What responsible educator believes that curriculum decisions, plus all other matters that concern teachers, can be handled in one one-hour meeting per month? Absurd!

Remember that the classroom teacher is the one person who is closest to the learners; he works daily with a group or groups of students. His classroom decisions are indeed curriculum decisions, regardless of negotiated agreements about time spent on curriculum work. The teacher cannot help being a curriculum builder. This role is not new and has not been changed by negotiations.

The assumption among teachers seems to be that administrators have operated under a plan that deliberately ignored their role in curriculum decisions. But a look at past practices and the literature of cooperative curriculum making proves the shakiness of such an assumption. (See, for example, *Organizing for Improving Instruction,* a joint 1963 publication of ASCD and AASA.) In their zeal for negotiating their role in curriculum decisions, teachers have left the impression that they have the sole right to negotiate educational policies. However, teachers who are experts in their own fields usually lack the broad background of experience and education necessary to oversee the total educational process. Teachers have not been trained in critical analysis for solving curriculum problems; they have not developed the skills needed to evaluate all parts of the curriculum field.

The Unsettled Curriculum Field

Now is an unsettled time for planning and organizing for curriculum change. Responsibility for curriculum decisions is unclear. Curriculum development seems to be taking on an increasingly bureaucratic and commercial flavor. Instructional systems are being developed that could be very efficient in accommodating individual learners. Cost accounting procedures are becoming a part of education, not only for budget processes but also for making curriculum decisions and for assessing learning outcomes. Commercial companies are increasingly developing instructional materials within their own staffs with less and less guidance from curriculum specialists. Curriculum workers are increasingly becoming the servants of an impersonal system as their prerogatives are dissipated.

One wonders how the indefinite, advising-without-authority role of the curriculum specialists managed to prevail as long and as satisfactorily as it did before anyone requested objective evidence of its effectiveness. Had not the academicians, the youth of America, the minority group parents, and the teachers demanded a greater voice in matters of curriculum and instruction, things might have continued indefinitely as they were. But the often disruptive demands of these groups could not be ignored or talked away. Action had to be taken. The role of the administrator as the "official leader" was quite clear.

A school system has to be operated. The superintendent is accountable for this operation. The school system of which he is in charge is actually a social system; its day-by-day operation shapes the behavior of the people in it. Some of the decisions to be made and procedures to be used by the superintendent are determined by the nature of the demands made on the system. For example, PPBS requires written behavioral objectives; some authority must make sure that each principal prepares the objectives with his staff according to the prescribed guidelines. In preparing for teacher evaluation an administrator must act quickly to determine the procedures needed to meet the legal requirements, including a deadline for initiating the plan; at the same time he must ensure suitable involvement of all people concerned. There is no time to sit back and wait for natural leadership to surface.

Given the urgencies of the times and the state of confusion about who is responsible for curriculum decision making, it seems inevitable that the superintendent must assume more and more of this responsibility if decisions are to be made and implemented in an efficient and dependable manner. For the sake of efficiency he may employ procedures that tend to be typical of management. However, this does not mean that he should proceed all alone. A successful superintendent must also prove to teachers and students that *they* can do something. Good staff and student relations depend on his recognition of the worth of each person and of a wide range of skills and talents. The way an administrator enables all people in his system to work together may be more important to the successful operation of the system than the things they accomplish. Decisions about priorities, roles, authority, and operational guidelines must be *cooperative* decisions. Whether or not the superintendent is actually involved in deciding how to operate some program or selecting new instructional materials, he is always responsible for the decisions. He can be held accountable.

The big curriculum job ahead is to rebuild. During the rebuilding years there may be few large curriculum movements of the type so prominent in the 1960's. Instead there may be a direct attack on improving instruction by individual teachers working with their students in a climate conducive to study and teacher experimentation. Behavioral objectives and accountability speak strongly for improving learning outcomes and being able to justify the amount of learning a child has acquired.

The administrator will be taking leadership in the following rebuilding tasks:

- *Defining the curriculum field,* or describing precisely whatever field may emerge to take responsibility for what is now "curriculum and instruction." It might be "individualization," the goal we say we are striving for. What are all the factors to be considered in providing an individualized program for each learner? The list will surely include everything from materials to people. Why not an assistant superintendent for individualization?
- *Defining roles.* The efficiency demanded by PPBS, accountability, and behavioral objectives makes it imperative that each person understand precisely the requirements of his role and accept the responsibility for meeting them. The role of all staff and students in decision making about instruction must be very clear, lest competing groups outside the school system usurp the decision-making process.
- *Developing new ways of working together.* Group dynamics have much to offer school personnel looking for effective ways to work with all groups that want to be heard in school matters, including volatile community groups. We in education have never really taken advantage of the resources offered by the other institutions of society—business, recreational, and social organizations, for example. We should also explore the use of teacher centers, pioneered in Britain. They are just what their name suggests, with physical facilities and self-improvement activities selected, planned, and run by teachers. The basic assumption behind the centers is that teachers change only when they are responsible for defining their own problems and getting help on their own terms.
- *Developing alternatives to what we have been doing.* This is the first step in finding solutions to new problems. Capitalize on the many options provided by free schools, open schools, and alternative schools. As experienced educators, we should be able to act offensively rather than defensively

and initiate new types of organization in anticipation of public demands.

Perhaps the curriculum scene has been described too pessimistically. Perhaps too much responsibility has been placed on administrators, and too much emphasis on the differences among categories of educators. Out of the difficult task of rebuilding the curriculum, or developing its successor, will come a revitalized school system with effective procedures for planning and organizing for what we now call curriculum change. As administrators we can profit from what we learn from the managerial procedures of industry, so long as we remain clearly dedicated to the concept of the learner as the central focus for all education decisions.

The period of rebuilding will not be easy; a period of redefinition never is. However, we may be able to develop a kind of coexistence among our pluralistic values, as illustrated in the following parable from Schopenhauer's *Parerga und Paralipomena* (1851):

> A company of porcupines crowded themselves very close together one cold winter's day so as to profit by one another's warmth and so save themselves from being frozen to death. But soon they felt one another's quills, which induced them to separate again. And now, when the need for warmth brought them nearer together again, the second evil arose once more. So that they were driven backwards and forwards from one trouble to the other, until they had discovered a mean distance at which they could most tolerably exist.

BIBLIOGRAPHY

1. AASA Commission on Imperatives in Education. *Imperatives in Education.* Washington, D.C.: American Association of School Administrators, 1966.

2. American Association of School Administrators. *Profiles of the Administrative Team.* Washington, D.C.: the Association, 1971.

3. Bailey, Stephen K. "Teachers' Centers: A British First." *Phi Delta Kappan* 53: 146-49; November 1971.

4. California Teachers Association, Research Department. *California Schools in 1971.* California Research Bulletin, No. 263. Burlingame: the Association, September 1971.

5. Cremin, Lawrence A. "Curriculum-Making in the United States." *Teachers College Record* 73: 207-20; December 1971.

6. Cuban, Larry. "Teaching the Children: Does the System Help or Hinder?" *Freedom, Bureaucracy, and Schooling.* (Edited by Vernon F. Haubrich.) 1971 Yearbook. Washington, D.C.: Association for Supervision and Curriculum Development, 1971. pp. 147-60.

7. Eisner, Elliott, editor. *Confronting Curriculum Reform.* Boston: Little, Brown and Co., 1971.

8. Farrell, Edmund J. "A Report to the Intercommission Committee Regarding the Current Pressures on Teachers." (Mimeo.)

9. Knezevich, Stephen J., editor. *The American School Superintendent.* Washington, D.C.: American Association of School Administrators, 1971.

10. Leeper, Robert R., editor. *Curricular Concerns in a Revolutionary Era: Readings from Educational Leadership.* Washington, D.C.: Association for Supervision and Curriculum Development, 1971.

11. Louisiana Association for Supervision and Curriculum Development. "Problems of Teachers." Baton Rouge: the Association, 1971. (Mimeo.)

12. McClure, Robert M., editor. *The Curriculum: Retrospect and Prospect.* Seventieth Yearbook, Part I, National Society for the Study of Education. Chicago: University of Chicago Press, 1971.

13. National Education Association, Research Division. "Curriculum Review in Negotiation Agreements." *Research Bulletin* 48: 106-108; December 1970.

14. ———. "Major Problems of Teachers." *Research Bulletin* 49: 103-108; December 1971.

15. Whipple, Guy Montrose, editor. *Curriculum-Making: Past and Present.* Twenty-Sixth Yearbook (1927), Part I. Bloomington, Ill.: Public School Publishing Co., 1926.

16. Wilson, Richard W. "Who Speaks for the Kids? (Negotiations and the Learning Environment)." *NASSP Bulletin* 55: 8-15; December 1971.

PHOTO CREDITS

Page 308
Ben Spiegel
National Education Association Publishing
Washington, D.C.

All other photos by Joe Di Dio
National Education Association Publishing
Washington, D.C.